CHRISTIAN THEOLOGY
IN OUTLINE

BY

WILLIAM ADAMS BROWN, Ph.D., D.D.

ROOSEVELT PROFESSOR OF SYSTEMATIC THEOLOGY IN THE UNION
THEOLOGICAL SEMINARY, NEW YORK
AUTHOR OF "THE ESSENCE OF CHRISTIANITY"

NEW YORK
CHARLES SCRIBNER'S SONS
1906

Library of Congress Cataloging in Publication Data

Brown, William Adams, 1865-1943.
   Christian theology in outline.

   Reprint of the 1906 ed. published by Scribner,
New York.
   "A classified bibliography": p.
   Includes index.
   1. Theology, Doctrinal. I. Title.
BT75.B83   1976   230   75-41044
ISBN 0-404-14648-1

Reprinted from an original in the collections
of the University of Iowa Library

From the edition of 1906, New York
First AMS edition published in 1976
Manufactured in the United States of America

AMS PRESS INC.
NEW YORK, N.Y.

TO MY STUDENTS

Past and Present

IN GRATITUDE AND HOPE

PREFACE

THE book which follows owes its origin to a practical purpose. It is the outgrowth of the author's experience as a teacher of theology, and is the attempt to meet a definite need which that experience disclosed, — that, namely, of a brief handbook, at once scientific and constructive, in which the subject-matter of Christian theology should be treated from the modern point of view, and the new conceptions and ideals which have been more or less consciously affecting Christian thought should be set forth in their inner consistency, and in their true relation to their antecedents in the past.

A considerable part of the material which the book contains was originally given to my students in the form of type-written notes, and has been tested by repeated use in the classroom. With the exception of the chapter on the Trinity, however, a part of which was included in an address delivered before the Alumni of the Union Theological Seminary, and since published under the title, " The Trinity and Modern Thought: An Experiment in Theological Reconstruction," no part of the matter here offered has appeared in print. The change of form has given a welcome opportunity of revision and enlargement. While the original purpose of the book as a textbook for the theological classroom has been strictly adhered to, I have not been unmindful of the wider public who are interested in theological questions. Many thoughtful laymen to-day desire to know how the great convictions which form the subject-matter of the

Christian faith appear when regarded from the modern, that is to say, the scientific, point of view. This question the book which follows attempts to answer. While I have everywhere studied brevity, I have tried not to carry condensation so far as to interfere with clearness. The spirit in which I have sought to write is suggested by the opening quotation from William Ames, a theologian who, in the clearness of his insight that the final test of truth is practice, suggests the genial modern philosopher with whose name his own has so many letters in common.

The purpose of the book explains its method. The positive treatment of doctrine is prefaced in each case by a brief historical introduction, in which the sources from which it is derived are indicated and the significance of the older statements explained. I am well aware that there are not a few thoughtful people in our day who, for causes into which it is not necessary here to enter, have moved so far in their sympathies from the historic forms of Christianity that any attempt to relate the living content of our present spiritual life to these forms seems to them misleading, if not disingenuous. I believe that one of the most important problems which face the Christian theologian at the present day is how to present the permanent elements in the Christian message in a form to appeal to those who have thus broken with the past. But, legitimate and fascinating as this attempt may be, it is not the task proposed in the present book. The public which it addresses consists of those who still feel themselves at home in the Christian church, who value the heritage which has come down to them from the past as a priceless possession, but who do not always see clearly how to relate this treasure to the world of thought in which they are living, and so find themselves in a situation of perplexity, if not of positive distress. To such the re-interpretation of old terms here proposed may serve as a help and not a hindrance, fostering that sense of spiritual unity with the past without which the religious life of the present must necessarily be impoverished.

It would be too much to hope that in a work which covers so wide a territory errors should have been avoided. No one is more conscious than the author of the many possibilities of mistake, or will more gladly welcome correction. Indeed, the desire to profit by the criticisms of other workers in the same field has been one of the strongest motives leading me to publication. The difficulties which confront the teacher of systematic theology in an age of transition render it desirable that those who are engaged in this important branch of instruction should share with one another whatever light they may have gained through their experience in the classroom. Improvement in method is possible only through the co-operation of many minds, and it is primarily as an essay in theological method that I should wish the book to be judged. If it shall serve in any degree to promote that closer co-operation which is so much needed for the most effective work in this particular department, one of the main purposes of its publication will have been fulfilled.

It was my original plan to furnish the text with notes, going more fully into difficult or disputed points, and including references to the more helpful and accessible literature. This plan I have reluctantly been obliged to modify, in order to keep the book within the limits originally designed. For the convenience of students, a classified bibliography of some of the more helpful books treating of the subjects under discussion has been added in an appendix. It is needless to say that the lists given make no claim to be exhaustive.

It remains only to express my thanks to the many from whom I have received stimulus and help. Where sources

of obligation are so numerous it is impossible to specify
names.   But I cannot refrain from acknowledging here my
debt to two honored friends, my former teacher, Professor
Adolf Harnack, of the University of Berlin, and Professor
William Newton Clarke, of Colgate University.   From
Professor Harnack I first learned to think of theology as a
progressive science, dealing with the living convictions of
living men ; to Professor Clarke more than to any other
recent English speaking theologian it is due that systematic
theology has been freed from the bonds of a scholastic
phraseology and taught to speak again an English pure and
undefiled.   For the example thus set, as well as for personal
kindnesses too numerous to mention, I desire here to thank
him.   Most of all I owe to the suggestions gained in personal intercourse with my colleagues, and to the questions
and criticisms of my students in the classroom.   Special
thanks are due to Dr. Francis Brown, Dr. George William
Knox, and Dr. Henry Sloane Coffin.   In the midst of many
and engrossing duties, the two former have found time to
read the whole, and the latter a considerable part, of the
proof, and to their helpful suggestions in points of detail I
owe much.

WILLIAM ADAMS BROWN.

UNION THEOLOGICAL SEMINARY,
        November, 1906.

CONTENTS

INTRODUCTION

PART I

THE POSTULATES OF CHRISTIAN THEOLOGY

PART II

THE CHRISTIAN IDEA OF GOD

PART III

THE CHRISTIAN VIEW OF THE WORLD

PART IV

OF MAN AND HIS SIN

PART V

OF SALVATION THROUGH CHRIST

PART VI

THE CHRISTIAN LIFE

APPENDIX

A CLASSIFIED BIBLIOGRAPHY

A Briefe Premonition, or Forewarning of the Author, touching the reason of his purpose.

Although I doe not assume this to myselfe, to comprehend in my minde all the thoughts of evill speakers, yet I foresee divers exceptions which this my endeavour (proceeding certainly from a very good intent) . . . . will fall into; the chiefe of which I purpose briefly to meete withall.

Some, and those indeed not unlearned, dislike this whole manner of writing, that the sum of Divinity should be brought into a short compend. They desire great Volumes, wherein they may loosely either dwell, or wander. Whom I desire to consider, that all have not so great leasure, or so vast a wit, as to hunt the Partrich in the Mountaines, and Woods : but that the condition of many doth rather require, that the nest itselfe, or the seat of the matter which they pursue, bee shewed without any more adoe.

Some doe not dislike this way, if the chiefe heads be handled in a Rhetoricall way, but they thinke that every particle is not so punctually to be insisted on. But indeed, when the speech is carried on like a swift stream, although it catch many things, of all sorts, yet you can hold fast but a little, you can catch but a little, you cannot find where you may constantly rest : but when certaine rules are delivered, the Reader hath, alwayes, as it were at any pace, the place marked where he may set his foot . . . .

On the other side there will not be wanting some who will require more exactnesse of the art of Logick, whom I could not fully satisfy if I would, through my own imperfection, neither indeed would I so much as I could, because of the weaknesse of others. I imagine there will not be few who will thinke that to set forth such institutions as these, after so many labours of learned men in the same kind, is superfluous, and but to doe that which hath been done before. Of whose opinion I should readily be, if anything of this kind were extant, which did please all in every respect.

Which notwithstanding, I would not have so taken, as if it ever came into my mind to hope any such thing of this writing ; but because I am not out of hope, that it may come to passe that two, or three or so, may fall upon this of ours, who may here find something more fit to instruct, and stir them up to piety, than they have observed in the more learned writings of others; which conjecture if it doe not faile me, I shall think I have done a work worth the labor . . . .

The drinesse of the style, and harshnesse of some words will be much blamed by the same persons. But I doe prefer to exercise myselfe in that heresie, that when it is my purpose to Teach, I thinke I should not say that in two words which may be said in one; and that that key is to be chosen which doth open best, although it be of wood, if there be not a golden key of the same efficacy . . . .

If there be any who doe yet find fault with, or desire other things, I would intreat them, that they would vouchsafe candidly to impart to me their thoughts, which may afford desired matter for a just apology, or due amendment. — WILLIAM AMES: *The Marrow of Sacred Divinity. Translated out of the Latine, for the benefit of such who are not acquainted with strange Tongues. Published by order from the Honorable the House of Commons. London (1642).*

INTRODUCTION

CONCERNING CHRISTIAN THEOLOGY

CHRISTIAN THEOLOGY IN OUTLINE

CHAPTER I

THE IDEA AND RELATIONS OF CHRISTIAN THEOLOGY

1. *The Definition of Theology.*

CHRISTIAN theology, or dogmatics,[1] as it is technically called, is that branch of theological science which aims to give systematic expression to the doctrines of the Christian faith. These doctrines have been variously defined. In what follows we shall understand by them the abiding convictions about God, man, and their relations, growing out of God's historic revelation in Christ, and verifying themselves progressively in Christian experience, which together make up the Christian conception of life, and the acceptance of which forms, on the intellectual side, the

[1] The name " dogmatics " is here used as a synonym for theology in the technical sense, as distinct from Christian ethics, and the various subsidiary sciences often grouped under that name. In this sense it has been used in Protestantism for over two hundred years (first in 1659 ; frequently since 1729). In Germany the word *Glaubenslehre* (science of the Christian faith) is often used as a synonym ; but we have no single equivalent in English. The popular association with dogmatism renders the word an unfortunate one ; yet in itself it is well adapted to the use to which it is put. As distinguished from doctrine (which may include opinion of every kind) the word dogma denotes truth of fundamental or authoritative character, and so appropriately describes the subject-matter of our science. It need hardly be said that in retaining the word, we do not use it in the legal sense in which it is understood in Roman Catholicism, but in accordance with the spiritual conception of religious authority which is characteristic of Protestantism.

bond of union between the members of the Christian church. Theology is the science which treats of these convictions. It is its function to point out their basis in experience; to explain their historic forms; to show their inner harmony and consistency, and so to relate them to present thought and life.

In the Seminary curriculum, dogmatics is usually classed with Christian ethics [1] and the philosophy of religion [2] as belonging to the department of systematic theology.

[1] The line between dogmatics and Christian ethics is not altogether easy to draw. Both deal in part with the same subject-matter (God, man, and their relations). Both are concerned with the same questions (*e. g.* freedom, sin, the church). The difference is rather one of point of view. Dogmatics looks upon the Christian life from the point of view of God and his will, ethics from that of man and his duty (Dorner). The first deals with the Christian view of reality, the second with the Christian ideal (Reischle). Both together are needed to give full content to the Christian view of the world and of life.

In the history of theology dogmatics and ethics have sometimes been treated separately, sometimes together. The latter is the ideal method, since it brings out most clearly the intimate connection between faith and conduct. On the other hand, a separate treatment proves more convenient in practice, the questions involved in the ethics of Christianity being too many and intricate to be effectively discussed in connection with the theological system. For this reason it is common to-day to treat Christian ethics as a separate discipline.

But if for convenience we decide to treat the ethical material separately, we must not forget that it belongs as rightfully to systematic theology as dogmatics itself. The moral ideal holds as essential a place in the Christian view of life as the conception of God. As ethics finds its presupposition and motive in the God of whom dogmatics treats, so dogmatics points forward to ethics as its necessary outcome, and tests the correctness of its doctrinal statements by their practical bearing upon the Christian life.

[2] The philosophy of religion is a new discipline which has recently made its place in the theological curriculum, taking the place of the older natural theology and Christian evidences. It discusses such questions as the nature and limits of religious knowledge, the origin, nature, and development of religion, the nature of Christianity, and our reasons for believing it to be the final and perfect religion. While it is true that a complete answer to these questions presupposes the results both of dogmatics and of ethics, it is equally true that our attitude to these preliminary questions will largely determine our method of treatment in both these disciplines. Here we find differences

Systematic theology occupies the centre of the theological curriculum, midway between the exegetical and historical and the practical disciplines. From the former it receives its materials; to the latter it furnishes their principles.[1] In this it is like philosophy in the curriculum of the university, which stands midway between the sciences and the arts. We may describe it as the philosophy of the Christian life.[2]

This conception of theology is to be distinguished (1) from the view which regards it as a purely Biblical or ecclesiastical science, whose task is the reproduction without inner appropriation of the doctrines presented in Bible or creed (dogmatics in the legal sense); (2) from that

of opinion among Christians with reference to which an understanding must be reached before it is possible to begin a systematic statement. It is the task of the philosophy of religion to consider these differences, and to define and defend the postulates which the later sciences assume. Thus it takes its place as the fundamental systematic discipline. In what follows we take its results for granted.

[1] The preparatory disciplines which affect systematic theology most directly are (1) Biblical theology, (2) symbolics, and (3) the history of doctrine; since these give the form in which the Christian convictions have received systematic expression in the past. But all the disciplines of the Seminary bear indirectly on systematic theology, since they increase our knowledge of the Christian life which is its ultimate source.

The attitude of the systematic theologian to the preparatory disciplines is one of receptivity. He cannot go back of their results, save as he himself becomes a historian or an exegete. On the other hand, he is not bound to include in his system all that they contain. Systematic theology is concerned only with the permanent elements in Christian truth. In determining what these are, the systematic theologian finds his freedom.

To the practical disciplines, on the other hand, the attitude of systematic theology is one of ministry. It gives them the principles of which they make use, and indicates the end toward which they strive.

[2] The similarity to philosophy appears not only in its position in the curriculum, but in its contents. It includes the Christian conception of reality (dogmatics = ontology), the Christian ideal of duty (ethics), and the fundamental principles by which both are justified (philosophy of religion, apologetics = theory of knowledge). Thus it is the constructive discipline *par excellence*, the keystone of the theological arch.

which regards it (with Schleiermacher) as a purely historical science, which is content to state the contents of the present Christian consciousness without raising the question as to the objective validity of its faith; and (3) from that which regards it (with Origen and Hegel) as a purely speculative science, whose object is the higher truths, which, while implied in the common faith of Christians, can be fully apprehended only by the initiated. In contrast to these views, it is here maintained that it is the task of Christian theology to state and to defend as true the convictions which are distinctive of Christianity as a historical religion, and which give inspiration and character to the Christian life. It is a normative science, whose function it is to discriminate that which is essential and permanent in Christian faith from that which is accidental and temporary, and to present the common Christian convictions in the form best fitted to give clearness to thought and definiteness to purpose.

Yet, while differentiated from each of the foregoing conceptions, the view of theology here presented recognizes the truth for which each stands and endeavors in its own way to make place for it. With the theology of the Christian consciousness it maintains (1) that theology has to do with religious convictions verifiable in experience. With the older dogmatics (Protestant and Catholic) it agrees (2) that these convictions have a definite historical origin (in the Christian revelation), and (3) that they form the bond of union between the members of a definite historical society (the Christian church). Finally, with the theology of the speculative school, it recognizes (4) that they abide in the midst of change, and hence need constant restatement to adapt them to the changing intellectual environment. These statements need fuller explanation.

2. *Theology and the Religious Experience.*

In the first place, the truths with which theology has to do are religious convictions; truths, that is to say, which have been appropriated by their holder, and which bear directly on his conduct. They are not purely theoretical propositions gained by abstract reasoning, but working principles verifiable in experience. While they include a theoretical element in that they describe the objects with which religion has to do, it is always in the practical connection in which these objects are presented in the religious life.

Among modern theologians Schleiermacher was the first to emphasize the dependence of theology upon the religious experience. Before his day the truths of theology were thought of as coming to men ready made, either from divine revelation, in church or Bible, or from reason in the form of a natural theology. He called attention to the religious feeling (*die Frömmigkeit*, piety) as a factor in the production of theology, and defined the doctrines of faith (*Glaubenssätze*), which form its subject-matter, as propositions which describe states of the Christian consciousness.[1]

The motives which led him to this definition were partly scientific and partly religious: scientific, in that he sought to assign theology a definite subject-matter capable of exact description and verification, and independent of the fluctuations of speculative philosophy; religious, in that he desired to substitute for the formulæ of a dry orthodoxy divorced from experience the language of a living faith. Both motives have continued to influence his successors; and it may be said that the necessary connection

[1] *Glaubenslehre,* Berlin, 1884, I, p. 94.

between doctrine and experience is one of the axioms of
modern theological thought.

But though theology must take its start from the religious life, it cannot stop there. Here is where Schleiermacher's definition is at fault. The subject-matter of
theology is not the religious experience itself, but the
God whom that experience reveals. Its doctrines are
not merely descriptions of states of consciousness, but of
" the unseen spiritual reality which it is the privilege and
duty of the Christian through faith in God's revelation in
Jesus Christ to experience." [1] Thus it is a philosophy as
well as a science, and, like every philosophy, professes to
give us knowledge of ultimate truth.[2]

3. *Theology and the Christian Revelation.*

Christian theology has to do not simply with the truth
implied in the religious experience in general, but with a
particular type of that experience — the Christian. This
still further limits its subject-matter. Nineteen centuries

[1] Reischle, *Christliche Glaubenslehre in Leitsätzen,* 2d ed. 1902, p. 30.

[2] The claim of theology to set forth ultimate truth raises interesting questions as to the relation between theology and general philosophy. Here
it is sufficient to say that while the two deal in part with the same subject-
matter, and their conclusions — within the ground covered by both — should
be consistent, the practical connection in which theology presents the objects
of its faith differentiates its method from that of philosophy, whose interest
is primarily theoretical or speculative. The philosopher seeks a comprehensive view of all reality, and the ethical and religious experience is but a part
of the phenomena which it is his business to explain. Hence, even when he
recognizes the legitimacy within its own sphere of the religious point of view,
and makes room for its contribution to his system, it is his effort to translate
the personal convictions in which the religious world of thought moves into
the forms of disinterested knowledge characteristic of science in other branches.
The theologian, on the other hand, takes his stand frankly within the religious experience, believing that through the practical insight which its judgments afford we have the true point of view from which to interpret life as a
whole.

ago there lived a man, through whom there came into the world new ideas of truth, new ideals of duty, in a word, a new *Weltanschauung*,[1] — a new conception of the world and of life. Christian theology seeks to express the convictions which are involved in this world-view. It takes for granted a historic revelation and the faith which it has called forth.

In this connection with historic revelation is to be found the answer to those who fear the subjectivity of a theology which takes its departure from the Christian experience. The reason why this fear is not well grounded is that this experience itself has an objective ground. Christian faith is not something self-created, the child of imagination or of fancy. It has its source in a historic revelation, and apart from Jesus could never have been. This connection separates it as something *sui generis* from other forms of the religious life, and gives Christian theology its distinctive subject-matter.

The objection is sometimes made that the restriction of theology to the Christian sphere is incompatible with its scientific character. It is unscientific, we are told, to separate a section of human experience from the rest, and in its light to interpret the whole. If we wish a trustworthy interpretation of the world, we must take in all the facts.

The answer is that restriction of some kind is inevitable. The only legitimate question is as to the grounds on which it rests, and the use which is made of it. If it is arbitrarily made, and persisted in, in the face of evi-

---

[1] We have no single word in English, which, like the German *Weltanschauung*, expresses that comprehensive view of the world and of life which is the outcome and expression of fundamental religious or philosophical conviction. Cf. Orr, *Christian View of God and of the World*, 7th ed. New York, 1904, p. 3.

dence to the contrary, the objection is well taken. **If**,
however, it is grounded in the nature of the facts, and
accompanied with an open mind toward all new truth,
this need not be the case. Progress in knowledge is
possible only through discrimination. Among the innu-
merable phenomena which the world presents, it is necessary to select those which have the most significance,
and to use these to interpret the rest. Every great philosophy which attempts a positive interpretation of life
practises such discrimination. In Christianity we have a
series of facts which, its adherents believe, shed the clearest light on the riddle of the universe. To set forth consistently the view of the world which is the result of this
conviction is not only scientifically legitimate : it is practically most important ; since it is only by the clear statement of any hypothesis that it is possible to determine
whether it is true or not.

More serious is the objection raised by those who deny
that there is any distinctive Christian view of the world.
Like everything else in history, Christianity, we are told,
is changing ; and what one generation holds to be Christian
is something entirely different from what the preceding
understood by that name. We may have a Protestant
or a Catholic, a Lutheran or a Reformed theology, but
Christian theology as such exists only in the minds of
those who set it forth.[1]

It must be admitted that there is not a little in the
history of Christianity which gives plausibility to this
objection. Among the multitude of sects which Christianity
has produced, the task of determining what belongs to its
essence is a difficult one. Yet that there is a distinctive
faith, having its source in the original revelation of Christ,

[1] Cf. Tiele, *Elements of the Science of Religion*, vol. I, pp. 124 sq.

and finding more or less complete utterance in each of the changing historic forms in which it has expressed itself, is the conviction of Catholic and Protestant alike. It is this distinctive faith which it is the aim of Christian theology to set forth, and which explains its dependence upon the various historical and critical sciences which deal with the origin and development of Christianity.

4. *Theology and the Christian Church.*

Christian theology is further differentiated from general philosophy by its close connection with the Christian church. Its interest is not simply practical, in that it seeks to promote the individual's understanding of his own religious life, but social, in that it provides the intellectual bond of union between the members of the Christian church. Men work together effectively in proportion as they understand one another, and are conscious of seeking the same ends. This understanding theology seeks to promote.

The higher the grade of civilization, the greater the importance of this intellectual understanding. In the lower forms of religion dogma has a subordinate place. Religion is a matter of ritual, or of social custom. Ceremonies are performed by the priest and witnessed by the worshipper often without understanding of their meaning. This is true to a large extent even in higher forms like Roman Catholicism. To many Catholics the dogmas of their church are concerned with mysteries rising above human reason, and the common people are not expected to understand them. It is different in Protestantism, which knows no priestly caste and offers its truths freely to the people at large. Here understanding is necessary, that worship may be intelligent, preaching effective and missionary work earnest and efficient. Without doctrines, that is, religious truths intelligently understood and heartily accepted, Protestantism, as we know it, could not exist. Its motive power would be gone. Hence the great importance of our science for the church.

Objection is often made to this close connection of theology with the work of the church. The pursuit of knowledge, we are told, to be successful, must be disinterested. But this attitude is difficult in the case of theological students, who are looking forward to the Christian ministry, and who are therefore definitely committed to the Christian view.

So far as this objection is thoroughgoing, it may be urged with equal effect against any attempt of men to instruct their fellows in the views which they hold true. It is directed, not against theology, but against the church, and ultimately against Christianity itself. It amounts to saying that no honest and impartial man can be a Christian. As long as Christianity exists as a missionary religion, so long its ministers must be trained in its distinctive tenets. They must know for what their religion stands, and the ends which it seeks to attain. We need not deny that this practical interest has its dangers. But this is not an argument for abandoning the study of theology, but rather for bringing to its pursuit the greatest possible caution, honesty, and openness of mind. The real question at issue is whether the Christian view of the world be true. If so, then the legitimacy of the theological method follows as a matter of course.

Yet, when considered as a criticism of the relation in which theological science stands to existing ecclesiastical institutions, the objection has much plausibility. It is true that in practice the church often seeks to commit her teachers to positions which limit their freedom; and there are theories of the relation of the church to secular learning which would render any true theological science impossible. These theories we shall consider in due time, and define our own position in detail.[1] Here it is sufficient to say that the only commitment which the Protestant church has a right to ask of her students is that which is the result of honest reflection based upon a genuine Christian experience.

5. *Theology and Contemporary Thought.*

Christian theology is not concerned with all the convictions which have been held by Christian people, but only with the abiding convictions, — those which maintain themselves through the changes of intellectual environment as permanent elements in the Christian conception of life. It seeks to present Christian truth as it appears to-day, freed from the accidental and transient elements with which it has been associated in the past. But this involves an intelligent appreciation of contemporary thought.

Under contemporary thought we include all the intellectual influences, scientific, philosophical, literary, which at any given time affect men's view of the world and of life. Some of these are of permanent importance ; others are transient. All together combine to produce a certain intellectual atmosphere into which the theologian is born, and with which he has to do.

The dependence of the theologian upon his environment is apparent on all sides of his work, critical, constructive, interpretative. He looks to science for the critical apparatus by which to determine what belongs to the essence of Christianity, and to distinguish its experimental

[1] Cf. Chapter V, section 4.

content from its changing forms. From philosophy he learns the nature and limits of human knowledge, the theoretical significance of the Christian contribution to the same, and its relations to other speculations concerning ultimate truth. Through literature he gains an insight into the intellectual habits and prejudices of his contemporaries, and so is taught the most effective method in which to approach them with his distinctive message.

A striking illustration of the intimate connection between theology and contemporary thought is found in the theories by which, from time to time, it has been sought to prove their independence. Thus the well-known division of theology into natural and revealed which Protestantism has inherited from Catholicism owes its present form to the new impulse given to theology in the Middle Ages by the rediscovery of Aristotle. In like manner the recent attempt of Ritschl and his school to secure an independent sphere for theology by distinguishing its truths as judgments of value from the theoretical judgments of philosophy and science is the application to theology of Kant's distinction between the pure and the practical reason. In each case, the apparent independence of theology is gained by a definition which arbitrarily restricts secular thought to a territory from which all that is distinctive of Christianity has been excluded, while the theologian reserves for himself the right to take over without acknowledgment such of its methods and results as he may find useful.

In contrast to such attempts to secure the independence of theology by an artificial delimitation of territory, it is to be maintained that the real guarantee of its freedom is to be found in the distinctive character and inherent worth of its subject-matter. Philosophy and science are only methods. They cannot create, but only observe and interpret. In Christianity something is offered for science to observe and for philosophy to interpret, and the result is Christian theology.

CHAPTER II

1. *The Sources of Christian Theology.*

WHAT has been said of the nature of theology determines our view of its sources. The ultimate source of Christian theology is the Christian religion itself with the revelation in which it had its rise. The proximate sources are the records which have preserved to us our knowledge of the origin and history of Christianity. Chief among these are the Bible, the creeds of the church, and the works of the leading Christian theologians.

The importance of the Bible for theology depends upon its close connection with Jesus Christ. As Christ is the centre of Christianity, and we get at Christ most directly through the Bible, it is evident that the Bible must be our chief source and the test by which all that calls itself Christian must be judged. Hence all that sheds light upon the Bible, its origin, its history and its interpretation, is of interest for the student of Christian theology. Specially important is an acquaintance with the religious teaching of the different Biblical books, as made known to us by the discipline of Biblical theology. This study shows us Christian theology in the making, and gives us the point of departure from which we are to judge the later development.

But though the Bible is the chief, it is not the only source of Christian theology. As the Christian revelation, while centring in Christ, includes also all the light which has been shed by him upon the life of men, so, with the Bible, theology must make room among its sources for all utterances of the Christian spirit which are the result and evidence of this wider influence. Most important among these are the creeds in which from time to time the church has made formal confession of her faith, and the systems in which she has tried to relate her convictions to contemporary thought, and to justify the Christian claim before the bar of reason. In these — with the Bible — the theologian finds his sources in the technical sense; the tools which his predecessors have used, and upon mastery of which his proficiency in his science depends.

The word " creed " is derived from the Latin *credo*, I believe. It denotes a confession of faith. Such a confession may be either individual or united. Peter's confession at Cæsarea was an example of the first; the Nicene creed is an example of the second. All the great creeds began as the utterance of individual convictions. Only gradually did they receive the common recognition which gives them ecclesiastical significance. The process was an entirely natural one, proceeding step by step by imperceptible transitions. Little by little the free spontaneity of the early creeds gave place to the formality and elaborateness of the later. The early connection with the Christian life was more and more obscured, and, instead of a confession, the creed became a symbol: that is, a law or rule of faith. It is important, however, to remember that this significance is secondary, not primary. Historically, the use of the creed as a confession precedes its employment as a standard, not *vice versa*. It is because the great creeds of the church do represent genuine convic-

2

tions based on experience — and for this reason alone — that they have a rightful place among the sources of theology.

The creeds of the church fall into three great families, corresponding to the three historic stages in the development of Christianity: the Greek, the Roman, and the Protestant. The first contains the so-called ecumenical creeds which centre in the doctrines of the Trinity and the Person of Christ (*e. g.* the Nicene and the Chalcedonian statements). The second contains the creeds of Roman Catholicism, beginning with the Council of Trent (1545–63) and ending with the Vatican Council (1870). The third contains the various Protestant creeds, of which the most important are those which belong to the Lutheran and Reformed groups.[1]

All three of these groups are in a true sense sources for the Protestant theologian, since all are outgrowths of the religious life which owes its origin to Jesus Christ. Nevertheless, in the nature of the case, the Protestant creeds will exercise the controlling influence, since they express the particular type of the Christian life to which he himself belongs.

The significance of the Protestant creeds is twofold. In the first place, they express the particular convictions by which Protestantism is distinguished as a distinct type of the religious life from the older types (*e. g.* the sole authority of Scripture, justification by faith, the universal priesthood of believers). In the second place, they give the point of view from which the doctrines taken

[1] In case the fourfold division suggested below (p. 62) should be preferred, we should have to add a fourth group, consisting of the modifications and revisions of the older creeds which have recently been undertaken in many of the Protestant churches, as well as those individual creeds without official authority, in which the spirit of the new age comes to expression.

over from the older creeds are to be understood. Of the two, the second function is the more important. Protestantism stands before all things for a new spirit; a new conception of the entire relation between God and man. It is a relation of freedom which gives each man a right to go back for himself to the source of divine revelation, and, in the light of that which he there finds, to judge all the later utterances of the church. This new conception modifies the doctrines taken over from Catholicism, as well as those peculiar to Protestantism. It involves in each case an appeal to the Christian experience not necessary on the older view, and this all along the line.

Scarcely less important than the creeds are the systems through which, from time to time, Christians of the past have endeavored to relate their faith to the philosophy of the time, and to justify the claim of Christianity at the bar of reason. It is through a study of these systems that we learn what our predecessors have regarded as central in their faith, and so are enabled to measure the progress which has been made in the understanding of the Gospel. It is through this study further that we become acquainted with the intellectual apparatus at their disposal, and so discover how far the methods they employed are applicable to the new needs and problems of the present.

Besides these technical sources the theologian must know the world in which he lives. Everything that helps him to such knowledge is a legitimate source of theology. The natural sciences are sources, since they shed light upon the physical universe which is the scene of man's religious development. Psychology is a source, because it treats of the constitution and laws of the human spirit to which the divine revelation is made. History is a source, since by its aid we retrace the record of God's dealings with mankind in the past. All the complex group of studies which it is customary to classify under the head of sociology (economics, law, politics, etc.) are sources, since they deal with the conditions under which man's social life has been formed, and the environment in which the Christian ideal must be realized.

Above all, the theologian must know the developments of contemporary religious life. It is from this study that he learns to know religion as a living force, and so to understand and to estimate rightly its utterances in the past. As the historic creeds and systems represent the impression of Christ gained by men of a particular age under a special environment, so the experiences of the present are giving rise to new impressions, and enlarging the evidence upon which any comprehensive view of his influence must be based. Specially instructive in this connection is the light shed by the foreign field. Here we see Christianity in daily contact with other forms of religion, and thus reproduce in a measure the conditions which obtained in the earlier history. By comparing the religious life of the present with the past, we learn to distinguish more accurately, in the case of any particular utterance of Christian faith, what belongs to the age and the surrounding, and what is of permanent importance for the race.

In making this discrimination we gain indispensable help from our own religious experience. As the first condition of understanding life is to live, so the primary condition of understanding religion is to be religious. The discrimination, difficult in theory, between form and substance, truth and setting, Gospel and environment becomes easy when doctrine is brought to the test of life. Here we learn the real meaning of the terms whose definition baffles the schools, and across the gulf of differing intellectual environments clasp brotherly hands with all who know by experience the Christian life.

This does not mean that we are to admit nothing to our theology which goes beyond our own experience. That would be to contradict the teachings of the Christian experience itself, the characteristic mark of which is to recognize in Christ a life richer, fuller, truer than our own. It is one of the merits of Ritschl that, in his emphasis upon the historic in Christianity, he has called attention, in contrast to the purely subjective method of Schleiermacher, to the objective basis of the Christian faith. Christian theology, as he rightly tells us, is not simply a description of individual experiences, but a witness to the Christ from whom new experiences come. But it is none the less true that if we are to understand the nature of the Christ of whom we speak, it must be by a study of the effects which he has produced in human life. Here our own experience gives us invaluable help. It is the key by which we enter into the understanding of men of other ages, and distinguish the permanent elements in their teaching from its transient setting.

In taking this view we have already adopted a definite philosophical attitude, — that namely which assumes that through the practical judgments of the moral and religious life we gain knowledge of objective reality, and insight into ultimate truth. This is distinguished, on the one hand, from the agnostic view which denies that knowledge of ultimate truth is possible, and, on the other, from the pure speculation which maintains that it is to be gained by reason alone, apart from the practical insight which comes through the feelings and the will. As Christians we believe that God can be known, and that the way to know him is through the experience which follows the doing of his will. It is this conviction to which Ritschl has given technical expression in his statement that the doctrines of religion are judgments of value (*Werthurtheile*): that is, truths whose justification is to be sought in their satisfaction of the practical needs of man.

The full justification of this standpoint belongs to the philosophy of religion. It requires us to show the place which the practical judgment holds in all our higher knowledge, the impossibility of any comprehensive or adequate theory of life which ignores the contribution of the ethical and religious nature, and, conversely, the possibility of making place for the principles and results of the natural sciences in the idealistic *Weltanschauung* to which ethics and religion alike point.[1]

But though the defence of the Christian standpoint as a whole belongs to the philosophy of religion rather than to dogmatics, the latter has its own contribution to make to the proof of Christianity. By working out to its full

---

[1] When we speak of a consistent *Weltanschauung* we do not mean necessarily a complete system of philosophy, in which all possible questions, cosmological, biological, psychological and historical find treatment. Such a system was the ideal of the great schoolmen, and was attempted by not a few of the older Protestant theologians. But the task proved too great, and the attempt defeated its own end. The only result was needlessly to commit Christianity to scientific and philosophical theories which succeeding generations have discredited, and so to obscure its distinctive message. We have no such aim. By a consistent *Weltanschauung* we mean simply such a statement of the fundamental Christian convictions as to God and the world as shall show their essential harmony, and their practical bearing on those vital questions in contemporary thought which directly affect the Christian life.

consequences the conception of life involved in the premises which it takes over, it makes it possible to test whether or no these are well taken. Thus the two sciences confirm each other. In the detailed questions discussed in the philosophy of religion it is easy to lose one's sense of proportion. But when the Christian view of life is set forth as a whole, it is possible to estimate it at its true value. Thus theology, through its subordination of the apologetic to the constructive interest, becomes itself the best apologetic.

2. *Method and Order.*

In the older theology the discussion of the special Christian doctrines was preceded by a section dealing with the nature and authority of the Christian revelation from which they were derived. This revelation the Catholic found in the church, the Protestant in the Bible. While both recognized that man could know something about God by reason, they were at one in believing that this knowledge was inadequate for salvation unless supplemented by supernatural revelation. Hence, the supreme importance given to the subject of revelation in the older dogmatics.

Modern theology is not less convinced of the importance of this subject, but it approaches its consideration from a somewhat different point of view. Instead of beginning with abstract considerations taken from the nature of the human mind, it begins with a consideration of the phenomena of the religious life itself. A closer acquaintance with the other religions of the world has disclosed unexpected similarities between them and Christianity, and forced into the foreground the question as to that which is distinctive in the latter. At the same time, a better psychology has made us familiar with the subjective elements which condition all impartation of knowledge, and so emphasized the part played by the religious experience itself as a channel and test of revelation. This widened horizon necessarily affects the problem of theological method and enlarges the range of topics with which theological introduction must concern itself.

Among the subjects with which the philosophy of religion has to do, three are of fundamental importance for theology : those of religion, of revelation, and of the church. Before we can set forth the Christian view of the world, we must know (1) what is Christianity, and what is its relation to the wider religious life of man ; (2) where to find the Christian revelation, and what are its nature, limits, and relation to the other subjects of our knowledge ; and (3) what is the nature of the society which is the outgrowth of this revelation, and especially of the organization through which it finds expression — the Christian church. These are the points at which the philosophical premises from which different theologies start show themselves in their clearest form, and in which the differences between the various Christian communions come to acutest expression. Our discussion of Christian theology falls accordingly into two parts, of which one treats of the postulates [1] of Christian theology, the other of the doctrines of the Christian faith. Under the first we take up in succession the Christian religion, the Christian revelation, and the Christian church. Only after we have come to clear views on each of these topics shall we be able to

---

[1] By the word " postulate," as used in this connection, we do not mean, of course, an assumption for which no proof can be given, but only a general statement which, for the purposes of the present discussion, we assume as already proved. The detailed verification of the positions assumed belongs to the philosophy of religion, whose results we here take for granted.

define intelligently the task of modern theology. This gives us the following divisions :

   I. The Christian religion.

   II. The Christian revelation.

   III. The Christian church.

   IV. The task of modern theology.

PART I

THE POSTULATES OF CHRISTIAN THEOLOGY

CHAPTER III

FROM the point of view of comparative religion, Christianity is one form among others in which the religious life manifests itself. From the point of view of Christian faith, it is the perfect or final religion, rightfully claiming the allegiance of all men. To understand Christianity, therefore, we must know: (1) what is the view of religion which it presupposes, and (2) what is its distinctive contribution to the religious life of man.

1. *The Definition of Religion.*

By religion is meant " the life of man in his superhuman relations " : [1] that is, his relation to the power on which he feels himself dependent, the authority to which he deems himself responsible and the unseen being with whom he is capable of communion. In the ideal of religion, dependence, responsibility and spiritual communion belong together. Historically, however, they have received unequal emphasis at different times. In the early stages of religion man recognizes many powers on which he believes himself dependent, and to which he is united by relationships of different kinds. Hence his religious life is one of divided allegiance. But so soon as he attains the conception of a universe, he perceives that the source of all power, authority and spiritual life is one, and finds this source in the supreme reality whom we call God. Hence, we may define

[1] Clarke, *Outline of Christian Theology*, p. 1.

religion briefly as the life of man in his relation to God.

The word " religion " is sometimes applied to forms of human experience which do not recognize the existence of any higher power (*e. g.* the religion of art or of humanity); and the use is justified by the example of Buddhism, which is based on an atheistic philosophy. Most scholars, however, regard the recognition of a deity in some form as an essential characteristic of religion. Apart from this criterion it is impossible to distinguish it from other forms of human life. Buddhism itself, studied in the light of its history, proves no exception to the rule that every religion must have a god.

Recognition of a higher power is common to religion and philosophy ; but religion differs from philosophy in its practical character, *i. e.* the personal relation which it conceives to exist between the worshipper and his object. This sense of personal identification, involving mutual relationships and expressing itself by the use of the personal pronoun, gives its distinctive meaning to the word " God." A god in the religious sense is an unseen being, real or supposed, to whom an individual or a social group is united by voluntary ties of reverence and service. Hence worship of some kind characterizes every form of the religious relationship.

As the life of man in his relation to God, religion affects all sides of man's nature, intellectual, emotional and practical. We may illustrate this in connection with the characteristic expression of the religious life, which is worship. Every act of worship, however primitive and superstitious, includes intellectual elements in the recognition of some object with which the worshipper stands in relation ; emotional elements in the feelings of fear, of need, of obligation or of gratitude which impel him to expression, and practical elements in the activities which result from these feelings; whether they be external, like fasting or sacrifice, or internal, like prayer. The history of religion is the record of the gradual spiritualization of worship under the influence of truer and purer ideas of God.

2. *The Origin and Development of Religion.*

Like every abiding human interest, religion has its roots in the constitution of man. Its psychological basis is found partly in the sense of dependence, which leads man to recognize his relation to a higher power; partly in the sense of need, which results from the contrast between the individual desire and the limitations of life; but above all, in the sense of worth, which leads man, as spiritual being, to feel his kinship to the unseen power on whom he knows himself dependent. In religion man's consciousness that he is made for higher things than his present life affords finds utterance. Negatively, it manifests itself in the cry for deliverance from specific evils, physical or moral; positively, in the longing for self-realization through communion with a higher spiritual power. Religion is the expression of man's faith in the possibility of salvation and blessedness through divine help.

Yet this faith alone would be inadequate unless it were answered by corresponding experiences. It is characteristic of historic religion that men have believed in the divine answer to their need, and have found evidence of this answer in specific phenomena both in the inner and in the outer world. These phenomena the religious sense interprets as revelations, *i. e.* disclosures of the divine will to man for practical ends; and in the correspondence between such divine communications on the one hand and human aspiration and need on the other, the reality of vital religion consists.

In the ideal of religion this intimate connection should determine all the manifestations of the religious life. Its doctrines are designed to express the relation of the worshipper to God, and its activities to promote communion with the Deity or to secure his help. In practice, however, the connection is frequently lost. This results from the fact that religion is not simply an individual, but a social affair. The revelation which the individual believes himself to have received he imparts to others. Hence arise religious societies with fixed institutions and traditions, designed to hand down to posterity the religious insight of the past. In this process the original connection which united doctrines and practices with experience is frequently lost. The former become purely theoretical propositions (often incomprehensible), received on authority; the latter, magical ceremonies, consecrated by custom, whose original meaning has been forgotten.

3. *The Types of Historic Religion.*

Apart from the contrast between vital and traditional religion already referred to, we find wide differences in the historic manifestations of the religious life. Some of these are due to fundamental differences of temperament (as between the mystic, the gnostic, and the ethical reformer); others are due to differences of intellectual or social environment. Many attempts have been made to arrange the historic religions in a series according to their distinguishing characteristics. Some of these attempts have taken their departure from the idea of God (*e. g.* henotheism, polytheism, pantheism, monotheism); others from the nature of the end sought in religion (*e. g.* nature and ethical religions, and within these, religions of law and of redemption). In practice, however, the complexity of the phenomena is so great as to make any satisfactory classification difficult. It is often impossible to tell where one religion ends and another begins; and within the greater religions almost all the types of the religious life may be found represented. Any description therefore must be of the most general character, leaving wide room for individual variation.

There is, however, one difference of fundamental importance: namely, between those simpler and more primitive forms whose origin is unknown, and in which tribal or national custom forms the bond of union; and those religions which are the outgrowth of an ethical revival brought about by a single individual, and which seek by missionary effort to make their ideal effective among men. In the latter class, to which the so-called universal religions belong, the personality of the founder stamps upon his religion a specific character which maintains itself in spite of all individual variations, and which no later changes are able permanently to obscure. To this class of founded religions Christianity belongs; and it is through the study of the person and work of its founder that its distinctive character is to be learned.

4. *The Place of Christianity in the History of Religion.*

Christianity is the religion founded by Jesus of Nazareth, who was crucified in Jerusalem under Pontius Pilate about the year 30 of our era for his claim to be the Jewish Messiah, or Christ. The bond of union among its adherents is found in their common recognition of his divine mission and authority. With this fact is given at once the close connection of Christianity with other religions, and its distinction from them.

As a historical religion, Christianity is the direct descendant of the religion of Israel. Jesus himself was a Jew, and found in the Scriptures of his people the direct preparation for his Gospel. Here we find the origin of the idea of the kingdom of God, which Jesus made central in his preaching. Here we find Messianic prophecy, with its hope of a God-given Saviour. Here, too, we find in germ much of the ethics of Christianity. Above all, here we find the revelation of God as a person, at once holy and loving; caring for men, and seeking their redemption. Along all these lines the later religion is the continuation and completion of the earlier. So much is this the case that at first Christianity was uncritically identified with Judaism; and even to-day many Christians do not distinguish between them.

Through Judaism Christianity touches the older faiths with which at various times the people of Israel were brought into contact (*e. g.* that of Egypt, of Assyria-Babylonia, and of Persia). As to the nature and extent of the connection, scholars are not yet agreed; but enough facts have been brought to light to make it probable that in the case of Babylonia and Persia at least, the influence was positive as well as negative. This influence, apparent at points in the Old Testament (*e. g.* the cosmogony of Genesis), is specially manifest in the later apocalyptic and pseudepigraphical literature of the Jews, and through it passed to the early Christian theologians.

Outside of Judaism, Christianity touches the religious life of mankind at many points. Very early in its history it was brought into contact with the religions of Greece and Rome. In modern times, through its missionaries, it confronts the great religions of the East (Confucianism, Hinduism, Buddhism, etc.), as well as the more primitive

forms represented among savage men. In all these it recognizes real though imperfect forms of the religious life,
and offers itself as the ideal toward which they are more
or less consciously striving.

The attitude taken by Christian theologians to the other
religions has varied between two extremes. The prevailing tendency has been to emphasize the contrast to the
sharpest extent. The ethnic faiths have been treated as
wholly degenerate and corrupt; or at least, so far as their
contribution to religious truth is concerned, as negligible.
Recently, however, the pendulum has swung to the other
extreme. The points of similarity between Christianity
and other religions have been rather over- than underesti-
mated, and the original contribution of the former to the
religious life of man minimized. Christianity is regarded
in many quarters as simply the reassertion in somewhat
clearer and more convincing form of truths common to all
the greater religions.

Obviously, the question as to the nature of the relation
between Christianity and other religions is one of fact, to
be determined by the researches of scholars. The interest
of the Christian theologian is confined to the significance
of the facts when determined. Here it may be said in
general that so long as the distinctive character and the
permanent authority of the Christian revelation are
assured, the greater the number of points of contact
between Christianity and other faiths, and the more
numerous the similarities between them, the easier will it
be to establish the universal character of the former, and
to defend its claim to be the final religion. Christian
theology is no less worthy of acceptance because Greek
elements as well as Hebrew have entered into its making.
If it shall be proved that Persia and Babylonia have added

their contribution, its claim to acceptance will not be less, but rather greater. The same will prove true of the religions of the farther as well as of the nearer East. Buddhism and Confucianism, as well as Islam, have no doubt each some lesson to teach mankind. If so, we may well receive it thankfully. It is a mark of greatness to be able to receive as well as to give. As the religion of humanity, it is the privilege of Christianity to take from each faith the element of truth which it contains, while supplying that which is needed to complete it.

But in order to maintain this position successfully we must be able to show that Christianity has something of supreme importance to give. Its comprehensiveness must not be so far emphasized as to obscure its distinctive character. For a world religion two things are necessary, a universal sympathy and a unique message. This combination Christianity provides. Hospitable to all good which the other religions contain, it has yet something of its own to offer them. This new gift is Christ himself. He is the original contribution of Christianity to the religious life of man. Everything distinctive which it possesses goes back directly or indirectly to him.

In the light of these considerations we may estimate the claim of some recent German theologians that Christianity is a syncretistic religion. By a syncretistic religion is meant a religion which consists of a combination of elements taken over substantially unchanged from earlier faiths, and without any distinctive character or new contribution of its own. As applied to Christianity, the term gains a certain plausibility from the fact that the Christian religion has always shown itself hospitable to new truth, that many influences have entered into its making, and that, in the course of its history, it has often appeared in association with elements indifferent, or even hostile, to its original character. But one may recognize the catholicity and many-sidedness of Christianity, while at the same time insisting upon the new contribution which it has made to the religious life of man. This new contribution is the direct result of the character of its founder. The personality of the Christ has stamped upon the religion which bears his name an impress which no later changes have succeeded in obliterating; and in the light of his character, teaching and influence, even those truths and experiences which it shares with other religions receive a new meaning.

We may illustrate the vitalizing and transforming influence of Jesus in connection with the Christian Gospel, the Christian ideal, and the Christian experience. It is at these three points that we see most clearly wherein the distinctive character of the Christian religion consists.

5. *Christianity as a Distinctive Religion.*

The Gospel of Christianity is that of the kingdom of God. It takes for granted the fatherhood of God, the brotherhood of man, and the infinite worth of the individual human soul. To the sinful it offers forgiveness; to the weak, strength; to the sorrowing, comfort, and to all, the opportunity of brotherly service and sacrifice. It seeks to organize mankind into a spiritual society, independent of race, nationality, education or class; in which love shall be the bond of union, and humility the test of greatness. But, unlike purely ethical systems, it finds its motive power in the redemptive love of the good God, who has given his Son to be the Saviour of the world, and whose fatherly purpose and character Jesus reveals.

While it postpones the complete realization of the kingdom to the future, it affirms that it is present here and now; and that entrance to it is possible to all who through penitence and faith accept the gracious invitation of the Master, and, denying themselves, take up their cross and follow him.

The ideal of Christianity is the character of Jesus. In him we find the divine purpose for man realized in a human life. Conscious of dependence upon God in the least things as in the greatest, it was his meat and drink to do his Father's will. Toward his fellow-men his attitude was one of unfailing sympathy and love. Yet sympathy never dimmed his moral insight, or caused him to lower his requirement. He claimed to be Master, and proved his right by his willingness to serve. In the suffering from which his disciples shrank, he saw a necessary incident in his saving work, and compared his shameful death to a covenant sacrifice, sealing the relation between his followers and God. Thus he reversed all previous standards of greatness, and created a new type of character, which he presented to his followers as an ideal for them to realize.

The new Gospel and the new ideal result in a new type of religious experience. The communion with God which the Master enjoyed is reproduced in the lives of his followers. The distance which in earlier forms of religion too often separated man from God is removed, and God is known as a present Spirit, realizing in men the ideal of character revealed in Jesus Christ. The sense of power resulting from communion with a present God is a distinguishing note of early Christianity, and gives freedom and spontaneity to the Christian life. Instead of slavishly following the precepts of a dead

Master, Christians are conscious of serving a living Lord, by whose Spirit they are led to new insight, and enabled to make new decisions, adapted to the changing circumstances in which they may be placed. The exact relation of this experience to the historic Jesus remains a problem for theology. The fact is patent, and must enter into any account of Christianity.

Thus Christianity, as the religion of divine sonship and human brotherhood, offers men a new Gospel, that of the kingdom of God ; a new ideal, that of the character of Jesus; and a new power, that of the divine Spirit, realizing the kingdom of God by transforming men into the image of Christ. It is the great redemptive agency, through which, in spite of imperfection and sin, God's saving purpose is being more and more accomplished.

6. *The Finality of Christianity.*

It follows from the nature of Christianity as a religion of freedom and life that it is not exhausted in the original revelation of God in Christ, but includes also the entire process through which that revelation is made effective among men. As the appointed means for realizing the kingdom of God, Christianity is a progressive religion. Growth is the law of its life, and this along all lines, — doctrinal, institutional, practical.

The progress thus implicit in the ideal of Christianity is exemplified in its history. Set in a changing environment and facing new problems, we see the Christian spirit creating new forms of thought, organizing new institutions, giving birth to new types of character. In this power of adaptation we have not only the secret of its past victories, but also the ground for faith in its continued influence and final triumph.

It is true that the development has not been uniform. Side by side with a growing insight into the spirit of Christ, we find a corresponding deterioration. This is due not only to the inherent tendency to evil in human nature, but also to a blind conservatism, which insists upon holding to forms and practices after they have served their day. The progress of Christianity realizes itself in spite of this tendency, and consists in the victory of the spirit of Christ over all the influences which seek to impede it.

In the light of these facts we have to estimate the claim of Christianity to be the absolute or final religion. This cannot be so understood as to exclude the variety and progress which its history shows, but must include and explain them. It is the expression of faith in the capacity of Christianity to gather to itself all that is good and true in human thought and life ; to purge away the errors and imperfections which have gathered about it in the course of human history, and so to prove itself the final and perfect religion for man. This capacity, which to the philosopher is a mere hypothesis whose truth or falsehood must be tested by the event, is to the Christian a doctrine of faith, based upon his own experience of the uplifting influence of Christ, and his conviction that in him are to be found resources adequate to the utmost human need. He believes that what he has found in Christianity others will find also. In this conviction he finds the law of his conduct, and the spring of his missionary enthusiasm. The end of all Christian activity is the establishment of the supremacy of Christ among men.

The ground for believing that Christianity is the final religion is the fact that it possesses Christ. Philosophies and institutions pass away ; he abides. After nineteen centuries his character still stands unsurpassed, and we know no better formula for religious progress than to describe it as the growing conformity of mankind to the spirit and principles of Jesus. So simple and human is his Gospel that it has been able to assimilate all that is good and true in the past; and there is every reason to believe that it will continue to do so in the future.

Thus the perfectness of Christianity is not like that of a picture or a statue which is finished once for all, and to which nothing can be added. It is rather like that of the human body which attains its end only through a process of growth. It is the perfectness of life, not of death. The great proof of the divinity of Christ is not so much that he once lived the perfect life, as that he is the source of an uplifting and transforming influence which is continuous.

Summing up our discussion in a concluding definition, we may describe Christianity as " the religion of divine sonship and human brotherhood, revealed and realized by Jesus Christ. As such it is the fulfilment and completion of all earlier forms of religion, and the divinely appointed means for the redemption of mankind through the establishment of the kingdom of God. Its central figure is Jesus Christ, who is not only the revelation of the divine ideal for man; but also, through the transforming influence which he exerts over his followers, the most powerful means of realizing that ideal among men. The possession in Christ of the supreme revelation of God's love and power constitutes the distinctive mark of Christianity, and justifies its claim to be the final religion." [1]

[1] The definition is taken from my *Essence of Christianity,* New York, 1902, p. 309, to which the reader may be referred for a fuller discussion of the problem connected with the definition of Christianity.

CHAPTER IV

As the source of the Christian religion Christian faith recognizes a divine revelation of permanent authority, by which the later development is to be tested, and that which is truly Christian is to be distinguished from all that is falsely so called. Theologians differ in their view as to the nature and extent of this revelation, and as to the grounds on which it is to be received; but there is general agreement that it centres in Jesus Christ, and that its essential features are preserved in the Christian Scriptures. As a help to a correct definition, it will be well to begin by considering (1) what is meant by revelation, and (2) what is the test by which a specific revelation may be recognized.

1. *What is meant by Revelation.*

By revelation is meant the self-manifestation of God. Like all impartations of knowledge, it involves subjective and objective elements. It takes for granted an apprehending mind, and consists in those activities by which this mind is made aware of new truth about God. Whatever facts, events or experiences have resulted in such increase of knowledge come legitimately within the scope of the term.

Revelation in the religious sense is distinguished from other impartations of knowledge, partly by its object, in that it has to do with God (here understood in the religious sense as the personal deity, as distinct from the ultimate of philosophy); partly in its end, in that it is designed to have a practical bearing on the conduct of man. Whatever else it may contain, it centres always in man's relation to God, and God's will for man.

Subjectively considered, revelation is always an individual experience. As the impartation of truth about God to the human spirit, it must repeat itself again and again in the experience of each new man. To speak of a revelation apart from such inner apprehension is a misnomer. In the apprehension of God no one can take the place of another. Each must know God for himself. In this sense revelation becomes co-extensive with true religious experience.

In practice, however, it is customary to restrict the use of the word to those impartations which have more than an individual significance. Experience in all its forms is the product of objective and subjective factors.[1] The stimuli which arouse our sensations and impressions come to us from the outer world, and this is just as true of the religious experience as of our knowledge of the physical universe. Moreover, just as in ordinary sense perception there are common objects which act upon many men and arouse similar impressions, so in the religious life. There are activities of God which act revealingly upon many different individuals. If it were not so, there could be no common religious life. To these sources of common insight we apply the term " revelation" in a special sense, distinguishing them from the wider revelation of the individual experience. The restriction — though often

[1] The word " objective " is here used in the familiar psychological sense to denote the object presented to consciousness, leaving the philosophical question as to the nature of the ultimate reality an open one.

abused — is not arbitrary, but rests upon an experimental basis: namely, the facts of the social religious life just described.

Historical study discloses a wide variety in the methods through which men have believed God to have revealed himself. In primitive religion, revelation is something arbitrary and sporadic, depending upon the presence of some individual specially favored of God. It comes through dreams and visions, through strange natural phenomena, and in other exceptional ways ; and concerns itself largely with the interests and welfare of individual men. As time goes on, and society becomes more highly organized, ethical considerations become more prominent. God's hand is seen moving in the affairs of nations, and his voice is heard speaking in the conscience of man. Revelation concerns itself with social as well as individual interests. Classes of men arise whose special function it is to discover and interpret the will of God. Lawgivers and priests embody the divine commands in precept and ritual. Prophets interpret the divine teaching in history and human life. The teachings of the past are gathered into sacred books and handed down for the enlightenment of future generations. Last of all, Nature itself is seen to be one great revelation of God.

2. *The Test of Revelation.*

The test of revelation is that it reveals: *i. e.* that as a result of it there becomes known to man some truth about God which was not known before, but which, once revealed, henceforth verifies itself in experience. This is the test of knowledge in all departments of life. The new fact or truth takes its place with others as part of the organism of truth. It relates itself to other facts and truths; verifies itself in experience; enables men to do work or to understand phenomena which they could not otherwise have mastered. So it must be if there is to be knowledge of the object of religion.

Self-evident as this might seem, it is far from being universally recognized. There is a widespread view which makes the test of revelation just the opposite: namely, the fact that it does not reveal. Instead of being regarded as the complement of reason, it is conceived as its antithesis; and may be described as the impartation, by supernatural means, of mysteries rising above the human understanding, and incapable, after communication as before, either of rational proof or of experimental verification.

The origin of this view is easy to explain. It is the natural expression of an age which has inherited from the past religious truths, whose origin and meaning it no longer understands. Its theoretical basis is an agnostic philosophy which banishes God to a transcendent realm where the human faculties are unable to follow him, and then tries to make up for its loss of direct communion by seeking indirect communications through supernaturally accredited messengers. But the relief is only in appearance; for the same difficulty which prevents us from knowing God obtains also in the case of his agents. So far as their message has to do with the divine, it introduces us into a world where our powers fail us, and we are shut up to a blind faith. The doctrines of religion remain mysteries received on authority, since there is no common standard either of truth or of right by which they may be tried. It is evident that, under the guise of affirming revelation, such a view denies it in any true sense.

Over against this agnostic view it is to be maintained that the relation between God and man is such that it is possible for him to reveal himself to man, and for man to receive his revelation. This has been the faith of the greatest theologians of the church, Catholic as well as Protestant. However much they have insisted upon the necessity for supernatural means for the impartation of truth, they have maintained that once revealed it could be explained and defended by its own light. Anselm's motto, *Credo ut intelligam*, well expresses the true spirit of Christian theology. Faith, *i. e.* practical acceptance of Christianity through the will, is the door to knowledge. The final proof of Christianity is that it gives a more satisfying view of the world than any other.

This is not to deny the presence of mystery in religion. No one knows better than the Christian theologian that all our knowledge of God is set in the midst of a great ocean of ignorance. His contention is merely that, so far as God is revealed, the mystery is diminished. What was before obscure now becomes clear. What was before perplexing is now seen to be reasonable. Even those truths in religion which go beyond present experience (as those which relate to the future) are expressed in terms of a possible experience, and gain assent because necessary to a completely rational explanation of the facts of the present life.

It follows that the proof of any particular revelation is to be sought not so much in the way it comes, as in what it brings. The position of the older apologetic, which magnified the extraordinary elements in revelation, and relied for its proof upon miracle, has been very widely abandoned. The mere fact of an extraordinary event, however inexplicable, proves nothing. Revelation begins when we discover a meaning in that which to others is extraordinary. And this is the case with the miracles of religion. They are not merely wonders; they are signs. Instead of being added to revelation from without to confirm it, they are themselves a means of imparting divine truth. Extraordinary as they appear, they are the disclosure of divine purposes and methods, which, to a deeper insight and a wider experience, prove part of a consistent whole. It is this fact which gives them their significance as revelation.[1]

3. *The Christian Revelation.*

By the Christian revelation we mean the disclosure which God has made of his nature and will in the person and work of Christ. Its content is the Gospel: *i. e.* the good news of God's redemptive love in Christ, calling men out of their sin and need into the righteousness and peace of the kingdom of God, and giving them as their ideal the organization of mankind in brotherly fellowship and mutual service after the likeness and in the spirit of Christ.

As applied to Christianity, the word "revelation" may be used in two senses. In the narrow sense Christ himself is the Christian revelation; since all that is distinctive in Christianity centres in him. But in a wider sense the

[1] This general point of view is quite consistent with different conceptions of the nature of the evidence by which revelation makes its presence known. In the older rationalistic theology the clearness and self-consistency of the truth presented was the controlling consideration. Recently, the part played by practical motives in determining our judgments of truth has been brought into the foreground. The point here made is simply that, whatever the principles which determine our acceptance of truth in general, it is through conformity to these that a revelation which professes to give us truth in the religious realm must be tested. The recent contention of certain theologians of the school of Ritschl, that religion has to do solely with judgments of value is not, as it is often represented both by its advocates and its opponents, a device for withdrawing religion from the control of the rational standards which determine the judgment of reality in other realms. It is simply a mark of a changed viewpoint which affects the philosophical concept of reality itself.

word may be used to include all God's manifestations, past and future; since it is only in the light of its antecedents and effects that the full significance of the Christian revelation can be understood. This fact is recognized by the church, which binds up in its Bible as integral parts of the Christian revelation, the Old Testament Scriptures, which contain God's preparatory revelation to Israel, and the Acts and the Epistles, which record the effects produced by Christ's spirit upon the lives of the men who came after him. This wider extension of the term appears in the phrase "person and work of Christ."

So far as the future is concerned, the legitimacy of the extension is clear. It follows from the nature of the Christian revelation as a Gospel of redemption and progress that its full significance can be understood only in the light of the experience which it creates. This fact is recognized in theology in its doctrine of the witness of the Holy Spirit. We learn of Christ not simply from his own words and deeds, but through the transformation which faith in him has wrought in the lives of his followers. So far as his influence works its appropriate fruits in human society, it is creating new objects by which God is made known to men. The clearest example of this is the New Testament. In the Gospels and Epistles we have the record of the effects produced by Christ upon the lives, feelings and thoughts of the men who stood closest to him. As such, they become one of the most important, indeed, the most important means of understanding Christ. They are in a true sense a new revelation, a new objective means by which God manifests himself to man. In fact, so valuable have they proved historically, that they have often obscured the earlier and greater revelation on which they depend.

What is true of the New Testament is true no less of the institutions of the church and of the lives of individual Christians. These two are fruits of the spirit of Christ, and, as such, means by which God reveals himself to men. The nearer we approach the New Testament ideal, the more numerous and effective should we expect these channels of revelation to become.[1]

But this is not all. There is a true sense in which Christ works backward as well as forward. In the light of his revelation, the earlier history of the race becomes full of unsuspected significance. God's revelations to Israel and in the ethnic faiths mean more to the Christian than to those who first received them; since he perceives the goal toward which they were moving, and so discovers meanings hidden from the men to whom they first came. So nature, studied in the light of Christ, yields lessons not otherwise to be learned. The laws which science discloses become methods of a Father's working; and forces, hitherto deemed ruthless or blind, are seen to be serving the Christian end. So everywhere in the universe, through Christ, the number of objects through which God is revealing himself is continually increasing.

Among the earlier disclosures which prepare the way for Christ, the clearest is found in the religious history of Israel. Beginning in exceptional communications to chosen individuals, this culminates in the teaching of the great prophets of the eighth and following centuries, who saw in Jehovah[2] the God of the whole world, and fearlessly

---

[1] The name "revelation," applied in 1 Peter (i, 13) to the second coming of Christ, shows that to Christian faith the supreme manifestation of the Christ remains for the future.

[2] In view of the lack of uniformity among English scholars in the transliteration of the Hebrew יהוה, I have retained the familiar Jehovah, in spite of its inaccuracy.

proclaimed the eternal principles of justice, mercy and love. In their writings we find the universal ideal of Christianity anticipated, and the foundation laid upon which its distinctive message rests.

These wider facts and relations we include in our conception of the Christian revelation. It is not something which stands apart from nature, history, and the religious experience, complete in itself. It is something which realizes itself through them, and whose full meaning becomes apparent only through the progressive apprehension in which they are determining factors.

When we speak of the finality of the Christian revelation, we mean that through all the stages of this progressive self-manifestation of God, the person of Christ remains the controlling factor; that he still keeps his place, and, we believe, will continue to keep it, as the highest realization of the divine ideal, and the most powerful means of realizing that ideal among men.

4. *The Nature and Function of the Bible.*

The contents of the Christian revelation are preserved in permanent and authoritative form in the Christian Bible.

By the Bible we mean that collection of writings, partly of known, partly of unknown date and authorship, containing the record of God's progressive revelation, first to the people of Israel, and afterwards to the world in Christ; which, at first consisting of two separate groups or Testaments, have since been united into a single volume, and are received by the Christian church as canonical, *i. e.* inspired Scriptures.

This definition brings out (1) the historical origin of the Bible; (2) its religious significance; (3) its function in the church.

(1) Considered historically, the Bible is a collection of writings by many different hands, extending over a period of many centuries. It is not a book, but a library; or, to be exact, two libraries. The Old Testament contains the classical literature of Israel; the New, the classical literature of early Christianity. While literary criticism can tell us much as to the origin and history of the several books, there is much as to the human authorship of the Bible of which we are still ignorant. Nor is the case otherwise when we consider the history of the Scriptures as a collection. Here, too, we have to do with a complex process extending over many centuries, in which different motives were operative, and which did not everywhere or always lead to uniform results. The traces of these early differences remain in the disagreement which still obtains between Catholics and Protestants as to the extent of the canon, and as to the grounds on which it is to be received.

(2) The unity which seems to many imperilled by the historical criticism of the Bible is found by the religious sense in its connection with revelation. The Old Testament gives us the record of God's revelation to Israel; the New tells of his wider revelation in Christ, and points forward to a continuing illumination through the Spirit. The justification of the union of the two groups of writings in a single volume is found in the intimate connection which has already been seen to exist between the Christian revelation in the narrow sense and its preparatory stages in Israel. Thus the unity of Scripture depends upon the unity of the progressive revelation it records, and it is on this connection that its permanent religious significance is based.

(3) Distinct from the religious significance of the Bible as the record of revelation, though intimately connected

with it, is its ecclesiastical function as a standard. It was, indeed, the desire for such a standard which first led to the collection of the Scriptures; and their normative authority, however differently conceived and defended, is still recognized by all the great branches of the Christian church. It is this function of the Scriptures which is expressed by the doctrine of inspiration.

5. *The Inspiration of the Bible.*

The term " inspiration " as applied to the Bible has a technical meaning. It refers to its use as a standard, and denotes the quality which fits it to act as an authoritative guide. This being the case, the fact of inspiration stands or falls with the fact of authority, and the theory of inspiration will depend upon the view taken of the nature of authority.

There are two chief views of the nature of religious authority. To the first, it is wholly external to the individual, beginning where human reason and conscience break down; to the second, it has its seat (not its source) within the individual, and consists in the appeal which is made by divine truth to the reason, conscience, and religious feeling of man. Where the first point of view obtains, the fact of a religious authority is established by purely external evidence (*e. g.* that of miracle, or of predictive prophecy); where the second is controlling, it carries its evidence within itself in its inherent excellence.

The view of authority which finds its seat in the individual conscience is not inconsistent with the acceptance of an objective standard. This is often asserted by those who maintain the other view, but wrongly. Man is a social being, and his life would be impossible unless there were common rules of thought and action by which his intercourse with his fellows could be regulated. The real question at issue is as to the ground on which such social standards are to be accepted : — whether they must be imposed by some external power, or whether their authority can be maintained on internal grounds, justifying itself in each case in the forum of the individual conscience.

The first of these points of view has been, on the whole, characteristic of Catholicism. The Catholic finds the evidence of the inspiration of Scripture in the extraordinary manner in which it was composed,[1] and relies for the proof of the canon upon the testimony of the church. Protestantism, on the other hand, has based its faith upon the inherent qualities of Scripture, emphasizing its perspicuity, efficacy, sufficiency and the like, and finding a sufficient proof of the inspiration of the Bible in the witness of the Spirit to the heart and conscience of the individual believer. Thus the Bible holds a more fundamental place in Protestantism than in Catholicism, since, instead of being one among other forms of the tradition principle, received on the authority of the church, it is itself the test by which the legitimacy of the later ecclesiastical development is to be judged.

In practice, however, Protestantism has not always drawn the full consequences of its spiritual conception of authority. While relying for its *proof* of inspiration upon internal evidence, it has retained in its *definition* qualities which have significance only on an external theory of authority. An instance of this inconsistency is the so-called inerrancy theory.

Inerrancy is the theory which extends the authority of the Bible to all the matters which it contains, historical and scientific as well as religious, and finds the evidence

[1] Cf. *Council of Trent,* " Spiritu Sancto dictante " (Schaff, *Creeds,* **II**, p. 78).

of its divine inspiration in the exact accuracy of all its statements. In its extreme form, as in the Helvetic Consensus Formula of 1675, it makes the Bible the result of immediate divine dictation, and holds that even the Hebrew vowel points were inspired. In its more moderate statements a distinction is made between form and substance ; and peculiarities of style and expression on the part of the Biblical writers are admitted. The arguments by which it is supported are partly theoretical and partly practical. The theoretical argument is based upon an *a priori* view of the divine perfection, which holds that the presence of error of any kind in Scripture would be inconsistent with the veracity of God. This appears most clearly in the theory of the so-called original autographs, in which all pretence of an experimental proof is abandoned, and perfection is asserted of a Bible which no man has ever seen. The practical argument takes its departure from the use of the Bible as a standard, and argues that the presence of error in any part of a book designed for such a purpose destroys its trustworthiness as a guide in all. This argument, too, proves at bottom to rest upon a theoretical assumption, namely, the inability of the human mind to recognize and respond to divine truth when presented in a human and therefore imperfect setting. Both difficulties are met by a truer conception of the nature of revelation, and a juster appreciation of those qualities in Scripture on which its significance as a guide depends.

6. *The Bible as Revelation.*

The qualities which give the Bible its permanent importance for Christianity are (1) the fact that it is the most ancient, direct and reliable source for our knowledge of the historic Christ, and (2) the fact that it is the most effective means for the awakening and stimulating of the present Christian life.

The union of these two qualities is not a matter of accident. The power of the Bible to enlighten and inspire is intimately connected with its historical function as a witness to Christ. As the Christian revelation *par excellence*, Christ is the source upon which the Christian life in every age must feed. But we get at Christ most directly through the Bible. In the Old Testament we have the spiritual food upon which his inner life was nourished, the divine revelation which he felt himself called to fulfil. In the Gospels we have the record of his life, and the original form of his teaching; in the Epistles and the Revelation, the influence of his spirit upon the men who stood nearest to him. His personality is central in the Bible, and binds its different parts into a unity.

This intimate connection with Christ explains the qualities which Christian faith finds in the Bible. It explains the clearness with which it presents the truths man needs to know, the adequacy with which it answers his questions and meets his needs, and the moving power with which it lays hold upon his conscience, and constrains his will. In these qualities (the perspicuity, sufficiency, and efficacy of the older Protestant dogmatics) resides the authority of Scripture. The life-giving power of the Master is found in the book which witnesses of him, and is the explanation of its continuing influence in the Christian church.

It is true that these qualities are not equally apparent in all parts of the Bible. Like all historical books, its earlier parts must be read in the light of the later, and its essential message distinguished from its local and temporary setting. It is not a law book from which one may quote proof texts at random, but a record of spiritual experience

which centres in Christ and must be tested by him.   Failure to remember this has led either to an allegorical
exegesis, in which the figure of the historic Christ has
been in danger of being lost, or to an artificial harmony,
in which lower and less advanced stages of divine truth
have been lifted to the same level as the most spiritual
teaching of the Master.   From this dilemma the literary
study of the Bible relieves us.   By showing the gradual
process through which our Bible has attained its present
form, and the diverse elements which have entered into its
making, it affords a scientific basis for the practical discrimination between the spiritual values of the different
parts which devout souls have instinctively practised in
all ages ; while, at the same time, by showing the real connection which unites the earlier stages of divine revelation
to the Christ to whom they point, it makes possible a use
of the Bible as a whole which is at once intelligent and
edifying.

Thus the Bible is at once a revelation and the record of
a revelation.   By its witness to the historic Christ, it
points the church back to the source from which its distinctive message sprang, and so affords a test by which
successive generations may test the purity and genuineness
of their Christian life.   Through its living message to the
needs and longings of the present, it lifts men, through
communion with the historic Jesus, to faith in the living
God from whom he came.   The union of these two
qualities constitutes the distinction of the Scriptures from
other writings, and justifies the unique place assigned to
them by the church as inspired, *i. e.* authoritative writings.

CHAPTER V

THE CHRISTIAN CHURCH

1. *The Definition of the Church.*[1]

THE religious life which has its source in the Christian revelation finds social expression in the church.

By the church of Christ we mean the religious society, tracing its origin historically from Jesus of Nazareth, and finding in him its bond of union in common worship, work, and life, in which the revealing and redeeming influence of Christ is perpetuated; and through which, under the influence of the divine Spirit, the Christ life is mediated to the world.

The word " church " is sometimes used in a wider sense to include the members of the patriarchal and Jewish dispensations; and in this sense, its foundation is carried back to Paradise. The usage has its analogy in the extension of the term " Christian revelation " to include divine communications before Christ, and its justification in the fact that the kingdom of God proclaimed by Christ is destined to gather into itself the devout and good of every name and age. But it is better in theology to restrict the term " Christian church " to the society which owes its origin to Jesus, and which is the direct result of the new and higher revelation which he brought. So understood, the term is a narrower one than the kingdom. The church is the divinely appointed means by which the kingdom of God is to be realized among men.

[1] Cf. chapter XXI, section 4, pp. 392 sq.

The church differs from other human societies in its
religious character, *i. e.*, the fact that the bond of union
between its members is the consciousness of a common
relation to God. This fact determines all its activities,
which are designed either to express this relation in worship, or to stimulate men to conduct which is its appropriate result. Yet, since the God who is worshipped in
religion is at the same time the Lord of the world, and has
expressed his will in ethical ideals which affect all human
relations, the church, in the fulfilment of its religious aim,
is necessarily brought into contact with all sides of human
life, and feels it its mission to organize society as a whole
in accordance with the religious principle. In this fact is
to be found the explanation at once of the independent
function of the church and of its intimate connection with
all phases of human activity.

A distinction is frequently made in theology between
the church visible, and the church invisible ; the former
term being used to denote the ecclesiastical organization,
the latter the company of the elect who shall finally be
saved. The distinction, which is common to Catholicism
and Protestantism, dates from the time when the church
of Christ was identified with a single ecclesiastical body ;
and was an attempt to account for the evil which this body
admittedly contained without giving up its divine and
authoritative character. Historically, the distinction has
served a useful purpose, (1) in emphasizing the fact that
not all who belong to the ecclesiastical organization are
members of the true church, and (2) in calling attention
to the fact that the redemptive influence of Christ extends
beyond institutional Christianity. In Protestantism, especially, it has proved an effective means of protest against
ecclesiastical tyranny. But it must never be suffered to

obscure the fact that the church of Christ exists to-day as a definite body in the persons of the men and women who have been touched by his spirit, and who live for the ends which he approves. This spiritual society, creating institutions, but not itself perfectly comprehended or expressed by any, is the true church of Christ.

As the religious society which finds its bond of union in Jesus of Nazareth, the church is one. When we take our departure from the ecclesiastical organization, this fact is either obscured, or preserved at the cost of ethical principles fundamental to the Gospel; but it becomes clear so soon as we consider the real character of the church as a spiritual society. Beneath the outward divisions and misunderstandings which separate different bodies of Christians, there is a common religious experience which is shared by all whose lives are lived under the influence of the Master, and which unites in sympathy, labor, and prayer, good men in every branch of the church. It is this common religious life, uniting in spiritual fellowship men of different ecclesiastical names and of none, which is the real foundation of the unity of the church.

2. *The Church in its Ideal and in History.*

In its ideal the church fulfils a double function. It is a school for training Christians in the knowledge and service of God, and it is the means by which the Christ life is imparted to those who have it not. Along both these lines it is the organ by which the spirit of Christ finds expression in the world.

The doctrine of the mediatorial function of the church has often been made the vehicle of sacerdotal theories foreign to the Gospel, but, properly defined, it is the most obvious of truths. The difference between a historic religion like Christianity, and mysticism, which confines religion to the individual experience, lies in the fact that, whereas the latter regards religion as a matter of pure feeling, and hence as incommunicable, the former believes that its revelation has a definite content, and therefore may be communicated from man to man. Since the work which Christ came to do was for society as well as for individuals, it requires for its accomplishment the creation of a body of men through whom his influence may be perpetuated, and his purpose accomplished. Mysticism knows no such society ; Christianity cannot exist without it.

The church perpetuates the work of Christ both as revealer and redeemer. The distinctive features which have entered into human thought through him are handed down by the testimony of his followers, and so become the permanent possession of the race. The self-sacrificing love, of which he gave the example, inspires like love in his disciples, and so gives rise to the church's varied ministry to human need. It is through the church that men come to know practically about Christ and are won to faith in the Gospel.

In the course of its missionary activity the church gives rise to institutions. Like every other human society, it has to create for itself organs of expression, and with the widening range of its influence and the growing complexity of its task, these become naturally more formal and elaborate in character. The witness which had first taken the form of personal testimony finds social expression in *creeds*. The writings which had at first been written for special occasions and for narrow circles are gathered into *Scriptures*. The worship which had at first been free and unrestrained becomes more formal, and assumes *liturgical* character. The simple rites of baptism and the Lord's

Supper become the first of a series of *sacraments*. The informal service of those who are older and wiser proves no longer sufficient, and we have the rise of a distinct *ministry*, which in time assumes *sacerdotal* character. Thus all the forms familiar in the history of other religions repeat themselves in the organization of the Christian church.

With the growth of institutional Christianity we note the reappearance of the conflict between vital and traditional religion, of which we have already spoken. The doctrines and forms which were the natural expression of the religious life of one generation are handed down to the next as unchanging laws. The organization which had its justification as means comes to be regarded as an end; and with growing emphasis upon ecclesiastical machinery the spirit of the Gospel is in danger of being lost. This contrast between ideal and history gives rise to the many reforming movements of which church history is full. Where the reforming spirit fails to find sufficient outlet within the limits of existing ecclesiastical institutions, it breaks away and creates new forms of its own. This is the explanation of the many sects into which historic Christianity is divided. They are, in part at least, the result of the effort of the Christian spirit to make its way and utter its message in a resisting environment.

The conflict thus indicated between vital and traditional Christianity is of fundamental importance for the history of theology. As Christian doctrine owed its origin at first to the effort to give intellectual expression to the new life brought by Christ, so all the vicissitudes through which that life has passed have left their traces in the history of doctrine. It is not the record of a uniform development according to logical rules, but the story of a conflict between different ideals, of which the various types of historic Christianity are the more or less complete expression.

3. *The Types of Historic Christianity.*

In the development of historic Christianity we note three stages which we may call the Greek, the Roman, and the Protestant.[1] Each of these has developed a distinct type of thought and life. In the Greek church attention is concentrated upon the past, and Christianity is identified with a body of doctrine once delivered, and a supernatural salvation preserved and mediated through an unchanging church. Roman Catholicism accepts in theory the traditional conception of Christianity, but makes room for progress by admitting a continual indwelling of the Spirit in the church, which renders possible new doctrinal definitions, with corresponding changes in the world of practice. In Protestantism the Bible takes the place of the church as the medium of revelation. In its pages God is thought of as speaking directly to the individual, and progress consists in the gradual appropriation by Christians, in thought as in experience, of the new impulse imparted to humanity by the Christ whose revealing and redeeming work it records. But, whereas in the earlier Protestantism the Bible is thought of as containing a

[1] The threefold division here adopted is the common one, as followed, for example, by Harnack, in his *What is Christianity?* and by Kaftan in his *Dogmatik.* It is a fair question, however, whether the true nature and relations of the different types of historic Christianity would not be more clearly exhibited by a fourfold division, namely, into Greek, Roman, Reformation, and modern. There is quite as much difference between the earlier and the later types of Protestantism as between the Greek and Roman forms of Catholicism. In each case the mark which distinguishes the later variety from the earlier is its more hearty acceptance of the principle of development; while the fundamental difference which separates Protestantism in both its forms from Catholicism appears in the nature of the standard which is accepted and the grounds on which it is received.

complete system of doctrine and morals, to be accepted unchanged by all succeeding generations; in the later it is conceived rather as giving the principles by which the church is progressively to develop her conception of truth and of duty under the continuing inspiration of the spirit of Christ.

Each of these stages, while dependent historically upon its predecessor, has a character of its own. Roman Catholicism takes over the result of the Greek dogmatic development, as preserved in the so-called ecumenical creeds, but modifies it according to its own distinctive spirit (*e. g.* the addition of the *filioque* to the doctrine of the Trinity, the doctrine of the infallibility of the Pope). Protestantism in its turn takes for granted the theological development in the Latin church, and has inherited many of its doctrines (*e. g.* the Augustinian doctrines of sin and grace, the Anselmic doctrine of the atonement). But its departure from Roman Catholicism is much more radical than that of the Roman from the Greek church, because of the fundamental difference in its conception of the relation of God to man. While Catholicism in both its forms is distrustful of the individual, holding that apart from the authoritative interpretation of the church he cannot be trusted to approach God for himself, Protestantism had its origin in the religious experience of an individual, and began with Luther's protest against any attempt on the part of the church to abridge his right of direct access to God.

It is a natural result of the character of Protestantism as a religion of freedom and individualism that its history should show greater variety in detail, and a more sensitive response to the changes of contemporary thought, than is the case with Catholicism. In place of a single institution like the Catholic church, we have to do with a

number of smaller bodies, differing in doctrine, in organization, and in the character of their religious life. These
differences are due partly to differences in intellectual or
social environment; partly to the influence of strong
religious leaders who have impressed their personality
upon the bodies with which they have been associated;
partly to the survival, in greater or less degree, of conceptions and practices inherited from earlier forms of Christianity. Yet these differences, important as they are for the
history of theology and for the understanding of special
doctrines, are consistent with a unity in fundamental conceptions and point of view which separates the various
Protestant bodies from Catholicism in all its forms, and
constitutes them a distinct class. This unity has its roots
in the new conception of religious authority which the
Reformers introduced, and its theological expression in the
principle of private judgment. Modern Protestantism
differs from the earlier forms in the clearness with which
it perceives this fact, and the consistency with which it
endeavors to apply it as a theological principle.

The practical effect of the difference between Protestant
and Catholic appears most clearly in the conception of the
church. While the Catholic identifies the church of
Christ with some existing ecclesiastical organization,
which is regarded as the vicar of Christ, the divinely
appointed agent for the exercise of his authority and the
mediation of his grace, the Protestant holds that the
church is found wherever the Gospel of Christ is preached,
and finds the sufficient proof of the divine authority of the
latter in its appeal to the conscience and in its transforming effect upon the lives of men.

It is true that this conception of the church has not
always been held by Protestants with equal clearness.

In its reaction against an excessive individualism, carrying the principle of private judgment to such lengths as to destroy the historic continuity and distinctive character of the Gospel,[1] Protestantism has sometimes taken refuge in a conception of the visible church inconsistent with the principles to which it owes its own life ; and we see the melancholy spectacle of one body of Protestants persecuting their fellows for exercising the same liberty of judgment which they claim for themselves.[2] But this is obviously a survival of an older conception of Christianity. The history of the church is full of such inconsistencies. Here, as everywhere, we must distinguish between theological principles and their more or less consistent ecclesiastical expression. It is the underlying theological difference between Protestantism and Catholicism which interests us here, not the special forms of its historical manifestation.

4. *The Catholic View of the Church.*

According to Catholic theory, the channel through which the influence of Christ is mediated to the world is the organization rather than the personalities who compose it. The ethical and spiritual marks of the church, while insisted on, are subordinated to those which are external. The proof of the true church is not primarily the Christlike character of its members, but direct descent from the

---

[1] As in the case of Carlstadt and the other revolutionaries whose excesses imperilled the cause of the newly established Protestant church.

[2] Calvin's burning of Servetus is perhaps the best known example of this Protestant ecclesiasticism. It appears in Luther's attitude to Zwingli and the Swiss Reformers in the matter of the Lord's Supper, and comes to full expression in the *jure divino* theories of the later Puritanism. The conception of the church as a society broad and many-sided enough to admit differences of opinion within itself on matters on doctrine is of comparatively modern origin.

apostles, and the possession of an unchanging ecclesiastical tradition. Hence the first condition both of knowledge and of salvation is submission to ecclesiastical authority.

This view of the church determines the idea of doctrine, of the sacraments, and of the ministry. Doctrine is the teaching of Christ through the apostles, preserved and handed down by the church in an unbroken tradition; to be received on the guarantee of her authority irrespective of its content. The sacraments are mysterious transactions, working *ex opere operato*, through which the store of divine grace committed to the church is made practically effective for the salvation of men. The ministry is a distinct order, a priestly caste, divinely set apart for the administration of this trust, both of truth and of grace.

In practice, this conception of the church is found associated with widely different forms of intellectual and moral life. It may be made the excuse for a purely stagnant religion, as in some forms of Eastern Christianity, or it may be consistent with constant change, as in modern Roman Catholicism. Its advocates may regard the Christian doctrines as mysteries rising above the reason, to be received on pure authority, or they may believe with Anselm in the possibility of their rational explanation and defence when once revealed. They may carry the doctrine of sacramental grace so far as to become indifferent to the most obvious ethical demands, or they may live lives as saintly as those of Francis of Assisi and Mère Angélique. But they agree in making the decision of the church as an institution the final arbiter in all matters of faith and morals. Those who deliberately refuse to accept her authority are denied the possibility of salvation, and those who remain within her pale do so with the understanding that if at any time a conflict should arise between her teaching and their conviction, it is in the former rather than in the latter that they must find the voice of God.

5. *The Protestant View of the Church.*

According to the Protestant view, Christ's influence is mediated to the world primarily by the persons who have been touched by his spirit, and who proclaim to others the truth by which their own lives have been changed. Protestantism recognizes the important part played by the church as an organization in the preservation and transmission of the Christian revelation. It accepts the Scriptures, the creeds and the sacraments, as divinely appointed means for the proclamation of divine truth. But it holds that all three fulfil their true function only as they so present Christ to men that they intelligently apprehend him, and heartily accept him for themselves. In Protestant theory the primary test of the true church is the possession of a Gospel that is making men Christlike.

This explains the fundamental place held by the Bible in Protestantism. It is through the Bible, as we have seen, that we gain most direct access to the historic Christ. In vindicating for the individual the right to go back for himself to the fountain head of divine revelation, and to interpret what he finds in the light of his own conscience under the guidance of the Holy Spirit, Protestantism has broken in principle with all ecclesiasticism, and substituted intelligent conviction for blind submission as the true bond of church union.

The substitution of the Bible for the church as the religious authority of Protestantism must not be understood as the substitution of one external standard for another. Such a change might have led to the reformation of specific abuses, but it would not have accounted for the radical change in the character of the religious life which the Reformation introduced. This change was due to the new sense of the freedom and worth of the individual which Luther gained through his own religious experience. The religious authority of Protestantism is not the Bible alone, but the Bible as interpreted to the individual by the Spirit of God. So understood, it is not a denial of the churchly principle, but its closer definition.[1] It is the expression of the kind of church in which Protestants believe: namely, a church in which the bond of union between the members consists in their common faith in the

---

[1] The popular view which contrasts the Bible and the church as exclusive principles is due to a failure to perceive the ambiguity of the term " standard." Strictly speaking, there is not one standard in theology, but several. The *formal* standard is philosophy (Cf. H. B. Smith, *Introduction to Christian Theology*, p. 61), or, as some theologians prefer to call it, human reason. All theologians, Catholic and Protestant alike, agree that nothing can enter into theology which contradicts the fundamental laws of the human mind (Cf. Vatican Council, quoted in Schaff, *Creeds of Christendom*, II, p. 249 ; Hodge, *Systematic Theology*, vol. I, pp. 49, 51). The *material* standard is the Christian revelation as preserved in Holy Scripture and progressively interpreted by the Holy Spirit. This, too, is admitted both by Catholic and Protestant, the only difference being as to the nature of the interpretation. The *ecclesiastical* standard is the creed of the particular branch of the church to which the theologian belongs. The significance of this is that it gives the sense in which the preceding must be understood, whether in the Catholic sense of a law to be interpreted by ecclesiastical decision and precedent, or in accordance with the Protestant principle of liberty. Historically, the three belong together. Common to all branches of Christendom, in some form or other, is the acceptance of the threefold standard, the Bible, the church, and the reason. The Protestant principle of the sole authority of Scripture is itself a creed statement, and, in so far, involves the recognition of the churchly principle.

Besides the threefold standard which is common to all Christians, every theologian has his own *individual* standard, by which is meant the specific principle or principles which he has gained from his study of the Bible in the spirit of the creed, and which he uses to guide him in organizing the wealth of material presented by the Christian experience into a consistent system.

Christ whom each has come to know, and freely to accept for himself, as he is presented to the reason and the conscience in the Bible.

This changed emphasis affects the Protestant view of doctrine, of the ministry, and of the sacraments. As the chief means of grace recognized by Protestantism is the *Word* (*i. e.* divine revelation preserved in the Scripture, and presented to the reason and conscience of the believer for his acceptance), so doctrine represents the common convictions of the whole body of intelligent Christians concerning revealed truth. The ministry is that portion of the body of believers who have received special gifts, fitting them for the spiritual instruction and guidance of their fellows. Their only authority is that of the truth they proclaim, and their office is fulfilled when they have presented the Gospel to others, leaving it to make its own appeal to the heart and conscience of those who hear. The sacraments are signs of spiritual realities, appealing to the faith of the individual, and becoming effective for salvation through intelligent apprehension of the truth for which they stand. Thus on all its sides Protestantism appeals to the intelligence of men, and has succeeded in building up a type of robust and thoughtful Christianity impossible to those whose religious life is nourished on the sacraments alone.

Yet, while thus emphasizing the independence of the individual, Protestantism recognizes the relative right of the principle for which Catholicism contends. Not all parts of divine truth are equally easy of apprehension, nor are all Christians equally mature. In religion, as in other departments of life, external authority has its legitimate place as an educational agency. As the child receives on trust what his parents tell him till the time comes when he is able to test it for himself, so the individual Christian

may well receive the testimony of the church with reverence and submission, knowing that it is the outcome of the
experience of men whose piety and insight were greater
than his own. It is not the principle of external authority
as such to which the Protestant objects in Catholicism,
but its exaltation from a means to an end. If the conflict arise between individual conviction and church teaching, to which we have already referred, the duty of the
Protestant is to follow his conscience, even if it take him
out of the church.

The two theories which we have thus contrasted corre-
spond to two permanent tendencies in human nature.
The Catholic is the conservative tendency, reverent of the
past, tenacious of its traditions, distrustful of the individual. The Protestant is the liberal tendency, living in
the present, intent upon progress, full of faith in the individual man. The day is past when it is possible for a
Protestant to think of Catholicism as wholly evil. It has
done and is still doing a necessary work in bringing in the
kingdom of God. Without its tenacious hold upon the
past much precious truth might have been lost ; without
its strong grasp upon the present much energy now
directed to useful ends might be dissipated. The weakness of Catholicism lies in its exclusiveness ; in its denial
of the legitimacy of the Protestant principle within its own
sphere. Protestantism has not always been free from this
exclusiveness, but it has had less excuse for it. The liberal,
if he be a true liberal, will be the first to recognize the
rights of conservatism. The way to meet the Catholic
claim is not to denounce it, but to understand it. This
will be our aim in the chapters that follow.

CHAPTER VI

1. *The Problem.*

ALL theology has for its aim the exposition and defense of the distinctive Christian doctrines. But in Protestantism this work is especially important because of the intimate connection which it assumes between doctrine and life. As the statement of the convictions which each Christian may win for himself from a study of the Bible, and which each should verify for himself in his own experience, theology becomes the common concern of all Christians. In contrast to the technical disquisitions of the schoolmen, Protestant theology began as the statement, in orderly and consistent terms, of the faith involved in the simplest Christian experience.

This fact explains two characteristics of early Protestant theology, — its Biblical and its practical character. The first dogmatic treatise of Protestantism (Melanchthon's *Loci* of 1521) was a brief handbook, designed to help men to a better understanding of the Bible by pointing out the fundamental truths (*Loci*) in which its message centres, and which each ought to be able by patient study to find for himself. Abstract and difficult questions were intentionally avoided, and those truths only were included which were believed to admit of experimental verification. It is true that Melanchthon recognized other Biblical doctrines, such as the Trinity, the two natures of Christ, etc., which were incapable of such experimental verification; but these he omitted from his book as likely to confuse the unlearned, and to lead to unprofitable discussion. In later editions he included them in order to show the attitude of Protestantism to the teaching of the older church, and to defend its adherents from the charge of radicalism. But in the later, as in the earlier editions, the practical interest is still prominent, and in his discussion of the more abstract and speculative doctrines Melanchthon is careful, as far as possible, to show the bearing of the unseen reality which is the object of faith upon the individual experience. This desire to relate doctrine and life is characteristic of all the Reformers.

Unfortunately this connection has not always been observed by their successors. With the doctrines of Catholicism, Protestant theologians too often took over its spirit and point of view. In theory still holding to a theology which should be at once Biblical and practical, Protestantism in its turn built up an orthodoxy whose contents were removed from any experimental test, and enforced acceptance of its teachings on grounds as external as those of Catholicism itself. So the original ideal of Protestantism, in which the bond of Christian union was the common redemptive experience produced by the Gospel, gave way to a confessionalism in which the creed took the place of the Bible, and the distinction between the technical points of philosophical theology and the fundamental convictions which are the spring of all Christian life was overlooked or denied.

Three causes have led to the breaking down of this traditional theology. The first is a better Biblical scholarship, which has shown the difference between the teaching of the Bible and the creeds for which its authority is claimed, and at the same time brought out the variety in the purpose and point of view of the various Biblical writers. The second is a revived religious life, which has emphasized anew the experimental basis of religion, and insisted that all the doctrines of Christianity be brought to a practical test. The third is a new philosophy, which has brought out the subjective elements which enter into cognition, and thrown discredit upon all attempts to gain knowledge of truth by a speculation which cannot be brought to the test of experience. Each of these causes has contributed its share to the revival of the original Protestant ideal of a theology which shall be at every point in close touch with life. It is the aim of modern Protestant theology, in all its forms, to set forth the objects of Christian faith in their distinctive character as modern scholarship has enabled us to see them; to show their experimental basis and their practical bearing; and so to commend them to all men as the truth they need.

While agreeing in the general ideal above described, theologians differ in their view of the method by which it may best be realized. Some, recognizing in the Bible at once the source and the test of Christian truth, are content to press back of the corruptions of the later ecclesiastical development to the historic revelation in which Christianity had its rise. Others emphasize the experimental basis of doctrine, and regard the task of theology as achieved when it has unfolded the contents of the present Christian consciousness. Still others, more philosophic in interest, seek to find, under the forms which history and experience present, the eternal principles of universal validity by which the claim of Christianity to final authority may be successfully defended. These methods, which we may call respectively the historical, the psychological and the speculative, are not necessarily exclusive. The ideal theology will recognize the right of each within its own sphere. It will turn back to the Bible to find what is distinctive of Christianity as a historic religion, and test the later ecclesiastical development by the Christ whom it reveals. It will set forth the convictions to which this study leads in the practical connection in which they are presented in the personal religious life, as saving truths to be verified in experience. Finally, it will seek to commend them to all men as the truth; partly by showing the function of the religious experience in life as a whole; partly by pointing out the unique answer of Christianity to the needs and longings to which this experience gives expression.

The bearing of the principles thus indicated upon theological method may be illustrated in the case of the central doctrine of the Christian system, — that of Christ.

2. *The Christological Principle and its Implications.*[1]

As the religion of divine sonship and of human brotherhood, divinely appointed for the redemption of mankind, Christianity is heir of all that is good and true in the past. The themes of which it treats are the same that have been the subject of theology in all ages, — God, the world, man, sin, salvation, the religious life. But that which is distinctive in its teaching is the new light which it brings to them from the person and work of Christ. Hence it must be our aim, both in our treatment of individual doctrines and in the system as a whole, to show the bearing of this new light on the older religious truths. In other words, our method must be Christological.

[1] The subject is more fully discussed in my essay, *Christ the Vitalizing Principle of Modern Theology*, New York, 1898.

But acceptance of the Christological principle without closer definition carries us but a little way; for Christ may be variously conceived. All the differences of viewpoint already discussed come to a head in men's thought of him. While some think of him primarily as the incarnate Logos, image and expression of the transcendent God, others see in him simply the ideal man, and regard any doctrine of metaphysical deity as involving logical contradictions destructive of his humanity. Still others seek to avoid the dilemma thus presented between a human and a divine Christ, by emphasizing the moral kinship between God and man which makes possible a divine indwelling in humanity, and the self-expression of God within the limits of a human life.

Where the first point of view obtains and Christ is thought of primarily as the divine Logos, there is danger that the distinctive features of Christianity as a historic religion may be lost. If the human life of Christ be but a form of the manifestation of the unchanging God, in which, for a brief time and for a special purpose, he has veiled his majesty and hidden his true nature, and if the distinguishing marks of the Christ are to be found in the supernatural attributes which separate him from man rather than in the ethical attributes which unite them, then the moral qualities revealed in his earthly life cannot be made the supreme criterion of Christianity. The Logos who has spoken once through the man Jesus may speak again by the mouth of his church, and the arguments which have been used to commend the first message may be employed with equal success to enforce the second. Even where the authority of the church is rejected, and revelation confined to the Bible, concentration of thought upon the divine Christ to the exclusion of the human has often led to so great an emphasis upon the transcendent and mysterious elements in Christian doctrine and life as to cause men to overlook the plain test afforded by Jesus' own teaching and example. So Christianity has been transformed into philosophic speculation or mystic ecstasy, and the qualities in which its distinctive character as a historic religion consists have fallen into the background.

On the other hand, when Christ is conceived simply as a man among men, we are confronted with the problem how to account for the place which his person has held in the Christian experience. Important as is the recovery of the human Jesus for the understanding of historic Christianity, it is equally true that to fail to see the divine significance of his person is to cut the spring of Christian faith, if the testimony of Christians themselves sheds any light upon its nature. The genius of Christianity as a historic religion consists in the fact that it sees in the human Jesus the revelation of the unseen God, and uses his life, teaching and example as a key to the understanding of the divine Father from whom he came.

The solution of the difficulty has been already anticipated. If we are right in our assumption that it is through the practical needs of the ethical and religious nature that we gain our insight into the highest truth, there is nothing unreasonable in the Christian faith in a Christ who is at once human and divine. It is through the experiences of love, holiness and sacrifice which become ours through contact with the ideal human life that we learn what the character of God is like, and so enter into relations with the ultimate reality. Such a life Christianity possesses in Jesus, and in him presents us not only with the highest ideal for man, but with the supreme revelation of God.

By the Christological principle, then, we mean the effort to trace in the ever-expanding revelation of God in humanity the vitalizing and transforming influence of the historic Jesus, that from our study we may gain new insight into the character and purpose of the God from whom he came, and so be able better to understand the meaning of the world in which we live and the end to which we are called. It is the method which arrives at God through Jesus, and uses the knowledge so gained as the final principle for the interpretation of life.

Such a method makes possible a sympathetic use of the older doctrines which Protestantism shares with Catholicism. We do not regard the interpretation of Jesus from the Godward side, as it meets us in the doctrines of the Trinity and of Christology, as mistaken or misguided ; though we recognize that it was often one-sided, and in many of its historic statements inadequate. We see in it the natural expression of Christian faith, witnessing, in the forms appropriate to the time, to the new life and light which it had found in Jesus. We, too, find light and life in the same Jesus, and regard it as the chief task of modern theology to give its answer, in the terms natural to our modern world, to the old question with which Christian theology began, — how God could be in Christ reconciling the world unto himself.

Acceptance of the Christological principle as thus defined is consistent with a wide variety of theological treatment. It is not necessary to begin with Christ in order to make him the controlling principle of the system. It is possible, with the older and some later theologians, to follow the so-called Trinitarian method, which groups its materials about the headings of the ancient creed, treating first of God the Father, then of Jesus Christ, and finally, of the work of the Spirit in the individual and the church. Or we may follow the synthetic method, characteristic of Calvinism, which begins with God as the source of all things, and then unfolds the system synthetically (*i. e.* by adding one new topic after another) through the decree, creation, providence, man, sin, Christ, etc., to the final issue. Or we may prefer to reverse the order and adopt the analytic method followed by Calixtus (1586–1656), and often employed by Lutheran theologians, in which we begin with the final issue of religion (blessedness, redemption, the kingdom of God) and reason back thence analytically (*i. e.* from effect to cause) to its source. Or finally, with Schleiermacher, we may make the Christian experience our point of departure, and gain our matter both as to past and future by a psychological analysis of the present consciousness of man. The order is not material, provided the point of view be correct and the treatment adequate.

In the present outline we shall find it most convenient to follow the common order, and to treat successively of the Christian idea of God, of the Christian view of the world, of man and his sin, of Christ and his salvation, and of the Christian life. This will give the following divisions :

1. The Christian idea of God.
2. The Christian view of the world.
3. Of man and his sin.
4. Of salvation through Christ.
5. Of the Christian life.

PART II

THE CHRISTIAN IDEA OF GOD

CHAPTER VII

THE ORIGIN AND RELATIONS OF THE CHRISTIAN IDEA OF GOD

1. *Of the Origin and Relations of the Christian Idea of God.*

THE word " God " has a different meaning in religion and in philosophy. In philosophy it is used as a synonym for the Absolute, and denotes the ultimate reality in the universe, however that reality may be conceived. To religion it expresses the unseen being or beings upon whom man believes himself dependent, to whom he offers worship, and from whom he invokes help. Hence in religion the word has a personal and practical connotation which is often absent in philosophy. Yet as man's thought grows more mature, and his experience enlarges, the two meanings tend to be identified, and the God who is worshipped in religion is seen to be the same as the ultimate reality of which philosophy is in search.

This identification — which may be studied in many different religions — is not arbitrary, but is the result of the unity of life, which combines the philosophic and the religious interest in the same person. With wider experience and deeper insight, the religious man comes to see that, unless his God be master of the world, the practical needs for which he seeks satisfaction in religion cannot be adequately met; while, on the other hand, the philosopher, seeking an explanation of the universe as a whole, finds it necessary to posit in the ultimate reality qualities which will account for the facts of the ethical and religious, as well as of the physical, life. Thus, while the religious interest constrains man to think of the personal God as absolute, philosophic motives lead him to attribute personality to the ultimate reality. The combination is characteristic in high degree of Christianity. The Christian God is at once personal and absolute, and the history of Christian theology is in large part the history of the effort to unite these two aspects of the thought of God in a consistent conception.

But there is a third element which must be noted in the Christian view of God, — namely, the conviction that the ultimate personality, after whom philosophy seeks and whom religion worships, has so revealed himself in the man Jesus that through his person and work we gain an insight, otherwise impossible, into the character and purpose of God. This conviction, which has found theological expression in the doctrines of the incarnation and the Trinity, is fundamental for the Christian view of God, and gives it its distinctive character in contrast to other forms of theism (*e. g.* Judaism and Mohammedanism).

Thus the Christian idea unites in itself three main elements. The first is personality, the second is absoluteness, the third is the possession by the absolute personality of the character and purpose revealed in Christ. Each of these has its own independent origin and history. Belief in a personal God is the inheritance of Christianity from Israel. The identification of this God with the ultimate of philosophy, while foreshadowed in the prophetic writings, is, in its fulness, the result of contact with Greek thought. The belief that the character and purpose of God are Christlike is the direct result of God's revelation in Jesus. The first two ideas are common to Christianity and other forms of thought; the last is peculiar to itself. All three are necessary to the complete Christian conception.

2. *Elements inherited from Israel.*

Christianity takes over from Israel its faith in a personal God, who is the creator and sustainer of the universe, and who orders all its affairs in wisdom, holiness and love. This faith, clearly expressed by the great prophets of the eighth and following centuries, has its roots in the earlier belief in Jehovah, the covenant God of Israel, who chose the Hebrew people from among the nations to be his own peculiar people, and the instrument of his world-wide salvation. In the course of the history we can trace a development along several different lines. The first is connected with a clearer recognition of the divine unity; the second is marked by a more spiritual view of Jehovah's purpose; the third manifests itself in the increasing importance attached to his relation to individuals. In the first, — which in the later Judaism is associated with a growing emphasis upon the transcendence of God — we have the point of contact with contemporary Greek philosophy. The second and third form the direct preparation for the revelation of Christ. Jesus recognized in Jehovah, God of Israel, the heavenly Father whom he knew, and found in the Scriptures of the Old Testament the revelation of the same wise, holy and loving character and purpose which he came to reveal.

The points of similarity between the Hebrew and the Christian conception may be observed both in the view of God's character and of his relation to man. In the Old Testament we see the same combination of holiness and love which is characteristic of the Christian view. While too pure to behold iniquity, and too righteous to leave unrepented sin unpunished, Jehovah is yet merciful and gracious, full of loving-kindness and compassion. His love surpasses human desert, and his faithfulness endures in spite of disobedience and sin. When Christians have sought words adequate to describe the greatness of God's love in Christ, they have turned instinctively to the pages of prophet and psalmist. There Jehovah's love for Israel is compared to that of shepherd for sheep, of husband for wife, of father for child, of mother for son. What human language can express concerning the love of God for man we find already uttered in the Old Testament.

In like manner, we find in the Hebrew conception of God the same combination of the ideas of the world governor and of the father of individuals which is so prominent in Christianity. With the idea of the kingdom of God as the goal of history, Christianity has also inherited from Israel that of the God who looks upon the heart, and who makes his abode with the man of humble and contrite spirit. Thus both the doctrine of the love of God and of his universal fatherhood are more deeply rooted in the Old Testament than it has sometimes been the habit of Christian theologians to recognize.

Yet, on the other hand, it is true that these profound and spiritual truths are associated in the Hebrew thought of God with national and legal limitations, from which Christian thought has freed itself. In the Old Testament the love of God seems often concentrated upon Israel to the exclusion of other peoples less favored. The relation of the individual to Jehovah is hedged about with legal restrictions which hide its spiritual nature. Often an exaggerated reverence so far separates Jehovah from the world that his character is obscured and his redemptive activity limited. This was notably the case in the theology of the later Judaism. In contrast to its distant God, known primarily as lawgiver and judge, and reserving his supernatural salvation as a reward for the righteous, Jesus' teaching concerning the heavenly Father who cares for the flowers and the birds, who receives the outcast and forgives the prodigal, and with whom the only condition of acceptance is a penitent and childlike spirit, came as a revolutionary Gospel.

3. *Elements inherited from Greece.*

The contribution of Greece to the Christian conception of God is the identification of the deity of religion with the Absolute of philosophy. By the Absolute we mean the ultimate reality which lies back of phenomena and which binds the various elements in experience into a unity. In Greek thought — both in its Platonic and Aristotelian forms — this reality was often conceived in an abstract and transcendent way. This is especially true of the later development which culminated in Neo-Platonism. Here God is thought of as standing over against the universe, acting upon it through intermediate beings like the Logos, but himself without part in its finite and imperfect life. This abstract conception of God is foreign to the genius of Christianity, and historically has been the source of many errors. Yet, on the other hand, by its emphasis upon the unity, the spirituality and the rationality of God, and the inherent unreasonableness of polytheism and idolatry, Greek philosophy served as a direct preparation for the Christian view; and, in the later history, furnished the forms through which it gained access to the world of educated men.

Some theologians, notably Ritschl, in their reaction against the abstract conception above referred to, have maintained that the idea of the philosophical Absolute should be banished altogether from Christian theology. This contention gains its plausibility from a narrow definition of the term, which obscures its positive significance and overlooks the religious motive which justifies its use in theology. This motive has been well expressed by Kaftan when he says [1] that by the term " Absolute " we denote " not what God is, but the place which the knowledge of God holds in our spiritual life." In other words, we assert of God that he is the ultimate reality of the universe, " the final goal of our aspiration, and the power which we recognize as everywhere supreme." [2] What the nature of the God may be to whom we thus attribute supreme authority, the term does not tell us. That we must learn from concrete experience, and especially from his historic revelation in Christ. But this knowledge once gained, we assert of the Christian God that he fills the same place in the universe which is assigned by the philosopher to whatever conception he may hold to be ultimate. What the materialist attributes to matter, the idealist to spirit, the pessimist to blind force or unconscious will, the agnostic to an unknowable somewhat incapable of closer definition, we affirm of the God and Father of our Lord Jesus Christ.

The difficulty with the early Christian theologians was that they did not always make Kaftan's distinction. With the general religious truth for which the idea of the Absolute stands, they took over the specific content which it had assumed in the contemporary philosophy. They asserted of the Christian God not only that he was the ultimate reality, but that he was such an abstract and

[1] *Dogmatik*, p. 161.   [2] *Ibid.*, free translation.

transcendent being as the later Greek philosophy conceived to be ultimate. Thus, instead of using the revelation of Christ to give content to the idea of the Absolute, they allowed a particular *a priori* conception of the Absolute to empty of content God's revelation in Christ. Under the historic conditions the process was entirely natural, and the evils which were the result, however regrettable, were perhaps inevitable. The philosophy of which the early Christian theologians made use was the common property of the educated world of the time, and that they turned to it for help in their effort to give a scientific expression to Christian faith was not a mark of retrogression, but of progress. The true remedy for the mistakes into which they fell lies not in banishing the idea of the Absolute from theology, thus renouncing the hope of a consistent *Weltanschauung*, but in so defining it as to show its religious significance and its true relation to the positive content of Christian faith.

4. *Elements distinctively Christian.*

The distinctive feature in the Christian conception of God is the conviction that the character and purpose of God are Christlike. This had its origin in the impression made upon the disciples by contact with Jesus. He declared himself the son of the heavenly Father, and lived in consciousness of daily communion with him. Hence the attributes which, in common with the Old Testament saints, he ascribed to God, received new meaning in the light of his own character and life. The disciples saw God revealed in Christ, and the conviction gave definiteness and certainty to their thought of God. In Jesus the far-off God had drawn near. He that had seen him had seen the Father.

So we find the disciples taking Christ up into their thought of God; using his life and death to illustrate the character and to interpret the plan of God; finding in God the same capacity for self-sacrifice which they had learned to know in Jesus; seeing in the cross, which to the thought of the time, both Jewish and Greek, seemed the culmination of all that was most undivine, the supreme illustration of God's love.

This definiteness has been at once the strength and the weakness of the Christian idea of God. It has been the point which opponents have been the first to attack. To many, in all ages, the thought of a God who can sympathize with men, who can even suffer on their behalf, has seemed unworthy, even incredible. When Celsus objected to the thought of a god who was crucified, he became the father of a long line of successors.

Yet, on the other hand, this concreteness has also been the strength of Christianity. No motive has drawn men with a more constraining power than the cross of Christ when regarded as the expression of God's love. If we ask what historically has given the Christian idea of God its distinctive character, we find that it is the note of divine self-sacrifice supremely illustrated on Calvary.

Thus it is not in any new teaching that we are to seek the distinctive Christian contribution to the thought of God, but in a living illustration of what the old teaching really meant. In Jesus we see one who lived in such constant consciousness of the divine love and care; who knew himself to be so at one with God in will and purpose, that men could find in him the revelation in human form of the unseen Father of whom he spoke.

In this conviction, gained less from explicit teaching than from the impression produced by contact with Jesus, and the effects which faith in him has wrought in human life, we have the experimental basis of the doctrines of the incarnation and the Trinity. The form in which these doctrines have come down to us was determined by the intellectual conditions of the time, and by the play of motives to which we have already alluded. Of both we may say that in their ecclesiastical form they represent the effort to relate the living content of the Christian idea of God to the philosophical conceptions which were current in the thought of cultivated men. What these were, and what was their effect upon Christian theology, we have now to consider.

5. *The Conception of God in Dogmatic Theology.*

With the rise of the Catholic church, involving as it did a close union with the intellectual and social forces of the Greek and Roman world, we find a disposition to magnify the abstract and transcendent elements in the idea of God. The personal and intimate features, so prominent in the teaching of Jesus and his disciples, fall into the background, and their place is taken by other ideas derived from contemporary thought. Three such conceptions may be distinguished, each of which has played a great rôle in Christian theology. The first is that of substance, the second that of will, the third that of law.

In the Greek theology the definition of God was obtained largely by a process of negation.[1] God's nature

---

[1] It is no doubt true that, side by side with this negative tendency, we find another stream of thought in the Greek theology. Where the rational nature of God is made prominent, positive arguments are given place in the determination of his being. Thus by the method of causation, inferences are drawn from the nature of the created universe to the character of the creative spirit who formed it, and by the method of eminence, a passage is made from the excellencies of the human spirit to the greater perfection of their unseen prototype. Both methods, the positive and the negative, pass

was found by thinking away all finite limitations and then affirming of the abstraction which remained all possible perfections. God was conceived as the one spiritual substance — far above human reach or comprehension — infinite, eternal, unchangeable, incomprehensible. Those attributes were thought most characteristically divine which most sharply expressed the contrast between God and man; and the Biblical terms like love, pity, patience, etc., which express the kinship between God and man, were emptied of their natural meaning. The centre of interest was shifted from the historic Jesus to the eternal Word consubstantial with the Father. Under the influence of such ideas, incarnation, involving as it did the union in one person of two contradictory sets of attributes, became a stupendous mystery, and the Trinity, instead of summing up the Christian conception of God's historic revelation, became the field of unprofitable speculations as to the nature of God in himself. In a word, the Christ in God was put into the background.

From the Greek theologians this conception passed through Augustine to the Latins. It is found in the theology of Roman Catholicism, and through the schoolmen has entered into our Protestant theological tradition. It has left its traces in the second article of the Westminster chapter on God.

Scarcely less important than the idea of God as absolute substance is that which represents him as arbitrary will. This view differs from the preceding in that it takes its departure from personality, but it finds the essence of personality in the power of unrestricted choice. God is

over to the later theology as an inheritance from the Greeks, and the problem of their reconciliation has been in every age a favorite puzzle for speculative theologians.

conceived as a sovereign who is bound by no law but his own good pleasure, and whose conduct, therefore, cannot be judged by any human standard. It follows that attacks upon divine revelation based upon reason and conscience are without effect.

In extreme form this view meets us in the Scotist theology of the Middle Ages, which found in it a convenient means by which to defend the authority of the church. The same idea lies at the root of the Socinian theology. It reappears in more moderate form in Arminianism, and furnishes the theoretical basis for the governmental theory of the atonement. In recent times Dean Mansel has reasserted it in his Bampton lectures on the *Limits of Religious Thought*.

In early Protestant theology we find still a third conception. The Reformers conceived God as the embodiment of the moral law, bound by his own nature to punish sin, and to uphold the eternal principles of righteousness and justice. In place of the arbitrary will which could remit penalty at its mere good pleasure, they put an immutable law which required a punishment commensurate with guilt. Hence the question how God could forgive sin became central in their theology, and the atonement the fundamental Christian doctrine.

Yet side by side with the emphasis on immutable law the old conception of sovereignty as unrestricted choice lived on. The reconciliation of the two is brought about in Calvinism by a distinction between the nature and the will of God. Nature is the sphere of necessity, will of freedom. The one we may know; of the other we can never be certain. Such attributes as omnipotence, holiness, justice, belong to the nature of God. The love and the mercy of God, on the other hand, are matters of will.

Just God must be, but he may or may not be merciful as he chooses. Thus a dualism is introduced into the being of God, and in the interest of his freedom, his redemptive love is robbed of its inner constraint. Those acts of God which are most Christlike become most arbitrary.[1]

We may illustrate this arbitrariness in connection with the Calvinistic doctrine of grace. " Grace " is a word which is used in the New Testament to denote the freeness of the divine love. It expresses the exceeding greatness and richness of that love above all human power to earn or to deserve.[2] The Prayer-book well expresses the idea in the communion office. " We are not worthy so much as to gather up the crumbs under thy table, but thou art the same Lord, whose property it is always to have mercy." In Calvinism, on the other hand, grace becomes a synonym for arbitrary choice. Instead of expressing the supreme law of God's nature, it denotes a series of signal and surprising exceptions to that law. The loss of the wicked is decreed " for their sin," [3] but for the salvation of the righteous no reason can be given but the " secret counsel and good pleasure " of God's will.[4]

At the root of this difficulty lies an inadequate psychology, which distinguishes between nature and will as

---

[1] It is one of the merits of the later Calvinism, as represented by Edwards and his successors, that it makes a consistent, and more or less successful, effort to overcome this dualism. Edwards makes benevolence, or love of being, the controlling theological principle. But this is conceived in such a highly abstract way that God himself, as containing within himself the maximum amount of being, becomes the supreme object of his own self-love. This love demands the display of all the divine attributes, of justice as well as of mercy, of wrath as well as of love. Thus the Edwardean theology, as truly as that of Calvin, requires a double issue for the universe ; and in the later theologian, as in the earlier, the historic Christ is relegated to a subordinate place.

[2] Cf. Eph. ii, 8.

[3] *West. Conf.*, c. III, 7.

[4] *Ibid.*, 5.

though qualities could be assigned to the one independently of the other. The motive which leads to this distinction is a laudable one, namely, the desire to magnify the freedom and the power of God. But the result is to obscure God's character, and to leave men uncertain of his purpose. In historic Calvinism, as truly as in both the older systems, the Christ in God is put into the background, and the full consequences of his revelation in Jesus are not drawn.

Yet here, as so often, men's practice proves better than their theory. While the ideas which we have criticized hindered the best expression of Christian faith, they could not prevent it. Side by side with the abstract and negative attributes derived from contemporary philosophy, we find Christian theologians in all ages trying to make place in their systems for the ethical and spiritual qualities which are central in Christian faith. What the logic of theology ruled out, a living piety supplied; and in the thoughts of the devout the memory of the lowly Jesus and the experience of his redemptive love kept alive that sense of God's fatherly forgiveness and grace which is characteristic of Christianity. What was lacking was a theoretical basis which made possible an adequate expression of this faith without doing violence to the principles which were current in the science of the day. Such a basis is supplied by modern philosophy.

6. *The Conception of God in Modern Theology.*

Under the influence of renewed study of the life of Christ, modern theology has brought into fresh prominence the ethical and spiritual qualities which were central in Jesus' thought of God. For the abstract Absolute of the earlier theology and the arbitrary will of the later, it substitutes the God and Father of our Lord Jesus Christ, and seeks to show that in his wise, holy and loving character we have the ultimate reality which philosophy calls the Absolute. In this attempt it receives aid from two different quarters. Through a better understanding of the nature of the will, modern psychology makes it possible to overcome the supposed opposition between freedom and law; while philosophy, through its renewed emphasis upon the immanence of God, opens a way for a conception of the Absolute which shall include the concrete features essential to Christian faith.

So far as the first is concerned, we are coming to see that it is not will but character which is fundamental for our conception of personality. That man is most truly free whose will is most completely dominated by a consistent moral purpose, and whose acts — given a knowledge of that purpose — we can most certainly predict. Character denotes to us such consistency of moral purpose; and law, so far from being a limitation of freedom, is its most effective means of expression. If then we are to have a real revelation of God, it must go behind his acts to the principles which determine them, and make known, not only the law of God, but the character which finds expression through it. Such a revelation we believe Christ has given us, and, because of that faith, we dare, in all humility and reverence, to fill up the " mere good pleasure " of historic Calvinism with the inner constraint of redemptive love.

No less significant is the help which modern philosophy gives theology through its better conception of the Absolute. Instead of conceiving the ultimate reality as the most abstract of all conceptions, we are coming to see that it must be the most concrete. We do not really explain the world by thinking away all that is most characteristic and meaningful in experience and then baptizing the colorless residuum God; but rather by studying experience, that we may discover amid the infinite variety which it contains what elements have greatest permanence and worth. Thus the conception of the Absolute becomes essentially teleological, denoting not simply the frame of thought, but the goal of progress; and the qualities which Christian faith finds central in God become those which are most needed for an explanation of the actual facts of life.

Thus, both in its conception of personality and of absoluteness, modern thought is removing the difficulties which have stood in the way of an adequate scientific expression of Christian faith. It is showing that the contradiction which has often been thought to exist between these two aspects of the divine being rests upon a misapprehension which more careful definition removes, and reinforcing the religious interest which makes Christ central in Christian faith with the philosophic insight that life is to be interpreted by its highest forms, not by its lowest. So long as Christ holds the place that he does in the religious life of mankind, a Christocentric theology is not only practically legitimate, but scientifically correct.

CHAPTER VIII

THE CONTENT OF THE CHRISTIAN IDEA

1. *Concerning Method.*

THE doctrine of God is usually treated in theology under the three heads of *Being, Attributes* and *Trinity.* Under the first, the nature of God is described as absolute Spirit. Under the second are enumerated the qualities which enter into the conception of God, such as omnipresence, infinity, mercy, justice, etc. The third treats of the divine *hypostases,* or God's threefold mode of existence as Father, Son and Spirit, — this being the form in which the Christian conception of God finds expression in the creeds.

It is safe to say that no part of theology is more unsatisfactory to the student than this. In place of a clear and simple statement of the Christian idea of God, he finds himself plunged into a maze of philosophical and theological distinctions in which all unity and consistency are lost. Many of these are a direct inheritance from the scholastics of the Middle Ages, and have long lost all meaning and interest for modern thought. The nature of God is treated as if it were something apart from his attributes, and the Trinity stands apart from both, as a doctrine of revelation, added to what can be learned of God from human reason, on the authority of the Scripture alone. The unity which the Christological principle requires is here conspicuous by its absence. One searches in vain for any trace of Christ in the sections on the being and the attributes. One is equally at a loss to find any foundation in God's nature for the doctrine of the Trinity. The one thing certain seems to be that the Christian doctrine of God is abstruse and difficult to understand.

While it is easy historically to understand the cause of this state of things, it is important that it should not be needlessly perpetuated. It is desirable, therefore, to realize at the outset that the subject-matter with which the three sections deal is the same, the only difference being in point of view. In each we have to do with the Christian idea of God. Under the nature of God we set forth as clearly and concisely as we can what is the distinctively Christian view of God. In other words, we give the Christian *definition* of God. Under the attributes we unfold this definition in detail to see what it involves. Under the Trinity we study the historic statements which have resulted from the effort to interpret God's revelation through Christ and the Holy Spirit in the light of the philosophical conceptions current at the time. If we are correct in our method, all that the later sections contain will be found included in germ in the preliminary definition.

In the present chapter the first two only of these topics will concern us. We shall consider what is commonly included in theology in the sections on the being and attributes of God, leaving the Trinity for later discussion. The reason for this is that the doctrine of the Trinity, involving as it does the use of technical terms whose meaning has become unfamiliar to us to-day, requires for its intelligent discussion a fulness of treatment out of proportion to that accorded other aspects of our doctrine. It is indeed, as its position in the old creeds makes clear, the comprehensive Christian doctrine, — summing up the entire content of Christian faith; and its treatment, as a sub-section under the doctrine of God, gives a wholly inadequate idea of its real significance and place in the Christian system. It will be enough if in our present discussion we can show its experimental basis, and indicate what are the elements in the idea of God of which it is the fuller expression.

A similar line of reasoning has led some theologians (*e. g.* Schleiermacher, Schweizer, Reischle) to separate their treatment of the attributes from that of the being of God. They argue that since the attributes express in large part the relation between God and the creature, they can be adequately treated only in connection with the Christian view of the world and of man. Thus Schleiermacher divides the attributes into three groups, — those which express the relation of God to the world in general, those which express his relation to sin, and those which express his redemptive activity, — and treats them at different places in his system, in connection with the corresponding doctrines of the world, of man's sin, and of Christ's salvation. The difficulty with this method is that it separates things which belong together in Christian thought, and fails to give that clear and comprehensive statement of the idea of God which it is the highest function of theology to furnish. For this reason it is better to follow the more common method in spite of its difficulties.

2. *The Christian Definition of God.*

God is "the personal Spirit, perfectly good," [1] who creates, sustains and orders the universe according to the wise, holy and loving character and purpose re-

[1] Clarke, *op. cit.*, p. 66.

vealed in Jesus Christ; and who, through his Spirit, indwelling in man, is ever at work in the world, calling men out of their sin and misery into the kingdom of God, and, by his redemptive grace, transforming individuals and society into the likeness of Christ. The name which best expresses his character, and which, since Christ, has become the characteristic Christian name for God, is Father.

Analyzing this definition, it is found to contain the three elements which we have seen to be fundamental in the Christian idea of God. (1) It includes personality, and that in the highest ethical form. God is the personal Spirit, perfectly good. (2) It includes absoluteness. God is the one who creates, sustains and orders the universe, — the supreme reality on whom all things depend. (3) It defines both God's character and his relation to the world in terms of the revelation of Christ. God creates, sustains and orders the universe according to the wise, holy and loving character and purpose revealed in Jesus Christ.

Of the three, it is the last which gives our definition its Christian character. Neither absoluteness nor personality is a distinctly Christian conception. Greek and Hindu believe in the first; the Jew and the Mohammedan accept the second. It is only when we reach Christ that we gain a principle of differentiation. Here we learn how the Christian conceives of the ultimate reality, and what is his view of the character of the personal God.

This definition further expresses the Christian view of the relation between God and man. It takes up into its thought of God the effects which his Spirit has produced and is still producing in human life. It regards the concrete features which have proved so great a stumbling-block in the older theology as necessary elements in an adequate conception of God. To Christian faith it belongs to the *nature* of God to impart himself in self-sacrificing love. The historic Christ and the present Spirit belong with the Father in the Christian thought of God, and the attempt to divorce the doctrine of the Trinity from its roots in experience, and to conceive God in terms of self-centred blessedness is the mark of a mistaken reverence.

The name which most concisely sums up the Christian conception of God is Father. In the divine Fatherhood Christian faith finds included the power and authority for which absoluteness stands, the kinship which is involved in personality, and the holy and loving character which Christ has revealed. This conception, gained from personal experience of God's redemptive love in Christ, Christian faith carries over to mankind at large, and regards Fatherhood, as we have come to know it through Christ, as expressing the true relation between God and his human children everywhere.

3. *Of the Divine Attributes.*

The content of the Christian idea of God is set forth in detail in the doctrine of the attributes. By an attribute is meant " any conception which is necessary to the explicit idea of God ; any distinctive conception which cannot be resolved into any other." [1] The attributes of God are the different elements which together make up the Christian thought of God, and the function of the doctrine is to define these elements more fully, and to unfold in detail the significance of the idea of God, which our preliminary definition has concisely expressed.

Some theologians define the term " attributes " more

[1] H. B. Smith, *Systematic Theology*, p. 12.

narrowly, distinguishing them as " those qualities which express a specific *relation* of God, but are not necessarily present in every Christian thought of God," from the " general properties of being " (*Wesensprädikate*) which are always present when we think of God.[1] There is a certain justification for this distinction in the fact that some qualities are more fundamental in our thought of God than others, but in practice it is difficult to carry through without artificiality. The danger is always present of regarding the most abstract and least distinctive elements as belonging to God's nature, while we leave the specifically Christian qualities to be added in the attributes. Thus Kaftan treats spiritual personality as a property of being, while he regards holiness and goodness as attributes;[2] and Clarke distinguishes love as an attribute from the affectional nature which belongs to God's being.[3] It is simpler, as well as more in accord with the usage of modern psychology, to regard the word " attribute " as a comprehensive term, including everything which can be affirmed about God but the bare fact of his existence, and to see in the doctrine a complete statement of all that is essential in the Christian idea of God.

From this point of view the vexed questions, so often debated in theology, as to the derivation and the classification of the attributes admit of an easy solution. We gain our knowledge of the attributes by analyzing the idea of God which we have already won from his revelation in Christ; and we arrange them in such a way as to bring the distinctive features of that idea to clearest expression. The analysis is necessary because of the great importance

---

[1] *E. g.* Kaftan, *Dogmatik*, p. 159.

[2] *Op. cit.*, pp. 159, 160.

[3] *Outline*, p. 76.

of the idea of God, and the danger of misconception in dealing with terms which have had so long and complicated a history. The arrangement is a matter of convenience, in which there is room for difference of opinion. Different theologians follow different methods, according to the elements which are most prominent in their conception of God. In general it may be said that the simpler and more natural the arrangement the better.

The order here followed grows naturally out of the preceding discussion. It groups the attributes about the three ideas of personality, absoluteness and Christlike character which we have made central in our definition. There are certain attributes, such as spirituality, unity, life, which are derived from our thought of God as person. There are others, such as holiness and love (the so-called moral attributes), which express the character which we attribute to this person. There are still others, such as omnipotence, omnipresence, etc. (the so-called attributes of nature), growing out of the absoluteness of God, which express the fact that the personal God whose character we thus define stands to the universe in the relation of supreme cause or ground. We shall consider them in the order named.

4. *Attributes of Personality.*

The fundamental attributes which grow out of our thought of God as person are spirituality, life, unity. These are all present in the Hebrew idea of God, and come to Christianity as an inheritance from Israel.

When we say that God is spirit, we express our faith that he is moral personality, having reason, conscience and freedom. His nature is not to be learned from the lower or physical side of man, which he shares with the brutes, but from the higher qualities of man's spirit. Between man, considered as spirit, and God, there exists a kinship; and hence, for all his majesty, he may be known and worshipped by those whom he has created in his own image.

The word " spirit" has had an eventful history. Formerly it was used to exclude anthropomorphic ideas of God. It was the affirmation, against those who attributed body to God, of the fact that his true nature is to be learned from that which is unseen in man; that it is reason, conscience, freedom, — in a word, the higher qualities of personality, which reveal God.

In our day, however, the word has very largely lost its concrete character. Instead of denoting the higher side of personality, it is used as a common term to include all that is not matter. As used in modern pantheistic systems, it means distinctly less than personality. Hence, for ordinary purposes it is better to call God person than spirit. In theology, however, the word still has its uses. It denotes the absence of the limitations of finiteness, and hence contributes something to the idea of God which person lacks. In this sense it is used in John iv, 24, to teach the lesson that the worship of God is not limited to any time or place, but depends solely upon the attitude of the worshipper. Clarke uses the term " personal spirit " as uniting both aspects of the Christian idea.

When we speak of God as life, we express the spontaneity and many-sidedness of the divine existence; the fact that there is in God the possibility of change, of initiative; that he is not bound in his activity to the results of the past. It is the negation of all that is dead and barren and monotonous and ineffective; the assertion of all that is fruitful and creative and inspiring. It is not the denial of law, but the affirmation of the highest law, namely, the law of personality, which is the sphere of freedom, and therefore of progress. A recent writer has well expressed the religious content of the doctrine in the phrase, " The God of the future is greater than the God of the past."

This conception, so prominent in the Old Testament, of God as living and the source of life, is of far-reaching importance for religion. It brings within the sphere of the divine interest and control the world of growth and change under the conditions of which human life is lived. It conceives of God as having a real experience, in some true sense analogous to that of man ; as working for ends which he conceives of value, and finding his interest and joy in their progressive realization in history. For the Greek ideal of the transcendent and self-centred God, it substitutes the Christian ideal of the self-imparting and self-revealing one. The bearing of this view on God's absoluteness will concern us later. Here it is sufficient to say that in Christian thought it is not the character of God which changes, but his activity and his experience. The fulness of the divine life consists in the progressive outworking of a consistent purpose.

Finally, when we say that God is one, we express the fact that this living spiritual God is the sole object of our worship and service. Hence all idolatry is excluded, whether it take the coarser form of the worship of supposed spirits or the more refined form of devotion to the world powers of selfishness, ambition, avarice or lust. The unity of God is fundamental in Christianity, as in Judaism. The doctrine of the Trinity itself, properly understood, is a confession of Christian faith in the unity of God.

The unity of God may be obtained in two ways, — by way of the divine absoluteness or by way of the divine personality. From our study of the universe we rise to the thought of a single principle; from our experience of God's personal dealings we gain the impression of a consistent character. Both are important, but only the second gives us the full Christian conception. The God whom we worship is one, because he is self-conscious and self-determining, binding together all things in the unity of a single consistent purpose.

5. *Attributes of Character.*

Since the character of God is a unity, it is not sufficient to learn the moral attributes from an induction of Scripture texts. Some principle of arrangement must be found which will bring this unity to expression. Such a principle is naturally suggested by an analysis of self-consciousness. The moral life, as we know it, may be regarded from three points of view, — from that of the intellect, of the emotions and of the will. The attributes which express these three sides of God's character are wisdom, love and holiness; all of which are less special qualities in God than names for the whole of his character regarded from these three different aspects.

It may be objected to this arrangement that it is anthropomorphic to attribute to God emotion as well as intellect and will. In the older theology this objection took form in the doctrine that God could not be the subject of desire. More recently, it has been revived by Ritschl in his interpretation of love as an attribute of will without emotional content. While in place as a protest against a weak sentimentality which overlooks the ethical quality in God's love, this interpretation cannot be defended in principle. With equal justice we might argue against attributing to God reason or will, both of which are known to us only through human personality. If we accept the Christian principle that God can reveal himself through man, then all that goes to make up the highest life in man must make its contribution to our thought of God. With reason and conscience, we must attribute emotion also to God, and interpret love as desire as well as purpose.

The true remedy for the danger against which Ritschl warns is to be found in the consistent application of the Christological principle to the doctrine of the moral attributes. This is the more necessary because in dealing with this subject we enter a field which has been the scene of so much controversy, and deal with terms which have had so long and so varying a history. What men call holiness has varied from age to age, and the same is true of all the terms in which men have sought to describe God's character. Justice, righteousness, goodness, faithfulness, anger, mercy, grace, — each sums up a long historic development, in which different ethical ideals have from time to time found expression, and which culminates in Christ. Here we are not concerned with the process, but with the result. We wish to know what is the conception of the divine character which has come to us through the revelation of Christ.

Thus, holiness to the Christian means the possession by God of the moral perfection which Jesus illustrated in his life. Positively, it expresses the fact that he ever wills for himself and for all moral beings that which is morally right. Negatively, it expresses his separation from and opposition to sin. This negative meaning was originally most prominent in the word; [1] but with deeper insight into the ethical character of God it was seen that that by which God was separated from other beings was his moral perfection, and the word came to have the positive meaning which our definition expresses.

Holiness has sometimes been contrasted as the characteristic attribute of the God of the Old Testament with love as the distinctive attribute of the God of the New. The distinction cannot be maintained. The truth is that Christianity has transformed and enriched both ideas. Its conception of the holiness of God is as much more profound than that of Judaism as its view of God's love is wider and more intense. Here the example of Jesus is conclusive. With love for man, and desire to help all who were in need, he combined the most exacting ethical standard and the most uncompromising condemnation of sin. Thus he becomes a revelation of the holiness of God as well as of his love, and those who seek to exalt one of these attributes at the expense of the other must seek their support elsewhere than in his teachings.

In God's dealings with men the divine holiness manifests itself as veracity and justice.

By the veracity or truthfulness of God we designate the manner in which he brings his holy character and

[1] The term " holiness " had originally a ceremonial rather than an ethical meaning. It denoted the difference which separated that which had been set apart for sacred or religious purposes from all that was secular and profane. Jehovah was a holy God, in the sense that he required of his worshippers the observance of certain rites and ceremonies without which he could not be properly approached. Israel was a holy people, because, and in so far as, its members observed this divinely appointed ritual. Cf Ex. xxix, 1, 29 ; xxx, 29 ; 1 Sam. xxi, 5. It is a striking proof of the extent to which the ethical has gained control in the Christian conception of God that the original meaning of the word should have been so largely forgotten, and the term " holiness " be understood to-day in Christian circles as a synonym of moral purity or righteousness.

purpose to expression in revelation. This is illustrated in Jesus' attitude to the men to whom he came as the revealer of God's truth. It was an attitude of mingled patience and sincerity, bearing with their inadequate ideas, as far as possible, but holding back no truth which was necessary for their moral good.

By the righteousness or justice of God we designate the manner in which his holiness finds expression in the government of the universe. In his dealings with moral beings God is at once searching and considerate, rendering to each, at each period in the progress of history as at its close, that which is morally right. The principles which determine his judgment find illustration in Jesus' attitude to his contemporaries; in the strictness of his ethical standards, his insistence upon the motive as everywhere determining, his uncompromising warfare against all sham and insincerity, as well as his tenderness and compassion to humility and penitence, wherever found.

The assertion of God's truthfulness and justice is the form in which the Christian confesses his faith in the rationality of the world, and in its moral order. The former is the guarantee of the trustworthiness of our faculties, and so of the possibility of science and philosophy. The latter is the assurance that man's struggle after a higher life and a better social order is not destined to fail. Yet it has often happened that a narrow interpretation of the relation which these attributes express has raised difficulties instead of solving them. Where attention is concentrated solely upon the relation of God to the individual, and the fact is overlooked that his government is concerned with society as well, the whole problem which is involved in revelation and redemption is misconceived. A revelation is looked for which stands in no relation to the intellectual environment, and a salvation expected which ignores the limitations which are involved in all social life. We need, therefore, to remember that God deals with men, not as individuals merely, but as members of society; that his method is a method of progress, in which both knowledge and character are gained by slow degrees; and that the convincing proof of his truthfulness and of his justice is to be found less in individual examples, however striking, than in the entire course of his government, with its evidence of the growing supremacy of the rational and the moral in the life of man.

By the love of God we mean his "desire to impart himself and all good to other beings, and to possess them for his own in spiritual fellowship." [1] This desire finds its completest expression in the gift of Christ, and its clearest illustration in his attitude toward men.

As thus defined, love is not merely self-impartation; it includes also the desire to possess the object cared for. This is true of the highest human love. To exclude this desire from God is to rob redemption of its deepest significance and worship of its highest joy. If God does not care whether or no men care for him, the supreme motive for the Christian life is cut off.

All the varying feelings, desires and emotions attributed to God in the Bible are to be understood as manifestations of love. This is obviously the case with such qualities as benevolence, pity, the longing to redeem, long-suffering, mercy. It is no less true of those feelings which express God's attitude to sin, such as displeasure, jealousy, grief, anger. In the one case, as in the other, we have the utterance of his desire to win men for himself, and of his

[1] Clarke, *op. cit.* p. 95.

opposition to any obstacle which stands in the way of his realizing his loving end.

Many, who have no difficulty in interpreting God's love in terms of feeling, regard the attribution of anger to God as an unworthy anthropomorphism. Yet it is difficult to see with what consistency we can affirm the first of God without admitting the second. If God cares at all for men, if he feels with or for them, he must feel opposed to that which hinders his loving purpose. So far as sin is deliberate, wilful, cruel, he must feel indignation against its perpetrator, and the better he loves him, the more indignant he must be. Here the example of Jesus is instructive, in whom compassion for the oppressed and indignation against those who have done the wrong go hand in hand.[1] Such anger is an element in the moral perfection of Jesus. It expresses the strength and virility of his character; the seriousness and fearlessness of his moral judgments. After such analogy must we conceive the anger of God. It is never fitful or wayward, but a holy indignation directed against sin. It is never called forth by personal slight, but always by wrong to others. It is an attribute of God as Father, and, as truly as his mercy, is the result and the manifestation of his redemptive love.

In relation to sinful men the love of God manifests itself as grace. By this term we express the freeness of the divine love, which is not won by any merit on the part of the creature, but comes " of its own accord to bless the undeserving." [2] Of this free love or grace, the life and death of Christ for sinful men are the supreme example.

Two errors need here to be guarded against: (1) the idea that the mercy of God is something arbitrary, shown

---

[1] Cf. Matt. xxiii, 13.
[2] Clarke, *op. cit.* p. 102.

to some and not to others, according to God's whim;
(2) the idea that it is something soft and sentimental,
open to every one without respect to the moral conditions
involved. Neither of these views finds support in the
attitude of Jesus. No sinner is so vile but he may hope
for forgiveness if he repent.[1] No love is so strong as to
justify forgiveness without repentance.[2]

In the love of God Christian faith finds the convincing
revelation of the dignity and worth of the individual man.
God, whose fundamental attribute is moral sincerity,
cannot give himself for an unworthy object. If then his
redemptive love embraces the sinner and the outcast, it
must be because he perceives in them the capacity of
spiritual growth and manhood. True love is always prophetic, embracing by faith what may be, but is not yet.
God's love is both prophetic and creative, — realizing the
capacity whose existence it assumes. This is the ground
for our hope in the future of humanity.

Finally, by the wisdom of God we indicate the adaptation of the means used by God to attain his holy and
loving end; or, since the supreme example of wisdom is
redemption, the manner in which God brings his holy and
loving character to expression in redemption.

As thus defined, wisdom is a moral attribute. As distinguished from omniscience, which has no necessary
moral content, it is the quality which enables God to do
the right thing. This may be illustrated by the means
which Jesus used to secure the ends he sought. His
wisdom, to be sure, appeared foolishness to the men of
his time. A Messiah who separated himself from the
rulers of his people, and ate and drank with publicans

[1] Cf. Luke v, 31 ; xxiii, 34.
[2] Matt. xxiii, 37; xix, 16–22.

and sinners, seemed to invite the failure which was his fate. And yet time has proved that Jesus was right. The despised Messiah has shown himself the wisdom of God (1 Cor. i, 24), and the cross, the power of God unto salvation (Rom. i, 16).

In the older theology a chief proof of the wisdom of God was found in the marks of adaptation in the physical universe. From the beginning, the wonders of nature have led men's thoughts up to God, and the glory of the sunrise and the silent beauty of the stars have borne their witness to the human spirit of a creative spirit kindred to itself. The modern poets but repeat in their own language the song of Hebrew prophet and psalmist, to whom the heavens are the tabernacle of the Lord and the earth his handiwork. The discrediting of the artificial teleology of the deistic period, in which God was conceived as a kind of gigantic carpenter, fashioning the universe as a man might make a house, has opened the way to a clearer insight into the spiritual meaning and significance of nature. None the less is it true that it is only when we reach man that we find convincing proof of the divine wisdom. Christian faith looks upon the world as the scene of a divine purpose running through the ages and centring in the cross of Christ, and it is in the light of this vision that the divine wisdom must be conceived.

On the wisdom of God Christian faith founds its hope of the solution of those problems of suffering and sin which, from the beginning, have baffled human thought. In the Christian experience we are conscious of a change of values, whereby that which to non-Christian thought seems irrational and evil becomes the means of the highest moral development, and the instrument of the most blessed spiritual experience. What Paul affirmed of the cross of

Christ [1] can be paralleled in every profound Christian experience. In this change of estimate we may find the key to much which still seems dark in God's conduct of the world.

All the attributes thus separately discussed are present simultaneously in every act of God. In all that he does he is at once holy, loving and wise. The possession of such a holy, wise and loving character constitutes the *glory* for which he deserves our worship, and is the ground of the *blessedness* which he desires us to share.

6. *Attributes as Absolute.*

When we say that God is absolute, we mean that the holy and loving personality whom Christ has revealed is really master of the universe. The world is his world. Hence he is able to bring his holy and loving purpose to a successful issue in it. The so-called natural attributes are only so many ways of expressing this truth.

This method of approach reverses the order which has been usual in theology, in which the discussion of the absoluteness of God precedes that of his personality and of his character. From the analysis of an abstract conception of the absolute a number of qualities are derived, such as infinity, aseity (*i. e.* self-existence), eternity, immensity, incomprehensibility, impassibility and the like, which, as commonly defined, are inconsistent with what we know as personality. Thus eternity is regarded as the negation of time, and the consciousness of God is declared to be timeless. The result is necessarily a contradiction in the idea of God. The true method is just the reverse. We should begin with the character revealed in Christ, and then assert that this is the ultimate reality of the universe.

[1] 1 Cor. i, 24.

This gives a positive content to even the most abstract of the attributes, and removes a large part of the difficulties which have been needlessly imported into this part of theology.

We may illustrate this method in connection with the attributes of omnipresence, omniscience, omnipotence, immutability and infinity.   Under these heads we may bring to complete expression what Christian faith finds involved in the absoluteness of God.

Thus when we speak of the omnipresence of God, we mean that at every point of space and at every moment of time this wise, holy and loving Father is present.   Immensity and eternity are the theological terms which express this truth in its twofold aspect, but they add nothing essential to its content.

When we say that God is *immense*, we do not mean that he fills space as a finite object might do, but only that space imposes no restraint upon his activity.   He is not hampered, as we are, by the limitations of distance.   Wherever he desires to act, there, instantly, he can call into play all needed reserves of power.

In like manner, when we say that God is *eternal*, we do not pretend to describe the nature of the divine consciousness (whether as containing within itself all time or as altogether removed from time relations), but only to express our faith that time imposes no limitations upon God's knowledge.   He is not hindered, as we are, by ignorance or uncertainty.   At every moment of time — as at every point of space — all the resources of his wisdom are at his disposal.

Both these convictions unite in the doctrine of God's omnipresence.   To Christian faith this expresses the fact that God's knowledge and power extend far enough to take in the remotest possible experience; that there are no limits, either in time or in space, which can remove man beyond his ability to help or to control. It is a practical conception, such as is expressed in the Psalmist's cry, " Whither shall I go from thy Spirit, or whither shall I flee from thy presence?" (Ps. cxxxix, 7); or, in the words of the modern poet: —

> " I know not where his islands lift
>   Their fronded palms in air;
> I only know I cannot drift
>   Beyond his love and care." [1]

When we speak of the omniscience of God, we mean that from this same wise, holy and loving God nothing is hid. He sees things as they are; their causes, their meaning, their end. He reads the hearts of men. Their secret thoughts are known to him; and because he thus knows them, he is able to deal with them aright.

The theoretical difficulties which have been raised in connection with the doctrine of the divine omniscience render it important to remember what is the Christian interest in the doctrine. It is an inference from God's function as moral governor, and extends just as far as the necessities of this government require. If, as some theologians have held, strict omniscience is not necessary to an effective moral government by God, it is possible in so far to limit God's knowledge. This is the position of Rothe, who holds that God's knowledge is necessarily limited by human freedom.[2] Such limitation seems to others to render impossible effective divine control, and accordingly they include the results of human choice in the objects of God's knowledge. If we are to trust God absolutely, he must

---

[1] Whittier: The Eternal Goodness.
[2] *Dogmatik*, I, pp. 110 sq.

not only know us as we are, but all that affects our welfare, past, present and future. To most men this has
seemed to require strict omniscience.

When we speak of the omnipotence of God, we mean
that this same holy and loving God is really Lord of the
universe, able to do in it all things which his character
and purpose may suggest.

This does not mean that God can do anything whatever;
that there is no standard, external or internal, to which
he must conform. Like every wise and consistent person,
God is determined by his character. It is morally impossible for him to do anything which is inconsistent with
this. He cannot sin; he cannot do that which is logically
contradictory. If he could, he would not be more but
less free than he is. But it *does* mean that there is
nothing in the universe as such which can prevent the
working out of the divine plan. God is not hindered, as
dualism affirms, by any foreign substance. Apparent
obstacles are there as part of the divine plan. Man
cannot prevent the execution of the plan. Sin cannot
prevent it. In his own good time, and in his own wise
way, the kingdom of God will surely come, and his will
be done in earth as it is in heaven.

This gives us the point of view for judging the questions which have played so great a rôle in theology as to
the relation of God's omnipotence to human freedom.
The problem of the relation of free-will and sovereignty
can best be discussed in another connection, [1] when the
terms it involves have been more carefully defined. Here
it is sufficient to say that whatever solution seems theoretically most satisfactory, the result is brought by Christian
faith under the point of view of God's plan. However

[1] Cf. chapter XV, section 2, pp. 245 sq.

much the Arminian may differ from the Calvinist in his theory of the will, he is at one with him in his belief that freedom is not inconsistent with divine control. The limitation which is involved in its existence is a self-limitation, promoting rather than hindering the realization of God's plan, and hence may legitimately be interpreted as an expression of God's sovereignty.

There is no doctrine which is practically more important than that of the divine omnipotence. It led Christ to go cheerfully to the cross, confident that his cause would triumph in spite of apparent defeat. It has given courage to the martyrs and saints of every age. It is the only sure stay of faith in the midst of the imperfections and discouragements of the world. In face of obstacles apparently insuperable, faith hears the promise, "With man it is impossible, but with God all things are possible," [1] and answers with the confession, "I believe in God, the Father Almighty."

When we speak of the divine immutability we mean that the holy and loving character in whom we have put our trust can never change.

This does not mean that God's action will never change. On the contrary, it must change constantly to meet the ever varying needs of his government. And with the change will come corresponding changes in the divine experience. But the change will never be an arbitrary one. Back of the varying action and the changing experience lies the unchanging purpose, giving unity and consistency to all God does.

This view stands in the sharpest contrast with that of the Epicurean philosophy, which represents God as standing apart from the world, unaffected by all which goes on

[1] Mark x, 27; Matt. xix, 26; cf. Jer. xxxii, 27.

in human life. In the Christian view, God's immutability is not due to carelessness or to indifference. It is rather a mark of intense moral activity. It may be defined as that moral changelessness by which all the powers of God's nature are brought under the dominion of a single consistent purpose.

Finally, when we speak of the divine infinity we express the inexhaustible greatness and majesty of this same holy and loving God.

This aspect of the divine being has been sometimes expressed in Christian theology by the ambiguous term "incomprehensibility." This does not mean that God cannot be understood at all, but only that he cannot be completely understood. The knowledge that we have gained through Christ is real knowledge, and valid as far as it goes ; but it does not exhaust God. After all is said, there still remain in him infinite reaches of wisdom, holiness, love and power, beyond our utmost ability to comprehend or imagine. We cry with Paul [1] ": O the depth of the riches both of the wisdom and knowledge of God ! How unsearchable are his judgments, and his ways past finding out ! " This is not the confession of agnosticism, but the affirmation of faith.

7. *The Consistency of the Christian Idea.*

It remains to consider certain objections which may be brought against the consistency of the Christian idea of God, as we have thus sketched it in outline. These objections have already been answered in principle, but the importance of the subject is so great that it may be well to consider them somewhat more in detail. They are based either upon an inadequate conception of absoluteness, or

[1] Rom. xi, 33.

of personality, and amount to this — that the two ideas are contradictory.

The first objection is based upon the assumption that the absolute must be the most abstract of all conceptions, and therefore must necessarily exclude the concreteness which is essential to our thought of personality. The second is based upon the assumption that the only possible form of personality is that of which we have knowledge in our finite and imperfect selves, and therefore that the conception is an unworthy one to be applied to God.

These difficulties are enhanced rather than removed by the various efforts which have been made to construct a picture of the divine self-consciousness. These attempts necessarily fall into one of two errors. Either they think away from the divine self-consciousness elements which are essential in our thought of personality; or else they uncritically carry over to the divine existence conditions which are only applicable to our own. An example of the first is the attempt to conceive the divine consciousness as timeless. Examples of the second are the various attempts which have been made (*e. g.* that of *scientia media* [1]) to solve the problem involved in sovereignty and freedom from the standpoint of the divine foreknowledge. The first removes God wholly from the relations under which human life is lived; the second subjects him to them completely.

The truth is that any attempt to construct a picture of the divine self-consciousness is bound to fail. It deals

---

[1] *E. g.* the theory that, though God's knowledge is limited by the uncertainty of human action, yet, through his perfect foresight of every possible contingency, he is able so to plan as to make certain the final accomplishment of his end. A modern example of this theory is Professor James' figure of the chessplayer in his essay on "The Dilemma of Determinism." Cf. *The Will to Believe*, pp. 181 sq.

with conditions of which we can have no possible knowledge, and ignores the evidence upon which our faith in God's absoluteness and in his moral personality is based. It is our own experience of life which leads us to conceive the ultimate reality in terms of personality, and the attributes which express the different aspects of God's nature are only the different forms in which we make real to ourselves the significance for our lives of this ultimate fact. The real question which we need to answer is not whether we can solve the theoretical difficulties involved in the conception of a divine self-consciousness, but whether the ideas of personality and absoluteness involve any inherent contradiction which renders it illegitimate to use them to give content to our idea of God. This question is to be answered by considering what is really involved in each.

So far as personality is concerned, we may readily admit that in the form in which we know it in ourselves it is associated with limitations and imperfections which, if applied to God, would involve a contradiction. We are housed in a physical organism, and limited by conditions of time and space. We gain knowledge by slow degrees, and win experience by constant mistakes. We are conscious of moral imperfection against which we strive in vain. If to be person means to be limited as we are limited, then we must agree with Pfleiderer[1] that in the interest of God's perfection we must deny him personality.

But is such limitation the characteristic mark of personality? Does it not rather indicate an imperfect stage of development? It has been well said by Ritschl[2] that

---

[1] *Religionsphilosophie*, Berlin, 1884, II, p. 290.
[2] *Christian Doctrine of Justification and Reconciliation*, Eng. Tr. III, pp. 233 sq.

we are not so much complete persons, as on the road to personality. Both as individuals and as a race we are growing up to self-consciousness; but full self-consciousness is for us, as yet, an ideal, not an attainment.

The significant thing is that in the measure in which this ideal is attained, the limitations of finiteness are overcome. What distinguishes man from the brute, and civilized from savage man, is the extent to which he is able to overcome what to the lower forms are insuperable obstacles. Consciousness, with its memory and its capacity for reasoning, enables us to annihilate space and time. We recall the past, and forecast the future. We combine in a single picture events most widely separated, and grasp the unchanging principles of logic and of morality which are equally applicable in all ages and in all worlds. Indeed, it may be said that the very qualities by which it has been sought to differentiate God's consciousness from that of man are known to us only through elements present in germ in our own. Eternity and immensity receive meaning to us through our own ability to transcend in thought the limits of time and space. Unity we know through the constant element in self-consciousness; immutability, through the persistence of the laws of thought, and the unchanging witness of conscience; even infinity, through our apparently limitless capacity, so long as life lasts, to receive new impressions and to grasp new ideas. Thus the way to conceive God worthily lies not in thinking away that which is characteristic of human self-consciousness, but in conceiving that which is highest in our own consciousness as present in God in supreme degree.

The same conclusion is confirmed by considering what is really involved in the idea of the Absolute. By the Absolute we mean the ultimate reality in the universe, and the question as to the nature of the Absolute is the question how that reality can be most adequately conceived. Here there are two possibilities open. We may begin at the bottom and interpret the Absolute in terms of the lowest forms we know, — those which are most abstract and least definite; or at the top, and conceive God after the analogy of the forms which are highest and most developed. In the first case we shall regard the Absolute as the changeless substratum of an unmeaning process; in the second, as the inspiration and the goal of progress. The latter view is most in accord with the methods of modern science, with its emphasis upon development as a universal law; and is the implicit assumption of all the great philosophies which have believed it possible to give a rational explanation of the world.

But if this be true, then the conception of the Absolute as personality is one for which philosophic as well as religious grounds may be urged, and the Christian idea of God may be defended as not only practically satisfying, but intellectually consistent. Whether it be *true* as well as consistent is another question. That depends upon the evidence which can be given for the positive content with which Christian faith fills up the idea of the absolute personality; and this, in turn, upon the place which Christ can be shown to hold in the moral and religious life of the race. This question will concern us in the next section. Here we have to do with definition, not with proof.

To sum up: In God Christian faith finds the ultimate reality of which philosophy has ever been in search; the source of all life, the standard of all truth, the goal of all endeavor; but it fills up the vague outlines of the philosophic conception with the warmth and color which come from the character and purpose of Christ. If it be objected that this method is anthropomorphic, that the concreteness of personality is inconsistent with absoluteness, the answer is that the same objection may be brought against any attempt to give positive content to our thought of the supreme reality of the universe. It is as true of the unconscious will of Schopenhauer as of the God and Father of our Lord Jesus Christ. Either we must take the extreme agnostic position and declare God essentially unknowable, or we have a right to interpret the universe by the highest we know. To the Christian the highest is Christ.

CHAPTER IX

THE GROUNDS FOR BELIEVING IN THE CHRISTIAN GOD

1. *What is to be Proved.*

In considering the evidence for the Christian idea of
God we must bear clearly in mind what is to be proved.
It is not enough to establish the existence of God.   It is
necessary to show that God possesses the qualities of character and purpose which Christ has revealed.   Many arguments, valid in their place, fail because they do not observe
this condition.

We may illustrate this failure in the case of two lines of
reasoning of great historic importance.   The first may be
called the method of speculation; the second the method
of authority.   Both together make up the traditional
proof for the being of God.

By the method of speculation is meant a method which
seeks to establish a conception of God, substantially
Christian, apart from the facts of the Christian revelation and experience.

This may be illustrated by the famous arguments for the
being of God, as they are presented in many modern text-
books.   Such, for example, are the ontological argument
(from necessary thought to being); the cosmological (from
change to cause); the teleological (from adaptation to
purpose); the moral (from ideal to a power adequate to
realize it).   All of these use common human experiences

to demonstrate the existence, and more or less completely to determine the nature of God. The evidence upon which they rely is such as is open to man apart from the special contribution which Christianity has made to the moral and religious life.

Our objection to these arguments is not the familiar one based upon the fact that, considered as strict syllogisms, they involve logical fallacy, assuming that which they profess to prove. The same criticism may be made of any conceivable attempt to establish God's existence by argument. It is, of course, impossible to demonstrate logically that which is the implicit assumption of all thought. The real significance of the arguments is analytic, not synthetic. They show the lines along which in all ages men's thought has risen to God, and the content which it has put into the idea when found. As John Caird has well said,[1] they represent "the unconscious or implicit logic of religion;" and as such they have the highest value. Our criticism is that, in the pursuit of this legitimate end, they have separated things which belong together. They have sought a rational proof of God which should ignore the evidence of the Christian revelation and experience; and, having omitted this most significant part of their data, it is not strange if the conclusion to which they come should seem to Christian faith inadequate. The God whom they prove may be God, but he is not the Father of our Lord Jesus Christ.

The procedure thus criticized becomes easily explicable, when we remember the historical origin of the arguments. They were not designed to prove the Christian idea of God, but rather to show that a rational proof of this idea was impossible. Their point of departure was the antith-

[1] *An Introduction to the Philosophy of Religion,* New York, 1880, p. 133.

esis between reason and revelation, and the necessity of the latter to supplement the former. Their function was to show that by reason we could know some things about God, but not enough to be saved. Given the premise, the method was entirely legitimate.

But when transplanted into our modern world, the case is different. We no longer recognize the antithesis between reason and revelation which the old theology assumed. To us life is a unity, and Christian experience takes its place as the highest and most perfect example of the religious life of man. Under the circumstances, it is an anachronism to conserve a method which perpetuates an artificial dualism which it is impossible to carry through consistently in practice. Christianity has so profoundly influenced our life that we are unable to ignore its results in thought even when we try; and treatises which profess to do so are the best witnesses of this unconscious influence. The God whom they seek to prove is no longer the God of the old natural theology, in whose nature no basis for redemption could be found, but a God substantially Christian, whose purpose includes the kingdom which Christ came to found, and whose character is defined in terms whose highest meaning we learn from him.

We have, then, this dilemma. Either our theistic treatises introduce into the idea of God which they claim to prove qualities which their professed premises are unable to support; or, sticking loyally to their premises, they yield a result which is less than is desired. This failure gives the method of authority its opportunity.

By the method of authority, we mean a method which despairs of direct proof of the Christian God, and so falls back upon external testimony. This method may be illustrated by the traditional argument for Christianity from miracle and prophecy. Its reasoning runs thus: God, whose true nature cannot be known by reason, has revealed himself by a supernatural communication evidenced by miracle and prophecy. The contents of this communication are embodied in the creeds of the church (or in the Scriptures), and are to be accepted by all men solely on this guarantee.

There are two objections to this reasoning. The first concerns its premise, the second its conclusion.

As to (1), the argument assumes that God is such a being that miracle and prophecy evidence his presence, and that man is so related to God that he knows this fact. But this proves either too much or too little. If God is so far removed from man as to be unknowable by reason, this invalidates the argument from miracle, as well as the more speculative reasoning to supplement which miracle is usually invoked. If, on the other hand, man can know God in part, there is no *a priori* reason why his knowledge should not extend further when the appropriate evidence is presented.

(2) But the most serious difficulty with the argument is with its conclusion. The God whom this proof claims to establish falls as far short of the Christian idea as that reached by the method of speculation. He is a being who reveals himself indirectly through testimony, instead of one with whom we come into direct contact in experience. But it is only through personal experience that we can know the Father of whom Jesus taught.

Thus both the method of speculation and the method of authority point back to the Christian experience. Here we find the real reason, and the only conclusive reason for believing in the Christian God.

2.   *The Basis in Experience for Faith in the Christian God.*

The basis in experience for faith in the Christian God is found partly in the response which the idea meets in the individual consciousness, partly in its growing supremacy over the reason, the conscience and the religious feeling of the race.

This method of grounding faith in God agrees with that of mysticism in that it is based upon an immediate experience of the soul. It differs from it in that the evidence on which it relies appeals to more than feeling. It includes the reason and the conscience as well, and hence can be stated in terms which can be understood. Herein lies the possibility of its scientific verification.

It is characteristic of mysticism in all its forms that it bases faith upon an incommunicable experience. It finds sufficient evidence for God's existence in the fact that one *feels* the presence of the divine. But this mysterious experience, common to all religions, is incapable of closer description. The mystic can point you to ways through which he has cultivated the sense of God, and recommend you to follow them, but he cannot put the idea of God which he has formed into definite words which will convey its content to others. God must be felt to be understood, and feeling is incommunicable.

There is an element of mysticism in every true religious experience. Experience has always about it something private and esoteric; something which must be felt to be understood. But in ethical religions like Christianity the characteristic feature is that the religious feeling is called forth by an object which is capable in part at least of definite description. The God whom Christ reveals is moral personality. He appeals to reason and conscience, as well as feeling. Because he is such a God, he may be preached to others. Faith in him may find utterance in common confession, and praise and prayer be offered in common worship. If this were not so, Christianity could not have become the world religion it is.

Thus, in describing the experience which is the basis of Christian faith, it is necessary to indicate the ways in which the Christian idea of God satisfies the needs of man on every side. We have to show how it satisfies the reason, giving a worthier explanation of the meaning and purpose of things than any which philosophy, apart from Christ, supplies. We have to show how it satisfies the conscience, presenting a moral ideal at once more comprehensive and more exacting than that which is found in any other ethical system. We have to show how it satisfies the emotional nature, providing an outlet for the affections adequate to the utmost human capacity. We have to show what light the Christian idea of God sheds upon the questions of daily duty which fill so large a place in human life; how in the kingdom of God it provides an end at once great enough to call forth the highest enthusiasm and enlist the most devoted loyalty, and yet many-sided enough to make place for the most widely varying talents, and to give meaning and dignity to the humblest work. In short, we must show how the Christian idea of God meets the practical needs of our nature on every side. The man who has gained this insight will have a basis for his faith which nothing can shake.

It is the merit of Ritschl that he has called attention to the positive elements in the Christian experience. In contrast to the self-centred ideal of mysticism, it is important that we should emphasize the ethical and practical interest of Christianity, and show how the Christian ideal gains its distinctive character from its close connection with the historic Jesus. It is possible, however, to carry the contrast so far as to overlook what the Christian experience has in common with all true religious life. Especially is it necessary, when we seek to establish the Christian idea of God, that we should bear constantly in mind the relation of Christian faith to the older lines of reasoning to which we have already alluded. What Christianity has brought into the world is not a new logic, but a new experience. The way to establish the Christian idea of God is not to discredit the ways in which men in other ages have sought to gain knowledge of the divine, but to indicate how the same methods, when applied to the new material which Christianity supplies, yield richer and larger conclusions. We may illustrate this in connection with the traditional arguments for the being of God.

Thus, when applied to existence in general, the cosmological argument yields only a first cause, — a purely formal and barren conception. Applied to a world which includes the Christian experience, with its peace and joy, it yields a cause adequate to produce such a result, — personal, moral, loving.

Applied to the physical world alone, as in the old Bridgewater treatises, the teleological argument yields at most reason, and has to face the apparent lack of adaptation in the moral world. Applied to the kingdom of redemption in which the problems of sin and suffering find their practical solution, it points back to a person wise and loving enough to devise such a plan, and finds him in the Father of our Lord Jesus Christ.

Again, the moral argument, considered apart from Christianity, will yield a result varying according to the ethical ideal which may be dominant at the time. At the best, it has to face the difficulty that in the world of experience we nowhere see the realization of the moral ideal. In Christ, Christian faith finds the missing link in the argument. Kant reasons: " Unless there is to be a dualism in the universe, I must believe in a power adequate to bridge the gap between moral ideal and fact." The Christian goes one step further and says: "In Christ I see the gap bridged."

Even the ontological argument receives new meaning in the light of Christian experience. Translated from its scholastic form into common speech, it expresses man's faith that this is an "honest world,"[1] and, therefore, that what is a necessity for human thought must have a corresponding counterpart in reality. Christianity, with its enhanced sense of the dignity and the meaning of life, reinforces this conviction; but it puts in place of the necessarily existing being of Anselm the God who gives meaning and joy to life.

Thus interpreted, all the arguments move in the sphere of what Kant would call the practical reason. They are not syllogisms of logic, leading to mathematical demonstration, but expressions of that moral probability on which our highest convictions rest. They state the grounds which, as a matter of fact, lead the Christian to believe that God is, and that he is such a being as we have defined. So far as our present discussion goes, they are individual and subjective, and it is open to anyone to reject them, who does not share the experience from which they derive their force. What gives them *scientific* interest is the fact that they are not purely individual. They express social as well as individual convictions, and have

[1] Clarke, *Outline,* p. 122.

maintained themselves progressively in history. In this fact lies the possibility of a scientific verification of the Christian idea of God. What is the nature of this verification, and what its limits, we have finally to consider.

3. *Method and Limits of Verification.*[1]

From the point of view of philosophy, the Christian idea of God is a hypothesis, which must be tested by its ability to explain all the facts of life. So long as it remains an individual conviction, its sufficient evidence is to be found in the fact that it meets the needs of the individual; but when it is put forth as an idea of universal validity, it must conform to the conditions of scientific proof. These are twofold, — universality and permanence. We call that theory proved (1) which is able to win and to hold the suffrages of all those whom we deem qualified to judge, and (2) which maintains itself in spite of all the additions to our knowledge brought by widening experience. Of two or more conflicting theories, we judge that most probable which seems most to admit the possibility of such progressive verification.

It is true that in the case of the highest ideas, such verification is only approximately possible. In the sphere of art, of morals and of religion, we have to do with objects which appeal to our sense of value, and hence which require for their apprehension quickness of conscience and sensitiveness of feeling. As the sense of beauty is necessary for the appreciation of a work of art, so the man who would know the Christian God must understand in his own

---

1 In what follows I am happy to find myself in substantial agreement with my colleague, Dr. George William Knox, to whose *Direct and Fundamental Proofs of the Christian Religion* the reader may be referred for a fuller development of the line of argument briefly suggested below. Cf. esp. pp. 30 sq.

experience what righteousness and love mean. In religion, as in art, it is the character of the witnesses which counts, rather than their number.

Yet, this limitation is counterbalanced by a corresponding advantage. If the number of those is limited, to whom at any time ideal interests appeal, it is capable of being increased. It is characteristic of the sciences which deal with the ethical and the spiritual that they help to create their own evidence. Considered as moral personality, man is not a constant, but a variable; and by appealing to that which is best in him, we develop the capacity whose existence we assume. In the highest things the experience of the few precedes and prepares the way for the experience of the many, and full verification belongs to the future. Thus the effort to realize the religious ideal in practice is an indispensable condition of its proof.

With this qualification, the conditions of proof are the same in religion as in other departments of knowledge. To prove a doctrine true it is necessary to show (1) that it is able to win the allegiance of the men and women of the greatest moral and spiritual insight, and (2) that it is able to hold this allegiance in spite of the changes which wider experience and enlarging knowledge may bring. In the case of an ethical religion like Christianity, in which the idea of God is inextricably interwoven with the ideal for man, this involves the proof that the principles to which it is committed are capable of realization in society.

Looked at from this point of view, the argument for the Christian idea of God appears at its full strength. It consists in the progressive verification to which it is being subjected, both in the experience of individuals and in society. We have to do with a conception which, beginning as the faith of a few individuals, has spread over a large part of the known world; which has maintained itself in spite of profound changes in intellectual and social environment, and which is held to-day by some of the most enlightened and civilized peoples of mankind. Among those who accept it are some of the finest intellects of the race, who, having studied all that the science and philosophy of their day could teach, have still found in the Father whom Christ revealed the highest object of thought and the most satisfying explanation of existence. Yet at the same time it has been the inspiration of some of the noblest characters the world has known, whose lives have been given to the effort to realize the kingdom of God among men, and who have left on record their witness that they have found in the Christian idea of God a practical solution of the perplexing problems which face every one who tries unselfishly to help his fellowmen.

This direct testimony is reinforced by a study of the effects which Christianity has wrought in society. It is true that the full force of this evidence is weakened because of the fact that much which calls itself Christian civilization is not really such. Yet when we ask what are the things in our modern life which we count most precious, those which differentiate it most clearly from that of savage or of half-civilized man, and on which our hope for the future is most confidently based, we find that they are those in which it conforms most nearly to the Christian ideal. Many of those, who, on intellectual grounds, question the Christian idea of God, accept the ethical principles of Christianity, and so give indirect witness to the facts on which faith in the Christian God rests.

Thus the testimony of the individual Christian, who in his limited experience has tested his faith and found it workable, is confirmed by that of the great company of men and women of all ages and races, who have been making a similar experiment, and who have arrived at like results. This consensus of Christian experience gives the argument from authority its real weight. Authority is the form in which the experience of the past is handed down and made available for the future. Its weight is proportionate to the amount and character of the experience on which it rests. Thus the place assigned to the Bible by the church is justified by the fact that in its pages we are brought into contact with the creative personalities of our religion, — the men in whom the transforming effects of Christian faith have made themselves most strikingly felt. The creeds have weight because they are the utterance — in forms, to be sure, determined by the intellectual and social environment — of convictions in which multitudes have found the answer to their questions and the inspiration of their lives. The same is true in greater or less degree of all the forms of the church's witness. That which makes it reasonable to accept it is the fact that it sums up in concise form the results of centuries of Christian experience. Traced to its source, the most abstract doctrine tells of a God who has been tested in some man's life in the past, and who invites to renewed test in the present and in the future.

What is true of Bible and church is true in supreme measure of the Christ to whom both point. That which justifies the unique place which Christ holds in Christian faith is the fact that in him the Christian idea of God finds its most striking practical test. Jesus reveals God, not by telling us things about him which we cannot verify, but by showing us in his own person what faith in God means for a human life, that we may test his message for ourselves. The convincing proof of his teaching lies in the fact that the ideal he reveals is capable of reproduction in the lives of his followers.

Thus the argument from authority in all its forms points beyond itself. For the individual it may be legitimate for a time to rely upon the testimony of another, without clear insight into the grounds on which his trust rests. That is a necessary consequence of the differences of capacity and of opportunity to which we have already referred. But for humanity at large continual verification is necessary, if the faith of one generation is to justify itself to another. Such a test Christianity invites. It bases its claim not only upon the satisfaction which individuals find in its teaching, but in the effects which it has wrought in society; and, above all, upon the succession of heroic personalities whom it has inspired, who from age to age have waged uncompromising war upon whatever in so-called Christian civilization has really been un-Christlike, and through whom the Christian ideal of brotherhood in service has been brought from generation to generation nearer its accomplishment.

Thus, both in the lives of individuals and in society, the Christian idea of God is in process of a progressive verification. It is no valid argument against it that so many still reject it. That is only to be expected in view of the character of the evidence on which it relies. The moral and spiritual qualities which Christian faith presupposes are found in unequal degree in a developing race, and no small part of the task of Christianity is the creation of the capacity to which its message must appeal. The important thing is that a beginning has been made. All that is necessary in order to prove our faith reasonable is to show that the Christian experience is increasing, and the Christian ideal gaining ground; that the better Christ is known, the more his supremacy is recognized; and that, in the regions where other masters hold sway, the needs and long- ings of man are such that apart from Christ they fail to find complete satisfaction. When Christian apologetics has shown this in detail for its own generation, its work is done. Complete proof must wait for the future, when the Christ whom faith calls Lord shall show himself supreme in fact.[1]

Yet, while theology cannot anticipate the final verdict, it may remove some obstacles which now tend to postpone it. Not all those who reject the Christian idea of God do so because of defective spiritual insight. Often the real diffi- culty is just the reverse. Our study has shown us how inadequate have been many of the forms in which the Christian idea of God has been presented in the past. When God is defined as self-centred blessedness or as arbitrary will, loyalty to the spirit of Christ may lead to the rejection of a doctrine put forth in his name. By a better definition theology can remove the occasion for such needless conflicts, and change many of those who are now counted as opponents of the Christian idea into its advocates.

To sum up: Our faith in the Christian God rests ulti- mately upon the appeal which Christ makes to that which is highest in us, together with the conviction that it is rational to interpret the universe by the highest we know. This argument fails (a) in the case of those who deny that it is right to use the highest we know to interpret the uni- verse, and (b) in the case of those who deny that Christ is highest.

As to (a), we can only point to the instinctive feeling

[1] Cf. my *Essence of Christianity*, p. 311.

of humanity, and the example of the great philosophies which have used this method in the interpretation of the world.

As to (*b*), we admit the limitation, but claim that its significance is less than is often supposed. For (1) there is a greater consensus than many believe, which waits only for correct definition to show itself; and (2) there is a growing acceptance of the Christian idea, which justifies our hope for the future.

In view of these things there is need not only of courage, but of patience. The debate upon which we are engaged has been going on for many centuries, and the end is not yet. So far as men's rejection of Christianity is due to misunderstanding, it is our privilege, as theologians, to try to remove it. But there is a better apologetic than that of the schools, and that is to live before men a life so Christlike that those who see it shall be moved to desire a like life for themselves, and so be introduced into that experience out of which alone a sincere faith in the Christian God can grow.

CHAPTER X

OF THE TRINITY, OR GOD'S THREEFOLD SELF-MANIFESTATION

THE Christian conception of God, whose contents we have thus far studied separately, is concisely summarized in the doctrine of the Trinity.

By the Trinity we mean that form of stating the doctrine of God which has resulted historically from the recognition of Jesus as the supreme revelation of God, together with the experience of God's present working which was the result of the new insight he brought. In its developed forms, as found in the so-called Nicene [1] and Athanasian [2] creeds, it is the view which distinguishes three different aspects or elements in the divine being, God the Father, God the Son, and God the Holy Spirit, and affirms that these three together make up the one God.

At the outset three things are to be borne in mind which

---

[1] The creed we call Nicene is attributed by the Council of Chalcedon (451) to the Council of Constantinople (381), and is regarded as their revision of the Nicene creed of 325, hence the name " Nicene " in the prayer-book. As a matter of fact, its author is unknown. It is a revision of the baptismal creed of the church of Jerusalem, embodying the Nicene doctrine of the person of Christ, and the later decisions concerning the Holy Spirit. The Council of Chalcedon gave it formal ecclesiastical sanction. Cf. Harnack, in Herzog, *Real Encyclopädie*, 3d ed. art. " Konstantinopolitanisches Symbol "; Hort, *Two Dissertations*, London, 1876.

[2] The authorship of the Athanasian creed is unknown. The one thing certain is that Athanasius did not write it. It is a Latin creed, probably composed in Gaul in the fifth or sixth century, and embodies the form of the doctrine which had been advocated by Augustine in his great work on the Trinity.

give us the proper standpoint for the understanding of the doctrine: (1) that the Trinity is not a supplement to the Christian doctrine of God, a new revelation added to that which is described under the divine nature and attributes, but only the fuller unfolding of what is there implied; (2) that it is not a purely speculative doctrine, but one which had its roots in experience; (3) that it is not a constant doctrine, and hence that its true significance can be understood only in the light of the entire history of which it forms a part.

1. *Sources and History.*

The New Testament contains no formal doctrine of the Trinity, though it gives us the sources from which the later doctrine grew. These are partly experimental, and partly philosophical. The experimental source is the historic revelation which God has made of himself through Christ, and the religious life which centres in him. The philosophical source is the doctrine of the Logos, or Word, through which it was sought to find a basis for this revelation in the being of God. The baptismal formula gives the framework of which the later doctrine was the development; but only the first step of that development falls within the New Testament, namely, the recognition in Christ of the incarnation of a pre-existent divine being.

To begin with the experimental source. The early Christians were monotheists. Like the Jews before them, they believed in one God, the creator and ruler of the world. Like the Jews also, they believed that this God was everywhere at work in the world, revealing his truth to men, and enduing them with power by his Holy Spirit. Unlike the Jews, they saw in Jesus, the Messiah, God's supreme revelation, the Saviour of the world. Consequently, Christ became intimately associated with their thought of God. They saw in him the one through whom God entered the world for man's salvation,[1] and the Holy Spirit, in whom, equally with the Jews, they believed, became to them the Spirit of Christ.[2]

This change was not arbitrary, but the natural result of the Christian experience. Side by side with the older ways through which God had revealed himself, and by which he might still be known, they were aware of a new and richer stream of influence which had come to them through his revelation in the historic Christ. As a result of his life and work, they were conscious of living in a closer and more intimate communion with God than they had hitherto enjoyed. God was known in their experience as an indwelling presence, and his revelation in nature and in history was answered by his immediate witness in the soul.

Thus, when the early Christians would describe the Christian life in its entirety, all three of these elements enter in, God the Father, Jesus Christ his Son, the Holy Spirit. Whatever may be the age of the baptismal formula, the apostolic benediction belongs to the first Christian generation; and many other passages — all the more impressive because of their practical character — show how closely the three were associated in Christian thought and life.[3] In this association, naturally suggesting itself from the facts of the religious life, we have the experimental source of the doctrine of the Trinity.

But this alone would not give us the Trinity of the creeds. For this we need to pass from God's revelation to

---

[1] Cf. 2 Cor. v, 19 ; John i, 1.

[2] Cf. 1 Peter i, 11 ; Rom. viii, 9.

[3] *E.g.* 1 Cor. ii, 1–5; Eph. ii, 18; Gal. iv, 6; Rom. viii, 9–11 ; 1 Cor. xii, 4–6.

his nature, and to attribute the differences which experience discloses in his outward manifestation to inner distinctions within his own being. Five steps may be distinguished in this process. The first is the identification of the pre-existent Christ with the Logos of Greek philosophy; the second, Origen's doctrine of the eternal generation of the Son; the third, the victory at Nicæa of the Athanasian formula, "homoousios"; the fourth, the definition of the distinctions between the Father, Son, and Spirit, as carried through by Basil and the Kappadocian theologians at the close of the fourth century; while the fifth and last is the transformation of the Eastern doctrine under the influence of Augustine, culminating in the Athanasian creed and the doctrine of the double procession.[1]

[1] Of the doctrine of the pre-existent Christ we shall speak in another connection. (See chapter XI, p. 179.) It is enough here to say that with this conception a point of contact was provided between Christian faith and the speculations, Jewish and Greek, which solved the problems of creation and of revelation by the assumption of mediating principles, like the Logos, through which the gap between the absolute God and the created universe was bridged. In the New Testament itself, however, the speculative interest is largely subordinated to the practical. The idea of the Logos is assumed as a familiar one, and the distinctive Christian revelation is found in the fact that in the human life of Jesus, the divine Word, who in all ages has been the source of revelation, has become flesh and dwells with men.

In the theology of Justin and the apologists we note a change of emphasis. Here the pre-existent Christ is formally identified with the Logos of Greek philosophy, and whatever the philosophers have attributed to the latter is affirmed of Christ. The human Jesus falls into the background, and the marks of limitation in his life are either overlooked or explained away. The Catholic Fathers, Irenæus, Tertullian, and Origen, vindicate the orthodoxy of the Logos, over against the simpler Messianic Christology (perpetuated in Adoptionism), and so determine the lines of the later dogmatic development. This is concerned largely with determining the relation of the Word, or Son, to God, and has as its result a shifting of interest from the practical problems of revelation and redemption to the speculative problem which concerns the nature of God in himself.

The transition between the two points of view is furnished by Origen's

This is not the place to retrace in detail the arduous path whose most conspicuous mile-stones have been thus indicated. It will be sufficient to note how natural and inevitable the entire process was. It is the fashion to-day to represent the older dogma as a corruption of the primitive simplicity of Christian faith by the admixture of a foreign substance, namely, Greek philosophy. The truth is just the reverse. The novel element in the compound was not philosophy, but the Gospel. The doctrine of the Logos and all that it implies was the common assumption of the culture of the time. That which was new was the identification of the Logos with Jesus, and the reinterpretation of God which this required. The steps which led to the formulation of the doctrine of the Trinity are the steps by which the Christian spirit made for itself a home in the existing intellectual environment. However speculative in form, every one of them was due to a practical interest.

This comes out clearly in connection with the controversy of Athanasius with Arius. It is easy to see in the

doctrine of the eternal generation of the Son. Before this time the Logos had been regarded primarily as a cosmological principle (*i. e.* a principle which expressed God's relation to the world), and hence it had been assumed that the Son had a beginning in time (cf. Tertullian, *adversus Hermogenem*, 3 : *fuit tempus, cum ei . . . filius non fuit*, "there was a time when the Son did not exist with him (*i. e.* God)"). This was the later Arian doctrine. To Origen also, the Logos was primarily a cosmological conception ; but since he held that creation itself was an eternal process, the Logos became of necessity co-eternal with God. In Origen's theology the connection with creation made this eternal co-existence compatible with a strong doctrine of subordination, and even with the use of such terms as "creature" to denote the relation of the Logos to God. But with the rejection of the doctrine of eternal creation, such a union was no longer possible, and the issue was clearly joined between the strict deity of the Son and his subordination as creature. This was the question in debate between Athanasius and Arius, which was decided in favor of the former at the Council of Nicæa. The Nicene creed denies that Christ is a creature, even the highest. He is very God, begotten not made, of the same substance (homoousios) with the Father.

discussions about "homoousios" and "homoiousios" an idle logomachy, and in the admission of the Athanasian formula to the creed a victory of the Greek metaphysical spirit.   Such a judgment, however, would be superficial. When we look beneath the words, we see that the much abused "homoousios" [1] is really the assertion of the fundamental reality of the Christian faith in spite of metaphysical difficulties.   What is at stake is the nature of God and his relation to salvation.   Against those who maintained that God stood outside the world and had committed the work of redemption to a creature, Athanasius contended that in the incarnation God himself was active, so that those who shared Christ's redemption entered into communion with God.   The deity of Christ, as Athanasius conceived it, meant the substitution of the present God of Christian faith for the abstract and transcendent God of philosophy.

The same may be said of each of the subsequent steps of the process.   The distinction between the terms "ousia" and "hypostasis," [2] carried through by the great theologians of Kappadocia at the end of the fourth century, was in the interest of the separate individuality of Christ, which seemed imperilled by the older terminology. [3]   The Augus-

[1] On the word "homoousios," cf. Strong, in *Journal of Theological Studies*, vol. II, p. 224, vol. III, p. 229 ; Robertson, *Athanasius*, in Nicene and Post-Nicene Library, second series, vol. IV, p. 30.   The term is ambiguous.   It may express the common possession by two different beings of the same nature or substance, or it may be carried so far as to affirm absolute identity. The last was the Sabellian position, and seemed to many conservative men to destroy the independent significance of Christ.   Moreover, the word had heretical associations, having already been condemned in connection with Paul of Samosata.   For both these reasons, as well as for its novelty, the word was vehemently opposed by a large section of the church, and received general recognition only after 381.

[2] On the meaning of the term "hypostasis," cf. p. 148, note 1.

[3] In the original Nicene creed the words "ousia" and "hypostasis" are used

tinian doctrine of the double procession, which proved so great a stumbling-block to the Greek church, and was one of the causes of the final separation, was the result of a desire to give clear expression to the unity of God, which was obscured by the subordination of the Eastern statement.[1] Putting ourselves back at the point of view of the men who made the decisions, and imagining ourselves faced with like questions, we should have been obliged to answer them in the same way.

as synonyms. To many conservative men this seemed to involve an identification of the Son with the Father (as in Sabellianism), and hence the denial of the independent significance of Christ. In the latter part of the fourth century the Kappadocian theologians (Basil and the Gregories) found a way out of the difficulty by distinguishing between the two words. " Ousia " was used to designate the divine substance, while " hypostasis " was set apart to denote the distinctions within the being of God. This terminology was adopted by Athanasius, and went far to secure the general acceptance of the doctrine.

The Kappadocian school also developed the doctrine of the Spirit, as to which, up to this time, wide difference of opinion had prevailed. Gregory Nazianzen tells us (Oration 31, in Nicene and Post-Nicene Library, vol. VII, p. 319) that some thought him God, others a creature, others knew not what to think. In other words, there was no uniformity of theological tradition. The definition of " hypostasis " put an end to this uncertainty. The Spirit, like the Son, was a divine hypostasis, a distinction within the Godhead, proceeding from the Father, and sharing his substance. Here first we meet the doctrine of the ontological Trinity in the proper sense of the term.

[1] The doctrine of the double procession, that is to say, the doctrine that the Spirit proceeds not from the Father alone, but from the Father and the Son, has proved the dividing line theologically between East and West. Finding its way, we know not how, into the Western editions of the Nicene creed, it was the subject of formal protest from the Eastern church, and with other causes not necessary to mention here, brought about the final rupture. With all recognition of the deity of the Son and of the Spirit, Eastern theologians insist that there remains a certain subordination in their relation to the Father. In Greek theology God the Father is the sole fountain of deity. From him is generated the Son ; from him, and from him alone, proceeds the Holy Spirit. It is otherwise in the West. Here under Augustine's influence the unity of the divine persons is so emphasized as all but to obliterate the distinctions between them. Instead of the Father being the sole fountain of deity, he shares this office with the Son. The Holy Spirit proceeds from the Son as well as from the Father ; and, with this recognition, the last trace of subordination disappears.

10

Yet when all is said, it cannot be denied that the victory of the Christian spirit over Greek thought was bought at a heavy price. With each step in the process of the formulation of the doctrine we note a tendency to greater abstractness of thought. The bond which unites the philosophical statement to its basis in experience grows weaker and weaker. The Nicene creed still betrays clear evidence of the motives which were originally controlling. It still puts in the centre of the creed the Jesus who for our sake was made man, who suffered under Pontius Pilate, and whose coming was foretold by the Spirit who spake by the prophets. But in the Athanasian creed the tie which unites the Christ of dogma to the Jesus of history is parted. The scene has shifted to a realm where neither reason nor experience can find entrance. The interest no longer centres in the word made flesh, but in the divine Son who was with the Father from the beginning. The Trinity has become a mystery dealing with the inner relations of the Godhead.

But, while the Athanasian creed marks the end of the dogmatic formulation of the doctrine, it is only the beginning of its theological history. The mind of man has never long been content with a doctrine incapable of rational explanation. Even while affirming that the mystery of the Godhead transcended human reason, and that the terms used in its description were only symbols to cover our ignorance, Augustine's venturesome intellect pushed out along a path of exploration on which he has been followed by many successors. He saw in the Trinity a revelation of distinctions in God's being which had their analogies in human life; and wherever the speculative interest has been strong, the search for such analogies has continued to exercise its fascination over the mind of man. To German idealism of the Hegelian type the Trinity is the truth of truths, the most rational of doctrines, the clearest philosophical expression of the being of God; and wherever the Hegelian influence is controlling, we find interest in the doctrine reviving, and giving birth to a series of attempts at speculative reconstruction.

Still a third phase in the interpretation of the Trinity has been introduced by modern historical study. A better acquaintance with the beginnings of Christianity has made it increasingly clear that the Hegelian construction does not adequately represent the convictions which led to the original formulation of the doctrine, or do justice to the motives from which it arose. It was not God as he is in himself with whom the early Christians were primarily concerned, but God as he had graciously revealed himself to them through Christ and the Spirit. In our day the experimental elements which underlie the doctrine are being emphasized anew, and its distinctive significance is found in its connection with the historic Jesus.

We have, then, three different methods of interpreting the doctrine, corresponding to three different types of theology. According to the first, the Trinity is a mystery transcending reason; according to the second, it is a speculative theory concerning the being of God in himself; according to the third, it is an interpretation of the Christian experience of God as revealed. We shall consider each in turn.

2. *The Trinity as a Mystery Transcending Reason.*

The clearest statement of the view of the Trinity as a mystery transcending reason is given in the Athanasian creed. According to this view, God is one substance (ousia, phusis, natura, essentia, substantia), in whom are three hypostases,[1] or principles of distinction (prosopa, hypostaseis, personae).   These hypostases are known technically as "persons," a term not to be confused with our word "personality," as is often erroneously done in the popular interpretation of the doctrine.   These three "persons" are equal, since all share the whole divine substance. They differ because each has its own hypostatic character. The Father is the begetter, the Son begotten, the Spirit proceeding.   The nature of these inner-Trinitarian distinctions language is not sufficiently accurate to describe. We use terms to denote them simply that we may not be silent.[2]

The impression of mystery and other-worldliness produced by this description is still further increased by the doctrine of the *Circumincessio*, or *Perichoresis*, in which the dogmatic conception of the Trinity culminates.   This is the doctrine of such a sharing of each person in the attributes of all the others that in the Trinity there is neither before nor after, beginning nor ending, greater nor less.   With this view the last trace of subordination dis-

---

[1] The word " hypostasis " means literally subsistence, *i. e.* that which underlies a thing, and gives it reality ; a real existence, as distinct from a mere idea.   Hence, its use as an equivalent of " ousia," substance.   As used in connection with the Trinity, it means a principle of individuation, or distinction (as distinct from a mere personification).   It does not necessarily mean a person in our modern sense.   This (mis-)translation is due to the fact that it has come to us through its Latin equivalent *persona*.   This is a theatrical term and means a mask.   It denotes the several parts which may be played by a single actor.   Hence, its use to translate " hypostasis," — a word which denotes a distinction grounded in a deeper underlying unity.   Our word " personality " gives a wholly misleading translation, and has been the parent of untold confusion.   It has resolved the unity of God into three distinct self-consciousnesses, and given us a view of God which is practically tritheistic. It is important, therefore, to remember that " person " in the Trinitarian sense does not mean personality.

[2] Cf. Augustine, *De Trinitate*, XV, 27, in Nicene and Post-Nicene Library, vol. III, p. 225.

appears, and with it the last reminiscence of the original source of the doctrine in the historic revelation that came through Jesus.

The acceptance of the Trinity in this form is common both to Catholicism and to Protestantism; but the significance which is attributed to it varies very widely. To many Protestants who take this view the Trinity is simply a mystery which is received upon authority because it is believed that the Bible teaches it, and then put upon one side as something which does not directly affect the Christian life. To intelligent Catholics, on the other hand, the Trinity is the doctrine of doctrines, central in worship as in the creed. It is the expression, in a form most strikingly calculated to impress the imagination, of that mystic conception of God as a being transcending knowledge which is characteristic of the Catholic type of piety.

Thus even that form of stating the doctrine of the Trinity which seems most remote from the present life of man proves to have its basis in the religious experience. The Athanasian creed is a fruit of that general change which came over the Christian religion with the loss of contact with the historic Jesus, and the substitution of the mystic type of piety for the ethical religion which finds its communion with God realized through social service. It is the attempt to express the inexpressible in words, a majestic hymn in which the august perfection of the ineffable finds utterance in human speech; and wherever the mystic type of piety survives, the Trinity of the Athanasian creed still remains an object of living faith.

But where this experimental basis is lacking, the significance of the doctrine is altered. To believe a mysterious doctrine because one's highest idea of God is mystery is

one thing.   To continue to describe God in terms incapable
of rational explanation when one has come to think of God
as rational is another.   Such a situation introduces into the
world of thought a condition as unstable as that of a building whose roof still remains standing after the main pillars
by which it is supported have been cut away.   Under such
circumstances there are but two safe methods to follow: to
remove the roof before its own weight brings it to the
ground; or to provide a new foundation better able to bear
the weight which is laid upon it.   It is the latter method
which is attempted in the next class of interpretations to
which we now turn.

3.   *The Trinity as a Speculative Theory.*

It is characteristic of all the constructions which we
class together as speculative that, like the Trinity of
dogma, they are concerned with the being of God as he
is in himself, apart from his historic revelation.   While
they use analogies drawn from human experience, it is to
illustrate the life of God as it is conceived to be lived
apart from all contact with human experience.   The difference between the two standpoints consists in the fact that,
while the former relies for its proof solely upon authority,
the latter sees in the Trinity a rational truth which may be
illustrated and defended by considerations whose validity
is recognized in other realms.   The most significant of
these have been drawn from a study of the personal life,
and the theories to which they have given rise may be
classed as psychological or social, according as the material
is derived from the analysis of a single self-consciousness
or is gained from a study of the social relationship.   Both
are very ancient, going back at least to Augustine.

Augustine distinguished in man memory, understanding

and will, in all of which the total mind is active. He further distinguished the mind, the knowledge which the mind has of itself, and the love which it has for itself. Through each of these analogies he gained a kind of trinity of the divine self-consciousness.

In modern times the psychological analogy owes its widespread acceptance to the influence of Hegel. Hegel saw in the Trinity the central Christian doctrine, and interpreted it as the expression in religious language of the fundamental truth of his philosophy, — the truth, namely, that the ultimate reality (or Absolute) must be conceived in the form of the synthesis of a logically preceding thesis and antithesis. Thus, the Trinity in its Hegelian form is simply the application to the absolute consciousness of the Hegelian formula of the trinitarian character of all thought.

As an example of this method we may take the recent treatment of Dr. Clarke, in his *Outline*.[1] He begins with an analysis of self-consciousness, as expressed in the formula, " I am I." Here we have the self as knower, the self as known, and the union of the two in the act of self-consciousness. But in us this trinity is never perfect, since we never completely know ourselves. There is always a difference between our subjective thought of ourselves and the reality. Not so with God. He is the perfect personality, in whom thought always corresponds with reality. In his self-consciousness, therefore, subject and object are completely one. He recognizes himself as perfectly mirrored in his thought of himself. So the circle is complete, and God is bound back to God in conscious unity. Thus (in contrast to pantheism) the perfect inner life of spirit exists in God.

[1] Pp. 172 sq.

In all this there is no difficulty. It is only the reassertion in different form of the familiar truth of the personality of God. The difficulty comes when it is sought to
relate this statement of the doctrine to its historic antecedents, and especially to the human Jesus whose revelation
the Trinity is supposed to explain. In order to do this it
is necessary to pass from the logical distinction of thought
to the metaphysical distinction of being. Dr. Clarke continues: "In finite and imperfect minds these mental movements pass half-noticed, and oftener wholly unnoticed."
But when we think of God, the perfect being, "it does not
seem impossible that to him each of the three should be a
centre of conscious life and activity, and that he should
live in each a life corresponding to its quality. The assertion that he lives such a life is the assertion of the divine
Tri-unity.[1] He lives as God original and unuttered, he lives
as God uttered and going-forth, and he lives as God in
whom the first and the second are united. He not only
lives and is conscious in these three modes, but from each
of these centres he acts from everlasting to everlasting.
His perfect life consists in the sum of these three modes of
activity. . . . They are not personalities in the modern
sense of the term, but separate aspects of one personality"[2]

It is just here that the difficulty begins. In spite of
Dr. Clarke's disclaimer, it is hard to see how these "centres of conscious life and activity" can be distinguished
from separate personalities. But for such a Trinity as
this, — a Trinity of three distinct self-consciousnesses,
our own personal experience as self-conscious spirits affords
no analogy. To gain a point of comparison, we are obliged

[1] Dr. Clarke uses the term "Tri-unity" to distinguish the ontological
Trinity, or the Trinity of essence, from the more familiar Trinity of manifestation.

[2] *Outline*, p. 174.

to abandon the standpoint of the individual, and to include the phenomena of social life. This is done by the other type of theory to which we now turn.

Like the psychological analogy, the social analogy goes back to Augustine. Long ago he noticed a trinity in love: the lover, the object loved, and the love which unites the two. In this he has been followed by many later theologians.

An example of the modern use of the social analogy is given by Dr. Fairbairn in his *Place of Christ in Modern Theology*. Here great stress is laid upon the fact that the Christian Trinity, with its Father and Son, involves the thought of social relations as belonging to the essence of God. "God is love," we are told, "but love is social, can as little live in solitude as man can breathe in a vacuum. In order to its being, there must be an object bestowing love; an object rejoicing in its bestowal. . . . If then God is by nature love, he must be by nature social." [1] It follows that in God we have one "in whom Fatherhood, and therefore Sonship, are immanent." [2]

This view has much to commend it. It starts from the Christian conception of God as love, and tries to solve a real difficulty, that, namely, of conceiving of a single isolated personality. How can God be just and loving, and all that we affirm him to be, if he have not from all eternity some object for these moral activities and relations? Such an object the doctrine of the Trinity seeks to supply.

Yet these advantages are counterbalanced by corresponding difficulties. Quite apart from the fact that in positing at least two, if not three, distinct self-conciousnesses in God, the theory carries us dangerously near to tritheism,

---

[1] *Place of Christ in Modern Theology*, p. **294**.
[2] *Ibid.*, p. **409**.

there seems no rational reason why the divine love should be confined to a single object. Why not Motherhood and Brotherhood as well as Fatherhood and Sonship in God? The social analogy would seem to lead to a multitude of different centres within the divine being in whose complete harmony and sympathy the perfection of the Godhead consists. Moreover, the place assigned to the Spirit in the analogy is unsatisfactory. Either the Spirit is regarded as expressing the bond of union between God and Christ, in which case the parallelism between the members is not maintained; or else the Spirit is treated as a third self-conciousness after the analogy of the Son, and assigned a special function in the economy of the divine redemption.

We would speak with great respect of those who think they can distinguish in their own experience the workings of the different Trinitarian persons. It is not for those whose experience is limited to set bounds which others may not transcend. It is sufficient to remind ourselves of certain unfortunate effects which have resulted from the attempt to press such distinctions beyond their rightful limit. When, for example, redemption is represented as the result of a bargain between the Father and the Son; or the failure of an expected revival explained as due to the jealousy of the third person of the Trinity because he has not received that portion of honor which is his own just due, it is easy to see that we are dealing with conceptions of God which are, to say the least, less than Christian. It was such tritheism as this, a Trinity of three separate Gods with independent rights and interests, against which the earlier Unitarianism protested; and we are bound to admit that its protest was justified.

Thus, while the psychological analogy gives us a God

who is but a single personality, the social analogy leads us to think of three, or at least of two, distinct self-consciousnesses. Each conserves one of the elements in the historic Christian faith,— the unity of God, the distinct significance of Christ. Neither does justice to both.

As a matter of fact, many modern writers waver between the two analogies; using now one, now the other, now both together, and refusing to discuss the vexed question how they are to be reconciled. God is person, and yet he is more than person. "Person" is only the word we use to describe his nature in default of a better. In him the limitations of finite personality are overcome. He is the type, not only of the unity of the individual, but of all the social unities, the family, the state, society itself. In short, to quote Dr. Fairbairn again, he is "the infinite home of all the moral relations, with their corresponding activities."[1] From this point of view the Trinity is simply another name for the richness and fulness of the life of God.

4. *The Trinity as an Interpretation of Experience.*

With the growth of the historical and critical spirit we find an increasing disposition to question the value of any speculative construction of the doctrine of the Trinity which separates it from its roots in the historic Christian revelation. This is due in part to a general distrust of *a priori* speculation, in part to a better acquaintance with the motives which led to the original formulation of the doctrine. We have seen that the process took its departure from the revelation of God in Jesus and in the experience which he created, and was the attempt to carry back the new insight thus attained to its source in God by means of

[1] *Op. cit.*, p. 406.

the philosophical conceptions common to the time.   This contact with historic revelation is still maintained in the Nicene creed.   Those who take the third position contend that this gives us the true point of view from which the doctrine is to be understood.   It is not a doctrine about God as he is in himself, but concerning God as revealed. It is the summary of the different ways in which one may know God in experience, and hence a framework in which the specific Christian view may be set.

According to this view, there are three different ways in which man may think of God.   They may think of him as the Absolute, the ultimate source of all being and life, himself surpassing man's ability perfectly to comprehend.   They may think of him as the self-revealing one, known to men through his revelation in nature, in history and, above all, in Christ.   Finally, they may think of him as the self-imparting one, known through direct experience in the consciousness of man as the source of the spiritual life.   These three aspects of the one God, each contributing its element to knowledge and its enrichment to experience, theology designates as the Persons of the Trinity, God the Father, God the Son, and God the Holy Ghost.

But it may be said, why confine the aspects in which God may be known to three?   Why not distinguish his revelation in nature, in history, in the church?   Or, if this be too much, why not sum up all our knowledge of God as revealed, under the single conception of the Son or Word?   Here the trinitarian character of consciousness, already referred to in connection with the psychological analogy, suggests an answer.   Inadequate when applied to the divine self-consciousness to give the Christian Trinity, this analysis is full of significance when applied to our own.   In the light of the distinction between subject and object which is involved in all thought, we can see why, in our apprehension of God, the objective revelation which culminates in the historic Jesus should be differentiated from the subjective appropriation which faith interprets as the working of the Spirit. Apart from the former, revelation lacks its definite content; apart from the latter, the objective presentation remains empty and barren. It is through a progressive revelation without, progressively apprehended within, that the nature of God, whose greatness surpasses man's ability at any time fully to comprehend (the Absolute), is made known to his human children. If there be no definite object through which God's purpose is made clear, the distinction between different religions disappears, and the religious life is resolved into vague sentiment or mystic ecstasy. If, on the other hand, the object remains unappropriated; if, when we hear the preacher's message or read the sacred page, there be no burning of the heart, no inner conviction of a divine voice speaking through the human lips, religion loses its personal character and becomes a mere matter of theory or of tradition. Yet neither objective revelation nor inner experience exhausts the full riches of the unseen being who manifests himself through both. Ever there remain riches of wisdom still to be explored, a boundless sea of truth from which those who shall come after may drink their draughts of light and peace. Till all these elements are taken in, our thought of God cannot be perfectly expressed. Thus the Trinity of consciousness becomes a form into which all knowledge of God can be fitted; and that which gives the Christian doctrine its distinctive character is not its philosophical construction, but the view taken of Christ as the one in whom the revelation on the objective side culminates.

But, if this be true, why, it may be asked, is it necessary to lay so much stress upon the philosophical aspects
of the doctrine? Why not be content, with Ritschl, to
dispense with speculation altogether, and to assert that in
Jesus Christ we find our clearest and most satisfying
revelation of God? Is it necessary, in order to express so
simple a fact as this, to make use of such abstruse terms as
" Logos " or " Absolute," "substance " or " hypostasis,"
which, in the course of history, have proved the source of
so much misunderstanding, and have been the cause of sus-
picion and of separation, rather than of union and strength?
Would it not be better once for all to have done with metaphysical theology, and to content ourselves with the plain
truths which find echo in the moral consciousness of man?

It might be a sufficient answer to call attention to the
practical difficulties to which such a plan is exposed. In
the quiet of the study or the classroom it is easy to speak
of banishing metaphysical terms from theology, but in
practice it is impossible. To do this would involve not
simply the rewriting of our theological systems, but of our
hymns, our liturgies, even of the Bible itself. The doctrine of the Trinity in its completeness may be a product
of the fourth century, but its beginnings go back to the
very threshold of Christianity; and the men who laid its
foundations are not Origen and Athanasius, but the apostle
Paul and the fourth evangelist. The Christ of the New
Testament is not simply the man of Nazareth, but the pre-
incarnate Logos, the Word that lighteth every man that
cometh into the world. Either we must be prepared to
break with historic Christianity altogether and banish large
parts of the New Testament from their place in our public
worship, or else we must be able to give some rational
account of the presence of the metaphysical element in

early Christian theology and of its significance for the present life of the church.

But we are not compelled to rest our case upon arguments of mere expediency. The reasons which prevent us from acquiescing in the proposal to banish the metaphysical element from our theology have a deeper root. They are to be found in the nature of the metaphysical interest itself. That interest is not merely speculative; it is intensely practical. It is the desire for a unified world-view which voices itself in the demand for a philosophical theology. It was this motive which influenced the writers of the New Testament when they pressed beyond the Jesus of history to the Christ of faith. They felt the need of a faith which should be at once catholic and consistent; a faith which should make place for all truth to which men had attained through their previous experience of God's working, as well as that which had come through this latest and highest disclosure. Such a comprehensive world-view the Logos Christology made possible. It was the means through which the specific revelation in Jesus of Nazareth was related to all the earlier revelations through which the unseen Father had been making known his will to man. It was the declaration of the Christian conviction that the revelation in Jesus, unique as it is, is not an isolated thing, but a part of a continuing process, which has been going on since the beginning of conscious life, and will continue till its end. It was the interpretation of this process as the progressive self-manifestation of an ethical personality whose true character and purpose through it all has at last been made manifest to the world in Jesus Christ.

The same desire for a unified world-view continues to make itself felt to-day. We are more modest than our fathers, and have less faith than they in the power of abstract speculation to reveal ultimate truth. We no longer believe that we can describe the divine nature as it is in itself, or determine the relation of the different elements in the being of God. The Word and the Spirit no longer denote to us realities in God which we can picture apart from our own experience, but are interpretations of that experience itself. Yet, none the less, they lend themselves to-day to the expression of the same conviction to which they gave utterance in the past. This is the conviction that through the historic revelation which culminates in Jesus Christ, as in the inner experience which appropriates him as Lord, we have to do not simply with human ideals, however exalted, or human aspirations, however sincere, but with the great God himself as he is manifesting himself in gracious, fatherly love to his needy children. It is not man with whom we commune in Jesus, but very God of very God. When we take upon our lips the historic terms, consecrated by so many centuries of Christian usage, we confess with all the saints of the past that the God of all the earth is a self-disclosing God, one whose very nature it is to utter himself forth to men in some objective form of revelation; and so we dare to translate the nameless Absolute of philosophy into the God and Father of our Lord Jesus Christ. We confess that the appearance of Jesus Christ was not an isolated phenomenon, but the consummation of a world-wide process, of which all other historic revelation is a part; and so we see in him the incarnation of that divine Word who has been the light that has lighted every man who has come into the world. We confess that God is not only a self-revealing, but a self-imparting God; that it is his very nature to dwell in the hearts of men and to give them insight into his truth; that the confession of Jesus Christ as Lord is only the highest utterance of an insight which has always been given to men in greater or less degree, and which is possible only through such divine indwelling; and so we add to our confession of the Father and the Son the confession of the divine Spirit who spake through the prophets and who speaks in us to-day. No other terms express so adequately that basis in unseen reality which is implied in the Trinity of Christian experience, and which is necessary to give it its fullest significance.

It is this sense of unseen reality which gives the doctrine of the ontological Trinity its practical value. In the past Trinitarians have been unwilling to stop with a Trinity of manifestation, because this method has seemed to them to resolve the doctrine into a mere analysis of human experience. Beyond all that was human and finite they have sought to press into the immediate presence of God, that they might find their rest and peace in him. We too, share the same longing for communion with the living God; but we believe that God is to be sought not without but within his world, and that the only way in which it is possible for us to know God as he is in himself is by unfolding the significance of the revelation through which he is made known to men. Hence, for us the antithesis between the Trinity of essence and that of manifestation disappears. The self-revealing God is the real God, — the only God we either can or need to know.[1]

[1] In the light of this discussion we are in a position to understand the questions at issue between Trinitarianism and Unitarianism. These are partly theoretical and partly practical. The theoretical question has to do with the metaphysical statement of the doctrine as set forth in the Nicene and still more in the Athanasian creed. Unitarianism, both in its earlier and later forms, has protested against this statement as inadequate and confusing, and has sought to press back of the elaborate metaphysics of the creeds to the simpler and more personal elements in Jesus' teaching. In

To sum up: The significance of the doctrine of the Trinity for Christian faith is twofold. Theoretically, it is the affirmation of a full rich life in God as distinct from all abstract and barren conceptions of his being. Practically, it is the affirmation that the true nature of God must be learned from his historic revelation in Christ, and from the experience which Christ creates. It includes the two elements whose combination is distinctive of the Christian

its older form this protest was associated with an abstract doctrine of the unity of God, which is itself open to just criticism. But in its later forms, as represented by such writers as Martineau and Wicksteed, it avoids this weakness, and is consistent with a sympathetic appreciation of those elements of truth for which the Trinitarian faith stands. Martineau, in his suggestive tract proposing a way out of the Trinitarian controversy (printed in his *Essays Theological and Literary*, II, pp. 525 sq.) calls attention to the fact that under the name of the Father, Unitarians have really been worshipping the forth-going and revealing God, whom Trinitarians call Christ, or the Son; and more recently Mr. P. H. Wicksteed, in a striking essay setting forth the significance of Unitarianism as a theology (printed in *Studies in Theology*, a volume of essays by Wicksteed and Carpenter, London, 1903, pp. 91 sq.) has pictured the enrichment of experience which is the result of the Trinitarian mode of conceiving God. The time has surely come when Trinitarians, on their part, may recognize the relative justification of the Unitarian protest, and join with their brethren in recognizing the central place of the historic Christ, and striving to conform their idea of God to his teaching.

Far more important is the practical question recently raised by a certain school of Unitarians, who deny the central position of Christ in religious history, and call for a theology which shall be theo- rather than Christo-centric. So far as this position has its roots in the desire to emphasize the divine capacity of every man and the extent of the work of God's Spirit in humanity, it has a certain justification, and may be regarded as an exaggerated statement of one of the truths which the doctrine of the Trinity itself affirms. So far as it denies the uniqueness of Christ and his central position as Master and Saviour, it overlooks the fundamental element in the Christian experience, and involves the abandonment of the distinctive truth for which Unitarians and Trinitarians alike have hitherto contended. No willingness to accept the Trinitarian formula on its philosophical side as a convenient summary of the different aspects in which God may be known can compensate for the lack of definiteness and the loss of inspiration which — if the lessons of the past have any light to shed for our guidance in the future — will surely follow any attempt, however persuasively defended, to relegate to a subordinate place the person and the revelation of the historic Jesus.

view of the world — the recognition of the supremacy of Christ, and the experience of progress. Thus it is at once the most concise and the most comprehensive statement of the Christian faith, gathering into a single phrase all the richness of content which has entered into the thought of God through the Christian experience of redemption.

PART III

THE CHRISTIAN VIEW OF THE WORLD

CHAPTER XI

EVERY doctrine of God carries with it a corresponding view of the world. The Christian view is expressed by Jesus in Matthew vi, 25–33. Analyzing these familiar words, we find that they imply four things: (1) that this world is God's world; (2) that his control and care extend even to the smallest matters; (3) that in a special sense man is the object of that care; (4) that the end to which all things tend is the kingdom of God. We shall consider in turn the source of these convictions and their history.

1. *Of the Sources in General.*

The sources of the Christian view of the world are the same as those of the Christian idea of God. This is true of every religion. As a study of the phenomena of the world leads men back of the world to God, so the view taken of God determines the conception of the world. The religious nature which ascribes personality to its God postulates at the same time a real object for his thought and care. The philosophical insight which recognizes the absoluteness of God requires as a consequence the dependence of the creature. The Christian experience which finds God disclosed in Jesus Christ assures the believer of the adaptation of the world to the end which he has revealed. The three main elements in the Christian view of the world are real existence, dependence, and adaptation to the Christian end; and they have their origin in the same sources as the corresponding convictions about God.

In studying the Christian view of the world, therefore, we have to distinguish its distinctive elements from those which it owes to older sources and shares with other faiths. This discrimination — everywhere necessary in theology — is here more than ever important; since it is in its doctrine of the world that theology is brought into closest contact with contemporary philosophical and scientific theories. While it is true that the interest from which these spring is different from that which gives rise to the religious view of the world — the former seeking to understand the universe for its own sake, the latter only so far as it is the necessary presupposition of the religious life — it is yet true that in practice the two cannot be divorced. The world in which the religious man lives his life is the same which science studies and which philosophy seeks to explain. He is dependent upon the former for the facts which his faith interprets, and upon the latter for the conceptions which make the interpretation possible. The idea of the universe itself, which has played so great a rôle in theology, is a philosophical conception which makes its appearance comparatively late in time, and which presupposes wide experience and a high capacity for reflective thought. A theology which shall be independent of the results of philosophy and science is a contradiction in terms, and the attempt to construct such a system can lead only to self-deception.

All the more important is it, in view of this necessary connection, that in the doctrine of the world the religious, and more specifically the Christian, interest should receive clear and adequate expression. The history of

Christian thought shows two dangers to which theology is exposed at this point: (1) the uncritical identification of some inadequate scientific theory with the Christian view of the world; (2) the sacrifice of some truth essential to Christain faith in the interest of supposed philosophical consistency. The first may be illustrated in the long series of alleged conflicts between science and revelation (*e. g.* that between geology and Genesis); the second in the various attempts to set forth the contents of the Christian faith from philosophical principles which deny one or more of its presuppositions. Examples of such inadequate theories are pantheism and dualism. Each of these takes its departure from an element in experience which Christianity recognizes, but it emphasizes it to such an extent as to exclude other truth which is equally essential. Pantheism insists upon the immanence of God, but carries it so far as to identify God and the world. Dualism takes its departure from the mystery of evil, but in its effort to defend the goodness of God, exalts evil to an independent cosmic principle. The former obscures the personality of God; the latter imperils his control. As opposed to these Christianity is theistic, and has inherited its view of the world from Israel.

2. *The Hebrew View of the World.*

Historically the Christian view of the world has its most direct preparation in the religion of Israel. Within the Old Testament we find clearly expressed two convictions of fundamental importance for Christianity: (1) that the world was made by God, and is at all times under his control; (2) that it is the scene of a divine purpose, whose end is the establishment of a righteous and redeemed community. These differentiate the Hebrew view of the world from that of the surrounding nations with which, in other respects, it has so much in common.

From the point of view of science, the cosmogony of Genesis may be paralleled in the creation stories of the Assyrians and Babylonians. The universe of both is geocentric, and the order of the several steps in the creative process is strikingly similar. But whereas in the Assyrian cosmogony, the universe owes its present form to the struggle of the opposing forces of good and evil, the first chapter of Genesis represents creation as the act of God's will, and the world which is the result as good (Gen. i, 3). Hence the physical universe has an ethical meaning to the Hebrew which it lacks to other peoples. It is God's creature, formed by his wisdom, upheld by his power, ministering to his purpose.

Rightly to understand the Biblical doctrine of creation we need to remember the practical connection in which it stands. It is the counterpart of the enlarged conception of God which has come with the experiences of the later monarchy and the Exile, and is the guarantee that the One in whom Israel is urged to put her trust is able to accomplish his redemptive purpose (cf. Isa. xl, 12–31; xliii, 1–4). Of speculative interest there is little trace. The question as to the ultimate origin of matter is not raised. In the great creation passages in Genesis (i), Proverbs (viii) and Psalms (civ), it is the formation of the world which is described rather than the creation of its substance. Yet when later the question was raised as to the origin of the primeval chaos, the natural answer from the Jewish standpoint was not that of dualism (cf. 2 Macc. vii, 28).

The world thus made by God is the scene of the divine providence. Jehovah orders all things according to a single, all-embracing plan. This plan centres in man, whom he has made in his own image (Gen. i, 27). More particularly it concerns Israel, whom he has chosen to be his own peculiar people (Deut. xxxii, 8, 9), and the instrument by whom his salvation is to be made known to all the world (Isa. ii, 2–4). But though centring in Israel, it is not confined to Israel. It takes in all men, all nations. No obstacle, either in the physical world or in the moral world, can prevent the accomplishment of Jehovah's purpose. The victories which lead Israel's enemies to think their gods mightier than Jehovah are only the means by which he accomplishes his judgments (cf. Isa. x, 5–15). They prove a love which knows how to use punishment as well as forgiveness, when punishment is needed to teach a moral lesson (Amos iii, 2).

Characteristic is the view taken of evil. That evil is real and terrible is the uniform assumption; but its origin is not in matter, but in rebellious will. It is sin which makes the tragedy of Hebrew history, grieving the heart of Jehovah and causing Israel's punishment, and all but destruction. Man's responsibility and guilt are insisted upon in the strongest terms, and his misuse of his powers is the explanation of the evil of which the world is full (cf. Gen. iii; Deut. xxx, 19; Isa. lix, 12).

And yet there is another side to the picture. While Jehovah does not desire evil, it is not beyond his control. He is able to use suffering, and even sin, as an instrument of good. The unfaithfulness of Israel and the opposition of her enemies may postpone, but it cannot prevent, the accomplishment of his plan. Indeed, through the consequences of her own wrongdoing, Israel learns lessons of the holiness and love of God not otherwise possible, and becomes the suffering servant through whom his message of redeeming love is conveyed to the Gentiles (Isa. xlii–xliv ;

lii, 13–15; liii). The last scene on the prophetic canvas
is always the triumph of Jehovah's kingdom (cf. Isa. ii, 2;
Mic. iv, 1).

This view of history as a moral process, having its goal in
the establishment of a righteous and redeemed society, prepares the way for the Christian view of the world. While
at first conceived as an earthly monarchy in which Israel
triumphs over her old-time oppressors, the kingdom of
God is given by the later prophets a moral and spiritual
content which renders it an appropriate point of departure
for Jesus' preaching. Israel is to conquer the world not
only with the sword, but by the might of truth. The old
oppressors, Egypt and Assyria, are one day to unite in the
worship of Jehovah, and be recognized with Israel as his
chosen (Isa. xix, 24–26). In the future commonwealth
Gentiles will take their place side by side with Jews and be
enrolled among the citizens of Zion (Ps. lxxxvii). Such an
ideal is little removed from the universalism of Christianity.

This view of the relation between God and the world
involves a clear perception of the transcendence of God.
The word "transcendence" may be used in two senses. In
the first it denotes distinctness from the world; in the
second, remoteness from the world. The former is necessarily involved in personality, and is the condition of communion between God and man; the second is an inference
from a false conception of the absoluteness of God, and
renders communion impossible. Both may be illustrated
in the history of Israel.

The God of the prophets is transcendent in the first
sense. He is in the world, but he is also above the world.
His life is the source of the world life, but it is not exhausted by that life (cf. Ps. xc, 2; 1 Kings viii, 27).
Transcendence in this sense is an expression of the free-

dom of God, of his ability both to plan and to accomplish that which he has planned. It is an attribute of sovereignty. God is the master who must be obeyed, the workman in whose hands men are as clay in the hands of the potter (Isa. lxiv, 8; Jer. xviii; cf. Rom. ix, 21), the father in whom it is safe to put one's trust.

Such a view of God's transcendence is entirely consistent with his immanence. While the theoretical questions involved in this doctrine are scarcely touched in the Old Testament, we have in the later books a practical recognition of the experience which it expresses. Thus the Spirit, which is often represented as acting upon men from without and evidencing its presence in extraordinary and miraculous ways, is elsewhere recognized as permanently present in the world, the source both of the physical and of the moral life. An example of the first is the One Hundred and Fourth Psalm; of the second, the Fifty-First. In the latter, with its recognition that God's indwelling Holy Spirit is the source of all right life in man, we have a striking anticipation of the Christian doctrine of the Spirit.

In the theology of the later Judaism, God's separateness from the world is carried to the point of separation. Jehovah is thought of as inhabiting heaven, which is conceived as the antithesis of earth. He no longer speaks directly to men, as in the days of prophecy, but makes himself known only through the medium of his revealed law. From this false conception of transcendence both revelation and creation become problems. To overcome the distance between creator and creature, philosophically inclined theologians begin to think of God as acting upon the world through intermediate beings, such as his Angel, his Word, his Wisdom, his Spirit. The unseen beings whose existence the Hebrews, in common with all ancient peoples, had taken for granted, but as to whose origin and relation to God they had not hitherto felt the necessity of speculating, now become the subject of explicit reflection.   They are divided into ranks and assigned special functions in Jehovah's government.   The good spirits are distinguished from the evil as God's ministers, and the latter are conceived as forming a kingdom under the leadership of Satan, who, in the earlier literature, appears as the messenger of Jehovah (Job i, 6–12; ii, 1–6). Thus the problem of the origin of evil is carried back into the angelic world, and the direct responsibility of God for sin in so far removed.   Under the same influence the poetic personifications of God's attributes in the Wisdom literature are transformed into hypostases, — *i. e.* real distinctions in the being of God.   This is especially true in the Alexandrine theology, which, under Greek influence, had developed the idea of the Logos, a creative divine principle, through which the problem of God's relation to the world was believed to find a solution consistent with his strict transcendence and absoluteness.   This conception, most clearly expressed by Philo, forms the point of contact between Greek and Jewish, as between both and Christian thought.

3. *The Greek View of the World.*

The speculative interest so conspicuously lacking in Hebrew thought is present in the Greek view of the world from the first.   Greek philosophy had its rise in the attempt to solve the problem of origins, and the cosmological interest characterizes it throughout its entire history.   Apart from the cruder theories of the earlier period, the most important types of thought for their influence on Christianity are the dualistic theory of Plato and Aristotle, and the pantheism which finds its chief expression in Stoicism. According to the first, the ultimate reality (or God) is contrasted as spirit with the world of matter (hyle), which is the imperfect copy of the divine thought. According to the latter, God is present in the world as its animating principle, as the soul is present in the body of man. The first emphasizes the transcendence of God; the second his immanence. Both have the conception of the Logos; but, whereas to Stoicism the Logos is the immanent reason of God, to Platonism it is the creative thought, which is ever striving to fashion into ideal forms the resisting hyle, but which is never able wholly to overcome its resistance.[1]

The dualistic character of Platonism appears most clearly in its view of evil. To a much greater degree than in

[1] This double aspect of the Logos idea — as immanent reason and creative thought — renders it especially fruitful and explains its far-reaching influence. It was eminently fitted to serve as a nucleus of the syncretism which characterizes the later Greek thought. Where the transcendence of God was carried to extreme lengths, as in the Alexandrine schools, the Logos offered itself as a mediating conception by which the interval between God and the world could be spanned. Thus in Philo, the Logos is at once creator and creature, equal with and less than God, sharing the divine nature, yet having its own distinct existence. It could be used to banish God from the world, or to affirm his presence; and the question whether it was to have the first significance or the second depended wholly upon the side from which it was approached. Where the redemptive interest was prominent the Logos brought God near; where the speculative interest was controlling it kept him at a distance. On the other hand, when God was thought of as immanent in the world, as was the case where Stoic influence prevailed, the Logos expressed the content of the divine thought as manifest in the course of things. It served to give all life a divine meaning, and to bring all history under divine control. It stood for the revelation of nature as distinct from the special revelation of grace. Interpreted in the Stoic sense, it was the foundation of all natural theology, as when taken in the Platonic sense (*e. g.* in the doctrine of the Trinity), it was the foundation of theology as revealed. In both these senses its influence may be traced in Christian theology; and the attempt — of which modern theology shows only too many examples — to interpret it from the side of dualism alone, leads necessarily to an estimate which is both historically and philosophically inadequate.

Hebrew thought, evil is to the Greek a cosmological conception. It has its origin in matter, the resisting raw material of things, which, as the essentially non-rational and non-spiritual, the Logos is not able perfectly to control. Hence the way to be delivered from sin is to be freed as far as possible from material contacts. The saint is the man of temperance and simplicity, the ascetic, the man who has gained the mastery of his body and is able to keep it under, as the skilful charioteer controls his unruly steed.

This realistic conception of evil has exercised a profound influence upon Christian theology. Here is the root of the asceticism which is so marked a feature of early Christian ethics, and which lives on to-day both in the theory and the practice of Catholicism. Here, too, is the source of the conception of sin as a semi-physical reality, having an objective existence apart from individual sinners, which plays so great a rôle in the traditional theology. The idea — so prominent in the Greek church — of sin as corruption rather than guilt, and salvation as deification rather than forgiveness, is traceable to the same source; and it was largely under this influence that the conception of the sacrament as a mystery, *i. e.* a device for imparting a new divine nature by physical means, arose.

But the realistic conception of evil was not the only one held by the Greeks. Side by side with it — often blending with it so closely as to be almost indistinguishable — we find another. According to this, evil is not a positive but a negative conception. It denotes simply the absence of reality. Sin is primarily ignorance, delusion, and the true remedy for it is knowledge. When you have learned to see evil as it is, it disappears. Hence the saint is the gnostic, the sage, the man of philosophic insight. This is the view taken of sin in the pantheistic philosophy of the

Stoics. This view, too, passed over to Christianity and, in combination with the other, played its part in the making of Christian theology.

Besides the philosophical conceptions thus described, Christian theology also inherited from the Greeks their scientific interest. In the writings of Aristotle we find the first attempt to give a systematic account of the universe as a whole, based upon exact observation. With him, therefore, the scientific as distinct from the philosophical conception of the world begins. Christian theology took over not only the result of these early scientific investigations, but also the interest which prompted them. The systems of the early theologians are in large part concerned with matters for which we should look to-day to treatises on natural science. Thus Origen in his *De Principiis* goes at length into cosmological speculation. Augustine applies to the solution of the problem of creation conceptions which have their nearest parallel in Aristotle.[1] John of Damascus includes in the contents of the orthodox faith the whole natural science of his day. In all this we see the Christian spirit passing from the naïve world of early Hebrew thought to the more complex and ordered universe of Greece; and, as it had mastered the former, striving to possess the latter for its Lord. If the means taken were often at fault, the end was legitimate, and the attempt necessary.

4. *New Elements Introduced by Christianity.*

Christianity takes over from the religion of Israel its view of the world as the scene of God's redemptive purpose. Its doctrine differs from that of the Old Testament only as the Christian idea of God and the Christian view

---

[1] *E. g.* the idea that the things which God made were not finished objects, but germs which had in them the capacity of development.

of his purpose differ from the corresponding Hebrew ideas. Both these differences are connected with the unique position assigned to Christ as the supreme manifestation of God. As Christ reveals God's character, and gives definiteness to his purpose, so also he is the key to history and the explanation of the world.

Historically this conviction appears in two forms: (1) Christ becomes central in the divine providence; the revealer and Lord of the kingdom for which the world exists. (2) Christ is identified with the divine principle of creation and revelation, taking the place filled in the Old Testament by such conceptions as the divine Wisdom and the Angel of Jehovah, and in Philo by the Logos. Both interpretations meet us in the New Testament. The latter is associated with the doctrine of the pre-existence of Christ, and gives Christian thought its point of contact with the cosmological speculations of contemporary philosophy.

To begin with the practical side. All the New Testament writers are at one in seeing in Jesus the central figure in human history. Looking back upon the past in the light of his Messianic claim, they see in him the one in whom all the Old Testament prophecies find their fulfilment. Turning forward to the future, they look for his complete supremacy in human lives as the great event for which the whole creation waits (Rom. viii, 18 sq.; 1 Cor. xv, 28). Seeking a conception to give unity and harmony to their thought of the world, they find it in his cross, by means of which the middle wall of partition between Jews and Gentiles has been broken down (Eph. ii, 14; cf. Rom. ix–xi), and through which the whole creation is at last to be reconciled to God (Col. i; Eph. i).

To understand the full significance of this interpretation, we need to remember wherein the kingdom which Jesus proclaimed differed from that for which his contemporaries looked. In his preaching we have the spiritual principles of the prophetic ideal freed from their local and transient setting. For a kingdom external, national, and in increasing measure transcendent and eschatological, he substituted a kingdom of the spirit, open to all who are penitent, humble and trustful, and which is already present in the persons of those who accept his message and trust the heavenly Father whom he has revealed.[1] For a conqueror who wins his victories by force, or a wonder-worker who compels belief by miracles, he substituted a suffering servant who uses only spiritual means to gain allegiance, and whose path to sovereignty leads by the way of the cross. How great was the revolution which this change involved we measure when we consider how imperfectly Jesus' Gospel was grasped by many of his own followers, and how long, in the form of chiliasm, an older ideal maintained itself in the Christian church.[2] It was only gradually that men came to see that to give Jesus the place assigned to him by Christian faith means to assert that the forces he reveals are the conquering ones in human history, and that self-sacrificing love is not only the noblest, but the most powerful thing in the world.

The practical recognition of Christ's lordship finds its speculative counterpart in the New Testament in the doctrine of the pre-existent Christ. In the letters of Paul, the Epistle to the Hebrews, and the Johannine writings, Christ is associated with the divine activities by which the life of the world is sustained and renewed. He is the revelation in human form of the divine Son through whom

---

[1] On the eschatological elements in Jesus' conception of the kingdom, see chapter XII, p. 185, note 1.

[2] On chiliasm, cf. pp. 185 sq.

God made the worlds, and by whom he sustains them (Heb. i, 2, 3). From the first he has been present in the world as the Logos, the source of light and of life (John i, 4, 5), inspiring the Old Testament prophets (1 Pet. i, 11), and preparing the way for his later coming in the flesh. Here we have the pre-existent Christ conceived as a cosmic principle, the agent of the unseen God in creation, revelation and redemption (cf. esp. Col. i, 16, 17).

The similarity of this line of thought to the cosmological speculations already described is obvious. Whether original or not, the connection, early made in Christian theology (*e. g.* by Justin) between the Logos of the Greeks and that of the Fourth Gospel, was as natural as it was inevitable. But the differences are no less obvious. In the former the speculative interest is controlling; in the latter the religious. The philosophers begin with the Logos idea, and use it to explain the world. John begins with the human Jesus, and asserts that in him we have the revelation of the creative principle in whose existence the philosophers believe, but whose nature they have been unable to discover. The word is the same, but it has received a new content. The transformation is similar to that which we have already observed in the case of the Messianic idea.

Of the importance of the conception of the pre-existent Christ for the doctrine of the Trinity, we have already spoken.[1] Here we are concerned only with its effect upon the Christian view of the world. This was twofold. On the one hand, it was the means of introducing Greek cosmological speculations into theology, and so of obscuring the primitive simplicity of Christian faith. On the other hand, by asserting the identity of the God whom

[1] Cf. chapter X, p. 142.

Christ revealed with the creative Spirit in which philosophy had come to believe, it proved the most effective barrier against dualism. The insight that the God of redemption was at the same time the creator assured the divineness of the present world, and so gave unity and consistency to Christian thought. The choice was not, as it is often represented, between the Logos doctrine and simple faith, but between a philosophy which made the Christian God master of the world, and one which set the two side by side as rival powers. When one remembers the strong dualistic tendency in early Christianity, which found theoretical expression in the systems of Marcion and the Gnostics, and practical embodiment in monasticism, and which, to so large an extent, influenced the theory of the church itself, we cannot be too thankful for the Logos doctrine, in its bearing upon the Christian view of the world.

The double interest which we have thus noted at the outset appears throughout the entire history of the doctrine. In the Christian view of the world, practical and theoretical elements have ever been closely combined. They have varied with the changing philosophy, but no attempt wholly to divorce them has been permanently successful. Even Ritschl, who is most uncompromising in his rejection of Greek cosmology, admits that the Christian connection of creation and redemption is an essential one,[1] and sees in Christ the unifying principle through which alone a consistent philosophical view of the world is possible.[2]

---

[1] *Justification and Reconciliation*, Eng. tr., III, p. 30.
[2] *Ibid.*, III, pp. 25, 207.

CHAPTER XII

OF GOD'S PURPOSE FOR THE WORLD, OR THE KINGDOM OF GOD

CHRISTIAN faith conceives the relation existing between God and the world as that of sovereignty on the one hand and of dependence on the other.[1] This sovereignty, extending to all parts of the universe, is expressed in theology by the doctrine of the divine decree. The decree may be defined as that consistent moral purpose by which all the events of the universe are determined, and of which, when taken in their teleological connection, they are the expression. This purpose Christian faith finds in the establishment of the kingdom of God.[2]

By the kingdom of God we mean that society of redeemed personalities, of which Christ is at once the ideal and the mediator, the union of whose members, one with another and with God in the community of holy love, pro-

[1] In their reaction from the extremes of Calvinism, some modern theologians discard the conception of sovereignty altogether, substituting in its place the idea of fatherhood. This substitution rests upon the mistaken idea that sovereignty and fatherhood are inconsistent conceptions. But this is not the case. Sovereignty means simply the right and the power to control. Its nature may vary as widely as the character of the sovereign. It may be the expression of the arbitrary whim of a despot, or of the consistent purpose of fatherly love. The sovereignty in which Christians believe is paternal, and is the expression of Christian faith that the universe as a whole is subject to the control of holy and loving will.

[2] This view of God's plan differs from that of the older Protestant theology, partly in its unity, partly in its definiteness. It substitutes for such abstract conceptions as God's glory, or the happiness of the creature, the concrete idea of the kingdom of God, and, in contrast to the double end presented in the Calvinistic doctrine of decrees, finds in God's purpose to establish his kingdom the sufficient explanation of the meaning of the world.

gressively realized in history, constitutes the end for which the world exists. The origin of the conception and its significance we have now to consider.

1. *The Place of the Kingdom in Jesus' Teaching.*

The conception of the kingdom of God is the inheritance of Christianity from Judaism. It denotes the righteous and blessed society which the redemption of the Messianic age is to introduce. The details of the picture vary. Sometimes attention is concentrated upon the institutions to be established, and the prosperity to be introduced at the Messianic era; and again, upon the moral and religious character of the redeemed society. In the earlier literature this earth is regarded as the scene of the kingdom; in the later, the universe is transformed to form a fitting setting for its glories. Sometimes Israel alone occupies the centre of the canvas; at others, the Gentiles also find their place in the picture. Sometimes the Messianic king in person is conceived as exercising the government; and again, it is Jehovah who is regarded as judge, ruling personally over his people. But through all varieties of conception these elements remain constant. The kingdom of God is the righteous and redeemed society in which God's gracious purpose for Israel finds its consummation. The ideal is at once social, ethical and religious.

In the later Judaism the transcendent and other-worldly elements in the ideal of the kingdom become controlling. The failure of the expectations which the restoration had revived led the devout few to despair of finding any satisfaction of Israel's longings under the conditions of the present life. For the pious individual, consolation was sought in the consciousness of a present communion with God in the spirit. For the community, the consummation

was postponed to a new æon, to be introduced by a great
catastrophe, when the Messiah should come on the clouds
with legions of angels, and the heavens and the earth be
transformed. It is this conception, anticipated in Daniel
(vii, 13, 14), voiced in the *Similitudes of Enoch* (37–70,
esp. 45, 1 sq.; 48, 2 sq.), and which has left its traces in
the New Testament itself, which is the background of
Jesus' teaching.

Jesus made his own his people's hope in the kingdom,
and declared himself the Messiah for whom they looked.
But he transformed both conceptions in the light of the new
experience of God's Fatherhood which was the controlling
feature of his consciousness. The spiritual and universal
elements which were implicit in the prophetic teaching,
but which had been obscured and often almost lost sight
of in the exclusiveness and ceremonialism of the later
Judaism, he put in the forefront of his teaching. To
Jesus the kingdom meant the presence of a society in which
the qualities which characterized his own relation to God
should be everywhere controlling. It meant a society in
which the national and legal barriers which in the past had
prevented the free access of the soul to God should be
broken down, and in which filial trust and brotherly love
should be at once the test of membership and the bond of
union. Hence, however distant might be the final consummation, the conditions of its realization were present
here and now. Unseen by men — as the seed swells in the
silent ground, as the leaven spreads in the receptive meal,
— the kingdom was present in the spirits of the men who
had been with Jesus and who accepted his message. To
the Pharisees, asking when the kingdom of God should
come, he answered, "The kingdom of God cometh not
with observation, neither shall they say, ' Lo here ! or, Lo

there ! ' for lo, the kingdom of God is (already) in the midst of you." [1]

This revolutionary teaching Jesus clothed in the language natural to his time, freely making use of forms familiar to his hearers. How far the apocalyptic imagery of our Gospels goes back to the Master is a question for scholars. That he used such language is entirely likely, and in no way inconsistent with the spiritual nature and universal scope of his Gospel. It is not in the inherited imagery, but in that which is new and revolutionary in his teaching that we are to find his distinctive message. Our task is to take this new message and to express it in the terms of our own thought even as the men of an earlier generation did in theirs. We shall be helped in this by a brief review of the history of the doctrine.

2. *The Interpretation of the Kingdom in Later Theology.*

There are three historic interpretations of Jesus' teaching concerning the kingdom of God, each of which contains an element of truth which we must conserve. We may call them respectively the chiliastic, the ecclesiastical and the individualistic.

(a). *Chiliastic.* By this name we describe a class of theories which look for a kingdom of superhuman triumph and prosperity to be ushered in by a sudden miraculous

---

[1] Or, as the Revision renders, " within you " (Luke xvii, 20, 21). What has been said of the kingdom as a present reality is entirely consistent with the fact that the term is often, and indeed most frequently, employed by Jesus in an eschatological sense. It follows from the nature of the Christian ideal as social and universal, that its full consummation belongs to the future. Modern scholarship is, therefore, quite right in emphasizing the eschatological element in Jesus' Gospel of the kingdom. When, however, this emphasis is carried so far as to obscure, if not altogether to deny, the present aspect of his teaching, we cannot help feeling that we have to do with an exaggeration which is, to say the least, equally misleading Cf. on this point the judicious remarks of Harnack, *What is Christianity ?* pp. 52 sq., esp. p. 54.

transformation of the present order of things. The word "chiliast" is derived from χιλία, a thousand, which is the Greek equivalent of the Latin *mille*. A chiliast is, strictly speaking, a pre-millenarian, that is, one who expects the second advent of Christ before the millennium, and who, because of that expectation, postpones till after the advent all hope of true progress or prosperity. More loosely, the word is used to denote unspiritual ideas of the future of whatever kind. The two meanings are often, but by no means always, associated. As here used, the word "chiliastic" is intended to denote the view which denies the divineness of the present world and postpones its hope of salvation to the future, whether that salvation be spiritually conceived or no.

The beginnings of chiliasm lie very far back. It is the revival within Christianity of the transcendent and eschatological ideal which we have seen to have been characteristic of the later Judaism. It was much strengthened by the wide acceptance among the early Christians of the apocalyptic literature of the Jews. In many of these books we find the expectation of a period of blessedness and triumph midway between this present evil age and the glorious age which is to follow it. Such an expectation meets us in the millennium of the book of Revelation (xx, 5, 7). Here we have the doctrine of a double resurrection and judgment. The advent of Christ is followed by a preliminary judgment, and by the resurrection of the martyr saints. These reign with him for a thousand years, after which follows the general resurrection and judgment.

Belief in such a millennial reign was widespread, though by no means universal, in the early church.[1] It meets us

---

[1] For the evidence in detail, see my article, "Millennium," in Hastings *Dictionary of the Bible*, vol. iii, pp. 370 sq.

now in more external, now in more spiritual form. Justin mentions it as an essential article of Christian faith (*Dial.* 80). It was a central feature in the teaching of Tertullian and Hippolytus. The extravagances of the Montanists tended to discredit the doctrine. With the dying out of the expectation of a speedy advent, it fell into the background. When Augustine identified the millennium with the earthly reign of the church, it lost all ecclesiastical standing.

But, though thus discredited, pre-millenarianism has never wholly died out in the church. In times of distress and failure, physical and spiritual, it has been sure to reappear. It is to-day the faith of not a few earnest and devout people. It has an extensive popular literature, and is carrying on an active and not unsuccessful propaganda. It is important, therefore, to understand the grounds on which it rests, and its practical effects on thought and life.

The exegetical basis of pre-millenarianism is found in a literal interpretation of the Biblical prophecies of earthly glory and prosperity for Israel. It is a revival of the Jewish ideal which Jesus rejected. The Messianic hope of his day centred in the expectation of the supernatural restoration of the national power of Israel. Jesus substituted for this an ideal which was spiritual. It was this which caused his rejection. The millenarian exegesis restores the older ideal. It practically says: "The Jews of Christ's time were right in their interpretation of prophecy. They possessed the true Messianic ideal. Their only mistake was one of date. They attributed to the first advent what properly belongs to the second. When we discriminate the advents all difficulty vanishes."

A deeper cause of pre-millenarianism is a pessimistic

view of life, which despairs of any real improvement through the working of present forces. This is a more serious evil. To Jesus, as we have seen, this world is God's world, and his kingdom is already present in germ. Many pre-millenarians speak as if the world were given up to Satan. The conception of development is repelled as misleading or dangerous. The world must grow worse before it can be better. Hence it is not uncommon to find pre-millenarians welcoming the disasters and misfortunes of the time as so many signs of the approaching advent.

If we ask what is the practical effect of this type of thought on the Christian life, we find that it is twofold. On the one hand, it produces great earnestness and strictness of life, and an intense interest in the salvation and ethical purity of individuals. On the other hand, if consistently followed out, it results in a lack of interest in, if not a positive opposition to, the wider social movements which seek to use existing social forces for human betterment. Its view of Christian duty is substantially that of Evangelist in Bunyan's *Pilgrim's Progress*. " Flee from the wrath to come." Here and there one will heed the testimony and repent, like brands plucked from the burning. Whether they hear or forbear, the preacher will have done his duty. When the number of his elect is made up Christ will come and usher in his kingdom. This must be the great object of the Christian's longing and prayer.

(b). *Ecclesiastical.* By this name we designate a class of theories which find the key to human history in the gradual organization of humanity into a single society under the government and control of the Christian church. This conception, first clearly expressed by Augustine in his *City of God*, finds its most complete embodiment in the

Roman Catholic church. To the Roman Catholic this world is a scene of probation. Humanity is being trained for the spiritual life, and the church is the institution which God has appointed to conduct the training. For this purpose he has endowed her with all needed authority, and the test of progress consists in the completeness with which she is able to make this authority effective in the world. Whatever resists her sway, whether in the realm of thought or of practice, is profane and evil, and ought to be put down by whatever force she can command. Hence, the distinction between the ecclesiastical and the secular, and the use of the former as a canon for testing spiritual values.

We have elsewhere discussed the Catholic theory of the church and need not repeat what was there said.[1] It is sufficient here to call attention to its practical bearing upon the Christian view of the world. To its credit must be reckoned the fact that it has helped to bring the present life under the religious estimate. It has recovered for divine uses and meanings many aspects of the world and of human experience which pre-millenarianism was content to abandon to evil (*e. g.* the state and the various social institutions which have grown up about it). It has planted the church as God's representative firmly in the midst of the life that now is, and in so far forth borne witness to the divineness of the present world. But it has done all this at the cost of a confusion of ethical values which has been the parent of new evils scarcely less serious. By identifying the religious with the ecclesiastical it has made the final test of progress a non-moral one; and, while not denying, has obscured those elements in Jesus' Gospel in which its distinctive character and revolutionary

[1] Chapter V, section 4, pp. 65 sq.

power is found.   To Jesus the kingdom is a phrase which he transformed by infusing into it a new content.   The government he would establish is paternal, and its type the family rather than the state.   To the Roman Catholic the church is a kingdom in the political sense, and the Pope as much an earthly potentate as Cæsar.   This is the reason why strife for temporal power has played so great a rôle in the annals of the Papacy.   From such a conception of the church as an earthly monarchy, the Reformation came as a needed deliverance.

(c). *Individualistic.*   As individualistic, finally, we designate all such views as think it possible adequately to express God's purpose for the world in terms of his relation to individuals.   The conception of that relation may vary.   It may be conceived in terms of individual probation as in Arminianism, or of electing grace as in Calvinism. But in each case the significance of life is made to depend upon the attitude of God to individuals, and the meaning of the world found in the fact that it is the scene of the execution of his purpose for them.

The formulation of this view into a distinct theological theory was the work of the Reformation.   Protestantism began as a reassertion of the rights of the individual.   The protest against Rome took different forms.   Luther emphasized justification by faith, Calvin the divine decree; the substance was the same.   In either case the necessity of ecclesiastical mediation was denied, and the essence of religion found in the relation between the individual soul and God.

This emphasis upon the individual had its good side.   It called renewed attention to the ethical and spiritual elements in religion, and reasserted the divineness of much which Catholicism had condemned.   By its insistence upon the Bible as the sole standard of truth for the individual, it helped to recover for mankind the memory of the Christ whose image the Bible enshrines. Especially important was its insistence upon the sacredness of the secular life, as expressed in the doctrine of the universal priesthood of believers. But it rejected the old cleavage only to introduce another, that between the elect and the non-elect. Mankind was divided into two camps, — one consisting of those who were to be saved, the other of those destined to be lost. The determining factor in each case was the divine decree; the end of both the manifestation of God's glory. The significance of the world consisted in the fact that it was the stage on which this double purpose worked itself out. The protest of the Arminian, important as it was in its bearing upon the theory of the will, did not essentially alter the outlines of the picture. To Arminius, as to Calvin, the world is still a world in which the most important fact to be considered is the relation of God to the individual.[1]

The practical effect of this view was to produce characters of strong personal independence (the Puritan type). In certain cases (*e. g.* Geneva, Scotland, the Puritan communities of New England), it succeeded in organizing small societies of a high degree of ethical strictness and purity. But it acquiesced more readily than did Catholicism

[1] It ought to be said, in justice to the Arminians, that it is to one of their number, Hugo Grotius, that the world owes the introduction into Protestant theology of the idea that God is influenced in his government by social as well as individual considerations. This idea, which lies at the root of the so-called governmental theory of the atonement, finds expression in the treatise *De Satisfactione Christi*, and was the germ from which much that is fruitful in the later theology of Protestantism has sprung. As expressed by Grotius, however, it is applied only to a single problem, that of the atonement; the prevailing individualistic conception of God's relation to man, and of his plan for the world, remaining unchanged. For the modern conception of personality as a social creation the times were not yet ripe.

in the idea of a divided universe; and during the days
when it had complete control, failed to realize the full
grandeur of Christianity as a missionary religion.

We are witnessing to-day a reaction against this exaggerated individualism.   It has become an axiom of
modern thought that the government of God has social as
well as individual significance, and the conception of the
kingdom of God — obscured in the earlier Protestantism [1]
— is coming again into the forefront of theological thought.
What this conception involves, and how it may be possible
to conserve the elements of truth in the earlier interpretations while avoiding their limitations, we have now to
consider.

3. The View of the Kingdom in Modern Thought.

The contribution of modern thought to the idea of the
kingdom of God consists chiefly in a clearer insight into
the social nature of personality, which is itself but a phase
of the modern recognition of the unity of life.   To present
day psychology personality is essentially a social conception, and the process by which the individual is formed
and trained by influences coming to him from his environment, a part of a larger process of development of which
the universe itself is at once the theatre and the subject.

When we say that personality is a social conception, we
mean two things: First, that what we call personality
owes its being to social influences; secondly, that it realizes its nature through social relations.   There is no such
thing as an isolated individual.   A man is truly himself
in the measure that he goes out in thought and love to

---

[1] So far as the conception of the kingdom is retained in early Protestant
theology, it is in the Catholic sense, as applied to the church visible (cf.
West. Conf., c. XXV, 2).

others; and his distinctive character as an individual consists just in this, that he has received such and such influences from his fellows, and reacts upon them in such and such ways. It follows that the individual and the community can never be dissevered in thought. They are the two poles of social thinking, each incomplete without the other. Both are essential, not merely to the completeness but to the existence of the personal life.

Translated into the language of Christian theology, this means that the kingdom of God is the all-comprehending theological conception. God's relation to the individual is not something apart from his relation to the Christian community, but is realized through it. As it is through the influences which the kingdom exerts that the character of the individual Christian is formed, so it is through the relations which the kingdom makes possible that that character finds expression. An unsocial Christianity is a contradiction in terms. Ecclesiasticism is simply the exaggeration of this familiar truth.[1]

This view of God's purpose has far-reaching consequences both for theology and ethics. It implies, in the first place, that the salvation of the individual can never be divorced as an end in itself from the establishment of the kingdom of God. The Christian ideal contemplates a society, — an organized body of persons, standing in definite relations one to another and to God. A man is saved only as he becomes a member of that society; that is, as

[1] The failure of ecclesiasticism, as we have seen, is due to its inability to distinguish between society and the institutions which it produces. In its zeal for the machinery of social life, it obscures its ethical basis, and treats acts which custom has made familiar as holy in themselves, apart from the moral and spiritual meaning which originally prompted them. Jesus teaches us that whatever promotes right relations between persons is sacred. Hence he gives a divine meaning to every form of human activity, and makes place for what men call the secular within, not outside of, the kingdom of God.

he enters into right relations to his fellows, and so helps to realize God's plan for the world.

Not less important is the bearing of this principle upon the ethical ideal of Christianity. It excludes all forms of ethical theory which state the ideal of human perfection exclusively in terms of the relation between the individual soul and God. Man's attitude to his neighbors is not to be regarded simply as a means of his own moral development, or even as a help in his approach to God, such that, when perfect holiness is attained, the relation of man to man will become unimportant, and only God remain. That is the mystic ideal, but it is not Christian. In Christianity the relation of a man to his fellows remains an integral element in his relation to God now and forever.[1]

Yet this does not exclude the complementary truth of the worth of the individual. On the contrary, it is matter of history that Christianity has emphasized the dignity of the individual as no other religion before or since. The reason is obvious. Such love and service as Jesus requires are possible only between ethical personalities, each conscious of his own worth, and so able to appreciate the dignity of his fellows. The value of society is measured by the character of the men and women who compose it. The Christian ideal as expressed in the kingdom contemplates a community in which the character of Jesus is the standard for the estimate of all human life. The reassertion of this truth, as against the unethical standards which had obscured it, is the supreme service of Protestantism, and its permanent contribution to the ideal of the kingdom.

We touch here that which is revolutionary in the Christian Gospel. It is the extension of the hope of social rec-

[1] Cf. Eph. ii, 19; Rom. viii, 16, 17; Eph. iv, 1–16; 1 Cor. xii, 12–31; Col. i, 13, and especially 1 Thess. ii, 19; 2 Cor. i, 14.

ognition and progress to the least favored members of the human family, through the interpretation of the possibilities of humanity at large in terms of the character of Jesus. This far-reaching change is the direct result of Jesus' teaching concerning the divine Fatherhood. Here we reach the real ground of Christian faith in the worth of the individual. As it is the experience of divine sonship that lifts man above the transient and the fleeting, and gives him his permanent abiding place in the universe, so it is the recognition of like capacities in his fellows which warrants him in extending a like judgment to them. Self-sacrifice in a worthless cause is not only foolish, but wrong. The supreme significance of divine Fatherhood lies in this, that it makes all men worthy objects of sacrifice and love.

Thus, according to the Christian view, the true end is neither the individual alone nor society alone, but the full development and realization of the individual in society. Extensively, society is more important than the individual, since it is only in society that we find a term comprehensive enough to describe God's plan. Intensively, the reverse is the case, since that which gives worth to society is that it is the training school of individual character. It is because of this reciprocal relation that Jesus, though an individual, can reveal to us the true social ideal. Narrow as was the stage on which he lived, his dealings with the men with whom he was brought in contact manifest the spirit which should characterize the relations of all men everywhere.

As a spiritual and universal ideal, the kingdom of God is contrasted with all ends that are partial and temporary. It is contrasted, for example, with the economic ideal, with the political ideal, and with the intellectual ideal. The economic ideal has for its aim the increased production and the more general distribution of wealth. The political ideal is concerned with the development and perfection of the state. The intellectual ideal tests progress by the advance of human knowledge. With these aims Christianity is not primarily concerned. As a spiritual religion, it has for its single aim the making and the training of persons. Whatever does not bear upon the formation of character is indifferent to it. On the other hand, nothing that concerns this is foreign to it.

The bearing of these principles may be illustrated by contrasting the modern conception of the kingdom with the chiliastic ideal. In the past chiliasm has taken two very different attitudes to the economic and political institutions of society. On the one hand, it has exaggerated their importance, conceiving the Christian ideal itself in economic or political forms, and finding in the kingdom of God an earthly commonwealth, in which the prosperity and righteousness impossible by natural means are to be supernaturally brought about. On the other hand, its attitude to the existing institutions of society has been one of uncompromising hostility. It has found the radical evil of the world in the fact that men have confused the spiritual end of Christianity with partial and subordinate ends, seeking salvation through change of environment rather than in change of heart; and for the disaster thus caused has discovered no remedy short of the destruction of the social organization itself with all its works.

Neither of these attitudes seems adequate to modern men. In contrast to the crasser forms of chiliasm, it is manifest that the aim of Christianity is purely spiritual. It is not to be identified with any form of political or economic organization, or tied to any particular philosophical or scientific theory. Yet, on the other hand, it is equally clear that no such absolute divorce as is contemplated in the opposing view is possible. Character is a complex thing, and many influences enter into its making. It is matter of common experience that inadequate forms of economic and political organization, as well as narrow and mistaken ideas, impose serious, often insuperable obstacles to our effort to help men to better moral lives. Where this is the case, loyalty to the Christian ideal leads us necessarily to attempt their removal. Thus political activity, economic reform and intellectual research, while discarded as ends, are given their place as means, and become part of the complex process through which the kingdom of God is built up among men. In the ideal society every legitimate human interest will find its gratification, and every form of human aspiration its outlet. Affirming chis, we affirm the truth for which chiliasm stands.

This comprehensive view of the kingdom, as including all forms of human activity, gives the key to the Christian view of the world. To the Christian the meaning of the universe lies in the fact that it is the scene of the progressive realization of the kingdom of God. This carries with it, on the one hand, its distinctness from God; on the other, its dependence upon him. Further, this explains the apparently conflicting attitude which we find Christians taking toward the world. So far as, at any time, it fails to realize the Christian idea, it is evil, — an enemy to be fought, and, if possible, to be subdued. So far as it is adapted to realize the Christian end, it is good, — the revelation and the creature of God. The latter is the fundamental Christian conviction, which expresses itself in the doctrines of creation and providence. The question how this fundamental conviction is to be harmonized with the fact of evil, forms the problem of the theodicy.

CHAPTER XIII

WE have seen that the three main elements in the Christian view of the world are (1) real existence, (2) dependence and (3) adaptation to the Christian end. It is time to consider more in detail what each involves.

1. *The World as Real Existence.*

Against pantheism, Christianity affirms the distinction between God and the world. The world is not simply a part of God; it has real existence for him, as the object of his interest, his affection and his care.

This is a truth which is common to philosophy and religion. The reality of the world is established for thought, partly by the fact of consciousness, with its distinction of subject and object, partly by the fact of will, with its experience of resistance. The religious experience contributes its own evidence in the sense of duty and worth, of stewardship and sonship. If man were not a being distinct from God, having an existence and responsibility of his own, the Christian life would be unmeaning.

These general considerations are reinforced by the fact of evil, in which the contrast between God and the world finds most acute expression. The Christian consciousness of sin assumes a present opposition between the will of the creature and God, which, however its existence may ultimately be explained, is real for God as for man, and constitutes an obstacle which it is God's ceaseless effort to remove.

Nor is real existence confined to the world of persons. It extends no less to the physical universe through contact with which the personal life is realized. The reality of the physical universe for God is involved for Christian faith in its reality for us. If God is to know us as we are, if he is to sympathize with our sorrows, our burdens and our cares, the world in the midst of which we live, this concrete physical world, must be real to him. And this is Jesus' teaching. The Father whom he reveals cares not only for men, but for the birds and the flowers.[1]

If, however, we insist that the world of human experience has a real existence and meaning for God, we must be careful not to confine the meaning of existence to that which we ourselves apprehend. The moral geocentricism which conceives the entire universe as having been brought into being for the sake of man is the result of a misinterpretation of the Christian doctrine of the kingdom. Early Christian faith conceived the human race as surrounded by a host of other spiritual existences, and included the angels with men among the moral personalities who through Christ were reconciled to God.[2] We are less ready than earlier generations to dogmatize about the unseen world. But surely no more flagrant example of dogmatism could be found than the assumption that apart from God man is the only moral and reasonable being in so vast a universe, and

---

[1] It is hardly necessary to add that this view is consistent with the acceptance of very different philosophical theories of reality. One may conceive reality realistically, after the fashion of the older ontological metaphysics, as that which has existence in and for itself ; or one may conceive it idealistically, as in the more critical epistemology which recognizes the part which the mind itself contributes to the construction of that which it perceives. The point is simply that, in either case, that which is perceived is regarded as having a real existence for the apprehending mind, and hence as fitted to serve as an object for thought, and an end for activity.

[2] Col. i, 16–20. Cf. Origen, *De Principiis*, book I, chapters 5, 6.

that the only spiritual meaning which it contains is that expressed in God's relation to us. What moral purpose and spiritual communion God may have with other beings in the boundless reaches of space and time which modern science has brought within our ken, we do not know. Our faith is simply that the meaning of all life everywhere is to be found in its relation to such a wise, holy and loving Father as Christ has revealed; and that the interest, the wonder and the joy which we, with our imperfect faculties and narrow insight, feel in our communion with nature, and in our relation to the so-called lower orders, must exist for God supremely.

With the doctrine of the reality of the world for God is given the transcendence of God. Transcendence is, as we have already seen,[1] only another name for the divine personality. It expresses the fact that while God is in the world, he is not exhausted by the world; that he is not only the source of life and power, but of standard and ideal. It regards the world not only as the place of his activity, but as the sphere of his purpose, and finds the explanation of its apparent imperfection in the fact that it is the scene of a divine will not yet realized, a divine plan not yet accomplished.

2. *The World as Dependent.*

The second element in the Christian view of the world is dependence. Against dualism, Christianity affirms that God, having made the world, is able to control and order it to his own end.

This recognition, too, is common to philosophy and religion. As the former carries back all that is to the Absolute, so the latter refers all to God. The truth which

[1] Chapter XI, p. 172.

the philosopher expresses when he speaks of the inter-relation of phenomena and the universality of law finds religious utterance in Schleiermacher's definition of religion as the feeling of absolute dependence [1] and the Westminster doctrine of the decree as that by which God "freely and unchangeably ordains whatsoever cometh to pass." [2]

The philosophical recognition of dependence is derived from the experience of relativity. However far back we go in time, we find the causes of things hidden in a remoter past. However far our thought travels in space, we discover the same interrelation and dependence. The course of the sun is just as much determined as that of the planets it controls, and the farthest star the telescope dis-covers proves part of the same system of forces which causes the apple to fall from the tree.

The same dependence characterizes human life. Man lives in surroundings he did not choose, and is subject to influences he did not create. The better he knows himself, the more clearly he recognizes the extent to which he is limited, both by heredity and environment. The freedom by which he seems to be differentiated from nature is crowded by psychology within narrower and narrower limits. Indeed, it is in the inner life that he first of all discovers the dependence which he afterwards carries over in thought to the world without.

The conclusion of philosophy is reinforced by the reli-gious experience. The truth with which Paul approached the Athenians, that in God we live and move and have our being (Acts xvii, 28), finds more or less clear recognition in all the great religions. But Christianity gives the old truth a new meaning through its revelation of the character

---

[1] *Glaubenslehre*, section 4, p. 14.
[2] *Confession of Faith*, III, 1.

of the God on whom we thus depend. It tells of a Father whose love and care are ever with his children, and invites to a submission whose result is perfect freedom. Those who are most advanced in Christian experience are most conscious of their constant dependence upon God, and most ready to testify that the life which they live is not theirs but that of God's indwelling Spirit.[1]

With this discovery of God's presence in all life, we have the recognition of the divine immanence. Like transcendence, this word has a moral as well as a metaphysical meaning. As used in Christian theology, it does not mean that God is present everywhere substantially, as a thing is; but in knowledge and power as a person. Thus the world becomes full of meaning and beauty, and life full of joy and hope. Wherever we look in this vast universe, in the tiniest atom as in the farthest star, in the lowest life as in the highest, but above all in the human spirit with its needs, its longings and its possibilities, we find present and active, working out his wise, loving and holy purpose the almighty Father whom Christ reveals.

3. *The Adaptation of the World to the Christian End.*

The third element in the Christian view of the world is adaptation. The world, dependent upon God, the scene of his purpose, is also fitted to realize that purpose; it is adapted to the Christian end.

This is true of the physical universe. The physical may not be an end in itself, but it is necessary to the realization of the Christian end. It is through contact with nature that the personal life is developed. From nature we learn lessons of the highest spiritual value, — the lesson of law, the lesson of order, the lesson of dependence, the lesson

---

[1] Cf. Paul's testimony in Gal. ii, 20, and Eph. ii, 8-10.

of humility. Through nature there is cultivated in man the sense of beauty and of mystery. Contemplation of her wonders awakens and deepens the sense of reverence. Deeply as he revered the moral law, Kant found the starry heavens no less awe-inspiring.

The physical universe, then, is good. It serves a spiritual end. Christianity rejects all theories of the essential evil of matter; and with them goes also the rejection in principle of all asceticism. Self-control and self-sacrifice are Christian virtues, but they have other roots than in the dualistic systems.[1]

This principle is true also of human life. Man is adapted to realize the Christian end. Indeed, it is in man that we first meet this end. Nature is but God's instrument; man is at once his servant and his child. In the human spirit faith finds qualities and capacities which are truly godlike, and longings which only divine sonship can satisfy.

The law of adaptation characterizes all human relations. The great human institutions are schools for teaching divine truth. In the home man learns to be obedient, faithful, trustful, loving. Through the state he is taught the practice of mutual helpfulness and brotherly co-operation on a large scale. He discovers an end beyond self, even beyond kindred; and is trained for the supreme end of the kingdom of God. The lessons of the state and of the home are gathered to a head in the church. Here the lesser relationships are shown in their divine meaning. Man's thoughts are lifted above the temporal and the fleeting to that which is unseen and abiding. Through his experience of human relations and friendships he learns to know himself a child of the divine Father, God.

[1] Cf. 1 Cor. viii; Rom. xiv, esp. vv. 14–21.

But we may go even farther. Of the evil in the world it is true that it is used by God to promote the Christian end. However difficult it may be to account for its presence, the fact remains that now that it is here, it is overruled for good. And this is true of both its forms, physical and moral. Through contact with suffering and sin, man learns lessons of inestimable value to himself, and becomes fitted to take part in the work of the kingdom. Struggling to overcome them, he not only grows in character himself, but he comes to understand more clearly the character of God. Even when the details are dark and the solution hidden, Christian faith has no doubt as to the outcome. Calvinist and Arminian may differ in their theories, but they are at one in the conviction that, when the end is reached, it will be found that even the experiences which seemed most un-Christlike have had their part to play in bringing about the Christian end.

With the mention of evil, we touch the fundamental problem in the Christian view of the world. How comes it to pass that in a universe which is by hypothesis under the control of a good God evil should be so ubiquitous and so persistent? How can we justify our faith that this world is really our Father's world, and serves his end? This is the problem of the theodicy. It has two phases, physical and moral, — the problem of pain and the problem of sin.

Apart from dualistic theories which attribute evil to a power other than God, the chief solutions of the problem of pain are of two classes. The first, or retributive, sees in suffering the result and just punishment of sin, either individual or racial. The second, or educational, sees in it an instrument of the divine training, first of the lower races, then of man.

The simplest form of the retributive theory is that which sees in individual suffering the evidence and consequence of individual sin. Thus, in much of the Old Testament we find the assumption that suffering is *ipso facto* a proof of guilt. More careful reflection, however, disproves this naïve assumption. Experience shows that the righteous suffer as well as the wicked, and some of the wicked do not seem to suffer at all. This is the problem with which the book of Job and many of the Psalms are concerned. From the standpoint of the individual there seems no solution, so long as attention is confined to the present life. With the rise of faith in a future life a way of escape is found in the theory of retribution after death, which makes possible the reference of all unsolved problems to the day of judgment.

A variation of the retributive theory is that which finds the explanation of the suffering of the individual in the race sin. The children suffer because they inherit the consequences of their parents' guilt; and mankind in general, because it is involved in Adam's fall. This is the answer of Paul in Romans, of Augustine and of Calvin. It emphasizes a side of truth which the individualistic theory overlooks, since it takes account of the facts of heredity, and recognizes that the problem of suffering is social as well as individual. Yet when taken as a complete solution it proves inadequate: first, because in explaining the children's suffering as the consequence of ancestral sin it avoids one difficulty, only to raise another; secondly, because experience proves that there is a significance in pain which cannot be expressed in terms of punishment at all.

The second solution of the problem of pain is educational. It sees in pain the means of the divine training, first of the lower races, and then of man.   It finds its support, partly in the observation of life which shows that through suffering man learns lessons of the highest importance for his welfare and training, partly in the Christian experience which sees in the cross of Christ the supreme illustration of its healing and uplifting influence.

The educational significance of pain is one of the lessons most clearly taught by modern science. While, from one point of view, science intensifies the problem of suffering by showing the length of time which it has been in the world, from another, it relieves its pressure by removing the arbitrary character which it acquires when isolated from its environment.   Modern psychology shows us that the capacity for pain enters into the very structure of consciousness, and is an indispensable element in our equipment for life.   By the law of contrast it makes possible our highest pleasures.   Through it we become conscious of our need, and are warned of the approach of danger; without it we should be left helpless in the struggle for existence.   The higher the development, the greater the capacity, and the more important the function, of pain.

These considerations relieve, even if they do not altogether remove, the difficulty which comes from the observation of pain in the animal creation.   However true it may be that animals do not know the more acute forms of suffering familiar to human experience, it is unquestioned that pain is a familiar and an important element in animal life.   For this fact the retributive theory affords no satisfactory explanation.[1]   The educational theory shows that

[1] An exception should be made in the case of the theory of transmigration. Here all living creatures are regarded as forming a single commonwealth under uniform ethical law. Under this law each individual passes through an endless series of existences, receiving in each, in a body adapted to his

pain is as necessary for the development of the animal as for that of man, and so gives it its place as one element in the complex system of divine government which culminates in humanity.

With the advent of man, the problem of pain enters upon a new stage. To the suffering of the body is added the suffering of the mind. Conscience awakes, and sin and guilt become familiar facts. Pain now becomes a means of moral, as in the animal world it is a means of physical, training, and suffering is recognized as retributive as well as disciplinary. From this point of view the problem of pain becomes inextricably interwoven with the problem of sin, and the Christian contribution to the solution of the former can be understood only in the light of its interpretation of the latter.

With sin we reach the ultimate problem of the universe. Pain may be explained by reference to higher ends. But moral evil seems to involve a permanent antimony which admits no theoretical solution consistent both with the goodness and the power of God. Hence many theologians have taken refuge in some form of dualism. The most common theory is that which accounts for sin by the fact of free will, with its power to the contrary. According to this view, God, in creating free agents, limited himself; and in this self-limitation, the necessary condition of the creation of moral beings, is to be found the explanation both of the possibility and of the fact of sin.

The difficulty with this view is that, if consistently carried out, it imperils the divine control, and hence removes the certainty of the realization of the Christian

ethical desert, the just reward for the deeds done in the life before. It is clear that from this point of view the problem of animal suffering is simply a phase of the larger problem of the suffering of moral beings which we have just been considering.

end.   If God, in creating man, could not prevent him from
sinning, what reason have we for believing that he will
ever be able to do so?   The device, so common in theology, of using freedom (in the sense of a real limitation
of God's power) to get sin into the world, only to reinstate
God in complete control so soon as sin is in, is more cred-
itable to the religious feeling of those who employ it than
to their intellectual consistency.   If God can control the
action of free beings to-day without destroying their freedom,[1] then he must always have been able to do so.   But,
if this be the case, then he must have had some reason
other than the fact of freedom for admitting sin.

Accordingly, we find many theologians applying the principle of education to the problem of moral evil.   Even
while affirming against thoroughgoing pantheism the
exceeding sinfulness of sin, they have maintained that it
has a necessary part to play in the unfolding of the divine
plan.   According to this view, it is not the possibility of
sin simply, but sin itself, which is an indispensable element
in the world's moral training.   On this common basis we
may distinguish two different types of thought.   The first,
which is the theodicy of historic Calvinism, sees in sin
an ultimate fact, destined to exist forever, and explains it
as necessary to the display and exercise of the divine attributes of justice and mercy.   The second, which is more
consistent with the view of God's character to which we
have been led, finds the justification for the presence of
moral evil in the world in the fact that through it there
has been brought about a closer communion with God and
a higher type of character in man than could have been
attained in any other way.   Or, in other words, it finds the
explanation of sin in the experience of salvation.

[1] Cf. Clarke, *Outline*, p. 150.

It is true that this is a practical rather than a speculative solution,— that is, a solution based upon the conditions of life as we find them. If anyone asks why the conditions are as they are, we cannot answer in the case of moral evil any more than in the case of physical evil. All that we can do is to show that in this world, as we know it, sin has a part to play in bringing about the highest end we know. We cannot think it away from the world without at the same time thinking away with it that which we recognize as supremely precious.

The educational effect of sin may be illustrated on all sides of the religious life. It affects our consciousness of communion, our ideal of service, our conception of God. Thus it is through sin, with its consequences in our own lives and in the lives of those we love, that we learn, as we could learn it in no other way, our need of God, our constant dependence upon him for salvation and strength. It is through sin, with its deadly havoc in the world, making appeal to the finest sympathy and the most complete devotion, that we learn the meaning of Christian service, the cost and the reward of Christlike ministry. Above all, it is through sin, with the cross by which it has been overcome, that we have learned to see God in Christ, and to measure the extent of the divine love.

In the light of such experiences, considered not as isolated but as parts of a system of divine training, the suffering of which the world is full receives a new meaning. So far from being the proof of a world which is undivine, it is the means by which God is teaching us his profoundest lessons, and fitting us for communion with himself. Through it there is being formed in us the type of character we see in Christ, and by it we are made capable of experiencing that finest joy which comes through sympathy at its best. Thus, in a very literal sense, it is true that to the Christian the cross has become the highest proof of "the wisdom of God."

The difficulty remains that all are not Christians. The Christian experience makes it possible to believe that all evil *may* serve a good end; but it does not of itself prove it. This proof remains for the future, when the transformation which has been wrought by the Christian spirit in a part of life shall be manifest in the whole. Here is the root of the Christian belief in immortality. If the Christian view of the world is to be justified, what we see now must be but part of a larger process, in which the work here begun, but not finished, shall be brought to completion, and the narrow experience and limited vision of this life be supplemented by the larger life and wider knowledge of the life beyond. The different forms which this hope has assumed, together with the grounds on which they rest, will concern us later.[1] For the present it is sufficient to note that not the least powerful of the influences which have called it forth and which keep it alive are the experiences of suffering and sin which together form the problem of the theodicy. Here — as everywhere in religion — we face the great venture of faith, of which the belief that God is like Christ is the highest expression.

---

[1] Chapter XV, section 3, pp. 250 sq.

CHAPTER XIV

In the light of the preceding discussion we must understand the doctrines in which theology has expressed the relation between God and the world. These are three, — Creation, Providence and Miracle. Each corresponds to one of the permanent elements in the Christian view of the world. Creation affirms the real existence of the world for God; providence expresses its dependence upon him; miracle evidences its adaptation to the Christian end. We shall consider each in turn.

1. *Of Creation.*

When we say that God created the world, we mean that the universe in which we dwell, as well as all its parts, owes its origin to the intelligent and deliberate action of that personal God whose character and purpose Christ has revealed. It is the affirmation of Christian faith that the reason and purpose which characterize the world as we know it to-day have been present from the beginning, and the guarantee that they will still continue to characterize it to the end.

As treated in the older theology, the doctrine of creation has to do chiefly with the natural world, God's creative activity in regeneration being treated under redemption. It is the assertion, as against dualism, that God is the author of the substance as well as the form of the world (creation *ex nihilo*), and this both material and spiritual (God, the maker of all things, visible and invisible). As to the time and manner of creation, we find considerable latitude of interpretation. While few theologians follow Origen in his doctrine of eternal creation, not a few agree with Augustine in regarding it as a process covering long periods of time. The widespread acceptance of the view, so common a generation ago, that the creative days were periods of twenty-four hours each, and that the world was made by God in a week, was the result of the literal exegesis which the Reformation fostered, and which, coupled with the inadequate conception of revelation already considered, has made the conflict between theology and natural science even more acute in Protestantism than in Catholicism.

In the reaction from the cosmological speculations of the older theology the question has been raised whether it is not possible for Christian theology to dispense with the doctrine of creation altogether. What matters it, we are asked, who made the world, or whether it was made at all, provided that now that it is here it is subject to the divine control? We may admit that what is essential to Christian faith is the fact of God's control, not the method by which it is brought about. But it is exactly this assurance of supreme control that the doctrine of creation is designed to express. The Christian interest here is the same which we have already considered in connection with the attributes of omnipotence and omniscience, and the principles which determine our attitude to the questions at issue are identical. Here, as there, it is important to distinguish those questions which are of predominantly philosophical and scientific interest from those which are distinctively religious. It is with the latter alone that Christian theology is primarily concerned.

The philosophical interest is concerned with questions of the nature of creation; whether a temporal or an eternal process; whether *ex nihilo* or positing some datum (*e. g.* space, as in Martineau's theory of creation [1]) on which the divine activity may work. All these matters are in themselves indifferent to Christian faith. The real significance of the doctrine of creation *ex nihilo* to the Christian is to be found in its denial of such theories (dualistic or emanistic) as are inconsistent either with the real existence of the universe for God or with its complete dependence upon God; and hence, with the adaptation of the world to the realization of the Christian end.

The scientific interest is concerned with the order of creation (the cosmogony). In the past Christian theology had an indirect interest in this question because of its supposed bearing upon the authority of Scripture. With a better view of revelation, this is no longer the case. Theology may leave to science with a quiet mind the study of the world process, reserving for itself the more important questions of meaning and end. Any view of the origin and development of the universe which is consistent with its dependence upon the Christian God and its adaptation to his purpose satisfies the requirements of Christian faith.

Yet, while Christian faith is indifferent to philosophical and scientific theories for their own sake, and experience shows that it can live with many different cosmogonies, it is of vital importance that it should be brought into harmony with the intellectual environment in which its adherents live. Thus, in a universe of the magnitude and unity which modern science assumes, it is most natural, instead of thinking of creation as a series of isolated and independent acts, to regard it as a permanent process,

[1] Cf. his *Study of Religion*, vol. I, pp. 382 sq.

expressing that continual relation between phenomena and their spiritual ground which is the form in which the idealistic philosophy conceives of the reality of the world. This conception of creation as a permanent process, anticipated in the older theology in its doctrine of preservation, is not only intellectually more consistent; it is religiously more satisfying. The God whom faith craves is not one who was once active in the past, and has since ceased from his labors; but one who is ever at work, and upon whose life-giving and transforming power man may therefore at any time confidently call. The surest support of the Christian conception of God as creator is the experience of the new life in Christ, of which we are daily partakers through his Spirit.[1]

That which is distinctive in the Christian doctrine of creation is the view of the God from whom the universe proceeds and of the end for which it was made. This end Christian faith finds in the production of beings like the good God, and in their union with himself in the fellowship of holy love. It is because the world as we know it to-day ministers to such a spiritual end that we believe it had its origin in the will of the holy and loving Father whom Christ reveals. Here, as always in theology, the teleological point of view is controlling. It is not the present world with its sin and evil accepted as a finality which is the subject of our doctrine, but the world transfigured by the cross of Christ in which faith has learned to see the training school for the kingdom of God.

2. *Of Providence.*

As the doctrine of creation carries back the origin of the universe to God, so that of providence expresses his present

[1] Cf. Eph. iv, 23, 24; Col. iii, 10.

relation to the world he has made. When we speak of the divine providence, we mean that the universe as a whole, as well as all its parts, is being sustained and ordered by God for the wise, holy and loving end which Christ reveals.

The older Protestant theology conceived the divine activity in providence as partly one of preservation, and partly one of government. In preservation God sustains in existence the beings he has made, both material and spiritual; in government he directs and orders them to the ends he has determined. Preservation carries on the work of creation. It is an exercise of power. Government realizes the end for which creation was undertaken. It is a work of wisdom. Both sides of the divine Providence are manifest in all that happens. God's sustaining and directing activity extends to the least thing as well as the greatest, to the evil as well as the good; yet it must not be understood as involving God's approval of what is morally evil, or as making him responsible for sin.

Within these general limits we find wide differences in the interpretation of God's relation to the world. Theological theories have varied all the way from deism to a view little removed from pantheism. At the one extreme it has been held that in creation God endowed the creatures with powers which they henceforth use for themselves. On this view the action of man is free, and, save as God deliberately interferes in the world through miracle, all that happens can be explained through the action of the second causes which he has brought into existence. On the other hand, we have the view that God not only sustains the creatures in existence, but that he acts with and through them, determining all that they do. On this theory, second causes are only one form of the divine activity, and the will of man is as much determined as the course of the tide. But here the moral question arises, How can God act through sinful men without himself becoming partaker of their sin? To meet this difficulty we find recourse to the theory of a *concursus*, *i. e.* a joint activity of God and man in every act. This was defined in the later Protestant theology as " that activity of divine Providence by which God exercises a general influence upon the action and upon the effects of second causes, in such a way that the effect is not produced either by God himself alone, or by the creature alone, or partly by God and partly by the creature, but in one single and sole and total efficiency both by God and by the creature." In this mysterious partnership God's action extended " *ad effectum, sed non ad defectum*," to that which was done, but not to the evil in the deed.

In the doctrine of providence, as in creation, we have to distinguish the philosophical and the scientific interests from the religious. The former are common to Christians and all educated men, but they have only an indirect religious bearing. The latter is concerned with the principles of God's government, so far as they bear directly upon the life and conduct of men. Yet in practice the line is a fleeting one, since in enlarging our knowledge of the laws of the universe science is at the same time giving us an insight into the method of God's government, which may at any time bear fruit in unexpected practical results.

The philosophical questions which meet us in connection with the doctrine of providence are of the same nature as those already considered in connection with creation. They have to do with the reconciliation of the supposed antithesis between transcendence and immanence; with God's relation to the creature, and the nature and limits of the latter's independence; with human freedom in its relation to divine sovereignty; with the possibility and nature of miracles (*i. e.* new beginnings not to be accounted for by their antecedents); in a word, with the problem of individuality in its many aspects. The older theology sought the solution of these questions in the region of abstract metaphysics. Modern philosophy has taught us that they are problems of personality, having in large part a moral root; and hence that their true solution is to be found, if at all, in the region of the teleological and the ethical.

Observation and experience disclose the following principles in God's conduct of the world: (1) It is uniform (according to law); (2) it is progressive; (3) it involves conflict; (4) it makes use of sacrifice.

(1) God's method is a method of *law;* that is to say, it is not arbitrary or irregular, but consistent, and in its great principles unchanging.

The universality of law is a conviction common to theology and science. But the significance of the principle is different for each. Science accepts it because it enables it to explain things; theology because it belongs to the Christian view of God's character.

It is important to emphasize this latter aspect, because it is so often overlooked. When personality is identified with arbitrary will, the moral significance of law is either obscured or denied. Instead of revealing God, the laws of the universe are regarded as concealing him. He manifests himself not through them, but in spite of them, by extraordinary exertions of power. Hence the sharp contrast already noted between the natural and the supernatural, and the definition of miracle as an event which is not only unexplained but inexplicable by law.

With a better conception of personality, we are relieved from this dualism. We see that law — so far from being a limitation of personality — is the expression of moral consistency, and hence the indispensable condition of revelation. In the laws which to science are ultimate we see the expression of God's character, and find the true basis of the uniformity of nature in his moral changelessness.

One reason why this truth has not been more generally perceived has been that men's conception of law has been so largely derived from a study of the physical universe. But the laws of nature in the narrow sense are only a part of the laws which science recognizes. Spirit has its laws as well as matter; and the freedom and initiative so vital to religion are themselves a part of the phenomena which make the world, and for which any comprehensive philosophy must make place. This leads us to note that

(2) God's method is a method of *progress;* that is to say, of growth, of development, of change from the less to the more perfect, according to an ideal determined from the first.

Progress is a personal word. It implies a comparison of values — a teleology. Although God's method is uniform, the world is not stationary. It is developing, moving toward an end. The scientific theory which expresses this belief is evolution. But the idea itself is more widespread than any theory. It dominates every department of modern thought and life. The astronomer conceives the physical universe as slowly evolving from a formless chaos into the system of suns and planets which fill our heavens. The biologist applies the same law to the organic world, and regards the more complex and highly developed forms of life as having slowly developed from the simpler. The historian writes the story of humanity as a gradual emergence from barbarism into civilization. The moralist accepts Paul's principle expressed in Philippians iii, 13, as the law of human character. The theologian revives Jesus' teaching in the parables by the sea, and conceives the kingdom of God as a growing thing, which, beginning as a grain of mustard seed, comes at last to be a mighty tree, under whose branches the peoples may find shelter.

Thus, for the static conception of perfection which thinks of all things as complete from the beginning, we substitute the teleological, which looks for the real meaning of things at the end. Instead of confining God's activity to a series of isolated interpositions (*e. g.* creation, revelation, regeneration, sanctification), each issuing at once in a complete and finished product (*e. g.* the Bible, the church, Christian doctrine, perfect moral character), we think of him as ever at work, forming, training and perfecting the moral personalities whom he has designed for union with himself. In the gradual development which science recognizes, from the lower forms to the higher, from the more simple to the more complex, we see the slow unfolding of God's providential plan. But the end to which science points, but whose nature it can only dimly guess, we find revealed in the kingdom of God.

With this conception of progress there is given the significance of the individual and the exceptional. Progress is possible only because some advance faster than others, and, breaking away from the prevailing type, set new standards both of thought and life, to which others are later brought to conform. New beginnings are as much a fact for the evolutionist as for the believer in special creation, and on the one theory as the other the origin of life, of personality and of character, as of countless steps between, remain mysteries which require for their explanation the initiative of a living, a personal and a holy God. To unite old elements into that which consciousness recognizes as new is as much an act of creation as to form from nothing the original elements themselves ; and this is what God is doing all the time.[1]

Yet progress is not uniform. There are irregularities and retrogressions. Both in biology and in ethics, degeneration and decay are familiar facts. This brings us to our next point, namely, that

(3) God's method is a method of *conflict ;* that is, a method in which progress takes place through struggle against obstacles, with the possibility of defeat or failure for those who fail to stand the test.

This too seems to be a principle of very wide range. It may be observed in all spheres of life — vegetable and animal as well as human, and has its analogies even in the inorganic world. Science tells us that the types we see are only the survivors of a much greater number that have passed away. And what is true of the types is true also of the individuals within each type. Of the countless numbers born into the world only a small portion survive; and of these only a few reach maturity. Wherever we look in nature, from the highest to the lowest, we find the same struggle; first for existence, then for a life which is rich and full.

What is true of the lower orders is true also of man. Such progress as he has attained has been through conflict. The races which are weak have yielded to those that are stronger. The prizes in every profession go to the few, and the many lag behind or fall by the way.

Nor is the spiritual life an exception. Here too progress takes place through conflict. The New Testament is full of figures taken from the race-course, the boxing-ring, the

1 See further, under section 3, pp. 223 sq.

battle. The Christian, like every other man, meets obstacles, inner and outer, and grows in strength and character by overcoming them. Jesus is the great example.

From this fact of conflict it follows that some advance farther than others in character and attainment, while their neighbors fall behind or drop altogether out of the race. In the interpretation of these facts men part company. Some find in the struggle for existence the last word in the explanation of life. It is God's will that the few should triumph and the many go to the wall. The theological name for this doctrine is election. In philosophy it finds expression in Nietzsche's teaching that might makes right, and the world belongs to the strongest. Others see in the struggle for self-development only one side of the divine government, whose obverse is the principle of self-sacrifice. This is the Christian view, and leads to our fourth point.

(4) God's method is a method of *sacrifice ;* that is, a method in which the voluntary renunciation and surrender of the more highly developed is the means of promoting the welfare and progress of those who are less advanced.

This principle too is one of widespread application. In animal life it meets us in the phenomena of motherhood (Drummond's "struggle for the life of others"[1]); but in man, with his sense of obligation and brotherhood, it is transformed from an unconscious instinct to a moral principle. In the measure that man develops in character and insight, sacrifice, in the sense of voluntary surrender and renunciation for others' sake, is recognized as a duty. In primitive, and even in many highly developed communities, its range is limited to the family, the tribe, or the nation. Christianity sets it forth as a law of universal

[1] Cf. *Ascent of Man*, p. 215.

application, foreshadowed in the Old Testament, exemplified in Christ, having its roots in the character of God.

This principle puts a new meaning into election. The fact remains that some are more highly endowed than others, and that it is their duty to make the most of the powers they possess. But the motive is transformed. It is no longer the desire for self-aggrandizement, but the means of more effective ministry. The stronger a man is, the larger and richer he is, the more he has to give.

The law of sacrifice is a consequence of the social nature of personality already considered. It has its ground in the fact that men are not isolated individuals whose interests can be divorced from those of their fellows, but members of a race bound together by manifold relations, physical and spiritual, so that the attainment of one may be the means of advancing the many, and the sacrifice of one the means of blessing all mankind. We find abundant illustrations of this law both in the lives of nations (*e. g.* Greece with its art; Rome with its laws; Israel with its religion) and of individuals (the heroes and martyrs of every age and of every profession). The philosophy of selfishness recognizes one application of this law when it justifies the service of the many to the few. Christianity is only going one step farther when it enjoins the service by the few of the many.

In the law of sacrifice is found not only the means of social progress, but also the key to individual happiness. Renunciation and suffering cannot be escaped. Resistance only makes their necessity more apparent and more painful. Christ teaches a better way when he finds in willing acceptance of suffering and limitation the means of deepening and enriching love. In his doctrine of self-realization through self-sacrifice [1] he gives us what is perhaps the profoundest insight we possess into the character, as into the law, of God.

3. *Of Miracle.*

A miracle is an extraordinary event in nature or in human life, the explanation of which religious faith finds in a special divine purpose connected with revelation. Every religion which has a personal God assumes such events, and sees in them evidences of God's interest in and care for man.   Christianity is no exception.

In discussing miracle we must distinguish the philosophical use of the word from the religious use.   In the first case emphasis is laid upon the exceptional character of the event; in the second, upon its function as revelation.   A miracle in the philosophical sense is a wonder, τέρας, something which cannot be accounted for by any known natural cause.[2]   A miracle in the religious sense is a sign, σημεῖον, that is, an event which in a special way reveals God.[3]   It is evident that the two meanings, however closely associated, do not necessarily belong together. There may be miracles in the philosophical sense without religious significance, and vice versa.   Moreover, the view of what constitutes each will vary with differences of intellectual environment and of religious insight.

In primitive times belief in miracle was universal.   Man believed himself surrounded by a host of unseen spirits, good and evil, to whose action he attributed such unusual events in nature or in human life as he could not otherwise explain.   Miracles were acts performed by such spirits,

---

[1] Matt. x, 39 ; xvi, 25 ; Mark viii, 35 ; Luke ix, 24.

[2] Cf. Mead, *Supernatural Revelation*, p. 97 ; Hodge, *Systematic Theology*, vol. I, p. 618 ; Shedd, *Dogmatic Theology*, vol. I, p. 540.

[3] Cf. Clarke, *Outline*, p. 133.

or by men who had received from them supernatural powers. The Biblical writers, like their contemporaries in Greece and Rome, took for granted the possibility of such acts, and believed that they might occur at any time. Neither in the Old Testament nor the New do we find any trace of our modern scientific difficulty, based upon the uniformity of law.

It is evident that, as thus defined, miracle is a philosophical rather than a religious conception. It is as much a part of the primitive view of the world as the universality of law is a part of the universe of modern science. Miracle acquires a *religious* significance only when men begin to see in the extraordinary events by which they are surrounded messages from the gods which may have bearing on their lives. Here everything depends upon the conception of deity, and the nature of the communication to be expected from him. Where the gods are thought of as fitful and arbitrary, the more mysterious an event is, the more divine it will seem to be. In the measure that God comes to be thought of as an ethical being, having a consistent purpose, the inexplicable in the miracle falls into the background, and attention is concentrated upon the moral lesson which it is designed to teach. We see the transformation begun in the Old Testament. In Christianity we find it completed.

Thus it is not on the philosophical but on the religious side that the distinctive contribution of Christianity to the idea of miracle is to be found. This consists: first, in the subordination of the merely marvellous to the moral and the spiritual; secondly, in the clear perception that whatever powers may be possessed by other spirits, the final control rests with the good God whom Christ reveals. These changes, which may be illustrated both in Jesus' teaching[1] and in that of the apostles,[2] and which are all the more impressive because of the traces of the older view which still meet us in the New Testament,[3] are the result of the transformation wrought by Jesus in the idea of God. Here, as so often, the religious insight anticipates truth, whose philosophical formulation and justification may be delayed for centuries.

The primitive conception of miracle which forms the philosophical background of the Biblical view must be distinguished from the more developed philosophical conception with which we are familiar to-day. The latter dates from the Middle Ages, and is the result of the sharp line of demarcation drawn by the schoolmen between nature and the supernatural, and the definition of the latter in terms of the arbitrary and the transcendent, rather than of the ethical and the spiritual. Thus, Thomas Aquinas distinguishes miracle as the direct work of God from the work of all subordinate spirits. "It is something which goes beyond the power of all created nature; something which God alone can do."[4] As such, it is the final evidence of deity, and the infallible guarantee of the divine origin of whatever truths or practices may receive its authentication. From the schoolmen this conception passed through the Reformers into Protestantism, and so has become part of our theological inheritance. Originally designed to establish the authority of the church, it has been used by Protestant apologists to prove the inspiration of the Bible, and is the common premise from which, until recently, both advocates and opponents of the Christian revelation have argued.

---

[1] *E. g.* Matt. xi, 2–5 ; xvi, 1–4 ; Mark viii, 11, 12 ; Luke xi, 29 sq.

[2] Cf. Paul's doctrine of the Spirit in 1 Cor. xii–xiv, and of the resurrection in 1 Cor. xv, 20 sq.

[3] *E. g.* the insertion, Matt. xii, 40.

[4] *Summa*, Part I, Qu. 105, art. 6, 8 ; 110, art. 4.

According to this conception of miracle, the religious value of an event is in direct proportion to its removal from the control of law or reason. We have here the reaffirmation, in more scientific language, of the primitive conception of deity as arbitrary or lawless. When we have found something which no conceivable experience can bring under law, we may be sure — so runs the reasoning — that we stand in the immediate presence of God. This is the major premise of the traditional apologetic.

In modern times two causes have combined to render this conception of miracle unsatisfactory. The first is scientific, the second religious. With the enlarged conception of nature to which modern science has led, men's confidence in their ability to make the distinction required by the older theology has been undermined. So much once thought miraculous in the narrow sense has been brought under law that we do not see how we can be sure of any conceivable event that it is " beyond the power of created nature " ; or, in other words, that no conceivable experience will make it possible for us to bring it, too, under law. This difficulty was recognized by the more acute of the older apologists. But they overcame it by maintaining that however difficult discrimination might be in many cases, the greater miracles could be recognized as such intuitively, with a certainty which precluded the possibility of mistake.[1] Such certainty, in a universe so vast and many-sided as that which modern science reveals, seems to many in our day no longer possible. The nature we know has proved so full of surprises that we dare not say of any conceivable event, " This lies outside the sphere of law."

Thus it appears that in our modern world the old position of the natural and the supernatural is exactly reversed.

[1] Cf. Thornwell, Works, III, pp. 246 sq.

The natural world is no longer conceived as a limited and narrow sphere surrounded by the boundless expanse of the supernatural. It is nature which is the all-embracing term, and the supernatural is the name we give to a certain portion of this vast territory. If we take the word in its technical philosophical sense as the exceptional, the lawless, it is that part of the world of nature which we do not yet, or perhaps may never, understand. If we take it in its wider historical sense as the revealed, it is that part of nature whose spiritual meaning we have come to fathom.

With this reference to spiritual meaning we have anticipated the second of the difficulties to which reference has been made. This has to do with the character of the evidence by which a divine revelation is to be established. Such evidence, we have come to see, must be like in kind to the being whose presence and activity it is designed to disclose. It is not simply that miracle in the old sense is hard to prove; but that, with our clearer perception of the rational nature and moral consistency of God, we no longer recognize the religious significance of acts of mere power, even if they could be proved. A God who is moral and spiritual, as we believe the Christian God to be, can make himself known only through evidence which is itself moral and spiritual.

The result of both these causes has been a transformation of the conception of miracle along the lines already noted in early Christianity. Instead of seeing in miracle something contrary to nature, as did the older apologetic, modern apologists regard it as the revelation within nature of a higher law;[1] and, leaving to philosophy and science the philosophical and scientific questions which its occur-

---

[1] Cf. Stearns, *Present Day Theology*, p. 63. "A miracle is a divine restoration of the true order of nature."

rence suggests, concentrate their attention upon the moral and spiritual qualities which give it permanent significance for Christian faith.

The question of miracle in the philosophical sense is the same which we have already considered in connection with creation and providence. It is the question of beginnings · the question how far that which comes into existence can be completely explained by its antecedents, and how far it requires for its explanation the assumption of creative power. Here modern science modifies the medieval conception of miracle in two ways. On the one hand, it makes it increasingly difficult to isolate any conceivable event from its antecedents and surroundings as the product in exclusive degree of new creative power. On the other, it makes it increasingly clear that nothing in the world can be wholly accounted for by its antecedents, but that in every transformation of the old into the new we are witnessing an act of creation. Thus, while from one point of view the field of the miracle is narrowed, from another it is wonderfully enlarged. Science recognizes no single miracle, because all the world has become miraculous.

This does not mean that to science all beginnings stand on the same level of importance. The transition from the lower to the higher levels of existence, *e. g.* from the inorganic to the organic, and from the animal to man, still remains for modern thought the problem *par excellence ;* and the number of steps introduced into the creative process by evolutionary theory serves but to make more manifest the impotence of that which is dead to produce life, or that which is non-rational reason. Science, too, has its great transitions to account for; and in these philosophy still finds the most signal proof of the presence of that creative spirit, to whose ceaseless activity all life is witness.

Thus, if from one point of view the result of modern science has been steadily to diminish the area of the supernatural as compared with the natural, from another point of view it has brought about a corresponding enlargement. The insight that law is universal is matched by the higher insight that it is only in consciousness that we find law. Thus, the supernatural receives its true meaning of the personal, and the false antithesis between nature and the supernatural is removed. The supernatural is the natural, seen in its spiritual significance. The natural is the supernatural, finding expression in forms which make possible the discovery of its permanent meaning and worth. As the natural, God is permanently present in the world in the laws which direct his activity and which express his character; that is, he is immanent. As the supernatural, he transcends the world, as personality always transcends even its highest expressions.

While this view of the supernatural does not diminish the importance of the individual and the exceptional in which from the beginning the characteristic mark of divine communication has been found, it guards its recognition against abuse by indicating what are the kind of events to which such revealing significance really belongs. Instead of being those which most bear the impress of mystery and unreason, they are those which, by revealing permanent principles which later experience may confirm, serve most to bring order and unity into life. Hence, the supernatural must be sought, primarily, not in the physical universe but in the world of spirit. It is through personal experience that we discover the order and the beauty of the world, and the meaning and value of life. It is through great personalities that we gain our most direct access to the divine mind. It is in the personal life, therefore, that we find miracle in the religious sense.

The question of miracle in the religious sense has to do with those higher beginnings in which man is conscious of receiving new knowledge and life from God. It is at bottom the question of personal religion ; the question, that is to say, of the possibility, and of the marks, of personal communication between God and man. Wherever man is conscious of receiving new insight and power through communion with God we have miracle in the religious sense. If outward events are given supernatural significance, it is only because it is believed that through them such insight and power may come to men. Those physical phenomena only are called miracles in the religious sense which are either the means or the result of divine revelation.

If this view be true, it is evident that miracle must be a recurring element in every true religious life. The sharp line of demarcation drawn between the Biblical miracles and those of later ages is neither justified in theory nor established by experience. The New Testament writers give no hint of it ; the men of the second century were not conscious of it ; the Catholic church does not recognize it. Protestantism itself has broken with it in theory in its doctrine of the supernatural character of the present Christian life, and in practice in its recognition of special providences and answer to prayer. If God be the personal God whom Christ revealed, and we his children, it must be possible for him to speak to us to-day, and for us to hear him when he speaks. In like manner, if this world be our Father's house — the scene of his continued interest and care — it must be possible for us to recognize him by his present working, as well as by his works in the past. This is a conviction which is finding ever clearer expression in modern Protestant theology.[1]

But the recognition of miracle as a permanent element in religion no more means that all events which faith calls miracles stand on the same level of importance than the discovery that life is a perpetual creation means that all beginnings are of equal significance. In miracle, as in revelation, we must distinguish between what has merely individual and what has social significance. Some events speak to me alone. Others proclaim God's presence and love to many. Some experiences have significance only to the man to whom they came. Others date epochs in the history of the race. In this fact lies the justification for the distinction between the apostolic age and the ages which come after. The events and experiences which centre about Christ and the great creative personalities formed under his influence have a significance for faith which is not found in the same degree in those which come after.

This gives us the principles from which to approach the miracles recorded in the Bible. In order to interpret them rightly, several distinctions are necessary. There is, first, the critical question whether or no the event really happened as recorded. There is, secondly, the philosophical question whether the event, granting that it happened as recorded, is a miracle in the scientific sense. There is further the religious question as to the meaning of the event; whether the truth which it is designed to teach is primarily of individual and temporary significance, or whether it is of universal and permanent importance.

From the point of view of the older apologetic, an ad-

[1] Cf. Bushnell, *Nature and the Supernatural,* chapter XIV; Ritschl, *Instruction in the Christian Religion,* Eng. tr., p. 189.

verse answer to either of the first two questions would destroy the apologetic value of the miracle. This does not necessarily follow from the modern standpoint. The story of Jonah may be as truly a divine revelation if it be interpreted as a parable as if the events it records really took place in history. In like manner, the bringing under law of many events once thought to be miracles in the strict sense (*e. g.* the miracles of healing; the casting out of demons; the passage of the Red Sea, etc.) does not alter the fact that they were, and still are, means through which personal communication between God and man has taken place, and religious lessons of permanent value have been learned by mankind.

The distinction between the individual and temporary and the permanent and universal in miracle is important; partly because of the light which it sheds upon the interpretation of the Bible, partly because of its bearing upon the present Christian life. The events connected with God's training of Israel have for us the significance of revelation because they show the steps by which the way was prepared for his fuller revelation in Christ. But it does not follow that the conception of the relation between God and man which the earlier portions of the Old Testament assume is the highest we know, or that we should expect or seek in our own lives evidences of the same kind of divine interpositions as it records. We stand in the full light of Christ's revelation, and should test both past and present by the principles which he reveals. In his person we find God's clearest word to man — the miracle *par excellence.* The final proof that any particular event is really a communication from God to-day is the fact that it promotes or strengthens in men the type of character which we see in him.

PART IV

OF MAN AND HIS SIN

CHAPTER XV

THE CHRISTIAN IDEA OF MAN

THE changes already noted in connection with the Christian view of the world require a like reconstruction in the doctrine of man. In the older theology, both Catholic and Protestant, the treatment of this subject was divided into two sections of unequal length. Under the first, or *status integritatis*, was described the state of man before the fall as holy and upright; under the second or *status corruptionis*, his present condition as sinful and corrupt. This division has an experimental basis in the contrast between the divine ideal revealed in Christ and the facts of man's past and present life. But the form which it has assumed in the traditional theology is unhistorical, since it carries back to the beginning of history the full realization and fruition which are possible only at its close.[1] We no longer conceive the divine nature of man

[1] A Biblical basis for this conception of the primitive state as including holiness as well as freedom was found partly in Gen. i, 27, which speaks of man as made in the divine image (here interpreted as including the divine character), partly in such New Testament passages as Eph. iv, 24 ; Col. iii, 10, which speak of the new man in Christ Jesus as renewed in knowledge and holiness after the image of him that created him. But its real basis is to be found in an abstract conception of the divine perfection, which ignores the part played by progress in the divine providence, and conceives of all God's works as issuing from his hands complete and perfect from the first. From this point of view the differences which meet us in the history of the doctrine become easily intelligible. Where the ideal for man is conceived as one of free self-development, in obedience to an ethical law once for all revealed, as in the Greek, and later in the Arminian, theology, the primitive state is

as an endowment imparted once for all, but as a capacity to be progressively developed in history; and the godlikeness which our fathers carried back to the childhood of the race is transformed for us into the ideal toward which we are to strive in the future.

The bearing of this upon theological method is plain. Instead of seeking to reconstruct the primitive state of man, modern theology asks what light the Christian revelation has to shed upon his nature and destiny. In raising these questions it enters a field which is already tenanted, and deals with subjects (*e. g.* freedom and immortality) which have long engaged men's thought. Again, therefore, it becomes important to distinguish between the distinctive Christian message and the truths which Christianity shares with other faiths, as well as those philosophical and scientific theories on which Christians themselves may differ. Here, as everywhere in Christian theology, it will be found that what is distinctive centres in Christ. In him faith sees the revelation of man's true nature, the example to which he is to conform, and the pledge of that which he is one day to become. In the light of these convictions we have now to consider what is implied as to man's origin, constitution and destiny.

thought of as one of innocence rather than of positive holiness; and the divine image is found in the possession of the reason and freedom that make right choice possible. Where the ideal is thought of as union with God through the indwelling divine Spirit, as in the theology of Augustine and of the Protestant Reformers, the first creation is regarded as involving from the start the holiness which is the characteristic mark of the second. Where, still again, as in the Semi-Pelagian theology of modern Roman Catholicism, the true relation of man to God is conceived as realized through the addition of supernatural gifts to natural endowments, the primitive state is marked by a similar union of qualities, and salvation is thought of as man's recovery, by the right use of his freedom, of the supernatural graces lost by the fall.

1. *The Origin of Man.*

To Christian faith the origin and the destiny of man belong together. As the adaptation of the world to the Christian end evidences its divine origin, so the presence in man of Christlike capacities and ideals proves his kinship to the heavenly Father, from whom Jesus was conscious of having come forth. Indeed, as we have already seen, it is only when we include man that the evidence for the divine origin of the universe can be stated at its full force. Apart from man, we can prove at most the dependence and the order of the world. It is only when we reach humanity that we discover an all-embracing end that gives ethical and spiritual meaning to all the intermediate steps in the process. As it is personality through which alone we can conceive creation, so it is only through persons that we can interpret creation. This unique position of man as at once the consummation of the universe and its interpreter, we express by saying that he is not only the creature, but the child of God. As creature, he is a part of nature, sharing its finite and dependent existence. As child, he is raised above nature by the reason and freedom which he shares with God.

The judgment that man is the child of God applies both to humanity as a whole and to each individual in it. It is characteristic of Jesus that, even while recognizing to the full the sin which obscures the true relation between man and God, he discovered in the most degraded, spiritual capacities which render them capable of uplift and progress. These common spiritual capacities, the mark and proof of the brotherhood of mankind, Christian faith explains as due to their common origin as children of the same divine Father.

Historically, the recognition of the divine sonship of the individual comes later than that of the sonship of the social group. It is characteristic of primitive religion that man's relation to God is thought of as realized mediately through the family, the tribe, or the nation of which he is a member. Only comparatively late comes the recognition that the individual as such has a worth for God, and a right of approach to him, quite apart from the social group to which he may chance to belong. All the more significant is it that the religious teachers of Israel, with their profound conviction of Israel's special relation to Jehovah, should have held fast the doctrine of the divine origin and unity of the race. This truth, expressed in Genesis in the account of the descent of all mankind from a single pair, is the presupposition for the spiritual ideals of the great prophets who most nearly anticipate the universalism of Christianity. Implied by Jesus both in his teaching and example, it is given theoretical expression in the New Testament (*e. g.* Acts xvii, 26), and is made by Paul the foundation of his theological system (the two Adams). The missionary activity of the Christian church rests on the conviction that God has made of one all the people that dwell on the face of the earth, and, therefore, that, wherever the Christian message comes, it may be sure of finding response. This conviction, which finds expression in the fine saying of Tertullian that the soul is by nature Christian,[1] opened the way for the Gospel to the submerged masses for whom the spiritual philosophy of Greece had no message, and made Christianity, in the strictest sense, a universal religion. To the follower of Jesus, not the wise or the mighty or the virtuous alone is the child of God, but man as man.

[1] " *Testimonium animae naturaliter Christianae,*" Apologeticus, c. XVII.

The doctrine of a kinship between God and man, grounded in the nature of each as free and reasonable, is of fundamental importance for Christian theology. It gives the standard for measuring the significance of sin. It renders possible faith in man's ultimate conformity to God in character. It is the ground for hope in immortality. It is the presupposition of the Christian doctrine of incarnation. Jesus Christ, though very man, is able to reveal God, because there exists between man and his Maker a spiritual kinship which can best be expressed in terms of fatherhood and sonship.

The conviction that man owes his origin to God must be distinguished from the various theories which have been held from time to time as to the manner of that origin. As in the case of the doctrine of creation in general, so here, a distinction must be made between the religious, and the philosophical and the scientific interest. However important it may be for the philosopher and the man of science to answer the questions which may be asked as to the manner in which man came into existence, and as to his relation to the earlier races which preceded him, for the theologian they have only an indirect interest. Any view of the origin of man which is consistent with his divine sonship and immortal destiny satisfies the requirements of Christian faith.

So far as the race is concerned, science tends to alter the view previously held as to man's origin in two ways. On the one hand, it gives the human race an antiquity far greater than that attributed to it in the older chronology. On the other, it substitutes for the doctrine of a special creation an evolutionary theory which regards the transition between man and the lower races as having been made gradually, through the slow development, out of materials already existing in whole or in part, of the capacities and endowments which we now recognize as distinctively human.

This raises perplexing questions as to the relation between man and the animals, and may require the modification in some points of the traditional estimate of the latter.[1] Yet nothing that science has brought to light has rendered untenable the fundamental Christian convictions as to the unity of the human race, and as to the

[1] The evolutionary theory raises many interesting questions as to the relation of man to the lower animals. The main points of distinction are clear. In man reflective thought has attained a development elsewhere unknown, and reason largely supersedes instinct as a guide of life. Man alone has invented machinery, and increased the fertility of the soil through agriculture. Man alone has developed a language and literature, and embodied his ideals in enduring works of art which remain as the inspiration of future generations. Man alone seems capable of a progressive moral and religious training in which the experience of the past raises those who come after to ever higher levels. Yet, on the other hand, at many points the sharp line of demarcation seems broken down. As the zoölogist traces the history of man's physical structure by a study of the anatomy and physiology of the so-called lower orders, so the comparative psychologist finds in the conscious life of the higher animals the germs of much, perhaps of all, that we know later as ethics, esthetics, and even religion. How far these germs may develop and bear fruit outside of man we cannot say, since we have no direct means of observation. But their presence warrants a higher estimate of the possibilities of the animal creation than has hitherto been customary in Christian theology. The belief that animals as well as men have an independent spiritual existence and destiny has been held, in one form or another, by a considerable portion of the human race. And while, as found in connection with the doctrine of the transmigration of souls, this belief rests upon a theoretical basis for which the evidence affords slight support, it is yet possible that it may point to a truth for which Christian theology, with its recognition of the divineness of all life, may well make room. If the spiritual capacities of even the lowest man be ground for believing in his immortal destiny, why is it unreasonable to believe that the higher animals may have a continued existence and development after death? If, on the other hand, the significance of the animal creation is exhausted in its contribution to the production of man, it may be argued with equal plausibility of the less developed members of the human race that their true function is to be found in their ministry to the more advanced. This is the position actually taken by many advocates of the theory of conditional immortality.

spiritual capacity and divine destiny of its members. The truth of these must be determined, not by any theory of origins, either ecclesiastical or secular, but by a study of man as he is to-day. On this point Christianity, through its missionaries, has its own evidence to offer of the highest scientific as well as religious value. To the similarities of physical structure and mental endowment on which science bases its belief in the unity of the race, it adds the witness of a common religious nature, through which man becomes conscious of kinship with God, and which has rendered even the most backward and degenerate races open to the appeal of the Gospel.

So far as the origin of the individual is concerned, no single theory has found universal acceptance. Apart from the doctrine of the pre-existence of souls taken over by Origen from the Platonic philosophy, Christian theologians have been divided between the theories of creationism and of traducianism. According to the first, God creates a new soul for each individual, which at birth unites with the body produced by ordinary generation, to form the new personality. According to the latter, man in his totality, soul as well as body, is derived by heredity from his ancestors. The former, which has been on the whole the prevailing theory, is the most natural for those who emphasize human individuality and freedom; the latter, which goes back to Tertullian, and was given currency by Augustine, rests on a realistic theory of the unity of the race, and is used to explain the complete corruption of man which is assumed in the ecclesiastical doctrine of original sin. Each stands for an element in experience which we recognize to-day, and whose reconciliation forms one of the fundamental problems of philosophy. On the one hand, man is conscious of an individuality which separates him

16

from all others and gives him an independence and worth of his own. On the other, he is bound by ties of heredity to the race whose character and endowments he shares.

This double position of man, as at once individual and member of a race, affects theology in two ways. It determines both the nature of the Christian ideal, and the means by which this ideal is realized. As the end for which man was made is not simply the salvation of individuals, but the establishment of a redeemed society; so the means taken to bring about this end are social as well as individualistic in character. In God's training of men, heredity and environment are determining factors, and theology, seeking to understand the divine providence, faces racial as well as individual problems.

The importance of the questions thus indicated was early recognized by theologians. Centuries before Christ, we find Ezekiel wrestling with the problem of the relation of heredity to individual responsibility.[1] In Paul, the theologian of the New Testament, the inheritance of Adam's sin is assumed as a familiar fact, and is the background against which he sets his great conception of a race salvation through Christ, the second Adam. Later theologians, following Paul in his doctrine of inherited sin, have treated salvation as a matter entirely between God and the individual. Recognizing heredity as a channel for the propagation of evil, they have denied it any corresponding significance as an instrument of good. Thus, conceiving God's method more narrowly than the facts justify, they have necessarily arrived at an inadequate conception of the end which that method is designed to promote.

In treating of the kingdom of God, we have tried to show how the truth of individualism may find recognition

[1] Ezek. xxxiii, 1-20.

in connection with the larger social ideal. Here it is only necessary to add that, not only in connection with the doctrine of God's plan, but at every point in Christian theology, the double position of man, as individual and as member of a race, must be borne in mind. Much of the confusion and failure of theology is due to the fact that this distinction has been overlooked; and judgments and experiences properly applicable to man in one of these relations have been uncritically transferred to the other.

2. *The Constitution of Man.*

The constitution of man answers to his origin as at once the creature and the child of God. As creature, he is a dependent being, sharing the limitations of finite existence. As child, he is moral personality, contrasting himself as reasonable and responsible with nature, of which he seems a part; and, through freedom, conscious of dominion over it.

This double position of man, as at once a part of nature and a free spirit contrasted with nature, raises perplexing questions as to the constitution and elements of human personality. While most theologians take over from common experience the familiar division of man into body and spirit, a few, following the example of Plato, insert between body and spirit a third element, the soul, or principle of animal life, through which the spirit, or divine part of man, is brought into contact with the body, which is the seat of the sinful passions and temptations. This trichotomy, or threefold division, which has its origin in a dualistic philosophy, has slight support either in Scripture or experience, and affords no real help in the solution of the problems on which it is designed to shed light. For theology, as for science and common sense, the natural

division of man is still that into body and spirit.   How
far this division represents a permanent distinction in the
nature of man, essential to the continuance and full expression of human personality, we shall consider in connection with the doctrine of immortality.[1] Here it is
sufficient to say that according to the Christian view the
body as well as the spirit of man owes its origin to God;
and that the imperfection by which he is contrasted with
his Maker is due to his nature as finite and dependent
rather than to any limitation imposed upon his freedom by
contact with matter.

   The dependence of man appears both in his physical
constitution and in his spiritual nature.   The body of man
is a part of the physical universe, and subject to its laws.
Chemistry analyzes it into its elements, and physics and
biology formulate the laws which regulate its activity and
direct its growth.   All three are only the application to
the special case of man of principles already proved valid
in other spheres of existence.   Nor is dependence less
manifest in the spirit of man.   Here psychology and
religion unite in their testimony.   As spirit, man owes his
origin to a source outside himself, lives his life in
obedience to laws he did not make, and realizes his ideal
through submission to a higher authority from which he
is conscious of receiving all that is best in his experience.

   Yet the dependence of which man is thus conscious as
spirit differs radically from that to which he is subject as
a part of physical nature.   Spirit is the sphere of reason
and of freedom, which transform blind submission into willing acquiescence and intelligent service.   As the child of
God, man can understand the reason for the limitations to
which he is exposed, and, accepting them, can make them

[1] Cf. section 3, p. 258.

his own. There is all the difference in the world between the dependence of a slave and that of a son. The dependence of the Christian is of the latter kind. It is not the negation of freedom, but the condition of its realization.

While accepting this general view of the relation of man to God as true as far as it goes, many theologians have gone farther, and held that man's freedom involves, in part at least, a limitation of God's power. They believe that, through the faculty of choice, man is raised above his position of dependence, and given a power to the contrary, which, within the limits of its activity, renders him as much a first cause as God himself. While Arminian theologians, inheriting the Pelagian tradition, regard such freedom as an inalienable constituent of human personality, Calvinists, following Augustine, restrict its possession to Adam before the fall. With the reconstruction of the doctrine of the primitive state along the lines already considered, this restriction has become increasingly difficult to maintain; and the debate between Calvinist and Arminian in its traditional form has been merged in the larger question in dispute between determinist and libertarian. This has to do with the nature of personality. More especially it concerns the relation of will to character in moral choice.

The question of freedom in the libertarian sense is the question whether the self, to which at any time we refer our "deliberate volitions," is "a self of strictly determinate moral qualities" [1] or not; whether, in other words, in any particular choice a man's action is completely determined by his character (understanding under the term the nature which he has in part inherited from his parents and which has in part been formed by his own past choices

---

[1] Sidgwick, *Methods of Ethics*, 5th ed., London, p. 61.

under the influence of his changing environment); or whether he possesses in the will a power raising him above his character and enabling him "at will" to choose independently of it. The determinist adopts the former alternative; the libertarian, the latter. We may express the difference between the two by saying that to the moral freedom, given in consciousness, on which the determinist founds responsibility, the libertarian adds metaphysical freedom in the sense of power to the contrary. Moral freedom is found wherever a man, facing two or more alternatives, one of which appears to him to be morally right, is determined to his action by no cause without himself. Metaphysical freedom involves the power of man, at least at certain times, to lift himself above himself. The libertarian regards freedom in the first sense as necessarily carrying with it freedom in the second. The determinist regards freedom in the second sense as an illegitimate inference from freedom in the first.

This does not mean that the determinist regards character as something fixed and unchangeable. On the contrary, he recognizes that it is the subject of a constant development (or deterioration), in which choice, with its resultant judgments of praise and blame, is the determining factor. His contention is simply that this whole process of training takes place under law, so that, if we knew all the influences which enter into the making of any choice, we could predict its outcome with certainty. The libertarian, on the other hand, maintains that there is in all choice an unpredictable element; or, to put it in other words, that arbitrariness is an essential constituent of personality on its ethical side.

It is clear that we have to do here with two contrasted ideals of personality. The libertarian ideal is individualistic. He insists upon the uniqueness of each moral personality, and sees in every character an original moral creation. The ideal of the determinist, on the other hand, is social. He emphasizes the wider relations of humanity, finds the end of individual development realized only through union with other persons, and explains the origin and growth of character by the system of moral relations which has its most complete expression in society, and its ultimate source in God. The libertarian regards the relation between God and man as most adequately expressed in terms of probation and retribution ; the determinist in terms of education and of discipline. The persistence of these contrasted types through so long a time and over so wide an area would seem to show that we have to do with one of those ultimate differences of interpretation which, having their roots in permanent elements in experience, will doubtless endure so long as humanity lasts. Any decision, therefore, must be individual, and with full recognition of the rights of others' opinion.

The view of the relation of God and man to which we have been led, finds most adequate expression in terms of determinism. As God's perfection consists, not in the possession of arbitrary power, but in the consistency and unchangeableness of his moral character ; as man is not simply an isolated individual, but a member of a society of brothers to whom he is bound by manifold relations, and through contact with whom he is being trained for communion with and likeness to God ; so we must conceive the entire process of this training as taking place under the divine law and control. The instrument of this training is the moral consciousness with its sense of freedom and of obligation, of responsibility and of guilt. Through freedom, man is lifted above the sphere of blind necessity and opened to influences that are spiritual. But spiritual influences, as well as physical, are at God's disposal, and through the use of these he is certain to accomplish his end.

Such spiritual control by God is a very different thing from the fatalism with which it has often been identified. The doctrine that all phenomena may ultimately be resolved into some form of mechanical causation is the destruction not only of freedom, but of all moral and spiritual life. The determinism of religion has a very different root. It is an inference from the rational nature of man, — the expression of the insight that he realizes his true ideal in the measure that his choice ceases to be arbitrary, and becomes the expression of a consistent character.

What gives libertarianism its plausibility is the fact that in most men such consistency of character is not as yet attained. Much of our choosing is still arbitrary and irrational, and we face each new crisis in the moral life with uncertainty as to the outcome. This is an incident in the development of personality, — a necessary stage in the slow process through which the spiritual in man gains its supremacy over the animal. But it does not follow that the sense of power to the contrary which characterizes our present stage of imperfect moral development is to be regarded as the permanent form of the moral consciousness itself; or that we should put upon those early choices, which fall in the days of mankind's greatest ignorance and weakness, the whole weight of the burden of man's responsibility and guilt. However important may be the part played by individual choice in the formation of character, it is not the only factor to be considered. Responsibility and guilt, like the personality which they express, are, in a very true and deep sense, social creations; and through the whole complex process by which the sense of both is awakened and intensified, the unseen God whom Christ has revealed is ceaselessly at work. If the mature Christian can realize his true freedom only through complete dependence upon his heavenly Father, we may be sure that the all-wise and ever merciful God has not left his human child to totter the first feeble steps of his moral life alone.

This has been, on the whole, the final word of the greatest Christian theologians. Origen, the leading spokesman of the Greeks, made freedom the cornerstone of his system; yet he held that in endowing man with the power of choice God had knit a bond between creature and creator, which, in spite of all wanderings, was certain at last to bring the prodigal home. Divine sovereignty, even to the point of absolute predestination, has been the cornerstone of Augustinianism and of Calvinism, the dominant influences in Western theology. If, in these systems, an apparent exception is made in the case of our first parents through the admission, for a brief moment, of freedom in the libertarian sense, it is only that the holiness of God may suffer no compromise through the entrance of sin. Yet, in the assertion that Adam's sin was not beyond the control of God, both Augustine and Calvin recognize that the real problem involved in the origin of moral evil admits no such easy solution. The final theodicy is to be sought, not in a temporary exception to the method of God's government, but in a clearer revelation of his character, and so of the end which that government is designed to serve.

Here is the deepest significance of faith in Christ. In Christ we have at once the revelation of God's character and of the end which it is his purpose to realize in man. In Christ we see how through a life completely one with God sin and suffering may be made to serve the highest end. In Christ, with the ideal for man, we have given also the motives through which that ideal is finally to be realized.

3. *The Destiny of Man.*

The Christian view of man culminates in the doctrine of immortality. This doctrine, which must be clearly distinguished from belief in a life after death, has had an eventful history. Foreshadowed by the Hebrew hope of a resurrection, and the Platonic belief in the indestructibility of the higher spiritual nature, it takes its departure in Christian thought from the resurrection of Christ, and stands or falls with the conception of the relation of God and man which he has revealed. To the Christian, life after death is necessary, not simply for the satisfaction of human longings or for the vindication of the divine justice, but that God's fatherly purpose for his children may be realized through their complete conformity to Christ in the kingdom of glory.

There are three distinct forms of belief in a future life: (1) the expectation of continued existence in an under-world without moral distinctions; (2) the belief in a judgment after death, with its accompanying rewards and punishments; and finally (3) the philosophical conception of strict immortality, *i. e.* the inherent indestructibility of the soul, or, at least, of its higher portion. In the course of its history Christianity has met all three of these forms, and an understanding of their origin and significance will help to make clear wherein consists its distinctive contribution to the subject.

1. *Life after death in an under-world without moral distinctions.* Belief in man's continued existence after death is one of the most ancient and widespread of human convictions. Among primitive peoples it takes the form

of belief in the continued existence of the individual in an unsubstantial and shadowy form, as a ghost or shade. Much early religion takes the form of such ghost worship. Later, the dead are conceived as dwelling in the under-world, Hades, or Sheol, where they live a dreamy shadow life, without hope or joy, appearing to their more fortunate comrades upon earth at rare intervals and unwillingly. Such is the conception in the earliest Greek religion. Such the belief which prevails in much of the Old Testament.[1] Such is the view which still survives among many of the less civilized races with whom Christianity is brought into contact through her missionaries. Between this conception and the Christian idea of immortality there is in common only the fact of continued existence after death.

2. *Judgment after death.* It is otherwise with those views of the life after death which give it moral quality. Of these there are two main types: (a) that of the Egyptians, which makes the under-world the scene of a divine judgment for the deeds of this life, and conceives the state of the dead as happy or miserable accordingly; (b) that of the Persians, which associates the future life with a resurrection, and makes the triumph of the righteous take place in the same world which was the scene of their probation. Both find illustration in the history of Israel, but it is the second which is the earlier and more characteristic.[2]

The doctrine of individual resurrection first appears in

---

[1] E. *g.* Ps. vi, 5; xxx, 9; cf. Salmond, *Christian Doctrine of Immortality*, 2d ed., New York, 1896, pp. 200 sq.

[2] Still a third form of the retributive theory is found in the Eastern belief in transmigration. Here, judgment after death takes place upon the earth, but under conditions radically different; there is a resurrection, indeed, but it is to a new body, not the same.

Israel after the Exile, and may have been due to Persian influence. At first it is restricted to the righteous (*e. g.* Isai. xxvi, 19). But later (*e. g.* Dan. xii, 2) we have the doctrine of a double resurrection, both of good and evil. In the apocalyptic literature this double resurrection is made universal, and associated with the coming of Messiah and the establishment of his kingdom. It was one of the distinctive tenets of the Pharisaic party, and the hope of the most devout Israelites in Jesus' day. From the Jews it passed over to Christianity and furnished the form in which the Christian hope of immortality first found expression.

In judging the doctrine of the resurrection, we have to distinguish between its religious content and its historic form. The former is the assertion of the continued existence after death of the full human personality with all its powers, and is the fruit of the ethical and religious revival which led to the discovery of the independent significance and worth of the individual. The latter is the result of the primitive philosophy which regarded the possession of this body of flesh and blood as necessary to the full development and expression of personality. It is clear that these two convictions need not necessarily go together; but that, should it be concluded that the continuance of the personal life is not necessarily dependent upon the continued existence of the present body, the religious motive for holding the doctrine of the resurrection in its original sense would be removed.

This is, as a matter of fact, what we find taking place in the centuries immediately before our era, in connection with the doctrine of the intermediate state. The new conception of the value of the individual makes itself felt, not only in the hope of future deliverance from Sheol, but in a new conception of the conditions and significance of the life immediately after death. Sheol is no longer a place of dreary monotony, but of active moral life. As in the religion of Egypt, the under-world comes to be thought of as the scene of a divine judgment in which the souls of men receive retribution for the deeds done in the body. There is a Paradise where the good man rests in Abraham's bosom.[1] There are prison houses where the souls of the wicked are kept in bonds under darkness against the final destruction.[2] Thus, the rewards and punishments of the last day are anticipated in the life immediately after death. Comparing the Hades of Homer and of Plato, we find a similar transformation in the Greek religion.

This new conception of the life after death is accompanied by a corresponding modification of the idea of the resurrection. Instead of involving the restoration of the individual to the conditions of this present physical existence, it is thought of as the means by which he is furnished with an organism adequate to the needs of the higher spiritual world. A striking example of such reconstruction is Paul's doctrine in 1 Corinthians xv. Here the body which is raised is not this present body of flesh and blood, but a different body, — as different as the plant is from the seed from which it springs (cf. esp. vvs. 36–39).

In the light of this history we are prepared to understand the real significance of the resurrection of Jesus. This was not in its proof of the fact of a life after death (since men already believed in such a life before Jesus' resurrection); still less in any definite revelation of the nature and conditions of that life (as to this we find after

---

[1] Cf. Luke xxiii, 43, with xvi, 22.
[2] Jude 6.

the resurrection, as before, differences of interpretation);
but in the assurance it brought that Jesus was what he
claimed to be, and, hence, in the renewed confidence which
it made possible in his teaching, ideals and promises. This
note of confidence is one of the most striking characteristics
of the New Testament view of the life after death. What
was believed or hoped before, is now realized. The sense of
mystery and dread is gone. Jesus' presence in the unseen
world transforms it from an unknown country to the Father's
house, and makes death only the exchange of the sorrows
of earth for a well-known and beloved fellowship.

3. *Strict immortality*. This religious conception of immortality, based upon the personal relation between God
and his child, must be distinguished from immortality in
the philosophical sense, *i. e.* existence which is strictly
endless. The last was the contribution of Greek philosophy, and finds its best known expression in Plato.
According to Plato, the soul belongs to the ideal world
to which alone reality in the strict sense belongs. As
divine, it includes within itself the principle of life, and is
therefore indestructible. Like the atom of modern science,
it is one of the ultimate forms of being, neither derived
from anything else, nor capable of resolution into it.
Hence, on the one hand, its pre-existence, on the other, its
immortality. Through contact with Greek thought such
conceptions were introduced into Christianity, and profoundly modified the older and simpler beliefs which it had
inherited from Israel. By Origen's time, and largely
through his influence, the theoretical basis of Christian
belief had shifted, and natural immortality had become an
accepted Christian doctrine.

As adopted by Christianity, the Greek conception of
immortality was modified in two ways. Where Plato

restricted immortality to the higher qualities of the spirit, Christian theologians conceived it as a property of the soul as such, and hence as equally applicable to the evil and the good. Where Plato based it on an inherent quality of spirit as original and indestructible, hence involving pre-existence as well as post-existence, they regarded it as a divine endowment imparted to the soul at creation, and having a beginning in time. In this restricted sense of immortality *a parte post*, — existence for all men that is strictly endless, it became one of the fundamental assumptions of orthodox theology, and the foundation of its doctrine of endless punishment. It was one of the few truths which passed unquestioned in the rationalistic criticism of the eighteenth century.

All the different currents of thought thus distinguished meet in the traditional eschatology. From Israel it has inherited the idea of the resurrection ; from Greece the conception of natural immortality. With the primitive church it divides the life after death into two periods, the intermediate and final states ; but, unlike the early Christians, it concentrates its attention upon the former rather than the latter. This is true both of Catholic and Protestant, though in different ways. Both agree that in the intermediate state, the soul, though disembodied, is yet in full possession of self-consciousness and memory ; enjoying the bliss, or experiencing the woe, to which its previous conduct has determined it. The Catholic makes place in this intermediate state for a purgatory, — *i. e.* a place of purification and training, in which through suffering, either individual or vicarious, those souls whose guilt still remains either wholly or in part unatoned may be gradually purified and made ready for their final blessedness in heaven. Protestant theology, on the other hand, holds the doctrine of

instant sanctification (or punishment) at death.   Historically justified as a protest against the abuses of Catholicism,
the practical result of this doctrine has been to break down
the line of demarcation between the intermediate and final
states, and to destroy the independent significance of the
latter.   If at death, as the Westminster Confession teaches,
" the souls of the righteous, being then made perfect in
holiness, are received into the highest heavens, where they
behold the face of God in light and glory," while " the
souls of the wicked are cast into hell, where they remain in
torments and utter darkness " (xxxii, 1); it is difficult
to see what can be added to the blessedness of the redeemed, by " the full redemption of their bodies," for
which they still wait, or what remains still to be accomplished by " the judgment of the great day," for which the
wicked are " reserved."   Evidently, in this connection the
last judgment has come to have simply a forensic significance.   It is merely the public registration of a decision
which has long ago been put in force.   In like manner, the
advent, with the resurrection which it brings, so far from
being the centre of expectation and the turning-point of
history, is simply the final consummation of a process whose
issues have been determined long ago, and of whose fruits,
whether for good or evil, men are already largely in possession.   We have here one of those changes of emphasis, of
which the history of theology is full, where receding
thought leaves old phrases stranded, like seaweed on the
beach, long after the original interest to which they owed
their origin has passed away.

In our own day many causes have combined to weaken
men's belief in immortality.   The rise of the critical philosophy has discredited the realistic metaphysics which
furnished the theoretical foundation of the traditional view

of natural immortality. In the enlarged universe which modern science has brought to light, it seems presumptuous to single out so insignificant a creature as man for endless existence. Again, the increased prominence of the social ideal seems to many to render the fate of the individual a matter of subordinate importance; and in the service of the community and the race they find compensation for the loss of faith in their personal survival of death. Add to these the prevalence of an agnosticism which despairs of knowledge of any kind that goes beyond present experience, and it is not difficult to understand the reasons for the present "eclipse of faith."

Yet the causes which first led to the rise of the belief still exist, and are bound in time to make themselves felt. Still man is conscious of capacities and ideals for which the brief span of this present life admits no satisfaction. Still the sense of justice cries out for some adjustment of the inequalities which are so painfully manifest in the lot of men. Still the religious experience warrants hope that the communion which now exists between the soul and God is prophetic of larger fellowship to come. The enlarged view of the universe may serve to exalt, as well as to belittle, the significance of the being who is apparently its highest product. The self-forgetfulness and devotion engendered by modern social service render the lives of those who exemplify them not less but more worthy of continuance. The breaking down of a crude philosophy but prepares the way for a larger conception of nature, in which the spiritual capacities and experiences to which Christianity witnesses may find their home.

Under these influences we see the beginnings of a new effort to lay a scientific basis for the doctrine of immortality. Sometimes this takes its departure from the theory

17

of evolution, as in Mr. Fiske's suggestive little book on the *Destiny of Man.* Sometimes it takes the form of a systematic investigation of the evidence for the existence of a spirit world, as in the elaborate researches of the late Mr. Myers.[1] Still again, as in Professor James' recent Ingersoll lecture,[2] the point of view is psychological, and interest centres in the question whether self-conscious life, as we know it, necessarily requires the human brain for its organ. Under the influence of these and similar discussions we see theologians pressing back of the traditional eschatology to the facts of experience from which it took its rise, and asking anew what is the distinctive contribution of Christianity to this doctrine, and what the permanent Christian convictions as to the nature of existence after death, and the grounds on which we believe in it.

So far as the first point is concerned, we note a growing reserve. Theologians are not so ready as they once were to dogmatize about the conditions of the life after death. The changes which modern science has introduced into our idea of the universe, and especially into our view of the relation of the physical and the spiritual, are such that the earlier discussions as to the nature of the resurrection body have largely lost their meaning. It is enough to know that the historic doctrine expresses man's instinctive faith in the continuance of the human personality under conditions which will admit its full expression and development. In general, the tendency of modern thought seems to be to lay less emphasis upon the contrast between this life and the next, more upon their continuity. We believe that in a true sense the life to come carries on the

1 In his *Human Personality, and its Survival of Bodily Death*, New York, 1903.

2 *Human Immortality : Two Supposed Objections to the Doctrine*, Boston, 1898.

life begun here, and that the principles which control God's government here extend their sway beyond the grave. Thus, the shifting of interest which we have already noted from the second advent to the life immediately after death is theoretically justified. The final state denotes rather the form in which we express our faith in the ultimate and complete realization of the Christian ideal than the introduction of any new and radically different conditions of existence. As death means for the Christian going to be with Christ and the company of his disciples who have gone before, so heaven means the gathering of all mankind into a society in which Christlike principles shall be everywhere and always controlling.

Even more important than the question of the conditions of life after death is that of the evidence upon which the belief in such a life rests. It is here that we find the distinctive contribution of Christianity. Science may help us to answer the various arguments which may be brought against the *possibility* of a life after death ; but only the new sense of the value of personality which Christ has brought can assure us of the *fact*. This is a truth which has been emphasized by the recent discussions of conditional immortality. In many of its statements (*e. g.* in its indeterministic view of the will, and in its practical denial of the unity of the race) the theory is open to just criticism. But in shifting the discussion of the grounds of immortality from such abstract considerations as the simplicity of the soul to the moral and spiritual qualities in which consists man's kinship to God, it has rendered a real service, and restored the emphasis to the place where Jesus himself put it, when he based his confidence in his own victory over death upon his experience of sonship.

It is in this experience of sonship that we find the one

sure support of faith in immortality. No less experience gives the individual life dignity and worth enough to warrant the expectation of its endless continuance. The world may perish ; God can make other worlds to take its place. But what " other " can take the place of a son in the Father's heart ? Here, as always, we turn back to Christ. It is impossible to believe that such a life as his should have gone out in darkness. Our own hope of endless existence is wrapped up with the faith that we too may become like Christ.

CHAPTER XVI

THE CHRISTIAN ESTIMATE OF SIN

THE same experience which reveals to man his ideal as son of God and heir of his kingdom shows him also his failure to realize it; or, in theological language, convicts him of sin. The nature of this conviction, as well as its origin and significance, we have next to consider.

1. *The Sources of the Christian Estimate of Sin.*

The word "sin" has both a moral and a religious meaning. It denotes an offence against God. It is evident, therefore, that the view of what constitutes sin at any time will be determined, partly by the prevailing ethical standard, partly by the dominant conception of God. In highly developed religions like Judaism and Christianity, where God is identified with the supreme moral principle, sin includes all forms of moral evil. In primitive religions, where the gods are conceived as limited beings, exercising a sway over but a part of life, this is not the case. Here sin is but a species within the genus "moral evil." It denotes that class of offences which is against the gods, even as crime denotes that class of offences which is against man. While all sin is wrong, not all wrong is sin. This distinction, theoretically overcome in Christianity, still maintains itself in practice in the separation of a class of offences as religious in the narrow sense from those acts which are forbidden by the wider moral code which has to do with matters secular. [1]

---

[1] We have here one root of the well-known distinction between the ceremonial and the moral which plays such a rôle in our estimate of early religion.

As a moral term the meaning of sin is affected by all the changes in contemporary ethical philosophy. The questions already considered as to the nature of freedom and responsibility necessarily affect men's judgment as to the nature and significance of sin. Still more important in their effects upon theological doctrine are the changes in contemporary ethical standards produced by the changing political and economic environment. The history of theology is in large part the record of the differences of interpretation to which these varying influences have given rise. All the more important is it in our survey of the doctrine to distinguish its experimental basis from its theoretical development; and, within the latter, that which is the distinctive contribution of Christianity from the wider questions to which this contribution has given rise.

The experimental basis of the Christian doctrine of sin is found partly in the facts of the individual moral consciousness, with its sense of wrong-doing and guilt; partly

What we call a ceremonial as distinct from a moral offence is an offence whose nature is exhausted in its relation to God, considered as an individual having rights of his own, as distinct from his interest in the maintenance of the common system of rights as between man and man, through which society consists, and which forms the subject of ethics commonly understood. The reason why, for us, the ceremonial elements in religion have fallen away, or become mere symbols of spiritual relations, is that our conception of God as an individual, asserting his own rights as against others, has so largely given place to that of the moral governor whose will is expressed in the entire system of moral relations which he has established; or, better still, of the Father whose personal satisfaction is so intimately related to the welfare of his children that he cannot be acceptably approached through any form of service which ignores their needs. Looking back from this vantage ground upon early religious ethics, we discard many of its provisions as merely ceremonial, *i. e.* temporary and symbolic. But from the standpoint of the early codes this distinction did not exist, since they had not yet attained the idea of God which it presupposes. The ceremonial laws were as essential as the moral; nay, if possible, even *more* essential, since they expressed the special claims of God, as an individual, upon men's service, as distinct from the divinely authorized claims of their fellows.

in a study of the history of mankind, which shows that this sense is not a temporary or isolated phenomenon, but a constant element in human experience, and a necessary condition of social as well as individual judgments; but above all, in personal contact with Jesus Christ, in whose holy and loving character man recognizes his true ideal, and by contrast to whom the true nature of sin is disclosed.

As a theological doctrine, the Christian conception of sin has its most direct preparation in the history of Israel. Here we find (1) the combination of the moral and the religious estimate of sin; (2) the inclusion, within the divine requirement, of right ethical relations between man and man, together with the development of the fundamental principles by which those relations should be determined; (3) the extension of the conception of sin beyond individual acts to include the nature and disposition from which they spring; (4) the recognition that this nature is not due wholly to the man himself, but goes back by inheritance to his parents; together with its corollary, that sin has social as well as individual significance; (5) the extension of this social judgment to include mankind as a race, with the corresponding judgment of its universal and all-pervading character; (6) the conviction that, while sin in all its forms, social as well as individual, is evil, deserving and certain to receive punishment, it is yet not beyond the control of God, but is destined ultimately to be overcome by him and brought to nought.

The distinctive contribution of Christianity to the doctrine of sin lies less in the disclosure of any new truth about it than in the new realization produced by contact with Christ of the significance of the sin of which men were already conscious. This reacted upon the older statements and

gave them a deeper meaning. In Christ men saw the revelation of the life they ought to be leading, and so were able
more clearly to measure their departure from the divine
ideal. Through him they gained an insight into the
character and purpose of the God against whom sin is an
offence, and hence were brought to perceive how inadequate
were the external standards by which they had sought to
measure the divine requirement. In particular, Christ's
doctrine of the love of God forced men's thoughts back of
all that was outward and temporary to the inner springs of
character, and so reinforced the tendency to regard the entire
nature of man as sinful which we have found characteristic
of the later thought of Israel. Still further, Christ's
teaching concerning the kingdom of God as a society of
brothers united in mutual love and service, and, above
all, his practical exemplification of these principles in his
dealings with others, intensified his disciples' sense of the
essential selfishness of society as at present organized, and
so reinforced their belief in its radical evil. Finally,
the new insight gained into the blessedness of the religious life rendered more dreadful the thought of failing to
attain it, and tended to turn men's thoughts from the
more external conceptions of penalty prominent in the
earlier history of Israel to the more spiritual view which
finds the supreme penalty in separation from God and
exclusion from his kingdom. The effect of all these
influences combined was to produce in the early Christians
a conviction of sin deeper and more intense than the world
had yet known, and to make redemption from *sin*, as distinct from suffering in all its forms, the supreme blessing of
the Gospel.

This deepened consciousness of sin had as its result an
increased interest in the problems connected with its origin,

its continuation and its final destiny. These problems had already begun to engage the attention of Jewish theologians. While some were content to explain the universality of sin as due to an inherent bias to evil in man's nature, others found its explanation in Adam's fall. The connection between Adam's fall and that of his descendants is reaffirmed by Paul in Romans, and through him has passed to the Christian church. While the Greeks thought of sin primarily as corruption, the Latins, following Augustine, emphasized its ethical character as guilt. Augustine conceived sin as inherent ethical corruption affecting man's whole nature, and from him the conception of original sin as inherited guilt passed over to the Reformers, and became a part of the theological tradition of orthodox Protestantism.

The changes already noted in the modern view of the world have modified the older conception of sin in various ways. Instead of regarding sin abstractly as infinite evil which is everywhere and always the same, modern theology seeks to indicate its psychological conditions, to trace the steps in its historic development, and to distinguish the various forms which it assumes among men to-day. Above all, it discriminates more clearly than did the older theology between the individual aspect of sin as personal blameworthiness and its social aspect as alienation from the kingdom of God. What is the bearing of these changes upon the theological formulation of the doctrine, we have now to inquire.

2. *The Christian View of the Nature of Sin.*

Like all ethical terms, the word "sin" has two aspects which we may distinguish as the formal and the material. By the formal element, we mean that element in sin which is present in every sinful act or state and which constitutes it sin. By the material element, we designate the positive standard by which at any time moral conduct is judged. The formal element is constant, and consists in the fact that in sinning man is doing that which he ought not, because it is contrary to the will of God. The material element is variable, depending partly upon the outward environment, partly upon the degree of ethical insight which has been obtained.

That which is distinctive in the Christian view of sin, on its formal side, grows out of the Christian view of the relation between God and man. Since man is the child of the Father God, sin is not merely transgression of law, but failure to realize man's true nature, through lack of conformity (either wilful or unconscious) with the fatherly will which seeks the highest good of his children.

This explains why the Christian ethics is so much concerned with the inner spirit and disposition of men. When it comes to the most intimate and sacred of human relationships purpose counts for more than act. With neighbors and acquaintance we are content to look upon outward appearances. If they do all that custom requires, we are satisfied. But with those we love it is another matter. In their case we press back of the outward act to the loving thought which prompts it, and value the former only so far as it is an index of the latter. If then God judge us by our motives, it is the highest honor he can show us. It proves to us that he looks upon us not as servants, but as sons; and so is unwilling to be satisfied with less than a filial service.

This explains further why unbelief (*i. e.* lack of trust), should hold the prominent place it does in the Christian catalogue of sins. Trust lies at the root of every true personal relationship. Without it spiritual fellowship cannot exist. A trustful attitude, therefore, is the first condition of right relation between man and God.

It follows that no attempt to express the nature of sin in terms that are external and legal can be satisfactory. While law (in the sense of external statute) is one of the means which God uses in man's moral training, it is not the highest or truest category for expressing his relation to man ; and any theory which attempts to solve the problems involved in punishment and redemption by its means alone is certain to fail.

On the material side, sin presents itself to the Christian as any failure to realize the ideal which Christ has revealed. For the individual this is a character like that of Christ ; for mankind, the organization of society according to his principles and in his spirit (*i. e.* the kingdom of God).

That which gives the character of Christ its uniqueness is its complete unselfishness. By this is meant not merely that his life was marked by the suppression of selfish desires and impulses through a sense of duty to others, but that he found his true self realized in ministry to others, and his highest happiness in the outgoing sympathy which made their needs and sorrows his own. For the individual to be perfect as Christ is perfect means that he must love men as Christ loved them. For society to realize the ideal of his kingdom means that Christlike love must characterize all human relationships.

Nor is this ideal valid only for man. It is true of God, as well, that his moral perfection consists in his outgoing love. It follows from the Christian conception of the kinship between God and man that to the extent to which man realizes his own true ideal as man he is at the same time growing in likeness to God. Hence the ethical precept, " Realize your own true nature, as Christ has revealed it," may equally well be stated in the language of religion, " Be ye perfect, even as your heavenly Father is perfect."

In the character of Christ as unselfish love we have to do with a standard once for all revealed, yet whose full significance is only gradually apprehended in the light of enlarging experience. This is due partly to the nature of man as a growing and developing being ; partly to the fact that the environment in which the ethical life is lived is changing. As an individual, Christ was limited by the conditions of his environment, ethical as well as intellectual. He could and did show men what the life of perfect unselfishness involved for a Jew at the beginning of our era who was conscious of having received a divine call to his unique work. But he could not, and he did not, anticipate the application of his principles to the new conditions and environment which later ages would bring. That application he left for his followers, as they should grow in insight and experience under the guidance of the divine Spirit. The history of Christian ethics is the history of the effort to apply the ethical principles of Christ to the new practical problems which the new generations bring, even as the history of Christian theology is the history of the effort to apply the religious principles of Christ to the corresponding intellectual problems.

The progressive apprehension of the Christian standard may be observed both in the case of individuals and of society. It is not those who are just beginning the Christian life who feel their own unworthiness most deeply, but those who are most advanced. The explanation is simple. They have come to apprehend the Christian ideal more clearly than their neighbors and, for that reason, judge themselves by a stricter standard. The better a man becomes, the more distinctly he perceives what he ought to be, the less he is satisfied with what he is. Thus progress in the individual Christian life is characterized by a continual revision of the ethical standard.[1]

Something analogous may be seen in the development of social standards. The ethical progress of society is marked by the extension of the judgment of moral disapproval to practices and conditions which have hitherto been regarded as ethically right or, at least, indifferent (*i. e.* slavery, polygamy, cruelty, wage slavery, etc.). This criticism of existing codes is the result of an awakened social conscience which has come to apprehend more clearly what is involved in the principles of Christian brotherhood, and to feel more profoundly the extent to which society, as at present organized, fails to realize them. The self-condemnation which results is not a mark of social deterioration, but of social progress.

Thus it appears that the sense of sin, whether individual or social, is not a passing phase of Christian experience, but a permanent feature of it, and a necessary accompaniment of Christian progress. Nothing more hopeless can be said either of an individual or a society than that it has lost its sense of sin. Here, as always, Christ is the great example. He was the perfect man, and for this very reason the one whose perception of sin was clearest, and whose judgment of it was most uncompromising.

But because the sense of sin is a necessary element in true Christian living, it does not follow that the form in which that sense expresses itself will always be the same. To expect of men in general the feeling of total unworthiness which was regarded as a normal accompaniment of con-

[1] Catholic theology recognizes this difference in its doctrine of a double ethics It judges the candidate for sainthood by a stricter standard than that which it applies to the common man

viction in some forms of the older theology, is to ignore the
working of psychological laws ; and the effort to produce
such a type of experience in the young, as practised by the
great revivalists of an earlier day, often resulted in serious
harm.   Such conviction as we find in an Augustine or a
Paul is a mark of unusual ethical sensitiveness, and presupposes a long moral training.   It is natural only in a
man who enters Christianity in mature life after long experience of non-Christian living.   In the normal Christian
life the sense of sin is a gradual development, the result of
a growing understanding of the Christian standard ; and
should be accompanied always by a corresponding insight
into the grace of God, which robs the discovery of its
terrors by pointing out at the same time the way in which
sin may be overcome.[1]

Nor does it follow that the intensity of a man's sense of
sin is to be measured by the extent of his consciousness
of personal ill-desert.   The great importance attributed
to this consciousness in the older theology was a result of
an exaggerated individualism, in which the saving of his
own soul was regarded as the all-important aim of man.
But, if the test of moral progress be conformity to Christ,
it may well be that the sense of personal guilt is not the
only, or the highest, form which conviction of sin may
take.   It is possible for a man to be so concerned about the
needs of his fellows as to lose all care for himself ; to be
willing even, with the apostle, to be anathema if thereby
his brethren may be saved.   Such loss of thought of self
in concern for others' welfare may well be more pleasing to
God than the most intense desire for individual salvation.
From this point of view, the abandonment of the intense

[1] This is the truth for which Bushnell contended so ably in his *Christian Nurture.*

individualism of our fathers for the wider view-point which finds its chief interest in the promotion of social righteousness, and its chief concern in the persistence of social wrong, is not wholly cause for regret. The one thing intolerable to the Christian conscience, and inconsistent with the spirit of the Master, is acquiescence in things as they are; whether acquiescence take the form of approval, or of indifference, or of despair.

In the light of what has been said we are prepared to understand the Christian affirmation of the universality of sin. This is not simply the affirmation of universal moral disorder, though it involves this, and is confirmed by the facts that establish it. It is the interpretation of this disorder in the light of the Christian standard. It is the assertion that there is in mankind as a whole, as well as in each of its members, the capacity, through progressive apprehension and appropriation of the Christian standard, to enter upon that experience of sin which is now found only in Christians, and in them imperfectly; but whose full development, both in individuals and in society, with the self-condemnation and repentance to which it leads, is the necessary condition for the victory of Christ's principles and the full establishment of his kingdom.

To sum up: By sin in the Christian sense we understand any lack of conformity with or disobedience to the will of the Father God, whether on the part of the individual or of the race. Since God desires the union of all men in Christlike love, service and worship, the supreme sin is selfishness; that is, the preference, from motives of self-indulgence, of any lower end to the kingdom of God.

3. *The Christian View of the Origin of Sin.*

There are two senses in which the question as to the origin of sin may be raised. The first is psychological.

How does the *consciousness* of sin arise? The second is metaphysical. What is the ultimate explanation of the facts of consciousness themselves?

The answer to the first is comparatively simple. Psychologically, sin begins with the misuse of freedom. It first makes its presence known through an act of the will in which man, being tempted, chooses evil rather than good. It has its antecedents, both inward and outward, in a nature capable of being tempted, and the temptation which makes the appeal. But it is not known and judged as sin till after the personal appropriation which manifests itself in choice.

We have, then, three elements which enter into the genesis of sin as a conscious experience, — a nature capable of being tempted, the temptation appealing to that nature, and the yielding of the will to the temptation. This is the way sin begins in the life of the individual to-day. So we must conceive it to have begun in the life of the race.

The great significance of the third chapter of Genesis lies in the fact that it sets forth in classic form the elements which are present in every sinful beginning. There is the temptation coming to man, as it always does, from without, but appealing to that which is within. There are the natural impulses and desires upon which it lays hold and in which it finds its strength, physical appetite (" good for food "), esthetic sensibility (" a delight to the eyes "), intellectual ambition (" to be desired to make men wise "). There is finally the yielding of the will to the temptation, and its consummation in an outward act. The account is all the more instructive because the transgression is not represented as wholly deliberate and wilful. It includes an element of self-deception which is most true to human experience.[1] It is only when the deed is done, and its consequences are faced, that its full significance is realized, and the judgment of self-condemnation and guilt follows.

The psychological analysis of the genesis of sin leads inevitably to the metaphysical question which lies back of it. This has to do with the relation of sin considered as a subjective experience to its antecedents, both inner and outer. Here we find three main theories, each of which takes its departure from one of the elements in experience which our preceding analysis has disclosed. The first finds the explanation of sin in the nature of man as a finite and limited being. The second seeks its origin without man, in the temptations which come from evil spirits, already living in opposition to God. The third finds its sufficient explanation in the nature of the will, with its God-given power of choice.

According to the first view, sin is not so much positive evil, due to deliberate choice, as failure on man's part to rise to the higher levels for which his spiritual nature and capacity fit him. It has its explanation partly in the limitation of man's knowledge which prevents him from perceiving his true ideal ; partly in the survival of earlier tendencies and habits, inherited from the animal creation from which he is sprung. These tendencies are in themselves entirely legitimate and necessary, but, if persisted in beyond the proper time, they become hindrances to progress, and so evil. Progress takes place through the gradual emergence of the spiritual in man, and its growing victory over the animal ; and the sense of sin is the consciousness which accompanies the process. So defined, sin is a neces-

---

[1] Cf. verse 1, " Yea, hath God said ? " with verse 4, " Ye shall not surely die."

sary stage in the evolution of humanity, — an essential element in God's training of mankind for higher things.

The strength of this view lies in the fact that the impulses to which temptation appeals, and in which it finds its strength, are, in themselves considered, innocent and legitimate. There is no sin which is not the exaggeration or perversion of some good. The weakness of the explanation consists in its failure to do justice to the positive aspect of moral evil. As known in consciousness, sin is not simply failure to attain the good, but often wilful choice of the evil. This positive aspect of sin is expressed by the word "temptation." When we speak of yielding to temptation we take for granted a world in which moral evil has already found its embodiment in other personalities through whom its appeal comes to us. To sin is not simply to remain on the plane of animal existence. It is to join the company of the wicked who are now living in active opposition to right. Without this environment of social evil, sin, as we know it to-day, could not exist. This is the fact of experience from which dualistic theories take their departure.

Strictly speaking, dualism is not a theory of the origin of evil. It is rather the denial that evil has any origin. Sin is made an ultimate fact incapable of further derivation. From the beginning the world has been the scene of the strife of rival powers, the evil and the good. Over against Ormuzd stands Ahriman warring against him, and seeking to defeat his purpose. Before Adam fell, sin existed in the angelic world, and from the devil, who was already in rebellion against God, came the temptation through which sin entered humanity.

The dualistic theory runs so counter to the prevailing tendencies of modern thought, and the forms in which it has found historic embodiment are many of them so fanciful and unreasonable, that it is easy to overlook the truth for which it stands. This is the fact that sin, as we know it to-day as conscious and deliberate, requires for its existence a social environment in which rival ideals shall be embodied, and out of which arise the temptations which play so prominent a part in the psychological genesis of sin. What is true of sin to-day dualism regards as always true, and founds thereon its conclusion as to the limitation of God's power in the world.

The third theory, or that of metaphysical freedom, has its origin in the effort to hold fast the absolute antithesis between good and evil, for which dualism stands, without giving up the ultimate sovereignty and control of God. According to this view, all sin, whether in angels or men, has its origin in the divinely implanted power of choice. As such, it cannot be explained by its antecedents, either external or internal. It is an absolute beginning, the one thing perfectly new under the sun.

We have already considered the theory of metaphysical freedom and seen the philosophical difficulties to which it is exposed. Bare will, apart from nature and environment, can as little create evil as these alone apart from will. Such an abrupt change as is posited in the theological doctrine of the fall is psychologically inconceivable. It makes man mightier than God, since in a single instant of time he has been able to accomplish what all the centuries of divine activity have been unable to undo. The difficulty of conceiving such an absolute beginning, in a world elsewhere everywhere characterized by limitation and relation, has been so keenly felt by some modern thinkers (*e. g.* Kant, Julius Müller), that they have sought to escape it by carrying the act of choice on which responsibility is made to depend back of all experience, and putting it in a noumenal world where conditions known to us here no longer obtain. But this is really to abandon all hope of solution, and to renew the old position of dualism in a more abstract and less defensible form.

None the less is it true that this theory, like both its predecessors, has its roots in experience. It stands for the fact that, whatever else may be necessary to account for sin, whether of inward tendency or outward environment, it becomes known and judged as sin only through that self-identification of the person which is revealed in choice. Apart from persons who choose, sin can have no existence ; and when we speak of it in the abstract and spell it with a capital S it is only a convenient way of denoting the sum total of all wrong choices together with the complex influences which have produced them and the manifold effects to which they have given rise.

Thus, from the philosophical point of view, no single explanation of the origin of sin is satisfactory. Each contains an element of truth which must find recognition in any comprehensive theory. The evolutionist is right when he finds the occasion for sin in the strife between the higher and the lower in man, taking place necessarily in the course of human development. The dualist is right when he calls attention to the part played by social influences in the genesis of sin, and his denial of the adequacy of any purely individualistic explanation. Historic theology is right in its contention that neither the animal nature nor the social environment are of themselves enough to account for sin. In the secret places of the human spirit takes place the strange change by which the non-moral is transformed into the immoral. We face here a mystery which we cannot explain, yet may not deny. It is the mystery of all beginnings, neither greater nor less.

It is not, then, in the region of philosophical speculation that we must look for the distinctive contribution of Christianity to the problem of sin; but rather in such dealing with the practical questions it presents as to make it possible to believe that a world in which it has a place may owe its origin to the good God whom Christ reveals, and may minister to the end he came to promote. This estimate Christ made possible, neither by reducing sin to illusion, as is the case in the pantheistic theodicy, nor by accepting it as final, as is done by dualism; but rather by revealing it for the first time in its true nature as an offence against the loving Father who ever seeks the highest good of his children, and in whose love, supremely manifested in Christ, is found the ground for faith that sin shall finally be overcome.

4. The Christian view of the Consequences of Sin.

The consequences of sin may be variously described according to the point of view from which it is regarded. Looked at from the moral point of view, sin issues in guilt; from the religious point of view, in estrangement; from the point of view of man's own character and habits, in depravity; from that of the divine government, in penalty.

It is clear that these terms emphasize aspects of the conception of sin which need to be clearly distinguished. Guilt and penalty are primarily legal terms and express man's relation to God considered as source and guardian of the moral law. Depravity is an ethical term, and describes the inherent evil of sin considered as a permanent habit or tendency. Estrangement is a personal word, and calls attention to the separation which sin effects between the divine Father and his child. Much confusion has resulted in theology from failing to distinguish these uses, and applying to one aspect of sin a term properly applicable only to another.

The difficulty is aggravated by the fact that in dealing with the effects of sin we cannot confine our thought to individuals, but must include its social consequences as well. As sin has a social as well as an individual origin, so its consequences affect society as well as the particular men and women who compose it. And this is true from whatever point of view we regard it.

The most obvious illustration of the social consequences of sin is furnished by depravity. By this term theologians designate that state of acquiescence in or subjection to evil which is the result of a long course of wrong action in the past. In the case of the individual, it is only the application to moral conduct of the familiar law of habit. What we have once done, we tend to do again, and with each doing it becomes easier. What at first cost effort, struggle, suffering, becomes at last natural, pleasant, almost inevitable. The deterioration which results from such persistence in evil affects all sides of the moral nature. The perceptions are blunted, and fail to respond to the Christian standard when presented. The feelings lose their sensitiveness, and are not easily stirred to enthusiasm for good. The will is weakened, and no longer responds to the call of duty. At last it seems as if the very capacity of doing right had gone. It is this aspect of sin which is described in the Bible in the familiar figures of blindness, darkness, hardening, bondage, death.

The tendency of sin to perpetuate itself may be observed also in society. Both through direct inheritance and through the environment which it creates, its consequences extend beyond the individual and affect those who come after. So far as it is evil the present character of society is the resultant of a multitude of influences, having their origin, many of them, in a remote past. Only in small part can the wrong which it contains be accounted for by the choices which fall within the conscious experience of its living members. Back of these lies an inheritance of social evil, reaching back to the beginnings of human history, and making itself felt in every age and in every relation of mankind. This is the fact of experience which lies at the basis of the doctrine of the fall.

Under the name of " inherited corruption " all theologians (except extreme Pelagians), recognize this sinful inheritance. They differ, however, as to its extent and its significance. While some make inherited depravity total, others regard it as only partial. While some consider it as guilty, others deny that guilt can properly be ascribed to it. Reserving, for the present, the latter question, a few words may be said on the former.

The doctrine of total depravity has often been misunderstood. Even in its extreme form [1] it is not the assertion that all men without exception are totally depraved; but only that they are so apart from God's Spirit. It is the picture of mankind which results when all the influences for good which we associate with divine grace have been thought away. As such, it has a real significance, as indicating the consequences to which an unrestrained indulgence in sin must inevitably lead. It is a reminder of the hidden capacities for evil which are present in even the best and purest of men, and a warning of the dangers to which we are exposed when, yielding to temptation, we turn away from the uplifting influences with which divine love surrounds us.

The difficulty with the historic doctrine is that it has

---

[1] *E. g. West. Conf.,* IX, 3; VI, 2, 4.

not been content to stop there. It has coupled with the assertion that man, apart from God, is wholly evil, the further statement that God has arbitrarily left a portion of mankind to themselves. The working of the Spirit has been confined to a narrow circle within the historic church, and the rest of mankind have been regarded as utterly devoid of spiritual life. The inheritance of evil has been matched by no corresponding inheritance of good ; and the virtues to which non-Christian history witnesses have either been denied or explained as mere devices to render the world more tolerable for the elect.[1]

Fortunately the facts of life do not bear out the restriction. The same heredity which is the channel of evil influences may be and is the means of transmitting the good. In spite of Antony, the good that men do lives after them, and the social evil which is typified under the natural headship of Adam has its counterpart in the social redemption which culminates in Jesus Christ.[2]

By depravity, then, we designate not so much a state as a tendency, present in some degree in all men, even the best ; varying in intensity according to the various stages of progress in the Christian life ; complete in those only (if such there be) in whom the working of the divine Spirit has wholly ceased ; wholly to be overcome only when the motives which influence men to good shall have gained such complete control as to make wrong conduct a moral impossibility.

From the Christian point of view the significance of depravity consists in the fact that to the extent to which it is controlling, it separates man and God. In the case

[1] Cf Cálvin, *Institutes*, Bk. II, c. II, 16 ; c. III, 3, 4 ; (vol. I, p. 318 ; pp. 339–341).

[2] 1 Cor. xv, 22 ; Rom. v, 20. Cf. Rom. vii, 19, with Rom. viii, 1.

of the individual this estrangement shows itself in the absence of that sympathy, trust and love, which is the characteristic mark of the true religious life. In the case of society it appears in the whole system of relations and influences which owe their existence to selfish impulses, and are designed to minister to their gratification. It is especially manifest in the widespread acceptance of the doctrine that the gratification of the individual desire is the highest law, and the dismissal as visionary and impracticable of any attempt to apply Christ's principle of self-sacrificing love to the solution of social problems. To the extent to which society is permeated by such principles, it is estranged from God, and constitutes a rival kingdom, controlled by interests and seeking ends of its own.[1]

It is the fact that we are surrounded by such an environment that makes temptation so hard to overcome. If we stood alone in our self-seeking, we should soon weary of it. But we are not alone. We are members of a great company, bound together by common pursuit of pleasure; supporting and encouraging one another in resistance to the higher voices which bid us deny ourselves for others' sake. This is what makes sin so tempting. It appeals to the social side of our nature, and finds excuse for its gratification in that which is itself good. To escape its dominion it is not enough to realize our individual relation to God. We must exchange our environment for one in which different influences are controlling. Indeed, we cannot do the first without the second.

Here is where Christianity meets us at our deepest need. In the kingdom of God it presents us with the new environment we need. Through contact with Christ, and the men and women who have been touched by his

---

[1] Cf Ritschl, *Justification and Reconciliation*, Eng. tr., III, p. 338 sq.

spirit, it shows us what the life of sonship to God really means. For the first time we become conscious of the significance of the life of selfishness which we have been leading; and the *sense* of estrangement which results is the first step in that turning of the soul to God which puts an end to estrangement as a *fact*.

CHAPTER XVII

1. *Guilt and Penalty.*

FROM the point of view of the divine government sin is judged as guilt, and is followed by penalty. It is in the interpretation and application of these terms that we find the most serious differences among theologians.

Guilt is a legal term which in the course of its history has acquired a moral meaning. The word originally meant debt; then the state of a man who was liable for debt. Later it was extended to cover any breach of law, and came to mean crime, and so the state of a man who had committed crime. A guilty man is one who has broken law, whatever its nature, and hence is justly liable to the punishment which is the invariable consequent of broken law. Since in theology we have to do only with the divine law, a guilty man is one who has broken the divine law, and hence is justly exposed to the divine punishment.

Thus it appears that the conceptions guilt and penalty are correlatives. Guilt means liability to penalty; penalty is the consequent of guilt. Both alike are the results of broken law. It follows that both guilt and penalty will vary with the conception of law. Where law is thought of as arbitrary or external — a matter of statute or precept — penalty also will be arbitrary, and guilt the state of a man who is liable to such penalty. Where, on the other hand, law is conceived as inner, carrying its own sanction to the conscience of the individual (*i. e.* as a moral and not merely a legal term), penalty will be the natural and

inevitable consequence of wrongdoing, and guilt, or the
state of just liability to such punishment, will carry with
it an element of personal blameworthiness not present in
the former case.   In ethical discussion guilt is commonly used in this narrower sense as a synonym for
moral blameworthiness.

In theology the use of the term has varied, according
to the varying views of God and of his relation to man.
Where God has been thought of as arbitrary and his law
external, guilt has been used primarily in the legal sense,
and penalty regarded as following upon transgression without reference to the motives which prompted it.   Much of
the penal legislation of the Old Testament, for example,
has to do with sins of ignorance or of accident; and one
of the purposes of the sacrificial system is to provide a
means of escape from their consequences.

With the increasing recognition of the significance of
the individual, and of his direct responsibility to God,
we find the legal conception of guilt giving place to the
moral view.   Guilt becomes the personal blameworthiness
which results from wilful disobedience, and penalty the
necessary satisfaction which justice demands for such
violation of the moral law.   At first, attention is confined to particular offences; but with deeper insight into
man's true relation to God, and the nature of the divine
requirement, the impossibility of such restriction becomes
apparent.   Not individual acts only, but the entire condition of man as selfish and wilful is made the subject
of moral condemnation, and the judgment of guilt is extended to the whole man, and ultimately to the society
of which he is a member and the race from which he is
sprung.   Such, for example, is the estimate which meets
us in the writings of Paul.   But, whatever the differences

in detail, in every case the concept of guilt expresses the relation between the moral state of man and those consequences, individual and social, which are conceived as resulting therefrom under the divine government. It is the interpretation of these consequences as penalty; that is, as the divinely appointed means for retribution and discipline. This connection between the sinful state and its penal consequences is sometimes described in theology as imputation.

The word "imputation" has unfortunate associations. To many people, to impute means to attribute to a person something which is not true. While the word has often been used in this sense in theology, it is important to remember that this is not its primary meaning. To impute means simply to reckon, and may apply to true judgments as well as to false. It is a term expressive of the moral estimate which is passed upon a particular act or state — what Ritschl would call the *Werthurtheil*, or judgment of value. It expresses the interpretation of the significance of conduct in the light of God's moral government. As such, the questions with which it concerns itself have a permanent place in Christian theology.

There are two questions which may be asked as to the relation between sin and its consequences. (1.) What part of the consequences of sin is to be reckoned penalty? (2.) What is the nature of the connection between sin and its penal consequences; and, more particularly, what is the result which this connection is designed to produce? The first is the question of the nature of penalty; the second, of its function.

2. *The Nature of Penalty.*

By penalty is meant the evil which God, in order to promote the ends of his moral government, has attached

to sin as its inevitable consequence.[1] To give any event
or experience penal significance, therefore, it is necessary,
first, that it should be adjudged evil, and, secondly, that
it should be regarded as taking place by God's will as
a part of his moral government.

It follows that the view of what constitutes penalty will
vary, partly with the view of the nature of God's government, partly with the estimate of evil. Where God's
government is regarded as primarily concerned with individuals (as in the theory of private or distributive justice),
penalty will be restricted to those evils which can be shown
to be the direct consequence and just recompense of individual sin. Where, on the other hand, God's government
is given social as well as individual significance (as in
the theory of so-called public justice), penalty may extend
beyond individual ill-desert and serve other than a retributive purpose.

On the other hand, it is equally evident that the conception of penalty will vary with the conception of evil.
Where those aspects of evil which are present to consciousness are exclusively emphasized, attention will be
concentrated upon the suffering which punishment brings.
Where thought presses back to the deeper causes, of which
the suffering is evidence, greater prominence will be given
to the limitation and loss which penalty involves. The
connection between the two elements and their relative
importance will appear more clearly when we consider
the function of penalty.

If we ask what experiences have been given penal significance we find wide differences of opinion. In primitive
times any misfortune or suffering which befell a man was
interpreted as punishment, and the only question to be

[1] Cf. Clarke, *Outline*, p. 248.

asked was as to the sin which had caused it. Thus, famine, pestilence, defeat in battle and physical death are examples of the penalties which God was supposed to inflict upon the individual or the nation that had transgressed his laws.

With the rise of belief in a life after death the conception of penalty is extended from this life to that which is to come. Those sinners who have escaped the consequences of their deeds here are thought of as reserved for a judgment after death, whose sentence will be all the more terrible because so long delayed.

As time goes on and man's insight deepens, attention is diverted from the external consequences of wrongdoing to its inner effects. The worst penalty of sin is seen to be the inner suffering which it brings and the moral weakness and degradation which it causes. In other words, depravity itself, with its resulting estrangement from God, is given penal significance.

The changes thus indicated may be illustrated in the use of the word "death" as a penal term. Originally taken in the literal sense as meaning the cessation of earthly existence (physical death), it became a synonym of the corruption produced in the moral nature by sin (spiritual death),[1] and at last for the complete separation of man from God which was regarded as the final state of the wicked (eternal death). Where early ages regarded death in the first sense as the chief penalty of sin, later generations gave penal signficance to the second and the third.[2] This is a part of the change from an external and legal conception of the divine government to one which is moral and spiritual.

[1] *E. g.* Eph. ii, 1 ; cf. Rom. i, 28–32.
[2] Cf. *West Conf.*, **VI**, 2, 6.

A similar change may be noted in the significance of the term "hell." Originally regarded as a place located beneath the earth, namely, that part of Sheol reserved for the punishment of the wicked, it has gradually lost all local significance, and come to be understood as that state of final estrangement from God which is the doom of the hopelessly impenitent.

Through all the changes in the Christian conception of penalty, the idea of alienation from God has remained a constant factor. In the complete separation from Christ and his kingdom, which is the inevitable result of surrender to a life of self-seeking, Christian theologians have always seen the supreme punishment of sin. If hell be conceived as a place, it is a place where no ray of love from the divine presence ever penetrates. If it be conceived as a state, it is the state which results when the last spark of the divine Spirit has died out of the human breast. In either case, it has its foretastes and its analogy here.

3. *The Function of Penalty.*

There are two main theories of the function of punishment corresponding to the views taken of the nature of God's moral government. Where the purpose of God's government is conceived to be primarily the manifestation of God's glory through the display of the divine attributes of justice and mercy, the function of punishment will be regarded as retributive, since the justice which it serves to display is manifest in the nicety with which it tempers reward to individual desert. Where, on the other hand, the end of God's government is found in the establishment of the kingdom of God in which all moral beings are to find their unity in love, the primary purpose of punishment will be disciplinary, since it is only through such discipline that the moral training through which men are fitted for the kingdom can be brought about.

It would be a mistake, however, to set these two theories in too sharp contrast. While retribution holds the primary place in the former theory and discipline in the latter, the two conceptions are not necessarily mutually exclusive. The retributive theory of punishment may make place incidentally for discipline, while the disciplinary theory recognizes clearly that retribution is a necessary element in moral training. The real difference between the two can only be clearly expressed when another element is taken into account. That which gives the retributive theory its distinguishing characteristic is the fact that it defines God's justice, and hence his punishment, primarily in terms of his relation to individuals; whereas, the latter conceives God's government in its wider social relations, and therefore admits a function of penalty which cannot be expressed in terms of individual justice. We may illustrate this difference in connection with the historic interpretations of the doctrine of original sin.

The doctrine of original sin had its origin in the attempt to interpret the facts of social evil already described under depravity in terms of individual blameworthiness. By original sin is meant moral corruption which is, at the same time, guilty, that is, justly deserving of punishment. Two assumptions underlie the theory in its older forms: first, that all social evil is to be interpreted as penalty; secondly, that all penalty is to be conceived in terms of individual justice. Since it is manifest that the individual cannot justly be held responsible for deeds in which he had no part, some way must be found to connect the later members of the human race with their first parents through whose free choice sin entered the world.

This explains the great importance given to the doctrine of the fall in the Augustinian and Calvinistic theologies.

The explanations of the connection which have been given are of two kinds. According to the first, or realistic theory, mankind as a whole is conceived as actually, not merely potentially, present in Adam, so that in his fall literally, and not merely figuratively, we "sinnèd all." Hence, in inheriting from him corruption, we are only suffering the just consequences of our own pre-natal act. According to the second, or federalistic, theory, the transition is made by a legal fiction. Adam as an individual is made by God the representative of the race, with the understanding that if he fails to stand the test, the consequences of his act shall be imputed to his descendants and they shall be treated as if they had sinned. It is manifest that if we are not prepared to accept either of these explanations one of two consequences must follow: we must either abandon the assumption that the social evil which is about us and within us is to be interpreted as penalty; or else, we must give the term a larger significance than the theory of individual justice admits. The former of these ways is taken by the Arminian theologians, the latter by the New School Calvinists.

According to the Arminian theory, guilt extends no farther than individual wrongdoing. So far as my nature has been tainted and my freedom limited as a result of ancestral sin, I cannot be held responsible, and so far as I suffer because of that sin my suffering cannot be interpreted as penalty. The Arminian solution, therefore, is found in narrowing the conception of penalty and admitting that there is much evil in the world which cannot be explained in this way.

The difficulty in the Arminian theory lies in the impossibility of determining the limits of individual responsibility. The course of modern thought has tended steadily to diminish the element of contingency in the moral life and to give an increasing rather than a diminishing importance to the social factor in sin. To empty of penal significance all those forms of evil which cannot be accounted for as a result of individual choice is to narrow the range of God's moral government and to weaken that sense of social solidarity which experience shows to be so potent a factor in moral discipline.

There remains the second possibility, to enlarge the conceptions of guilt and of penalty to take in the consequences of social as well as of individual sin. This is the view taken by the later Calvinism, which substitutes for the distributive justice of the older theories a public or governmental justice, and for immediate imputation, both in its realistic and federalistic forms, a mediate imputation in which guilt attaches to the evil act or state itself, irrespective of the conditions by which it has been brought about.[1]

Singular as it may appear, repugnant though it be to the individualism in which we have been trained, this is the view which, on the whole, seems best to account for the facts of experience. In moral evil we have to do with a social phenomenon which can only be adequately treated when looked at from the point of view of God's progressive education of the race. So regarded, guilt, as truly as depravity or estrangement, may have a social as well as an individualistic meaning. It expresses the true signifi-

---

[1] Historically the two theories are closely connected, and the line between them is often hard to draw. It was an Arminian, Hugo Grotius, who, as we have seen, first applied the conception of public justice to the solution of the problem of the atonement, and the governmental theory of which he was the father has been widely held in Calvinistic circles.

cance of man's selfishness and alienation when judged
from the point of view of God's moral government. It is
prophetic of the individual judgments of self-condemnation which will be called forth when the men who are now
living in ignorance or in indifference are brought face to
face with the Christian standard, and realize at last the
true meaning of the life they have been leading. It is the
acceptance, as morally justifiable and necessary, of all
those social consequences of sin which — from the point
of view of individualistic ethics so perplexing — are the
most effective proof that man's true ideal is not individual
but social, and hence to be realized only through a redemption which includes the entire system of persons of which
he is a part.

We distinguish then between guilt and the sense of
guilt. The first is objective, and consists in the divinely
appointed relation between wrong and its consequences,
both individual and social, whether those consequences
are consciously realized or not. The second is subjective, and consists in the progressive realization of the
moral significance of sin, both in its individual sense as
personal blameworthiness, and in its social aspect as failure
to realize the kingdom of God. The farther one advances
in the Christian life, and the more completely one's judgments are controlled by the principles of the Gospel, the
more the personal aspect of guilt will tend to be subordinated to its social significance, and concern for one's individual shortcomings give place to the deeper sorrow which
results from the hindrance of God's loving purpose for
mankind.

It is from this point of view alone that the cross of
Christ is seen in its true perspective. From the point
of view of the individualistic theory it is impossible to

account for Christ's experience on grounds of justice, and we are reduced to the various forms of legal fiction which meet us in the older theories of the atonement. But, if God's government be social as well as individual, and justice be concerned with the promotion of the welfare of mankind as a whole as well as of the individual units who compose it, then the voluntary acceptance by the innocent of the consequences of social wrongdoing may prove the means by which the moral progress and ultimate salvation of mankind is to be brought about.

We are now in a position to see the true relation between the different elements in penalty. Two such elements may be distinguished, suffering and loss ; and the question naturally suggests itself whether both are essential and, if so, which is primary.

According to one view, which we may call the vindicatory theory, it is suffering which is the primary element in punishment. The loss which it involves has for its main object the production of pain, and it is in the latter that the real penalty consists. When the horizon is limited to this life, the divine punishment is found in the various misfortunes and sorrows which befall man on the earth, and physical death is the supreme penalty because (according to primitive theory) it removes him from the pleasant conditions of life here to the dreary shadow world of Sheol. When, with the moralization of Sheol, the future life becomes an object of desire, the same principles are extended to the after life, and Gehenna is conceived of as a place in which the wicked, who seem to have escaped in this life without due recompense, are visited with the suffering which their guilt deserves. Where guilt is thought of as infinite, suffering is regarded as lasting forever, and the final doom of the wicked is an eternity of torment. This is the genesis of the traditional conception of hell.

The great difficulty with this conception of punishment is its acceptance of sin as an ultimate fact. It is not the eternity of suffering which is most perplexing to faith, but the endlessness of sin. If God be like Christ, how can the presence in his universe of men and women who, to all eternity, resist his fatherly love and remain alien to the life of his kingdom, be other than a mark of defeat? Either God does not really desire the ultimate salvation of all, or else we must admit that sin defeats God. It is the courageous acceptance of this dilemma that explains Jonathan Edwards' famous sermons. Unwilling to admit the latter alternative, he adopts the former. To Edwards sin contributes positively to the glory of God. It is the means through which his justice is made manifest to all creation, and the time will come when the contemplation of the sufferings of the wicked in hell will become an element in the blessedness of the redeemed. With our conception of the character of God, such a theodicy is no longer possible.

The difficulty to which the retributive theory is exposed is avoided by the disciplinary theory. According to this view the main object of punishment is the reclamation of the offender, not his destruction. The most serious consequence of sin is not the pain which it brings, but the deterioration of character which is its inevitable consequence, and the estrangement from God which is its necessary result. Punishment is God's means of calling man's attention to this fact and so leading him to seek amendment before it is too late. The suffering which it brings is, therefore, a cause for thankfulness and not for regret. If it were not for this, men might lose all that was precious to them before they realized it. Friends and self-respect and life itself might go and they be never the wiser. This danger is prevented by the psychological connection between loss and pain. Our hope for mankind, present and future, lies in the suffering which in the providence of God follows individual and social sin.

This is not to deny the retributive element in penalty, but to put it in the right place. The essence of retribution consists in the inevitable connection between moral conduct and its consequences, and the inevitableness of the connection is itself an element in the discipline which it is designed to promote. The dilemma, retributive or disciplinary, is a false one, every true punishment being at once retributive and disciplinary. The point is simply that in the purpose of God retribution is not the ultimate fact, but is itself a means to a higher end, namely, the bringing in of the kingdom of God which Christ has revealed. Historic theology has recognized this in part in its interpretation of the sufferings of the elect as chastisement; but it was prevented from drawing the full consequences of the principle by its narrow view of God's plan. With our enlarged view of the kingdom of God as the final end of the universe, the way is open for the interpretation of all punishment as discipline.

The question remains whether the end of the discipline is primarily racial or individual; whether God's plan contemplates simply the gathering, out of the wider humanity of the natural which is destined to destruction, of a smaller spiritual society of Christlike men to constitute his kingdom; or whether each individual who has ever lived has a place in his redemptive purpose. The former is the view of conditional immortality; the latter of universalism.

According to the former view it is not simply heaven but life itself which is the prize of the faithful. Punishment is conceived in terms of loss and not of suffering, and the final outcome of sin for the hopelessly impenitent is regarded as literal destruction. When all has been done, and the last spark of spiritual life has died to ashes, those who persist in evil will be allowed to pass out of existence. In the redeemed universe which is to be the scene of God's kingdom sin can have no place.

There is much to be said for this view. It claims to be scriptural, and it certainly has a strong Biblical basis. It has many analogies in God's method of dealing in other realms. It harmonizes the doctrine of the final loss of some with the complete triumph of God's kingdom. But it has one great difficulty. It limits the power of God's love. In this view too, though in a different and less painful way, sin defeats God.

It is this sense of defeat which gives the advocates of universalism their chief strength. Against the passages which seem to imply the final loss of some individuals, they set Jesus' teaching concerning the Fatherhood of God, and the apostolic faith in the sovereignty of love. They argue that God will not really overcome sin until his Spirit conquers the power of evil, not merely in the great mass but in each individual. Not at once, or in this life, or without heavy cost, but in the end, God will overcome the resistance of the last rebellious will and win back the last wandering child.

It is a great mistake to think of universalism as easygoing sentimentality, afraid of the thought of suffering. No doubt there is such a universalism, but we are not concerned with it here. The universalism here in question is not only consistent with future punishment; it requires it. It holds that every sin brings with it suffering and loss; that the longer sin continues, the more man will have to suffer, and the more difficult and arduous will be the way of recovery. But it believes also that such recovery is possible to every child of God; and that through the power and love of God, such recovery is certain. Sooner or later, at whatever cost, God will have all souls.

On a matter of so great difficulty it becomes us to speak with reserve. We have to do with one of those ultimate problems, in the solution of which men will probably always differ. More important than the theoretical conclusion we adopt is our attitude to the practical problems with which the fact of sin confronts us. Here it may be said with confidence that the effect of Christ's Gospel has been immensely to enlarge men's estimate of the spiritual capacity of mankind, and to bring within the range of missionary endeavor peoples and individuals whom earlier ages had been content to leave without the pale. Whatever may be true in theory, in practice it is certain that the more widely our hope extends, the better we shall be able to fulfil the task to which we have been called, and to hasten the day when all mankind shall own the supremacy of the good God whom Christ reveals.

We may sum up our discussion of the principles which determine the Christian thought of the final issue of sin in the following propositions:

(1.) That salvation, whether in this life or in the life to come, means transformation into the likeness of Christ, and is brought about in every case by repentance and faith.

(2.) That as long as sin continues it must be punished; and the longer it continues, the greater will be its penalty, and the longer and more difficult the way of recovery.

(3.) That the final control rests with the good God whom Christ reveals; and therefore, that we may safely trust him to bring his purpose to a successful issue in spite of every obstacle.

PART V

OF SALVATION THROUGH CHRIST

CHAPTER XVIII

THE CHRISTIAN IDEA OF SALVATION

1. *The Antecedents and Relations of the Christian Doctrine.*[1]

THE word "salvation" means primarily deliverance, and takes for granted in every case some danger or evil, in rescue from which salvation consists. It follows that the meaning of salvation will vary according to the nature of the evil from which it is a deliverance. Where the evil is external, such as misfortune, defeat or death, salvation also will be outward, a change of surroundings or of condition ; where it is internal, such as sin, salvation will be inward, and involve transformation of character. The Christian idea of salvation is of the latter kind, and corresponds to the conception of sin we have already considered. It may be provisionally defined as the process through which man, both as an individual and as a race, is delivered from the corruption, guilt and estrangement caused by sin, through the removal of the causes which have produced them. On the religious side, it involves the realization of the right relation between man and God, through the substitution of the filial spirit of trust and obedience for the attitude of indifference, rebellion, or fear. On the ethical side, it involves the transformation of human character through the substitution of the principle of self-sacrificing love for that of individual self-seeking. In both these aspects it has its source in God's free grace, progressively

[1] Cf. my article "Salvation," in Hastings' *Dictionary of the Bible*, IV, pp. 357 sq.

revealed in human history, and finding its most signal evidence in the person and work of the historic Christ. While it has its beginnings here and now in the assurance of individual pardon, and the consciousness of new desire of, and strength for, service; its full consummation belongs to the future, when the peace and joy which are now experienced by but a part of mankind, and by them imperfectly, shall become the common possession of all men, and society as a whole be organized according to the principles and animated by the spirit of Christ.

The most direct preparation for the Christian view is found in the Old Testament. Before Jesus, Jeremiah[1] had taught that salvation is an inward spiritual experience, involving deliverance from sin and transformation of character in the individual. The same conception finds expression in the Psalms.[2] Here, as elsewhere, Jesus builds upon a foundation already laid. What is new in his teaching is the extent to which he combines this ethical and spiritual conception of salvation with the social ideal, as expressed in the idea of the kingdom. But greater than any teaching was the redemptive influence exerted by his life and self-sacrificing death. In Jesus men saw what the life of sonship and brotherhood really meant, and so were able to conceive what it would mean for the world if the principles of Jesus found universal acceptance. Touching him, they became conscious of a gracious influence lifting them above themselves to new heights of purity and peace. In him they saw God's promised Messiah, the Saviour who was to come; nay, more, in him they found the ancient promise fulfilled that God himself would some day draw near to his people for their redemption. Hence the person

---

[1] Jer. xxxi, 31–34; xxxii, 40.
[2] *E. g.* Ps. li; cxxx, 8.

of Jesus became intimately associated with their thought of God's redemptive activity. The history of the Christian doctrine of salvation is the record of the effort to relate the new insight and uplift which came with Jesus to the older hopes and experiences by which the way for his Gospel was prepared.

In particular, three conceptions may be distinguished which have played a great rôle in human history and which have powerfully affected Christian thought. According to the first, salvation means deliverance from suffering and misfortune and takes place in this world. According to the second, it is deliverance from the world itself to a heavenly existence where the conditions which govern life here no longer obtain. According to the third, it involves the deification of human nature through the introduction of heavenly powers and influences into the present world. The two first conceptions find illustration in the history of Israel; the third has its nearest parallel in Greece. [1]

(a) *Salvation as Deliverance from External Evil.*

In the earlier portions of the Old Testament salvation means deliverance from misfortune and suffering. Since the chief evil to be feared is defeat in battle, the word is often used as a synonym for victory, and successful warriors are called saviors. Jehovah's saving activity is identified with his watchful care over Israel as a nation, specially manifest in his raising up such leaders to deliver them in war. With the experiences of the Exile, involving as they did the destruction of the Jewish state, the hope

[1] The conception of salvation as deliverance from future punishment, so prominent in the theology of Roman Catholicism and of Protestantism, is really a combination of the first and second of these conceptions. Like the first, it conceives salvation as deliverance from suffering; but, like the second, it postpones this deliverance to another world.

of national deliverance is postponed to the future, and the word "salvation" acquires the technical meaning of the divine deliverance through which the glory and prosperity of the Messianic age are to be ushered in. Yet, even here the early associations continue; and the kingdom which the Messiah is to establish is long thought of as an earthly monarchy involving the defeat of enemies and the restoration of conditions, more glorious indeed than those which prevailed under David and Solomon, but in other respects similar to them. Traces of this view still linger in the New Testament in the popular expectation of a leader who should overthrow the Roman domination, and echo in the disciple's question to the risen Jesus, " Lord, dost thou at this time restore the kingdom to Israel ? " [1]

Jesus rejected the popular ideal of a conquering Messiah, and with it the conception of salvation as deliverance from external misfortune. The kingdom which he came to establish was not of this world; and its marks were inward, not outward. None the less, he recognized the truth for which the older ideal stood. He looked with compassion upon human suffering and misery. He healed the sick,[2] comforted the sorrowing and enjoined upon his disciples a life of brotherly helpfulness and charity. If he laid down no programme of political reform, he gave the principles whose application to human life has been the inspiration of all the great reforming movements. The social spirit which is everywhere setting itself to the betterment of the

[1] Acts i, 6.

[2] Tenderness for human suffering has characterized the Christian religion from the first. The hospital has found its place side by side with the church, and the physician and the nurse have accompanied the preacher and the evangelist on their missionary journeys. In our own day, Christian Science owes much of its strength to the conviction that the principles which Jesus himself applied to the treatment of disease must be of permanent validity.

conditions of human life to-day gains its motive power from the estimate of man which Jesus introduced. It is because man is not simply a creature of time or of sense, but an immortal spirit, born of God and capable of communion with him, that it is worth while to expend every effort to make his present environment worthy of the priceless jewel of which it is the setting.

(b) *Salvation as Deliverance from this World.*

With the growing transcendence which characterized Israel's later conception of God, the Messianic salvation took on a supernatural character and was transferred from this world to that which is to come. Despairing of present communion with God, man postponed his salvation to an indefinite future and conceived it as a reward to be earned by fidelity to the ceremonial law, either on the part of Israel as a whole or of individual Israelites. A similar transformation took place in the idea of the Messiah. Instead of being an earthly monarch, he was conceived as a semi-divine being, sitting upon a heavenly throne, destroying the wicked with the breath of his mouth, and gathering before him for judgment all the mighty of the earth.[1] To be saved meant to escape the punishment which this divine avenger was to inflict, and to enter the heavenly blessedness which God had appointed for those whom he found faithful.

This eschatological and legalistic conception of salvation also has left its trace in the New Testament. It meets us not only in the Epistles and the Revelation, but in the apocalyptic discourses in the Gospels; and not a few scholars have been found to argue that it truly represents Jesus' own idea of salvation. A closer survey, however, shows that this is not the case. However it may be

---

[1] Cf. *Similitudes of Enoch*, chapter LXII, 2, 3 (Charles' ed., pp. 163, 164).

brought about, salvation is to Jesus always an inward spiritual experience, involving repentance from sin, faith toward God and brotherly love toward one's neighbor. To be saved means to become partaker in such an experience, and so to be made a fit subject for the life of the kingdom. It is not punishment from which Jesus comes to save man, whether in this world or the next, but sin; and this is a salvation which begins here and now.

Yet here again, while rejecting its exaggerations, Jesus makes place in his teaching for the truth for which the other-worldly ideal stands. Just because salvation involves the complete conformity of all men to the spirit of the Master, it is impossible to be satisfied with the imperfect foretastes which the present life affords. The ideal which Jesus proclaims is one of brotherhood as well as of sonship; and salvation in its completeness includes not only the transformation of individual character, but the organization of all the relations of life according to the principles which he has revealed. Such an ideal can be realized only if God's redemptive activity is conceived as reaching beyond the limits of this present existence, and including the unseen world into which already so many of mankind have passed, and in which alone therefore a social salvation can find its consummation.

It follows that the eschatological element so prominent in the New Testament teaching is not to be regarded as of merely transient significance; a form which may be put aside without loss of content. Throughout the later history, it has maintained its place as a permanent element in the Christian hope. The picture which has been formed of the conditions under which the future redemption is to be realized has varied with the changing world-view. Sometimes the contrast between this life and the next has been so emphasized as to rob the present world of all independent value or significance ; and again the life to come has been regarded as simply the consummation and fulfilment of that which is here begun. But, whatever the differences in detail, Christians have been at one in the conviction that the salvation which Christ brings is large enough to include the future as well as the present, and to unite this world with that which is to come as the scene of one all-embracing redemptive purpose.

(c) *Salvation as Deification of Human Nature.*

With the dying out of the older chiliastic ideals men's thoughts were turned again from the future to the present, and their view of the nature of salvation was insensibly transformed. While salvation in its completeness was still postponed to the future, it was believed that it had its foretastes here and now in the change of nature made possible through the incarnation of Jesus Christ. In Christ the incorruptible God himself had entered humanity ; assumed man's nature with all its limitations and weakness, and through that very assumption transformed it into the likeness of his own glorious and divine life. In the words of Irenæus, " He became what we are, that he might make us what he is." [1] This change, potentially realized for all in the incarnation, was made actual in individuals through mystic rites called sacraments, by which divine grace was imparted to men by physical means. In baptism men's sin was washed away and a new nature was born within them. In the Eucharist they were actually brought into contact with the incarnate Christ, and, feeding upon his glorified body, became partakers of its incorruption.

This conception of salvation, too, has its anticipations in

[1] *Adv. Haer.* Bk. V, Preface (*Ante-Nicene Fathers*, vol. I, p. 526)

the New Testament. In the letters of Paul, and still more in the Johannine writings, we find salvation conceived as a transformation of nature brought about through union with the risen Christ. The Christian is to Paul a new creature, — one for whom old things have already passed away; while to the mystic vision of John the difference between time and eternity has all but vanished, and judgment and resurrection are present realities, fulfilling themselves daily in the experience of men. In Jesus of Nazareth, the divine Word who was with the Father in the beginning has become flesh, that through his grace and truth, made manifest in crucifixion and resurrection, he may draw all men unto himself.

We have elsewhere seen how the doctrine of the Logos formed the transition between the Greek and the Christian view of the world.[1] It remains to consider its bearing upon the doctrine of salvation. Here again we note a twofold influence. On the one hand, by its emphasis upon the present aspect of salvation, it was the means of deepening and spiritualizing the Christian view; on the other, where salvation was carried back of experience to its basis in unseen reality, there was danger that the ethical and spiritual elements characteristic of the Christian view of salvation would be obscured. This is what actually happened in the later history. The intimate and personal features, so prominent in Jesus' own teaching, fell into the background. Instead of being conceived as a change of personal relationship in which the conscience and will of man are actively concerned, salvation became a mysterious change of nature, taking place in a region below consciousness and mediated by non-rational means. This physical (or to speak more accurately, metaphysical) conception of

[1] Chapter XI, section 3, p. 180.

salvation is known technically as sacramentarianism. It is the form in which the present redemption which Jesus proclaimed found natural expression in a world in which sin was regarded as a matter of nature rather than of character, and defined as corruption rather than as guilt or as estrangement. It is the counterpart, in the region of soteriology, of the realistic conception of God as absolute substance whose inadequacy we have already considered.[1]

Yet, here again, the error is only the exaggeration of a truth ; the truth, namely, that salvation is not a matter of change in external conditions, whether in this life or in that which is to come, but involves a radical transformation by which the entire personality is renewed, and life, as a

---

[1] It would be unjust to the Greek theology not to recognize the presence of other tendencies besides the one just criticized. Where the rational element predominates in the conception of God, we find a different view. Here the evil from which man needs deliverance is regarded as ignorance rather than corruption, and salvation comes through the impartation of a higher knowledge. This knowledge, or Gnosis, is brought by the Logos, the divinely appointed teacher of men. In his instruction all generations have shared to some degree. The Greek philosophers were his pupils as well as the Jewish law-givers and prophets. Still clearer are the lessons which he has taught in the incarnation, and still teaches in the institutions of the church. But these, too, are only partial, parables needing fuller interpretation. Salvation in the full sense is for those only who can press back of the outward appearances even of sacred things to the divine mysteries of which they are types. This higher Gnosis is the special theme of Christian theology, which consists in the fuller investigation and interpretation of the eternal truths, whose summary statement is given in the creed. No one can read such a book as the *De Principiis* of Origen without feeling the deep religious interest which animates it. In studying the divine mysteries, its author believes himself to be communing with the living God, and thinking his thoughts after him. In his pages cosmology becomes soteriology, and the story of the stars is but a chapter in the record of that all-embracing redemptive process through which, by devious ways, God is winning all rational intelligence unto himself. With a conception at once so broad and so noble, it is impossible not to feel sympathy. What is at fault in this type of theology is not its intellectualism, but the dogmatic spirit which has sought to stereotype forms which must of necessity be changing, and to forge out of the free speculation of one generation chains by which to restrain the liberty of *its* successors.

whole, is brought under the control of a new principle. This consciousness of inward renewal, brought about by contact with spiritual reality, gives sacramentarianism its strength, and explains the attraction which it has exercised in every age over so many devout and sensitive spirits.

With the sacramental system the realistic conception of salvation which it presupposes passed from Greece to Rome; but its development in the Latin theology followed independent lines. While some theologians, notably Augustine, regarded it as an ethical renewal manifesting itself in faith and love,[1] the prevailing tendency was to a legalism which conceived salvation primarily as remission of penalty.[2] The guilt of sin was emphasized rather than its corruption; and God was thought of as a law-giver whose dignity, outraged by sin, must be propitiated by atonement. This change of emphasis appears both in the view of Christ's work and of the means by which its benefits are made available for man. In both we see the application of formulæ derived from the Germanic criminal law to the religious problems of sin and redemption. The death of Christ was regarded as laying up a store of merit which might be transferred to man's account by the authorities of the church; and, through the sacrament of penance, and the indulgence system which was based upon it, a complicated machinery was devised by means of which this transfer was made possible. This combination of a realistic conception of salvation, with a legalistic view of the means by which it is brought about, is characteristic of the traditional theology of Roman Catholicism.[3]

---

[1] Cf. Augustine's well-known formula for justification, *Justificere = justum facere. De spiritu et littera*, c. 45 (Nicene Library, vol. V, p. 102).

[2] Cf. p. 303, note 1.

[3] I say, the traditional theology of Roman Catholicism, for it must never be forgotten that, side by side with this legalistic conception of salvation, we find in the Latin theology many evidences of a more spiritual view.

All these different strands of thought have entered into the making of the theology of Protestantism. Side by side with the deeper moral and spiritual truths which the Reformation reasserted we find traces of the older ideals, against which it was a protest. The Reformers, like other men, were children of their age, and were obliged to express their thought in the forms which they found ready to their hand. These had been largely wrought out under the influence of a Catholic conception of the church, and did not lend themselves readily to the expression of the new religious insight of Protestantism. The legalism against which Luther had so valiantly contended lived on in the theology of his successors ; and such terms as " covenant," " merit " and " imputation " became catchwords of Protestant theology. So we find in the great Protestant creeds the same combination of a profound spiritual ideal and an artificial and scholastic phraseology which we have already observed in the creeds of Catholicism. Nowhere is it more important to return to the original sources of Christian doctrine, and to seek a statement which shall

Sometimes this takes the mystic form of longing for the immediate vision of God ; sometimes the language used is personal, and the Christian ideal is conceived in terms of the imitation of Jesus. To Augustine salvation involves ethical renewal, evidencing itself in love ; while Abelard replaces the legal interpretation of the Atonement by one of moral influence. The distinction, so deeply rooted in the ethics of Catholicism, between the religious and the secular life, has its doctrinal counterpart in the conception of a twofold way of salvation. The saint, like the Gnostic in the Greek theology, may dispense with the machinery of satisfaction provided by the church, and approach God directly on the basis of his contrition alone. But for men and women in general, the sacramental system is the indispensable condition of salvation ; and where contrition is lacking, attrition, or the repentance that comes from fear of punishment, may at a pinch be made to serve. This combination of a profound and spiritual ideal of salvation and an external and legal view of the means by which it is ordinarily brought about, is characteristic of the official theology of Roman Catholicism, and is the background against which we must set the new insight of the Reformation.

give clear and consistent expression to its distinctive message.

In the older Protestant theology the doctrine of salvation falls into two parts, of which the first treats of the person and work of the Saviour; the second, of the application of that work to the individual and the church. We shall find it more convenient, in the present chapter, to follow a different order, and to precede the discussion of the several doctrines in which the different aspects of the Christian redemption are treated in detail, by a general survey designed to show the relation which each holds to the others, and the special contribution which each has to make to the doctrine as a whole.

If we analyze the conception of salvation, we see that there are three different points of view from which it may be regarded. We may consider salvation (1) as a work of God, (2) as an experience of man, (3) as a process, progressively realized in history. While the former takes precedence, both in the order of logic and in that of religious importance, it is more convenient to postpone its consideration to the last; since it is only through a study of the experience of the individual and of the history of the race that we can understand wherein the divine salvation consists and how it is brought about.

2. *Salvation as an Individual Experience.*

As an experience of man, salvation has a twofold aspect, corresponding to the double significance of sin as religious and ethical. As a religious experience, it involves the consciousness of reconciliation between God and man, manifesting itself on God's part in forgiveness and acceptance, and on man's part in repentance and trust. Since the God with whom man is thus reconciled is at the same time the guardian of the moral law, salvation involves also the removal of the consciousness of guilt, so far as that consciousness acts as a barrier between God and man. It is the substitution of the attitude of the son for that of the servant, and has its fruits in the assurance of pardon and peace. This consciousness of present acceptance and forgiveness is expressed in theology by the doctrine of justification.

The doctrine of justification by faith is the reassertion, in theological language, of the truth put more simply by Jesus in his teaching concerning the childlike spirit.[1] It describes the substitution of the attitude of personal trust which is characteristic of sonship for the legal relationship which is expressed in terms of good works, merit and reward. It has its psychological basis in the insight, won by Luther from a painful experience, that any attempt to earn or to deserve forgiveness by good works does but lead to deeper self-condemnation and distrust. Historically the way was prepared for it by the revival of Biblical scholarship, with its resulting rediscovery of the Pauline theology. From Paul Luther learned that the only sure way to find assurance and peace is to abandon all hope of self-righteousness, and to seek in personal commitment of the soul to God the spring of a higher life. Catholicism had recognized the legitimacy of this course in the case of exceptional individuals. Protestantism laid it down as the law of normal Christian living.

The consciousness of reconciliation with God does not necessarily carry with it the cessation of all the evils which are the consequence of past sin, but it gives them a

[1] This connection is recognized in the parallelism of the doctrines of justification and adoption in the later Protestant theology. In adoption the truth which the doctrine of justification states in legal phraseology is repeated in more intimate and personal language. Cf. *West. Conf.*, chapter XII.

new significance. They are no longer felt as punishments expressing man's separation from God, but as discipline, designed to bring about his closer union with him. Hence they are accepted in humility and submission, as evidences of love as well as of justice, and become means of grace, promoting that moral transformation which is the other side of the experience of salvation.

As a moral experience, salvation involves a change of character, manifesting itself in the adoption of Christ's principle of self-sacrificing love as the guide of life. It leads to the subordination of the desire for individual gratification to the wider aim which finds self realized through service of one's fellows, and has as its fruit the joy which is the invariable accompaniment of self-forget-fulness in a worthy cause. The full significance of this transformation is only gradually apparent, as the habits formed during the period of self-assertion and of self-indulgence are superseded by new habits appropriate to the new principle which has become dominant. Till this is the case, the battle with sin continues, and the experience of the redeemed may include the consciousness of moral defeat, with its resulting self-condemnation and self-distrust. But this defeat, instead of leading to carelessness or to despair, is only a motive to greater watchfulness and closer dependence upon the divine leader, in whom is strength sufficient for every need, and through whose help the final victory is assured. This progressive victory over sin, culminating at last in perfect conformity with the character of Christ, finds expression in the doctrine of sanctification.

These two aspects of the redeemed life, while closely associated in the Christian experience, are not identical. The religious experience of acceptance with God is not the same as the ethical experience of the realization of the moral ideal; nor is it necessary to wait for the latter in order to enjoy the former. The true relationship is rather the reverse. It is the religious experience of acceptance and forgiveness which makes possible the realization of the ethical ideal. When a man abandons all hope of self-righteousness, and turns to God in penitence and trust, to find in grateful dependence upon him the spring and power of a new life, then, and not till then, is he conscious of the moral renewal whose full outworking will involve the complete transformation of the character into the likeness of Jesus Christ. This is the truth for which the reformers contended in their distinction of justification and sanctification.

If we seek to describe in a word the Christian conception of salvation considered as an individual experience, we may say that it is the substitution of the outgoing for the self-centred life. On the religious side, this consists in the abandonment of the hope of individual self-righteousness for the filial relation of submission and trust (justification by faith); on the ethical side, in the substitution for the individualistic principle of self-love of the social principle of love to others (sanctification). Both changes are made possible through the discovery of a system of wider relations in which the narrow and divisive ideal of individual self-seeking is superseded by the wider ideal of sonship and brotherhood. But this leads us over inevitably from the point of view of the individual experience to that of the historic process of which it is a part.

3. *Salvation as a Historic Process.*

From the point of view of history, salvation is the process by which the divine ideal is realized in society through the

establishment of the kingdom of God among men. This
process has two main aspects. On the one hand, it consists
in the progressive revelation of the divine will; on the
other, it involves the progressive realization of that will
in society. In both cases it is made possible through the
appearance of exceptional individuals, who, as teachers and
preachers, proclaim God's will to man, and by their character and example set in motion the influences by which it
is ultimately to be realized. Among these Christian faith
assigns the place of central importance to Jesus Christ.

The social influences by which the divine salvation is
brought about are of two kinds. They are directed in part
to deepening and clarifying the sense of sin through the
revelation of the divine ideal; in part to providing a means
of deliverance from sin through the disclosure of God's redemptive love. This double method is recognized in Protestant theology by the distinction between the Law and
the Gospel. By the first is meant the sum of all those
influences (moral as well as legal in the technical sense)
by which the divine ideal is revealed to man, and he is
made to feel his own inability to realize it. By the Gospel,
on the other hand, is meant the sum of all those influences,
inward as well as outward, by which God's redemptive
purpose is not only made known to man, but is actually
made effective for his salvation.[1]

---

[1] In its traditional form, the treatment of the distinction between the Law
and the Gospel is open to criticism from two quarters. It is defective (1) in
the legalism which dominates the entire treatment (*e. g.* the conception of the
Gospel as a covenant); (2) in the lack of historic sense which carries back
that which is the distinctive contribution of Christianity to the beginning of
human history (cf. *West Conf.*, chapter VII, section 6, not two covenants, " but
one and the same under various dispensations "). None the less is it true that
it stands for a fact of experience of permanent importance, the fact, namely,
that the process of redemption is at the same time a process of growing apprehension of the divine ideal, and of deepening conviction of the impossibility of
any independent realization of it, In this sense the Confession is right when it

In connection with the doctrine of sin, we have already traced one side of the process, noting how the external and legal conception of the divine will gives place to one which is moral and spiritual, and the ideal of outward conformity is superseded by that of inner harmony of spirit. A similar change may be observed in connection with the conception of salvation. The outward machinery provided for the removal of the consequences of legal and ceremonial offences in systems of sacrifice and purification is felt to be inadequate to deal with the guilt and estrangement caused by sins of the heart. Especially significant in this connection is the Old Testament restriction of the efficacy of sacrifice to sins of inadvertence or of ceremonial defilement, when compared with the prophetic teaching concerning Jehovah as a God with whom there is forgiveness for the worst offender, if only it be sought in sincere penitence, and accompanied by amendment of life. Here we see how a deepened conception of sin goes hand in hand with a more spiritual idea of salvation.

This moral and spiritual conception of salvation has its counterpart in a corresponding change in the idea of mediation. Mediation in one form or another is a fundamental religious fact. It is simply the expression in the sphere of religion of the dependence of the individual upon his fellows which is the law of all social life. In the early stages of religion, this dependence is expressed in crude and superstitious forms, as in the savage's reliance upon the charm of his medicine man. But, with more spiritual conceptions of God, the idea of mediation is correspondingly altered, and the true mediator between the divine Father and his

says that the " uses of the law are not contrary to the grace of the Gospel, but do sweetly comply with it, the Spirit of Christ subduing and enabling the will of man to do that freely and cheerfully which the will of God, revealed in the law, requireth to be done " (chapter XIX, 7).

child is seen to be the one who most perfectly understands the character of God, and most worthily exemplifies the ideal for man.

This change is most conspicuously illustrated in the Christian view of Christ. In him we see the earlier conceptions of mediatorship spiritualized and transformed. He is the prophet who reveals God's will to man, the priest who represents his fellows before God and offers acceptable sacrifice in their behalf, the king who fights the battles against their enemies, and will finally gain the victory. But as applied to Christ the old expressions receive a new meaning. His revelation is one of character as well as word. His sacrifice is not outward but inward, even that of obedience unto death. His victory is over foes of the spirit, temptation and unbelief; and the kingdom which he establishes is a spiritual society whose marks are righteousness and peace and joy in the Holy Ghost.

In their reaction against external and unspiritual theories, we find many in our day who hesitate to apply mediatorial language to Jesus, lest it seem to limit the privilege of direct access to God which is the heart of his Gospel. The instinct which lies back of this unwillingness is a sound one, and it cannot be denied that there is much in traditional theology against which protest is in place. But the remedy is not in the denial of the fact of mediatorship, but in its proper definition and application. From the historic point of view which here concerns us, it is simple fact that apart from the work and influence of Jesus we should not know God as we do, and so should not enjoy that free access to him which is now our privilege. It is historic fact that through him there has come into being that sum of spiritual influences which we call Christianity, under which our lives have been trained and developed, and to which we owe the religious insight and spiritual freedom which are now our heritage. When we say that we approach God through Jesus we mean that in place of all external and legal devices for securing the divine favor, we put the spiritual principles which he has revealed, and learn from him the way by which the divine Father may rightly be approached.

In this spiritual conception of mediatorship, we find the real basis for the idea of vicarious atonement, which has played so great a rôle in Christian theology. Where the relation between God and man is conceived as external and legal the conception of atonement presents no difficulty. It is simply the presentation to God, either in the form of satisfaction or penalty, of a service or suffering judged equivalent in amount to the injury which he has sustained by man's sin. So long as sin and guilt are conceived as objective realities which may be isolated in thought from the person of the sinner, there is no reason why atonement should not be made by a substitute as well as by the original offender, — as indeed we find constantly to be the case in the sphere of the civil law. When, however, the relation between God and man is conceived as personal and moral, legal categories break down, and the attempt to state the problem of salvation in terms of external substitution is seen to be fruitless. But this does not mean that vicarious atonement has no place in the redemptive process, — only that it must be conceived in moral and spiritual terms, analogous to those which express the relation between God and man along other lines. The doctrine of vicarious atonement expresses the inevitable cost of redemptive love in a world where sin has a social as well as an individual significance. It is the price in patient endurance and sympathetic suffering without which the mes-

320 OUTLINE OF CHRISTIAN THEOLOGY

sage of God's holiness and grace cannot be brought home
effectively to men who are enslaved by selfishness and
blinded to truth. In the case of Christ himself it is the
supreme expression of the law of redemption through the
vicarious suffering of the good which was anticipated by
the second Isaiah, and applied as a universal principle by
the apostle Paul.[1]

With the recognition of the spiritual nature of mediatorship is given at the same time the true conception and
function of the church. We have already defined the
church as " the society in which the revealing and redeeming work of Christ is continued, and through which, under
the influence of the divine Spirit, the Christ life is mediated
to the world." [2] The church is the company of all the men
and women who have been touched by Christ's spirit, and
are working for his ends. It includes all who are bearing
others' burdens, grieving for their sins, and giving themselves for their salvation. So defined, the process of salvation is parallel with the growth of the church; and the
goal of salvation will be reached when the line which now
separates the church and the world (*i. e.* those who follow
Christ in unselfishness and trust from those who are living
in self-reliance and self-seeking) shall be obliterated by the
complete victory of the former.

From the point of view of the individual experience, we
defined salvation as the substitution of the outgoing for the
self-centred life. This definition is confirmed by our study
of salvation as a historic process. The history of redemption is the history of mankind's progressive victory over
selfishness and distrust; and Jesus is the mediator *par
excellence*, because he is the one in whom this victory is
complete.

[1] Isai. liii; Col. i, 24.   [2] Chapter V, p. 57.

But we cannot stop here. It is characteristic of religious, and especially of Christian, faith that it conceives salvation in all its parts as the work of God. Both the individual experience and the historic process are carried back to him as source ; and it is the task of theology to interpret their significance from this point of view. This gives us a new set of conceptions which we have now to consider.

4. *Salvation as a Divine Work.*

To begin with the historic process. The words of the prophet and the sacrifice of the priest gain their significance to the believer because through them the unseen God who is the sole object of true worship makes his will known, and his grace effective. They are his representatives, chosen by him, and acting for him in their mediatorial work. The doctrine which expresses this relation is that of election.

By election is meant God's choice of individuals or of nations for special service connected with his redemptive work. At first applied only to exceptional messengers and to unusual service, the range of the doctrine has been gradually extended till it takes in all individuals who have any part in the work of the kingdom of God. Since the way of service is also the way of salvation, election to service is at the same time election to salvation. But the separation of the latter conception from the former, as we find it in Protestant dogmatics, is an unfortunate one, since it divorces two things which belong together, and gives an arbitrary and individualistic interpretation to that which is essentially a social and historical conception. It follows from the nature of the Christian ideal, as we have already learned to know it, that God's choice of individuals is never arbitrary, but always for special work and special service in connection with the upbuilding of his kingdom.

21

By the doctrine of election, the entire course of human history is brought under the control of the divine will and interpreted as the expression of the divine purpose. Beneath the strife of human interests and wills, faith detects a consistent plan, slowly unfolding to its appointed end ; and, in those outstanding personalities whose witness brings God closest to men, sees evidence of an all-embracing providence, which is equally present, if less clearly manifest, in the humblest life.

What is true of the historic means by which salvation is mediated is true also of the individual experiences in which it is realized. These, too, faith recognizes as the work of God. In justification and sanctification, the Christian is conscious of a new divine life which he did not originate, but which has its source in the indwelling Spirit of God. [1]

The doctrine of the divine Spirit has varied historically with the conception of God. Where God is thought of as transcendent in the exclusive sense, the Spirit is an external influence, acting upon men from without, to fit them for special work. Where he is conceived as immanent, the Spirit is an abiding presence, the source and the support of the higher life of man. It is the latter conception, most fully developed by Paul and John, which has become characteristic of Christian thought. Here God is conceived, not only as revealing his will to men through prophets and seers, but as himself imparting the life which makes conformity to that will possible. This consciousness of new powers and ideals — the fruit and evidence of God's presence and activity in the soul of man — finds expression in the doctrine of regeneration.

Both lines of thought meet in the Christian conception

[1] *Larger Catechism,* questions 67–69.

of Christ. Jesus is not only God's chosen instrument, the elect servant, through whom his will is revealed, and his purpose accomplished; he is the one through whom God himself enters humanity, to manifest his own character and purpose in a human life. The doctrine which expresses this self-manifestation from the divine point of view is the incarnation; from the human point of view, the deity of Christ.

The idea of incarnation — in one form or another — is found in many of the non-christian religions.[1] As held in Christianity, it expresses the fact that God, who from the beginning has been present in human history, revealing and redeeming, has in the fulness of time found expression in the person of Jesus Christ; revealing the divine character and purpose to man through his life of righteousness and love, and by his self-sacrificing death on Calvary preparing the way for that complete indwelling of God in humanity which constitutes the ideal of the kingdom.

At the root of this conception lies the idea of God as essentially self-imparting. To Christian faith God is not simply the Sovereign who commands, but the Father who loves, and who, because he loves, gives. Between him and his human child there exists a kinship, which even sin cannot completely obscure, and which makes possible the divine indwelling in humanity.

It is this kinship which gives its great significance to the doctrine of the deity of Christ. By it, that which would otherwise involve an irreconcilable contradiction is translated into the most natural of truths. When we say that Christ is God incarnate we express our faith that the God who holds the universe in his hand is bound to us by

[1] *E. g.* the religions of India and of Greece.

such ties of kinship, moral and spiritual, that it is possible for him to express himself through man without ceasing to be God.   We affirm that self-impartation and self-sacrifice, such as we see exemplified in Christ, belong to the nature of deity ; and that the ideal which realizes itself in the perfect man is at the same time the self-revelation of the unchanging God.

In another chapter we have seen how this conception of God as self-imparting and self-sacrificing has been crossed and, in part, neutralized by other conceptions (*e. g.* that of God as self-centred and self-sufficient).   Where this is the case, incarnation and atonement are isolated from their wider relations, and conceived as wholly exceptional devices to remedy an abnormal situation.   God's redemptive work for humanity is conceived as exhausted in the person and work of the historic Christ, and the gulf which separates him from his fellows is one which can never be bridged.   The motive which leads to this isolation is an entirely natural one ; namely, the desire to find an objective basis for faith, independent of the fluctuations of the individual experience.   But the end is gained only by the sacrifice of other interests equally precious.   In one form or another the greater Christian theologians have always sought to lay a basis for God's special manifestation in Christ in his wider relation to humanity.   This effort appears in the Johannine conception of the Word as the light which lighteth every man who cometh into the world, — an idea which passes over into Greek theology in the doctrine of the Logos spermatikos.[1]   It finds utterance in the conception — specially common in modern Anglican theology — of the church as the continuation of the incar-

---

[1] *I. e.* the doctrine that the Logos is present to some degree in all men, as the *sperma*, or germ of such truth or goodness as they possess.

nation. Most clearly of all is it expressed in the faith, suggested by 1 Corinthians xv, 28, that humanity as a whole may at last become as completely the organ and expression of the divine life and character as is now the case with Jesus himself. In all these we have various forms of the conviction that the incarnation of God in Christ was not an exception to God's method of dealing with man, but only the supreme manifestation of that which is destined in time to become its universal law. This is the truth which lies at the heart of the doctrine of the Trinity, in which God's special revelation in Jesus and his wider revelation in the church are both carried back to the same divine source in the nature of God.

With this conception of God as one whose very nature it is to express himself in humanity, there is given a profounder conception of the atonement. The sufferings and death which were the inevitable result of Jesus' life of fidelity and love are seen to be the expression in humanity of that abiding pain which the sins of his children have ever caused the divine Father. The cross of Calvary becomes, at the same time, the revelation of the heart of God; and salvation through sacrifice is shown to be the universal law.

Thus from the divine point of view, as truly as from that of the individual experience or of the historic process, salvation may be defined in terms of the outgoing life. It is that progressive self-impartation of God to humanity, which has for its goal the complete conformity of mankind to the divine character as revealed in Jesus Christ. In the light of this fundamental conception we have now to consider in detail the special doctrines, in which Christian faith has expressed the different aspects of this comprehensive truth.

CHAPTER XIX

OF CHRIST, THE MEDIATOR OF SALVATION

ALL the different interests which we have thus separately considered meet in the doctrine of Christ. In him Christian faith sees at once the ideal of humanity (the second Adam); the historic mediator of salvation (the Messiah); and the revelation of God in human life (the incarnate Word). He is at the same time true man, unique man, and God in man. The effort to relate and harmonize these different elements constitutes the problem of the person of Christ.

This problem may in turn be analyzed into two parts, corresponding to the twofold source from which the doctrine of Christ is derived. The first is historical, — the problem of the consciousness of Jesus; the second is philosophical, — the problem of the incarnation. The doctrine of Christ's person will be determined at any time, partly by the view taken of the facts of his earthly life and ministry, partly by the conception of the relation of God and man which these facts suggest. Without the historic basis Christology becomes abstract and barren; without the speculative development it remains shallow and inconsistent.

In the reaction against the older metaphysical Christology, the necessity for philosophical construction is often overlooked. It is not our place, we are told, to decide *a priori* how the incarnation must have taken place, but rather to study the life of Christ as revealed in the Gospels, that we may learn what the facts actually were. The difficulty is that the more earnestly we apply ourselves to historical study, the more inevitably we are led at last to questions which history as such cannot answer.[1] As Kähler has well shown,[2] the question between the so-called Jesus of history and the Christ of faith is not between a purely historical and a purely speculative conception, but rather between two different types of theoretical construction. The true criticism to which the old Christology is open is not that it was philosophical in character, but that it was based upon a philosophy which too often ignored, instead of interpreting, the facts of history which it professed to explain. This will become plain as soon as we consider the sources from which the Christian conception of Christ is derived.

1. *The Jesus of History and the Christ of Faith.*

The sources of the traditional Christology are partly historical and partly philosophical. The historical sources are the life, character and teaching of Jesus, the impression which he produced upon his immediate disciples, and the influence which he has exerted upon the life of mankind. The philosophical sources are the conceptions, derived from contemporary thought, through which Christians have endeavored to make clear to themselves and to others the significance of his person and work. Two of the most important of these conceptions we have already considered in other connections. The first is the Messianic idea; the second, that of the Logos. The former is the inheritance of Christianity from Israel; the latter comes to it from Greece.

---

[1] *E. g.* the question of the consciousness of Jesus.

[2] In his suggestive little book, *Der sogenannte historische Jesus, und der geschichtliche biblische Christus* (*The so-called Historic Jesus, and the Historical Biblical Christ*), 2d ed., Leipzig, 1896.

From the point of view of history, the effort to reconstruct the portrait of Jesus in detail is subject to all the
difficulties which beset similar attempts in the case of other
great men. Some things about Jesus' life can be determined with certainty ; for others a strong probability may
be established ; while as to still others the question will
probably always remain an open one. Concerning Jesus
we know that he lived in Palestine in the first quarter of
the first century of our era. We are acquainted with the
environment in which he grew up, the main facts concerning his outward ministry, the Gospel which he preached,
the causes which led to his rejection and subsequent crucifixion, and the impression which he produced upon those
who stood nearest to him. But as to many points upon
which we would gladly be informed (*e. g.* as to the length
of his ministry, the proportion of his time he spent in
Judæa, the origin and growth of his Messianic consciousness, and the time and circumstances under which he first
made known his claim to others), the evidence is not such
as to make final certainty possible. What we have in our
Gospels is not so much a series of lives of Jesus, as a series
of character sketches, picturing the impression made by the
Master upon the disciples who stood nearest to him. In
each the living personality comes to us framed in the conceptions of the time, and colored by the personal experience and religious faith of the painter. It is as true of the
Fourth Gospel as of the Epistles, and of the Synoptics as
of the Fourth Gospel, that their subject is not so much the
Jesus of history as the Christ of faith.[1]

The content of the picture the Gospels present can
be described in two words as a character and a consciousness. In the first place, our Gospels present us

[1] Cf. Mark i, 1 ; John xx, 30, 31.

with a character of unexampled beauty and simplicity; trustful in its attitude toward God, brotherly in its relation toward men; quick to respond to every appeal of need; sensitive to every influence of beauty; uncompromising in its opposition to meanness, injustice and hypocrisy; marked by a singular absence of any consciousness of sin. At the same time this character is rooted in the consciousness of a unique relation to God. The Jesus of the Gospels knows that he is come forth from God; that the authority he exerts and the works he performs are divine. This consciousness expresses itself in the Synoptics in Jesus' claim to be the Messiah; in the Fourth Gospel, in the sense of a union still more intimate, a sonship not temporal simply, but eternal. The Jesus of the Fourth Gospel is one who, though very man, transcends this present world of time and sense. Even now he shares the light and life, the peace and joy in which the blessedness of the divine existence is found.

Throughout all the later history these two elements have remained central in the Christian thought of Christ. He is at once the ideal man and the incarnate God. The supreme question for Christian faith is as to the origin and the validity of these convictions. Do they go back to the consciousness of the Master himself? Or are they later additions, supplied by the devotion of the disciples? Can they maintain themselves to-day in face of all the new knowledge which the new age has brought? Or must they be relegated to the past as conceptions, which, however serviceable in their own day, are destined to be superseded by new ideas better adapted to the new needs of the present? These are the questions which lie at the heart of the modern discussions concerning the historic Jesus.

It is obvious that they are questions which cannot be

answered by historical means alone. To press back of the
picture given in our Gospels to the Jesus of whom it is a
portrait requires an effort of the constructive imagination
which involves the use of agencies as subjective at least as
those which they are designed to replace. Criticism may
enable us to fix a date, or to determine the original form of
a saying ; but when it comes to the question of the nature
of consciousness or the possibilities of character, it leaves us
in the lurch. Here there are but two possibilities open ;
either to make that which we ourselves already know the
limit of the possible, and hence to reject as mythical or
legendary whatever in the Gospel picture of Jesus surpasses
the standards and attainments of his day, or to see in Jesus
one of those creative forces which meet us now and again
in human history, initiating new lines of development, and
to regard the picture in the Gospels as the transmission —
in terms, to be sure, conditioned by the insight and environment of those through whom it comes — of elements
essential in the consciousness of Jesus himself.

The Christian church in all ages has adopted the latter
alternative. She has seen in the Christ of the Gospels the
creator rather than the creature of the Christian experience,
and ever turned back from the imperfection of her own
attainment to the undying ideal there presented. Here she
has found the goal of her endeavor, the solace of her disap-
pointment and the stay of her faith. It has been easier for
her to believe that a character so exalted and a personality so
satisfying was drawn from the study of a human original,
than that it was the creation of men whose moral and intellectual limitations at so many points the Gospels themselves clearly reveal.

If then we accept the Christ of the Gospels as giving us
a picture which in its essentials accurately preserves the

features of the historic Jesus, it is not because we deny the rights of scholarship or question the value of its contribution to our knowledge of the Gospel history; but only because we recognize that when it comes to the deepest secrets of personality, the methods of science break down, and the last word must always be spoken by the human spirit. The spirit has its own way of recognizing spiritual reality, and by it alone the possibilities of the personal life can be determined. Among the sources for our knowledge of the historic Jesus, therefore, not the least important or reliable is the experience of those later generations which have ever seen in the Christ of the Gospels the ideal which they would attain, and found fulfilled in him that divine indwelling through which alone the true life of man is made possible.

But if we recognize in the Christ of faith the legitimate interpretation of the Jesus of history, this does not mean that his person presents no problem for our thought. As the men of the New Testament expressed their faith in Christ in the forms natural to their day, and by the aid of a philosophy accepted at the time; so in every age Christian thought has busied itself with the problem of the person of Christ, and sought in its own way to give clearness and consistency to the confession of its faith. Sometimes the human Jesus has been the point of departure; again, faith has reached past the human form to the unseen God of whom it was the expression. Where the prevailing type of theology has been mystic, the person of Christ has been construed in terms of a union of natures; where ethical considerations have been dominant, the concrete features of his life have been emphasized, and the supreme mark of his divinity has been sought in his moral character. It would be strange indeed — in view of the difference of viewpoint which separates their philosophical presuppositions from ours — if the Christology which satisfied the men of the fifth century should prove in all respects adequate to the needs of the men of the twentieth. We may illustrate this difference by contrasting the Chalcedonian Christology with the modern theories in which our contemporaries have sought to express their view of the person of Christ.

2. *The Christology of Chalcedon.*

The formula of Chalcedon (451) was a compromise, adopted under Roman influence, with a view to reconciling the different theological parties in the Greek church.[1] It affirms the union, in the person of Christ, of two complete and distinct natures, one divine and one human, each retaining after the union, "without confusion or change,"

[1] The understanding of the early Christological controversies is confused by the fact that some of the theologians engaged in them have been condemned as heretical, whereas others have maintained their orthodox standing. This gives rise to an artificial classification which obscures the real significance of their teaching. For example, Cyril is regarded as an orthodox man, while Eutyches is condemned as a heretic. Yet the two are much closer than many who hold the Chalcedonian creed. So Nestorius was condemned by the Council of Chalcedon, yet the Chalcedonian formula was the triumph of principles for which he contended. A careful study of the history shows two tendencies at work; one, which interprets the person of Christ from the point of view of his deity, and has no place for a separate human personality; the other, which interprets his person from the point of view of his humanity, and hence desires to make the separation between the human and the divine natures as distinct as possible. The Alexandrine theologians inclined to the former view. They emphasized the unity of nature between God and man. Their favorite phrase for Mary was "mother of God," and their formula for the person which resulted from the incarnation was the "one nature of the Word made flesh." The school of Antioch, on the other hand, saw in Jesus a particular man, like Peter or Paul, with whom the divine Spirit united ethically, as he might unite with any other good man. We shall be most apt to put the different theologians in their proper place in the development of doctrine if we judge their views with reference to their relation to this fundamental difference.

the same properties which it possessed before.[1] Its philosophical basis is a view of God which isolates him from the world as a being of totally different nature from man ; its practical interest the desire to show how, consistently with the maintenance of the reality and completeness of both natures, this difference has been overcome in the incarnation. Against the prevailing Greek Christology[2] which so emphasized the union of the natures as practically to obliterate the distinction between them, it insisted that after incarnation, as before, each nature retained its properties unchanged. But it found the solution of the rival school of Antioch[3] equally unsatisfactory ; and, for the ethical union of two distinct personalities, substituted the union of two impersonal natures, the bond of union being furnished by the person of the Logos, who assumed humanity at the incarnation, while, at the same time, retaining his divinity unchanged.

In estimating the significance of this Christology we have to distinguish its philosophical form from its religious content. Like the Nicene doctrine of the Trinity on which it depends, it has for its presupposition the transcendent and

---

[1] The exact language is as follows: " We teach men to confess one and the same Son, our Lord Jesus Christ, the same perfect in Godhead and also perfect in manhood : truly God and truly man, of a reasonable soul and body ; consubstantial with the Father according to the Godhead, and consubstantial with us according to the manhood . . . one and the same Christ, Son, Lord, Only-begotten, to be acknowledged in two natures, unconfusedly, unchangeably, indivisibly, inseparably, the distinction of the natures being by no means taken away by the union, but rather the property of each nature being preserved and concurring in one person and subsistence, not parted or divided into two persons but one and the same Son and Only-begotten of God, the Word, the Lord Jesus Christ." This is taken, in substance, from Leo's letter to Flavian.

[2] That of Cyril of Alexandria, represented in heretical form by Eutyches and afterwards perpetuated in Monophysitism.

[3] Represented by Theodore of Mopsuestia and Theodoret, and in heretical form by Nestorius.

other-worldly conception of God, whose inadequacy we have more than once noted. Regarding God and man as mutually exclusive terms, it is forced to conceive of the incarnation as a stupendous miracle, involving the union in a single person of two sets of mutually contradictory attributes. This difficulty had been in part avoided in the Alexandrine Christology by the doctrine that, whereas there were two natures before the incarnation, there was only one after it; the human nature being endowed with supernatural attributes through its union with deity in the person of Christ. This mystic solution the fathers of Chalcedon rejected. Retaining the Cyrillian conception of incarnation as the union of two natures in a single person, they attempted to combine it with the truth for which the rival school of Antioch contended, namely, the persistence of the full humanity of Jesus. But in place of a distinct personality united to God by ethical harmony of will, they substituted an impersonal nature assumed by the Logos, and so lost the vividness and naturalness of one theory without securing the simplicity and consistency of the other.

Yet the very qualities which make the weakness of the Chalcedonian statement, judged from the point of view of philosophical theology, contribute to its strength when considered as an ecclesiastical formula. It is not by their philosophical consistency, but by their practical aim that creeds are to be judged. Here the Chalcedonian statement has much to commend it. In an age when two rival parties were struggling for the mastery, each striving to exclude all who disagreed with them from the pale of orthodoxy, it sought to find a middle path of safety and peace. It affirmed indeed the three great elements which enter into the Christian thought of Christ: divinity, humanity, and the union of the two in their integrity in the person of the historic Jesus. It repelled all theories, however attractive, which rejected or weakened any of these three members; but it condemned also the attempt to add any further test of orthodoxy. Under its capacious shelter there is room for widely different Christologies, as the later history has abundantly shown. Thus viewed, it stands for breadth, not narrowness, and is not unworthy of its place as one of the historic expressions of Catholic Christianity.

The difficulty of making any consistent theory of the person of Christ, from the point of view of a philosophy which assumes a fundamental contradiction between the divine and the human, may be illustrated by the later history of the Chalcedonian formula. Neither in the East nor in the West has it succeeded in bringing about uniformity of thought. In the East it was followed by a period of long and bitter controversy, during which large bodies of Christians holding a Monophysite Christology broke away from the established church. In the West we see Lutheran and Calvinist, both professing to accept the Chalcedonian Christology, carrying on in the form of an interpretation of its statements, the debate long ago begun by Nestorius and Eutyches. The Lutheran, laying chief stress on the union of the natures, affirms a Christ whose consciousness during his earthly life is practically divine. This he does by distinguishing between nature and attribute, and declaring that while the former remains distinct, the latter may be interchanged (*communicatio idiomatum*) [1]. The Calvinist, on the other hand, following the Nestorian tradition, insists upon the sharp distinction between the human and the divine in the incarnate Christ,

---

[1] Cf. Formula of Concord, VIII, 2–12, quoted in Schaff; *Creeds of Christendom*, vol. III, pp. 148 sq.; Bruce, *Humiliation of Christ*, pp. 83–107.

and solves the psychological difficulties to which this
hypothesis leads by the hypothesis of an alternating
consciousness, now divine and now human.[1] Both Christologies are exposed to the polemic of the Socinians, who,
making earnest with the transcendent idea of God which
the older theories assume, see in Christ simply a man who
has been raised by God to divine honors, and is to be
worshipped accordingly.[2]

The practical difficulties to which, both in its Lutheran
and Calvinistic forms, the older conception of Christ's person was exposed, were in a measure relieved by the doctrine of the states of Christ. By this doctrine a contrast
was made between the earthly life of the incarnate one
and his pre-incarnate and post-resurrection existence. The
earthly life was distinguished as a state of humiliation
from the state of exaltation to which he was restored
by the resurrection. As to the exact nature and extent of
the humiliation theologians were not agreed. Some held
that the divine glory (or in other words, the attributes possessed by the Logos as God) was simply obscured by the
incarnation (the kryptic theory); others, that during the
earthly life he actually refrained from making use of it
(the kenotic theory). All agreed that by the resurrection
the humanity as well as the divinity was exalted to the
right hand of God; but, while the Lutherans were per-
suaded that through the interchange of attributes the
human nature became possessed of the divine qualities of
omnipresence, omniscience, omnipotence, and the like, the
Calvinists maintained that, for all its dignity, the human
nature of the risen Jesus, like our own, remained separated
from that of deity by an impassable gulf.

[1] Cf. Shedd, *Dogmatic Theology*, II, pp. 314 sq., esp. pp. 319, 321.

[2] *Racovian Catechism*, section V, chapter I (London, 1818, pp. 189 sq.).

3. *Modern Theories of the Person of Christ.*

Two influences have led to the reopening of the Christological question in modern times. The first is historical criticism, which, through reinvestigation of the sources of the life of Jesus, has led to a new realization of his humanity. The second is modern philosophy, which, as the result of a better understanding of the subjective conditions of knowledge, has discredited the uncritical ontology which lay at the basis of the older theories, and substituted for its purely transcendent God, a God who is immanent. Modern thought concerning the person of Christ may be described as the effort, by means of a better philosophy, to do justice to the new facts concerning Jesus which historical criticism has brought to light.

This change appears in the shifting of interest from the nature to the consciousness of Christ. The earthly life of Jesus is the point from which all modern theories take their departure. What was the nature of Jesus' experience; the law of his development; the conditions and limits of his inner life? Such are the questions which engage men's thoughts to-day. The psychological interest takes precedence of the metaphysical. Whatever else a Christological theory may do, it must give us the picture of a true human consciousness.

Under these influences, a variety of theories have come into being which have this in common, that they make earnest with the humanity of Jesus. We may take as representative of different types (1) the theory of the kenosis, (2) Dorner's theory of progressive incarnation, (3) Ritschl's interpretation of the divinity of Christ as a *Werthurtheil.*

According to the theory of the " kenosis," the human

consciousness of Jesus has its explanation in the fact that, in becoming incarnate, the Logos renounced for the time being some or all of the attributes of deity. Its Biblical basis is Phil. ii, 7 ; its theoretical foundation the doctrine of the *communicatio idiomatum*. It is at one with the older Lutheran Christology in the belief that incarnation involves a change in the natures which are united. But, whereas the latter emphasizes the deification of the humanity, kenotic theologians begin at the other end, and teach that in the incarnation God becomes subject to human limitations. In some cases the renunciation is carried so far that the consciousness of Jesus becomes purely human. Yet, in the most extreme kenotic theory, there is this difference between the experience of Jesus and that of other men, that, whereas both share the same limitations, he is conscious of a prior existence in which these limitations were removed. It is the paradox of his unique consciousness that he who exists as man knows himself to be God, and remembers the time when he exercised the attributes of power and knowledge which for the time being he has laid aside.[1]

The philosophical difficulties of this theory are so obvious as to need no extended comment. The picture of the consciousness of Christ is no less contradictory than that presented by the older theories. What manner of being is this who knows himself to be God, yet is destitute of the attributes of God? Attributes are not independent entities added to the being of God, which can be laid aside without affecting his essence. They are only our analysis of God's essential nature. We cannot think away a single one without at the same time destroying God. If we

[1] Cf. Godet, *Commentary on John*, Eng. tr., vol. I, pp. 358 sq. ; 394 sq., esp. p. 397.

start with an impassable gulf between God and man, no trick of logic will make it possible for us to bridge it. The only way out of the difficulty is to revise our original definition so as to remove the contradiction. This is the method taken by a class of theories which emphasize the immanence of God and his kinship with man. We may take Dorner as representative of this class.[1]

According to Dorner, it is God's nature to communicate himself to man, and incarnation, so far from involving an alteration of his previous method of working, is only the complete realization of that which has been his plan from the first. The Logos, who has been the creating and revealing principle from the beginning, in the fulness of time unites with himself a human nature; and, as a result of this union, there comes into being a new personality, namely, that of Jesus, the Christ. The life of Christ is a true human life and, as such, is subject to the law of growth. But it is also a divine life, because the basis of its personality is the Logos, who ever communicates his perfection to the humanity, as it is able to receive it. This does not involve any change in the Logos, for it belongs to his nature to communicate himself to man; nor does it destroy the humanity of Christ, since God has made man capable of receiving the infinite. But it does involve the creation of a new type of consciousness, neither strictly divine nor strictly human, but divine-human, even that of the perfect or ideal man.

In conceiving incarnation as the realization of the ideal relation between God and man, the Christology of Dorner represents a distinct advance over the theory of the kenosis. But, in explaining the person of Christ as due to the union of the Logos with an impersonal human

[1] *System of Christian Doctrine*, Eng. tr., vol. III, pp. 279 sq.

nature, the theory still moves in a region of abstract metaphysics where it is difficult for men trained in the concrete methods of modern science to follow.it. Such terms as " Logos " and " humanity " are words which express our interpretation of the significance of Christ's person; not independent entities through whose union it comes into being. This is the point of view which is represented by the Christology of Ritschl.[1]

According to Ritschl, the divinity of Christ is not so much a theoretical as a practical conception. It is a *Werthurtheil*, or judgment of value, expressing the place which Christ holds in the life of the church. It expresses the fact that in Jesus of Nazareth his disciples find the ideal of humanity realized, and are conscious through him of being brought into contact with a power which is able to raise them above the iron law of necessity into the freedom and joy of the kingdom of God. Hence, to the church, Christ has the value of God. For God, as he is known in religion, means just this practical power to help and to deliver. What God is in himself we cannot say, and it is futile to inquire. Hence, any attempt to construct the person of Christ by the aid of abstract conceptions like the Absolute, or the Logos, which have no basis in experience, is to invite failure. The true task of the theologian is to study the human Jesus, that he may learn from an analysis of his life and work what are the features of his character and ministry which give him his unique power to uplift and to transform human life. When we have done this we shall have learned what his divinity means, for we shall have learned how it comes to pass that in him we find that practical power to help, which we call God.

[1] *Justification and Reconciliation*, Eng. tr., vol. III, pp. 385 sq.

Accordingly, we find Ritschl calling attention to the qualities which give the historic Jesus his unique place in the life of humanity. He points out his consciousness of his vocation as revealer and founder of the kingdom of God; his fitness for his vocation in character and endowments; his willingness to accept the limits and pay the price which fidelity to his divine calling involved; and finally, the success with which he has realized his mission by bringing into existence the society in which the life of freedom and brotherly service is actually realized among men. It is a fact that, through contact with Jesus as revealed in his church, men are justified and redeemed, and instead of being slaves to the world and to sin, become conscious of victory over both. But this means that through Jesus men meet God and find in him their Saviour.

In taking his departure from the humanity of Jesus Ritschl is representative of the prevailing tendency in modern Christological thought. In two points, however, his own view is defective. (1) In his reaction against an abstract metaphysics, he does not always do justice to the facts of experience for which the ontological terms which he rejects stand. (2) In his emphasis on the uniqueness of the historic Jesus, he does not sufficiently emphasize the wider relation between God and man, of which Jesus is prophecy and type. In both these respects we see his Christology being supplemented and corrected by his successors. While Kaftan [1] works back through the historic Jesus to the absolute God who is revealed in him, Troeltsch [2] seeks to show by a comparison with other religions that in Jesus the true ideal for humanity is real-

[1] *Dogmatik*, pp. 437 sq.
[2] *Die Absolutheit des Christentums und die Religionsgeschichte*, Tübingen, 1902.

ized. The result is an enrichment of Christology through a fuller recognition of the different points of view which have entered into the making of the historic doctrine.

Outside of these more distinctly theological theories we find many in our day who have adopted a purely humanitarian view of Jesus. To a certain school of modern Unitarians, for instance, Jesus is simply one of the great leaders and teachers of humanity. In their reaction from the artificiality and abstraction of the older Christology, they have gone so far as not only to deny the metaphysical deity of Jesus, but to call in question his moral perfectness. In part this position is due to a lack of sympathy with certain elements in the New Testament picture of Jesus; in part to the theoretical difficulty of conceiving of a perfect individual in an imperfect environment; in part, also, — and this not least — to a passion of brotherhood, which, in joy at the recovery of the human Jesus from the clouds of dogma behind which his life has been obscured, is impatient of any barrier which separates him from other men. Such a barrier moral perfection seems to be; and it is for this reason rather than because of any lack of reverence for his person, that we find some in our day hesitating to affirm the sinlessness of Jesus.

Taking recent Christological thought as a whole, we note the following general characteristics : (1) The effort to *realize* instead of simply *affirming* the humanity of Christ ; (2) the disposition to find the proof of his divinity in his unique character and historic influence rather than in a metaphysical construction of his person ; (3) the tendency to emphasize the naturalness of incarnation as the fulfilment of the true relation between God and man, together with the corollary that in God's special indwelling in Christ we have the type and pledge of a wider incarnation in a redeemed humanity. In connection with these three points we may bring to expression the distinctive Christian convictions concerning Christ.

4. *The Permanent Elements in the Christian Thought of Christ.*

(1) The true humanity of Jesus has always been a fundamental article of Christian faith. It is as essential to John as to Mark ; to Cyril as to Nestorius ; to Luther as to Calvin. The difference between the older and the more recent theology is not a difference of faith, but a difference of conception. Whereas the authors of the Chalcedonian formula and their successors were content to treat humanity as an abstract idea which could be isolated in thought from its embodiment in a particular man or men, to modern theologians humanity is an unmeaning abstraction apart from its realization in individual lives. This difference is due in part to a different philosophy ; in part it represents a difference of ideal, the mystic conception of a change of nature through the impartation of a superhuman life, having given place to the ethical ideal of the full realization and development of human personality in a transformed and perfected society.

When, therefore, we study the life of Jesus we are not content simply to note the marks of genuine humanity which the Gospels present; the facts of birth [1] and of death ; of development, physical, mental and spiritual ; of limita-

[1] It is the desire to emphasize the reality of the birth rather than its exceptional character which explains the place given to the doctrine of the virgin birth in the Apostle's creed. Against the docetic tendency to resolve all elements of weakness and limitation in connection with our Lord's life into a mere semblance, the creed asserts that he was really born and that he really died (*i. e.* descended into Hades, the place of departed spirits). The same interest finds expression in the familiar phrase in the *Te Deum,*

tion and dependence; of suffering in body and mind; of temptation and struggle. We seek to reconstruct the environment in which Jesus lived, and to show how, under the particular conditions in which his life was lived, his experience came to take the form it did. We see how the universal truths he taught, and the unchanging ideals he revealed were necessarily framed in local and temporary settings from which it has ever since been the task of his followers to disengage them. In a word, we see in Jesus the embodiment of the ideal in an individual life, with all that that implies.[1]

The doctrine of the human individuality of Jesus, so far from weakening his universal significance and authority, is the indispensable condition of securing both. It is the means through which the divine truths he reveals and the divine life he exemplifies are brought into vital relations with the conditions under which all human life is lived. The individuality which separates him from every other man is at the same time the bond which unites him to all men, by making him partaker of the limitations which they share. If Jesus, living the life of a Palestinian Jew of the first century, could realize the divine ideal for man under the conditions which surrounded him, then such realization must be possible in the jungles of India or in the slums of London. Environment becomes an opportunity instead of a barrier, and all turns upon the spirit

---

"When thou tookest upon thee to deliver man, thou didst *humble* thyself to be born of a virgin."

[1] The unwillingness of the theologians of the fifth century to admit that Jesus was an individual is readily understood in view of their philosophy, which made such a doctrine equivalent to the denial of his representative or universal character. It is not easy to see, however, why modern theologians who no longer hold this philosophy should hesitate to admit a fact so patent on every page of the New Testament.

with which it is met. It is here, in the character and quality of his inner life, that we find the most striking difference between Jesus and other men, and the secret of his unique influence over them. This uniqueness finds expression in the doctrine of the Messiahship of Jesus.

(2) In applying the Messianic conception to Jesus, Christian faith ascribes to him two qualities of fundamental religious importance, (1) authority, and (2) saving power. He is the one through whom we receive the authoritative proclamation of God's will. He is at the same time the one through whom we are conscious of receiving power to realize it. In both these respects he does for humanity at large what the Jews expected the Messiah would do for Israel; and it is in his performance of this double function that his unique significance consists.

In the interpretation of the uniqueness of Christ, we find differences analogous to those which we have already noted in connection with his humanity. Where the problem is approached from the point of view of abstract metaphysics, the uniqueness of Jesus is found in the possession of supernatural endowments separating him from other men; where historical and psychological considerations are controlling, his uniqueness is found in his moral character and in the transforming influence which he has exerted on the spirits of men.

A study of Jesus' own conception of his person and work shows that the authority which he claimed and the influence which he exerted were of the latter kind. His transformation of the Messianic idea consisted largely in restoring to their place the ethical and spiritual qualities which the apocalyptic conceptions of the later Judaism had obscured. Refusing the appeal to miracle, in the sense of wonder, he made his appeal directly to the conscience and the will of his hearers, and went to the cross rather than invoke the aid of external force in support·of his claim. Throughout the later history his greatest triumphs have been won by spiritual means, and the blood of the martyrs has been the seed of his church.

To men trained to think of God as an arbitrary and transcendent being whose fundamental attribute is force, this reliance upon spiritual means has ever proved a stumbling-block. Accordingly we find men interpreting the human life of Jesus as an episode in the process of the divine self-manifestation; an exception to God's ordinary method of dealing with men. The incarnate life is contrasted as a state of temporary humiliation with the glory which the Christ possessed before his birth, and the exalted state to which he was restored by the resurrection. The attributes which are regarded as most characteristically divine are the metaphysical properties which separate Jesus from all other men, rather than the moral qualities which unite him to them. From this point of view, humanity with all that it involves becomes a problem for theology, and divinity is proved not through it, but in spite of it. Either, as in the various forms of docetism, Christ is regarded as concealing from men's knowledge the divine attributes he possessed; or, as in scholastic Calvinism, his consciousness is regarded as alternating, now divine and now human; or else, as in the theory of the kenosis, he is regarded as temporarily renouncing those attributes which are inconsistent with deity, to resume them again at the resurrection.

With a truer conception of the nature of God, and of his relation to man, this difficulty disappears. The moral qualities and influences on which Jesus relied during his earthly ministry are seen to be those which are most characteristically divine; and the proof of his uniqueness is found less in his ability to use supernatural means not open to his fellows than in the extent to which he showed himself master of the moral and spiritual influences to which the deepest in man responds. In Jesus we hear the voice of God speaking to our conscience, as nowhere else in history, and through submission to him we are conscious of a moral and spiritual transformation which requires God for its explanation. This is why we give him a divine significance we do not attach to other men.

This sense of Jesus' unique mission and authority finds expression in the doctrine of the deity of Christ. The true meaning of this doctrine has been often misunderstood. It is not the declaration that God is to be found only in Jesus, but that he is everywhere and always like Jesus. It is the confession of Christian faith that in Christ we have the revelation of the true nature of the ultimate reality who is the source and law of all things. In contrast to the dualistic view which holds that outside the moral realm where the principles of Christ are supreme there is another whose law is force, to which his authority does not extend, it is the affirmation that the God who reveals himself in Jesus is master of both realms, the physical as well as the moral. This is a conviction which is of the highest importance for Christian faith. As we have elsewhere seen,[1] in connection with the doctrine of the Trinity, it is the means by which we bring unity into our world-view, and make Christianity a rational as well as an ethical faith.

But it is one thing to hold that moral forces are supreme in the universe, and another to suppose that this supremacy must show itself by physical means. The difficulty with

[1] Chapter X, pp. 159 sq.

the older conception of Christ's deity was that it did not always observe this distinction. It is characteristic of moral supremacy that it can manifest itself only by moral means; and the effort to supplement the moral proof of Christ's deity by the evidence of physical power, as in the traditional form of the argument from miracle, is really the denial that the righteousness and love which we have seen to be supreme in God are the world-conquering powers which Christian faith affirms them to be.

In the light of these considerations we are in a position to see what is the real significance of the doctrine of the pre-existent Christ. It is not a means of carrying back the consciousness of the human Jesus into a divine realm of whose conditions and laws we are ignorant; but of asserting our faith that in him we have the revelation in human form of the unchanging God of whose progressive self-revelation all history is the story, and who is destined at last to win all men unto himself.

In like manner when we affirm our faith in the continued existence and supremacy of the risen Jesus, we do not presume to picture the conditions under which his life is at present lived, or to catalogue and classify the different elements, human and divine, which enter into his consciousness; still less to explain in detail the exact relation which his heavenly life holds to our present life on earth. It is enough to know that the Master who drew men with such persuasive power while upon earth still lives and loves those for whom he showed his care here; that his spirit still watches over his disciples, restraining them from evil, and winning them to good; and that at last, when life here is over, those who have followed him in humility and trust will join him in the Father's house whither he has gone before to prepare a place for them. This is a truth which is consistent with very different conceptions of the life after death, and has its support less in any detailed information derived from the early witnesses of the resurrection than in our present experience of Jesus' continued influence, and the witness of history to the growing supremacy of his kingdom among men.

It is evident that from this point of view the proof of Christ's divinity is not something which can be conducted without reference to his influence upon his followers. As, at the beginning, faith in Christ owed its origin to the redemptive experience of which he was the mediator, so it has continued to maintain itself because of the vitalizing and transforming influence which he has exercised in the life of his followers. Like every other theological doctrine, that of Christ's divinity has a teleological character, appealing to the future for its full justification, and standing or falling with his continued moral supremacy in the life of the race.

Here is where the historical method, which from one point of view has seemed to imperil the supremacy of Christ, is proving itself an unexpected aid to faith. By setting Jesus in his environment as a man among men, it prevents us from judging him by an abstract standard of perfection which has no possible application to the conditions of real life, and so helps to reveal for the first time the originality and grandeur of his character. Such a life, lived under such conditions, has more than an individual significance. It has typical or representative character, and constitutes an ideal for the race. This leads us to the final point in the Christian estimate of Christ.

(3) The doctrine of the representative character of Christ holds a fundamental place in the New Testament. The profound interest which the apostolic writers take in the divinity of Jesus is due to the fact that they see in him

the type to which his disciples are destined to conform.[1] The same interest continues throughout the later history. When we substitute for the artificial constructions of the older theologians our more historical and psychological conception, we are seeking to accomplish the same end which inspired their endeavor; namely, the attainment of a view of Christ which has representative character, or, in other words, which presents us with a genuine human ideal.

We have already seen that in their desire to emphasize Jesus' brotherhood with men, some contemporary writers think it necessary not only to reject his metaphysical uniqueness, but also to deny his moral perfection. Since sin is a characteristic feature of human life as we know it, they believe that Jesus must also have shared it. To separate him from all other men as the ideal for imitation is from this point of view as gross an inconsistency as to make him the sole object of worship. Thus, in the supposed interest of the true humanity of Jesus, his representative or ideal character is denied.

So far as this position is a reaction against the application to Jesus of an abstract standard of perfection which ignores the conditions of individual life, it has a relative justification. So far as it involves the theoretical denial of the legitimacy of finding the ideal for the race realized in a single individual, it is based upon an inadequate estimate of the part played by exceptional individuals in promoting social progress. Progress along any line is possible because some individual anticipates the attainments of his fellowmen; and, realizing in his own person that which for them remains an ideal, proves the means of raising them to the higher level on which he himself stands. If this be so, there is nothing impossible in the supposition that the

[1] Cf. Rom. viii, 16, 17; 2 Cor. iii, 18; 1 John iii, 2; John xvii, 22, 23.

moral ideal of society may be realized at last through influences proceeding from a single individual, in whose character the ethical possibilities which lie latent in other men attain their full development, and in whom the goal toward which they are moving is anticipated.

This is what Christian faith affirms of Jesus. In him it sees one who, on the stage on which his own life was lived, has completely embodied the principles through whose universal application the social ideal would be attained; and who, because of this fact, becomes the type toward which social progress is tending. The perfect man, as Christianity conceives him, would be one who should unite in himself the consciousness of untroubled communion with God and the self-forgetting love of man which characterize the experience of Jesus, as our Gospels portray it to us.

It is from this standpoint that the doctrine of the divinity of Christ receives its deepest significance. When we see in Christ the incarnation of God, we interpret in the light of his character and purpose the unseen being who is at once the source of history and its goal. Throughout the universe we find God at work in the spirit and for the ends which Christ has revealed, preparing the way for his fuller revelation in Jesus. It is not that in Jesus we have the manifestation, for a brief period, of divine powers and relations normally absent from human life; but that in him for the first time there has been completely revealed in a human life that abiding relation between God and man which gives life its profoundest significance, and which warrants our faith in the ultimate realization of the divine ideal in humanity.

With this conception of incarnation as the expression of the ideal relation between God and man, we are in a position to see what is the truth for which the doctrine of the kenosis stands. This is not metaphysical but moral; not a matter of the renunciation of attributes, but of contact with sin. If it be God's chief desire to impart himself to man, his entrance into humanity in incarnation cannot constitute his humiliation. The real humiliation consists rather in the fact that, because of sin, his loving purpose has been so long delayed. In like manner the exaltation of the incarnate one consists not in his removal from human limitations, but in the triumph of his love; not in the cessation of his sacrifice, but in its success. Here, as so often, difficulties which seem insoluble, when looked at from the standpoint of abstract metaphysics, vanish when the problem is approached from the teleological point of view.

Thus the special incarnation in Christ requires as its complement the wider incarnation in humanity; and the life of Jesus remains incomplete till it is contemplated in relation to the larger social ideal whose realization it is designed to promote. This is the standpoint from which we must approach the conception of the work of Christ.

CHAPTER XX

1. *Concerning Terminology.*

THE mediatorial work of Christ is commonly treated in Protestant theology under the formula of a triple office (*munus triplex*), — prophetic, priestly, kingly. The terms come from the history of Israel; but the conceptions for which they stand have been so transformed by the Christian spirit as to be misleading without interpretation. Hence, some theologians have proposed to discard the traditional terminology in favor of some less ambiguous terms. The difficulty is, however, no greater than that which meets us in the case of other Christian doctrines, and there is an advantage in relating our modern statements to the older forms about which historic associations cluster. In themselves the terms are well adapted to express the main aspects of Christ's mediatorial work. As prophet, he reveals God to man. As priest, he represents humanity before God. As king, he shows himself the spiritual leader of mankind, deserving and receiving the allegiance of those who love and serve the good. It is important, however, to remember that in using different terms to describe Christ's work, we have to do not with three separate and independent functions, but only with three different aspects of the same redemptive work. The supremacy of Christ is realized through the spiritual activities for which the prophetic and the priestly titles stand.[1]

[1] Cf. Ritschl, *Justification and Reconciliation*, Eng. tr., vol. III, p. 428.

In like manner, the prophetic work is not something apart from the priestly; but Christ's revelation is made in large part through the self-sacrificing service which culminates on Calvary.

The treatment of the subject is further complicated by the ambiguity of the term Christ, the word being used in theology, now to denote the historic Jesus, now the divine Word of whom his human life is the expression. In the latter case, the work of Christ is as wide as humanity, including all the influences, both before and after the appearance of the historic Jesus, by which mankind is redeemed from sin, and the kingdom of God established among men. In the former case attention is concentrated upon the special part played in this world-wide process by the historic Jesus. It is in the narrower sense that we shall use the term here. All the more important is it therefore to remember that to Christian faith the special ministry of the earthly Jesus is only a part of a continuing divine work, which runs throughout all history and makes use of many agents. This truth finds striking recognition in our terminology. When we call Jesus prophet and priest, we describe him as one who inherits older ideals and carries to completeness a ministry already begun.

2. *Christ as Prophet.*

We have already treated the prophetic aspect of Christ's work so fully in connection with the doctrine of revelation that little need be added here. As applied to Christ the word is used in its wider sense of preacher, revealer ; not simply in the narrower sense of one who predicts the future. In Old Testament prophecy, prediction was a subordinate function. This is still more the case in Jesus' revelation, the characteristic of which was to bring the distant God near.

As prophet, Jesus reveals God to man — and this both on the side of his holiness and of his love. In his life and work, we have the manifestation in time of God's abiding attitude toward sin. We learn through him the seriousness of God's estimate of sin and its inevitable consequences, but at the same time the depth of his loving purpose. We see him drawing men to himself, bearing with their weakness, enlightening their ignorance, forgiving their sins, and at the cost of infinite patience and suffering restoring them to their true position as sons of God and members of his kingdom.

As prophet, Jesus further reveals man to himself. In him we see the ideal which God has for the individual, and so the standard by which he judges him. We learn how far even the best of men fall below the possibilities of human achievement, and the extent of their need of divine help; but we learn also the greatness of human opportunity, and the divine capacities which lie latent in even the worst of men. This is the truth which is expressed in the doctrine of Christ as judge.

And as Jesus reveals the individual, so he makes known also the true social ideal. In the kingdom of mutual love and self-sacrificing service which he came to found we have at once the goal toward which social progress is tending, and the standard by which all existing forms of social organization must be tested.

This revelation Jesus gives not only in the form of teaching but of example. In him men see truth made incarnate. He draws men with the magnetism of personality, appealing not only to the intellect but to the affections and the will. Learning of him, his disciples

become transformed into his image. They, too, feel the
prophetic call, and go forth in his spirit, to proclaim by
word and life the saving truths which they have learned
of him.   Thus, as revealer of God, Christ acts in a representative capacity, being in his own person what it is the
divine purpose that all men should become — a divine
word or utterance of God in humanity, the expression
of the divine thought in terms of character and life.

This representative character is made still more apparent
in the second term used to describe Jesus' work — that
of priest.

3. *Christ as Priest.*

A priest is one who represents his fellows before God
in worship, offering sacrifice on their behalf, and making
intercession for them.   It is a term which expresses the
social solidarity which is so prominent a feature in early
religion; and its significance must be determined by a
study of the activities through which the priestly function is realized.   Among these the most important is that
of sacrifice.   The conception is so foreign to our modern
methods of thought that a brief historical review may
prove helpful.

In its simplest meaning, a sacrifice is a gift offered by
man to the deity to express some religious feeling or to
attain some desired end.   It is a recognition of the intimate relationship between the god and his worshippers,
and of the former's right to a share in all that is theirs.
Hence we find great variety both in the materials used
in sacrifice, and in the conditions under which it is
offered.   In an agricultural people, sacrifice may consist
of corn or of wine; among a pastoral people, of a sheep or
a bullock.   There is abundant evidence that in early times

human sacrifice was a widespread custom; and it is not unlikely that it was practised in the Canaanitish religion with which Israel was brought into intimate contact during the period of the judges.

With the growing centralization of religion, the freedom which characterizes early sacrifice is gradually curtailed. Instead of the worshipper being his own priest, a special order of men arises, whose function it is to offer the sacrifices prescribed by the official religion. In place of a multitude of local shrines, we have a single central sanctuary; and the various forms of sacrifice which had grown up naturally to meet special needs are classified, and the manner and details of their observance rigidly prescribed. The primitive meaning of sacrifice as a gift to God tends to disappear, and is superseded by the conception of a ritual observance instituted by God, and gaining its significance because of its divine appointment. This is the conception which meets us in the later codes of Israel.

As the sense of sin grows more profound, the sacrificial system is brought into closer relations with the moral problems of guilt and of forgiveness. Originally no more important than the other offerings, the sin-offering becomes the sacrifice *par excellence*. The life-blood shed by the priest is conceived as purifying the worshipper from the stain of sin, and so restoring the fellowship between God and man which sin has impaired. All the other sacrifices of the year culminate in the great ceremony of the Day of Atonement, in which the high priest, taking two goats, offers one for a sin-offering, while he lays upon the other the sins of the people, that he may carry them away into the wilderness to Azazel.[1]

[1] Levi. xvi. 10.

To understand the significance of the sin-offering, we must bear in mind (1) that the death of the victim is not thought of as a punishment, but as a means of purification; the sins of the people being conceived as covered, or wiped away, by the precious blood which is sprinkled upon them. In the ceremony of the Day of Atonement, where we approach nearest to the language of substitution, it is the living goat, not the goat which is slain, which is conceived as carrying away the sins of the people. (2) The efficacy of the sacrifice is due to its divine appointment, and is necessarily conditioned upon the penitence and amendment of the people. (3) It avails only for sins of inadvertence and ritual defilement. Wilful moral offences, whether against God or man, are beyond the reach of the sacrificial system, and are only to be dealt with by the free forgiveness of God.

It is against this background that we must set the priestly figure, in order to appreciate its significance as applied to Christ. Speaking to an audience familiar from their childhood with the sacrificial ritual, the writer to the Hebrews declares that in Jesus we have one who, by his perfect self-sacrifice even unto death, has made possible that free access of men to God which the old system was designed to promote, but which, through its limitation to ceremonial offences, it was unable to secure (vii, 11–25). In him we have one who for the first time presents to God on behalf of humanity that perfect sacrifice of obedience and service which he desires, and so shows men what is the true gift with which they may approach their Maker. This is not the outward offering of ritual observance, but the inner gift of obedience and loyalty (xiii, 15, 16). Thus, by his ministry he has once for all opened the way for his brothers into the true holy of holies, *i. e.* the immediate presence of God, whither he expects them in due time to follow him (ix, 24; x, 19–25).

We have here the same combination of the exceptional and the representative which we have already noted as characteristic of the Christian idea of Christ. It belongs to Christ's priesthood, as conceived in the letter to the Hebrews (1) that in Jesus God should see his ideal for humanity for the first time completely realized in a human life; (2) that the purpose and effect of this realization should be the reproduction of relations of similar intimacy in the case of all those who through Jesus have found the true way of access to God. Thus, with the substitution of a moral for a ceremonial conception of sacrifice, the necessity for priestly mediation in the old sense disappears, and the way is opened for the spiritual relationships which Jesus made central in his teaching and example.

In the later history, the priestly work of Christ is associated with ideas of expiation and punishment derived from other sources. His offering is conceived in terms of penal suffering rather than of 'obedience and service, and so the original meaning and significance of the sacrificial conception is lost.

The idea of expiation through suffering is a very ancient one. Where a wrong has been done for which the ceremonial system affords no remedy, atonement must be made by the death of the offender or his substitute. This conception finds striking expression in I Chronicles xxi, where David's sin in numbering the people is atoned for by a pestilence in which seventy thousand of the people perish. It is the pre-supposition of the well-known passage in Isaiah liii, in which the stripes of the righteous servant are the means by which the wicked are healed. In the New Testament it has its most signal illustration in the Pauline conception of the crucifixion as the vóluntary acceptance on Christ's part, as a result of his self-identification with humanity, of the consequences in suffering, shame and death, to which their sin had made them liable.[1]

Side by side with the ceremonial conception of purification through sacrifice, and the legal conception of atonement through suffering, we find a third set of figures applied in the New Testament to Christ, in which his death is compared to a ransom or purchase price, by which sinners are delivered from the bondage of sin.[2] The comparison was suggested by the provision made in the law for the enfranchisement of slaves upon the payment of certain specified sums of money, or by the familiar custom of the ransom of prisoners taken in war. What these money payments accomplish in delivering those in bondage from temporal captivity, the death of Christ is conceived to effect in securing the deliverance of transgressors from the deadlier bondage of sin.

Logically, the conception of Christ's death as a ransom admits two very different interpretations, according to the view taken of the power to whom the price is paid. Where dualistic or semi-dualistic ideas obtain, the death of Christ may be regarded as a ransom paid to Satan, as the prince of evil, under whose dominion man is brought by his sin. Where the sovereignty of God is the controlling principle, it is God who, as the guardian of justice, exacts the penalty which sin deserves; and it is God, therefore, who requires of Christ the sufferings and death which are the price of the redemption of humanity.

In the interpretation of Christ's priestly work the different lines of thought thus briefly indicated cross and

---

[1] *E. g.* Phil. ii, 5–8 ; Gal. iii, 13, 14.
[2] *E. g.* Mark x, 45.

recross. Christ's death is regarded now as a ransom paid to Satan, now as a sacrifice offered to God; and, where the Godward point of view is controlling, as has been the case on the whole since Anselm, its efficacy has been found, now in its moral quality as obedience, now in its penal quality as suffering. Often the two points of view are found side by side, as in the Westminster association of the active obedience of Christ with his vicarious suffering.[1] Still again we find other viewpoints controlling, as in Abelard's discovery of the efficacy of Christ's death in its moral influence as a revelation of God's love,[2] or in Luther's view of the atonement as the Saviour's victory over Satan and all the powers of evil.[3] In this whole matter of Christ's saving work we have to do with a conception so complex that no single formula can hold all the truth for which it stands; and it is not strange, therefore, that we should find theologians often led by the richness and many-sidedness of the Biblical imagery to break the bounds which their own logic has set.

With the growth of legalistic conceptions of the relation of God and man, we find a disposition to isolate the death of Christ from its surroundings, and to give it independent significance. Anselm sees in it an infinite satisfaction, equivalent in value to the wrong done to God's honor through man's sin, and graciously accepted by him as a substitute for the obedience they have failed to render.[4] Protestant theologians, replacing satisfaction

---

[1] *Conf. Faith*, chapter VIII, 5.

[2] In his *Commentary on Romans*, III, 22–26 (in Migne, *Patrologia*, vol. CLXXVIII, pp. 833 sq.).

[3] Cf. Köstlin, *The Theology of Luther*, Eng. tr., Philadelphia, 1897, II, pp. 409 sq.

[4] *Cur Deus Homo?* Eng. tr. in Deane, *St. Anselm*, Chicago, 1903, pp. 171 sq.

by penalty, retain the same language of substitution and equivalent. To them the death of Christ means his endurance of an amount of penal suffering equivalent to that which the infinite sin of man deserves. Calvin does not shrink from saying that on the cross Christ endured the torments of the damned, or to interpret the descent into Hades as a literal suffering of the pains of hell.[1] This suffering, by imputation transferred to the account of the elect, and appropriated by their faith, relieves them of the necessity of like suffering, even as the active obedience of Christ, accepted as a substitute for their imperfect righteousness, is the ground of their justification. Thus in different forms, the conception of Christ's work as representative is replaced by the very different idea of its substitutionary character.

In Roman Catholic theology, the effects of this change are in part neutralized by the parallel doctrine of the merits of the saints. Here we have the reassertion — to be sure in artificial and legal form — of the representative character of Christ's work. While for those of weaker faith an easy way of salvation is open through the store of merit laid up by Christ, to be administered by the church, the highest life is inspired by very different ideals. It is the ambition of the saint to give as well as to take. Through his own obedience and renunciation, if need be, even unto death, he seeks to add something to the store of merit which shall be available for his weaker brethren. Thus, even in the highest sphere of redemptive love, Catholicism holds out to its disciples the possibility of the imitation of Christ.

Traditional Protestantism, rejecting as it does the idea of churchly mediation, and relating the salvation of the

[1] *Institutes*, Bk. II, chapter XVI, 10, 11 (Eng. tr., vol. II, pp. 60, 61).

individual directly to the death of Christ, has found it less easy to recognize the representative character of his atoning work. The result has been that in its protest against one class of evils, it has fallen into others scarcely less serious. Not only has it expressed the significance of Christ's death in legal terms which fail to do justice to its moral and spiritual meaning — in this following the example already set by Catholicism — but it has given it a purely individualistic reference which ignores both the historical conditions under which it took place and the social consequences it was designed to promote. The death is represented as simply the fulfilment in time of a condition entered into by Christ in his eternal covenant with the Father, as a result of which the latter promised, in return for the price paid him, to give salvation and eternal life unto all those for whom the Son had purchased it.[1] In a transaction of this kind imitation would be as impossible as it is needless.

It is the merit of the governmental theory[2] that it breaks with this transcendent and individualistic conception, and seeks to relate the death of Christ to its historical environment. Rejecting altogether the ideas of legal substitution or of mathematical equivalence, it sees in Christ's death a necessary outcome of the social consequences of sin, and explains its saving efficacy by its moral influence in bringing about repentance. Its weakness lies in the fact that

[1] Cf. *Conf. Faith*, chapter VII, 3; chapter VIII, 5.

[2] By this name we describe a view of the atonement first set forth by Hugo Grotius in his famous treatise on the *Satisfaction of Christ*, and given currency in America by the New England theologians and the new school Presbyterian divines whose theology was formed under their influence. Its major premise is the denial of the principle of equivalence insisted upon by the penal theory, and the substitution of a public justice, which makes the welfare of society the controlling aim, for the private justice in which all turns upon the desert or ill-desert of the individual.

the categories which it uses are still those of law, instead of ethics or religion (public justice instead of private justice); and the motive on which it relies is that of fear rather than of love. These errors it is the effort of more recent theories to correct. While Campbell [1] describes the nature of Christ's atoning work in the personal terms of repentance and confession, Bushnell [2] calls attention to the vicarious nature of love, which identifies itself with its object, even to the bearing of his sins, and so proves the strongest influence leading to repentance. Ritschl [3] on his part describes the death of Christ as the inevitable outcome of his fidelity to his calling, and so as typical of the kind of service which God expects of every one.

With the substitution of the historical and psychological point of view for that of abstract metaphysics and law, the way is opened for a new appreciation of the representative character of Christ's work as priest. As the moral excellence which for the time separates him from his fellows constitutes him at the same time the type to which they are to conform, so the self-sacrificing ministry which culminates in Calvary should have its counterpart in the disciples' willingness to spend and be spent in others' service. The Christian ideal is not that of a society in which there are no priests, but one in which priesthood is a universal experience, each man bearing his neighbor's need upon his heart, and unsparingly giving himself for his salvation. It is because Christ's work issues in the production of such a society that we recognize him as the unique mediator between God and man.

[1] *The Nature of the Atonement*, 6th ed., London, 1886.

[2] *The Vicarious Sacrifice grounded in principles interpreted by human analogies.* New edition, 2 vols, New York, 1891.

[3] *Op. cit.*, pp. 472 sq.

Thus the atonement of Christ proves to be not an isolated thing which can be understood apart from its environment, but the culmination and expression of the entire relation in which he stands to God and man. It has its presupposition in the social ties which unite the different members of the human family, and its necessity in sin, with its resulting estrangement from God. Its characteristic mark is a sympathetic self-identification of Christ with sinful men, by which their sins and sorrows were felt as his own, and his capacities and ideals by faith transferred to them. Its saving efficacy consists in its moral influence in arousing repentance and faith; while its ultimate ground is found in the love of God, of whose eternal purpose to save the life and death of the historic Jesus are the most signal manifestation. In all this it is typical of the true attitude of man, both toward God and toward his fellows, and prophetic of the part, which, under God, his disciples may play as fellow-workers with Christ for the salvation of the world.

The fundamental presupposition of the Christian idea of atonement is the unity of the human race. We have seen that it follows from the nature of the Christian ideal as social that the relation of the individual to God is realized in part through his relation to his fellow-men. But this means that mediation is not simply a device artificially introduced to remedy the evils caused by sin, but an abiding element in human life.

None the less is it true that the character of mediation is profoundly affected by the fact of sin. We have studied elsewhere the consequences of sin,[1] and seen how profoundly it affects all human relations, estranging men

---

[1] Chapter XVII, section 4, pp. 277 sq.

from God, and preventing the realization of his loving purpose. It follows that the first task of any one, who would help men to realize their true relation to God, must be to turn them from the pride and selfishness which separate them from their Father in heaven. But this means that he must put himself into opposition to the prevailing tendencies in human society, and be prepared to pay the price, in suffering and shame, to which such opposition will inevitably lead.

In this condition of things we have the psychological explanation of the sufferings of Christ. The historical situation indeed determined why these sufferings should take the particular form they did; but the underlying causes were deeper than any particular historical situation — even the permanent opposition between good and evil which abides through the changing centuries, and leads everywhere and always to similar results.

The Christian church is therefore entirely right in refusing to consider the significance of Jesus' sufferings as exhausted in the historical causes which led to them. It has always interpreted them as a bearing, on the part of humanity's choicest representative, of the burden of the world's sin. In the crucifixion of Jesus, the perfect man, by the representatives of the highest authority in church and state, we see as nowhere else in history the awful consequences of sin. By the purity of Jesus' life, the unselfishness of his purpose, the breadth and intensity of his love, we measure the blindness and ingratitude which could thus reject and destroy one whose sole desire was to save and bless. In this consciousness of rejection by those he came to help, of failure where he had hoped to deliver, we may well find the bitterest drop in the cup of Christ's agony, and the explanation of the cry which theology has interpreted as the sense of his own personal rejection by God.[1]

Yet, inevitable as were Christ's sufferings, we do not understand their saving efficacy till we consider the spirit in which they were met. This was at once a spirit of submission and trust toward God, and of love and hope for man. There is no trace of rebellion against the divine will, only a filial acceptance of the cup which the Father has given him to drink.[2] There is no tinge of bitterness toward his persecutors, but only the prayer for their forgiveness as those who know not what they do.[3] Bitter as is the sense of his personal failure and loneliness, there is yet no despair for the future, but a firm faith that the love which has led him to the cross shall not fail of its fruit, but that, in the end, he shall yet see of the travail of his soul and be satisfied.[4]

It is the qualities of faith and love which give the death of Christ its value for God. Not its penal character as suffering, but its moral quality as obedience makes it acceptable in the divine eyes, and constitutes it the fulfilment of the ideal of sacrifice. In Jesus, God sees his own estimate of sin reproduced in man. From his lips — to use Campbell's striking phrase [5] — he hears, in response to his holy judgment, the Amen from humanity for which he longs. In Jesus, at the same time, he sees one in whom his loving purpose has become incarnate, and who is willing to die that his brethren may live.

[1] Matt. xxvii, 46.

[2] Matt. xxvi, 42.

[3] Luke xxiii, 34.

[4] Cf. Matt. xxvi, 64. The cry on the cross (Matt. xxvi, 46) must be interpreted in the light of the preceding prophecies (*e. g.* Mark viii, 31 ; ix, 31 ; x, 33, 34), in which his rejection is foreseen, and his suffering accepted as a necessary element in his redemptive work.

[5] *Op. cit.*, p. 117.

It is this union of faith and love in Christ's suffering which explains no less its saving efficacy for man. Such formulæ as that of the legal imputation of merit and guilt have a certain significance in that they represent the end of the redemptive process, as anticipated in God's judgment of the sinner from the first. But from the point of view of man, the problem is a different one. His question is how he may be actually delivered from the power of sin, and restored to fellowship with the divine Father whom Christ reveals. Here there are only two possibilities, either that of an impartation of new life through subconscious and non-moral means, as in the mystic idea of baptismal regeneration, or of a personal appropriation, through repentance and faith, of the moral impulse received through contact with Jesus Christ.

It is the characteristic feature of Christ's sufferings that in all ages they have been the means of producing such moral transformation. In the spectacle of Jesus, willingly suffering for others' sins, praying for forgiveness on his murderers, firm in faith that his loss would issue in others' gain, men have seen a new revelation of the possibilities of humanity, and of the victorious power of love. Conscious in themselves of the same selfishness and pride as that which nailed Christ to the cross, they have been led by the contemplation of the faith and love of the dying Jesus to a new hope and to a new resolve. Turning to God in penitence and faith, they have found in him the strength which they have elsewhere sought in vain, and been conscious of an inward renewal in which fear has given place to trust, rebellion to submission, shame to hope, and selfishness to love. Thus Christ has proved in very truth the mediator of salvation unto those who come unto God through him.

But this saving influence is possible only because in

Christ we have the revelation in human form of that redemptive love which has been in God from the beginning. Christ is mediator, not because he propitiates an angry God, but because he shows those who have been wandering in self-imposed orphanage what is the real character and purpose of their heavenly Father. In the last analysis, salvation belongs unto God; and we gain the full moral influence from the atoning death of Jesus, only when we look through him up to the divine sin-bearer who through all the ages has been carrying the burden of the world's sin and suffering upon his heart.

We see now why it is possible to give the atonement of Christ a representative character without imperilling the completeness and sufficiency of the divine salvation. It is not that we by our sacrifice and renunciation supplement the inadequacy of Christ's work (though the apostle Paul does not scruple on one occasion to use such a figure [1]); but that it is our privilege by imitation of Christ's self-sacrificing ministry to help make known to men that unchanging divine love which is the final ground, as it gives the sole assurance of salvation; and so to hasten that good time when all men shall know by experience the peace and joy which come from trust and service.

Thus the priestly work of Christ, no less than the prophetic, points forward to the future, and cannot be completely understood without reference to the redeemed society in which it issues. This future reference is still more prominent in the third of the mediatorial terms applied to Christ — that of king.

[1] Col. i, 24.

4. *Christ as King.*

The kingship of Christ is only another form of expressing his Messianic office.   It stands for the authority which
he exercises and the power he exerts as God's representative in the founding of his kingdom.   As such it is the
complement of the priestly idea.   As that represents Christ
in his renunciation as suffering servant, this emphasizes
the victory to which the renunciation leads.   It is a word
of triumph, of attainment.

The kingly work of Christ has been differently interpreted according to the different views taken of his person.
Where the evidence of his deity is found in his possession
of the attributes of omnipotence, omniscience, etc., his
kingship is thought of as exercised in those acts which
most conspicuously display superhuman power, such as his
resurrection from the dead, his ascension to heaven, his
sitting at the right hand of God, and his coming again in
glory to reward his disciples and to judge the wicked at
the second advent.   Where, on the other hand, the proof
of Christ's divinity is found in his moral perfection, his
kingship is given a spiritual interpretation.   It is found
in the authority which he exercises and the influence which
he exerts by virtue of his character.   It is the expression
of that transformation in human life which we have seen
to be so conspicuous an effect of his ministry.   This being
the case, it is not necessary to confine the kingly work,
as is commonly done in traditional theology, to the post-
resurrection life.   We find examples of it during his
earthly ministry, and not least in the manner in which
he met his sufferings and death.[1]   It is indeed his mastery

[1] This is a point which has recently been emphasized by Ritschl. Cf.
Justification and Reconciliation, Eng. tr., vol. III, p. 460.

over the temptations and evils which have proved too strong for other men, which explains the influence which he exerts over the lives of his disciples.

This mastery is apparent first of all in his own person. It appears in his victory over temptation; in his patient endurance of suffering; in his indifference to adverse judgments; in his independence of public opinion; in his refusal to be moved from the path of duty either by love or by fear. It appears in his self-poise and self-command; in his reserves of sympathy and patience; in his calm and untroubled consciousness of God. In all these we see marks of the life of attainment; of a consciousness able to bring the divine into the midst of the human, and rejoicing here and now in the presence and the peace of God.

The mastery of Jesus is further apparent in his influence over others. The same qualities which distinguish his own character reappear in greater or less degree in the lives of his disciples. Through him, they are conscious of being delivered from the life of bondage and fear, and of being made partakers in the freedom and the peace of God. This consciousness of discipleship, manifesting itself through the different centuries in the most varied forms, is the evidence in experience of the spiritual supremacy of Jesus.

The consciousness of discipleship in the Christian sense must not be identified with that blind submission to authority which has sometimes been put forth as the supreme religious virtue. It is the consciousness of having been brought by Jesus into that personal relation to God in which he is known by direct experience. It is marked by the same immediacy and freedom which is found in the consciousness of the Master himself, who, in his kingly, no less than in his priestly and prophetic work, represents the type to which every true man should strive to conform.

Accordingly we find the authority which characterizes the teaching of Jesus perpetuated in the preaching of his disciples. They too speak what they do know, and testify what they have seen; and they, like him, win others to their cause by the inner constraint of truth and love. So the Christian church grows from age to age, as the work of Jesus is carried on by his disciples, and his spirit is reincarnated in their lives.

Nor is the influence of Jesus apparent only in those who consciously confess him Lord. It is seen in the transformation of standards and of ideals which is apparent in society as a whole. In our own day it appears in the widespread dissatisfaction with the individualism and selfishness of the present economic system; in the growing protest against war as a means of settling disputes between nations, and in the rise of ideals of international brotherhood and peace. Not least is it seen in the new social spirit to which the settlement movement among others has given voice, which aims to break down the artificial barriers created by class distinction, and to find a common meeting ground for man as man. In all these we see evidence that the spirit of Jesus is making itself felt in society, and his principles winning the allegiance of men.

Nor should we be surprised if in the upward movement of humanity we find other centres of spiritual influence which cannot be traced historically to Jesus. If Jesus be in truth, as Christian faith believes, the expression in human form of the unseen God of whose redemptive influence all history is the scene, we should expect to find, as we do, that the stream of truth and power which has its rise in Jesus, is met and reinforced in its onward course by other tributaries tending toward the same end. The proof of the spiritual supremacy of Jesus is not to be found in the number of those who call him Lord, Lord ; but in the fact that the principles and ideals to which he has given the highest and purest expression, prove themselves the dominant forces in the life of men.

In this growing influence of the Christian ideal, faith sees a foretaste and a prophecy of that complete embodiment of the principles of Jesus in the life of individuals and of society, which constitutes at once the goal of history and the consummation of salvation. Not through an abrupt catastrophe, it may be, as in the early Christian hope, but by the slower and surer method of spiritual conquest, the ideal of Jesus shall yet win the universal assent which it deserves, and his spirit dominate the world. This is the truth for which the doctrine of the second advent stands. What this involves and how it is to be brought about we shall consider in another connection.[1] Here it is only necessary to say that it cannot be by the abandonment of the spiritual principles which we have seen to be characteristic of Jesus' ministry, in favor of the method of external constraint and force ; but only by following out to their final successful issue those methods of appeal to the conscience and the heart whose study has thus far engaged us.

[1] Chapter XXIII, section 2, p. 416 sq.

PART VI

THE CHRISTIAN LIFE

CHAPTER XXI

THE NATURE OF THE CHRISTIAN LIFE

1. *General Characteristics.*

THE Christian life may be variously described, according to the point of view from which it is regarded. In relation to God, it is a life of filial dependence and trust, in assurance of his fatherly forgiveness and care, expressing itself in obedience, worship and prayer, and having its fruit in peace and hope. In relation to men, it is a life of brotherly service, and of labor for the advancement of Christ's kingdom, having its motive in love, and its fruit in joy. In relation to the forces of evil, it is a life of effort and conflict, characterized by a continual struggle against sin, and a growing victory over it; and having its fruit in a character conformed to that of Jesus Christ, in purity, sincerity, humility and sympathy.

Along all these lines it is a life of growing likeness to Christ, through progressive appropriation of his spirit.

This general conception of the Christian life is consistent with great variety in detail. Apart from the differences which are the natural result of various degrees of proficiency, and which tend to diminish with advancing experience, we find permanent differences of type. All the more important forms of the religious life are reproduced within Christianity. One man's piety is of the mystic type, leading him to minimize the importance of the historic and the concrete, and to seek communion with God in the immedi-

acy of feeling. In another the intellect is dominant, and
the energies of the religious nature are directed primarily
to understanding the nature of God, and to tracing the
outworking of his purpose in nature and history.   To still
another the test of true religion is found in conduct, and
the Christian life described in terms of the imitation of
Christ. These differences are the religious expression of
permanent differences of human character and endowment.
Christianity, the heir of all that is human, has not obliterated them, but only informed and transfused them with
the Christian spirit.

None the less is it true that the Christian experience has
a distinctive character.   This is due to the fact that it has
been formed under the influence, direct or indirect, of the
historic Jesus. Even of the mystic type of Christianity
it is true that the God with whom direct communion is
sought is one who takes up into his infinite being the
wealth of content which Christian history has associated
with that august name, and is described in terms of love
and grace which gain their fullest meaning through reference to historic revelation.   It is Jesus through whom the
mystics are conscious of having been led into the immediate presence of God, even if they part company with him
there.   Still more obviously is this the case with those
whose religious experience is more distinctly intellectual or
ethical in type.   Here both the idea of God and the ideal
of conduct have been formed under influences into which
the personality of Jesus has entered as a determining
factor, and the character of the resulting piety is necessarily
affected thereby.

Characteristic of Jesus' religious experience was the extent to which he succeeded in harmonizing two elements
which in our own commonly appear as contrasted, — the

sense of attainment and possession which gives quiet and poise to life, and the firm grasp of ideals whose realization lies still in the future. From one point of view Jesus is the one who, through his revelation of God as a present factor in experience, has brought into human life a peace unknown before. From another point of view, as the preacher of the kingdom of God as the supreme good, he has shown himself the most radical of reformers. These two aspects reappear in greater or less degree in every succeeding expression of the Christian experience, and the Christian ideal is realized through their perfect reconciliation and harmony. To understand the nature of the Christian life, therefore, we must consider it, first in its religious, and then in its ethical aspect.

2. *The Christian Life in its Religious Aspect.*

In its religious aspect, the Christian life is a life of communion with God. It is a life in which God is not only recognized as the giver of every good and perfect gift,[1] but as himself the supreme good, whose presence and fellowship give life its highest meaning and joy.

Communion with God, as thus defined, must be distinguished from the pantheistic ideal of absorption in the divine being. Communion is an ethical and spiritual term. It implies the fellowship of persons, and has as its result the development, rather than the destruction, of the individual self-consciousness. In the Christian experience God is known as Father and Friend; and the loss of self, which is the ideal of religion, has as its result that discovery of the true self, which is the inevitable consequence of all outgoing toward a worthy object.

This explains the important place held by the historic

[1] James i, 17.

Jesus in the Christian experience. It is through Jesus that we have come to know God as we do. In his life and character we see the clearest revelation of the unseen Father from whom he came. Under the influence of this impression our idea of God has been formed. It is inevitable, therefore, that the thought of Jesus should be indissolubly associated with our thought of God. The Father with whom we commune is no unknown deity, but the God and Father of our Lord Jesus Christ. In the measure that this association falls into the background, our religious life tends to lose its distinctively Christian character.[1]

But this is a very different thing from saying that we have no direct communion with God in experience, and that all our knowledge of him comes to us indirectly through inference from his historic revelation in Jesus. All true religious life involves the recognition of God as present. The Christian life differs from other religious life only in its conception of the God with whom communion is had, as a God personal and moral, revealing himself in man's present experience as the possessor of the attributes of holiness, wisdom and love, which have their supreme illustration in Jesus.

In this conception of God as personal and moral, we have the explanation of a further feature of the Christian experience, namely, its religious estimate of all life. Since God is the Lord of the whole world, present in all life, and manifesting his loving purpose throughout all history, every phase of human experience may furnish an occasion of communion with him. Especially is this true of our relation to our fellow-men. Since all men are our Father's children, among whom it is his purpose to establish his

[1] This is the truth emphasized by Herrmann in his well-known book, *The Communion of the Christian with God.*

kingdom, every effort to help and serve men is at the same time an effort to further his purpose, and should have as its effect a more vivid consciousness of fellowship with him. The ideal of the religious life is realized in Christianity, not by forsaking the world that one may lose oneself in God, but by carrying the sense of God's presence and purpose into all life. It is not that the world-consciousness is swallowed up in the God-consciousness, but that it is transfigured thereby. The means by which this is brought about is faith.

Faith, in the Christian sense, may be defined as personal commitment of self to "the unseen but living God, as he is revealed in gracious character in Christ, the Saviour of men." [1] It is not simply belief, though it involves an intellectual element in the recognition of God's character as revealed in Christ. It is an act of the will which involves the personal commitment of self to God in trust, and has its expression and evidence in obedience. So defined, faith is the fundamental religious virtue, and the necessary condition, as it is the only means, of salvation.

While especially associated in Christian thought with that initial act of consecration to God with which the Christian life in its higher forms commonly begins, faith is by no means confined thereto. On the contrary, it abides as a permanent element in the religious life. It is not only the instrument of justification, but of sanctification as well. It is the presupposition of all the higher religious virtues, and enters so indissolubly into the making of the Christian life that the words of the apostle are literally true : " Whatsoever is not of faith is sin." [2]

---

[1] Clarke, *op. cit.*, p. 403.
[2] Rom. xiv, 23.

The test of true faith is obedience.   Apart from this we may have belief in the sense of intellectual assent; we cannot have the trust which is essential to religion.   Trust is confidence which expresses itself in conduct.   As distinct from belief, therefore, saving faith may be defined as trust enough for obedience.

Psychologically, religious faith has its analogy in that attitude of mind which leads to the practical acceptance, as working principles of life, of fundamental assumptions in themselves incapable of rational demonstration.   In science it shows itself in the acceptance of such a generalization as the universality of law, which in turn is only an application of the larger assumption of the rationality of the universe.   In ethics, it shows itself in the acceptance of a moral order, evidencing itself in the sense of obligation, and giving the universe as a whole ethical significance.   In both cases we see postulates of feeling (*Werthurtheile*) raised to the dignity of intellectual hypotheses, and justified as such by their practical results.   Faith, as thus defined, is presupposed by all our living, since it is only through such postulates that we grasp unseen reality.

Religious faith differs from other faith simply in its object, which is God ; Christian faith differs from that of religion in general, in its conception of God as Christlike. Psychologically, the process in all three cases is the same, and the methods of verification in practice are similar.   Of the nature and limits of this verification in the case of the Christian idea of God we have already spoken in another connection.[1]

The communion with God upon which man enters through faith expresses itself in worship.   By worship is meant that reverent outgoing of the spirit toward God in

[1] Chapter IX, section 3, pp 132 sq.

adoration and praise, which is the result of seeing in him the supreme source of truth and of beauty, of holiness and of goodness, of life and of love. In view of the personal relation between God and man which is involved in the conception of God's Fatherhood, Christian worship takes the form of prayer, that is, of personal address of the soul to God, with desire and assurance of response.

In its larger definition, prayer is only another name for the personal communion of man with God. It is the form which worship takes when consciously addressed to a personal being capable of responding, such as the God and Father of our Lord Jesus Christ is conceived to be. It includes adoration, praise, thanksgiving, confession and aspiration, as well as petition in the narrower sense. As Dr. Clarke has well said, " All confidences enter into it, and no genuine speaking to God is excluded from its range." [1] The common identification of prayer with petition unduly narrows it, and gives an inadequate conception of its real importance and significance in the Christian life.

Yet, though petition is not the whole of prayer, it is a legitimate and necessary part of it. This results from the fact that both in the individual and in society the Christian life is still incomplete. We are conscious that we ourselves are not yet what in God's plan we ought to be, and no genuine speaking to God can ignore the fact. So with praise and thanksgiving go inevitably the petitions for forgiveness of sins and deliverance from temptation. Again, when we seek to follow Christ in labor for his kingdom, we are aware of a thousand obstacles which thwart, and often seem utterly to defeat our efforts. So prayer that is natural and sincere must ever include as one of its

[1] *Op. cit.*, p. 413.

elements the petition that these obstacles may be removed, and God's kingdom come.

Nor in considering prayer as petition is it easy to draw any hard and fast line between what are sometimes called material and spiritual blessings. The bond between the physical and the spiritual is so close that often we cannot clearly distinguish where one ends and the other begins. Even in the realm of the spirit, we cannot always be sure what will best promote God's loving purpose. Hence every petition must be qualified by the proviso: "Not my will, but thine, be done."

It is not in its objects, then, so much as in its spirit, that the real test of Christian prayer is found. In all that he asks, the Christian should recognize that it is God and not man who must be the final judge as to what is best. Opening up our hearts before him, with all their desires, as children to a father, we leave them with him to deal with as he thinks best, knowing that " he doeth all things well."

This is the true meaning of the formula, " through Jesus Christ," with which Christian prayer is commonly concluded. We come to God through Christ or in his name, not as though through him we had gained a right of access not otherwise open to us ; or as though on account of his merits God might be induced to do for us what he would not otherwise have done; but because it is through Jesus that we have learned the true way of approach to the Father, and we would offer all our petitions in the spirit of which he has set us the example.

In the light of these principles, we are in a position to approach the vexed question as to answers to prayer. It follows from the relation of God and man, as we have defined it, that the possibility of answer in the sense of personal response by the being addressed is of the very essence of prayer. Apart from this there could be no communion, and worship would resolve itself into esthetic admiration or ethical enthusiasm.

But this does not mean that our requests work any change in the purpose of God. The conception of prayer as a means of influencing an unwilling God to do that which he would not otherwise have done rests on a theory of the relation of the divine will to the human which we have seen to be equally unsatisfactory to ethics and to religion. The true conception of prayer is that it opens the way for the impartation of the divine blessings by providing the necessary condition of their bestowal, and this all along the line. Even in the realm of the physical it is true that while our prayer may work no change in the laws which express God's method in this realm, and hence in the specific event which is in question in our prayer, it may yet produce a change in our attitude to the event, and so in its significance for our life. It may turn what we might have interpreted as an evidence of God's indifference or alienation into an indication of his loving purpose, and so bring into our lives that sense of his presence which is the chief blessing of religion. Still more is this the case with those prayers which have for their direct object victory over temptation or deeper spiritual insight. They are the necessary means for bringing their own answer; since it is only through the sense of personal communion with God which prayer promotes that we can gain the added power or knowledge for which we ask.

What experience shows to be true of petition in our own case is our encouragement for its use in the case of others. If there be no other result of our prayer, it will certainly have its effect in a changed attitude on our

25

own part. I cannot pray honestly for another without working for him, and so helping to answer my own prayer. The case of the apostle Paul is a conspicuous example. Yet there is no reason for confining the influence of our prayers to such reflex action. As the Father of spirits, God has direct access to the spirits of all men; and we know not what part in the complex system of spiritual influences through which his kingdom is advanced may be played by the prayers offered in faith and love by Christians on behalf of their fellows who are in need. Here the example of Jesus is full of instruction. No one knew so well as he the loving purpose of the Father toward his children; yet this did not prevent him from praying for them. If we pray for men in the spirit of Jesus, we may be sure that our prayers will not be in vain.

As a life of communion with God manifesting itself in trust, obedience and prayer, the Christian life is characterized by the filial spirit. It is indeed best described as the life of children with their Father, and is marked by the qualities which this life, in its ideal form, is adapted to promote. These are humility, confidence, freedom and peace.

In the first place, the Christian life is a life of humility. By humility is meant that disposition to subordinate one's own individual interests and claims which is the result of long association with one who is wiser and better. It is the spirit of teachableness and receptivity; the reverse of pride and self-assertion. In the Christian life it manifests itself in cheerful acceptance of whatever lot God may assign, and whatever suffering he may send, because of trust in the wisdom and love of the sender.

Yet, at the same time, the Christian life is a life of confidence. This is due to the knowledge of God's loving purpose as revealed in Christ. It is the spirit of the child who, conscious of his own dependence and need, knows also his father's love and power, and therefore comes to him with boldness, sure that nothing which is really for his good will be refused. It is this aspect of the Christian life which received special emphasis at the Reformation through Luther's insistence upon the doctrine of assurance.

The true significance of Christian assurance has been often obscured by its association with the doctrine of election. The result was to turn men's thoughts from the present to the future, and concentrate them upon final salvation. But it is not a future but a present state which is the primary object of religious assurance. It is God's present forgiveness and acceptance of which we have experimental knowledge, and which is the ground of our confidence. None the less is it true that since the God with whom we have present communion through Christ is at the same time the Lord of all life, our thought reaches out inevitably to the future, and the consciousness of present acceptance and forgiveness passes imperceptibly into hope of final salvation.

The Christian life is further a life of freedom. With the knowledge of God as our Father, to whom we stand or fall, and with whom alone we have to do, all artificial barriers which restrict the freedom and spontaneity of life fall away. This is true not only of the outward barriers of public opinion and of law (considered as external precept received on authority), but of the inner tyrants, fear and care. In sorrow and suffering the Christian learns to see God's messengers, sent to teach him some lesson he could not otherwise learn, and hence powerless to do him harm. Death becomes the door which leads from one room to another in the Father's house. Sin itself loses its terrors as, through the cross of Christ, he learns to know the power of redeeming love, and anticipates by faith the final victory over evil, of which God's present forgiveness gives him the foretaste.

Finally, the Christian life is a life of peace. By peace is meant that inner harmony and self-mastery which comes from the complete subordination of all man's powers to a single controlling and all-embracing purpose. To know all in God's hands and ourselves his children, is to have the discords of life resolved into harmony, and its rest-lessness exchanged for quietness of spirit. This rest in work through trust in God is that Christian peace which passeth understanding.

So to live as a child of God in humility, confidence, freedom and peace is to realize the ideal of the Christian life in its religious aspect.

3. *The Christian Life in its Ethical Aspect.*

In its ethical aspect, the Christian life is a life of brotherly service, having its motive in love and its fruit in joy. The description of this life in detail belongs to Christian ethics. Here we can indicate only in a word its leading characteristics.

As a life of love, the Christian life is essentially social, and its nature in the individual can be described only in terms which describe or assume his relation to others. The ethical ideal of Christianity is that of a life in which each man, by faithfulness to his own special function in society, promotes the welfare and advances the happiness of others. It is the ideal of the family in which a common life is real-ized through many members, love providing at once the bond of sympathy and the motive to service.

The love which is the distinguishing characteristic of the

Christian life is not the love of indulgence which is content to gratify desires already existing. It seeks to realize the higher life which Christ has revealed as the ideal for man. Like the divine love from which it springs, it has a prophetic quality, embracing by faith that which it cannot yet see. It does not ask what is easiest or pleasantest, but what is best. Hence, if need be, it is not afraid to say No; or to bear the misunderstanding and reproach which refusal may bring.

This aim determines the character of Christian service. It is not the self-conscious ministry which has for its object the acquisition of individual merit (as in the Catholic conception of almsgiving). It is the expression of that truest sympathy by which one enters into the feelings of others, identifies his interests with theirs, and makes their joys and sorrows his own. Hence it is not content with the indiscriminate application of general principles, but seeks by patient study of the desires and capacities of the individuals to be helped, to find what is their supreme need and how it can most wisely be met.

In this loving identification with others' needs is found both the occasion and the necessity for sacrifice. Sacrifice, in the Christian sense, is not simply that renunciation of lower aims and purposes which is the inevitable price of the pursuit of an ideal end. It is the cheerful acceptance of the specific consequences in misunderstanding, reproach and shame which follow from seeking an end in conflict with the prevailing tendencies and desires of one's fellows. It is not all sorrow, but such sorrow as is the special result of Christlike ministry. As the pathway of loving service along which Christ chose to walk led inevitably to the cross, so it must be in the case of the disciple. There is something of Calvary in every true Christian life; and the truer it is, the more completely will it exemplify the meaning of sacrifice.

As the effort to realize the Christlike ideal in a resisting environment, the Christian life is further a life of conflict. This is true not only of its outward, but of its inward aspects. The enemies which oppose without (prejudice, misrepresentation, slander, contempt, social indifference and inertia, as well as active opposition of every kind) are reinforced by allies within. Old feelings of pride and self-esteem, old habits of self-indulgence, the natural love of ease and comfort, the instinctive desire to stand well with one's neighbors, the human craving for response from those we love : — all these war against the Christian spirit, and can be held in check only through ceaseless vigilance. Again and again the Christian is conscious of having fallen below the divine ideal ; of having unworthily represented his Master. Constantly, as he turns to God for the help and strength he needs, he is conscious of the need of forgiveness for new sins. So repentance enters as a permanent element into experience.

By repentance we mean not merely sorrow for sin, but the actual forsaking of it, and turning to God " with full purpose of, and endeavor after, new obedience." [1] It is the converse of faith; the turning from evil which is implied in every true turning to God. Like faith, it is an essential element in true religion, and holds a place of fundamental importance in the Christian life.

The necessity for continual repentance should not be due simply to the repetition of the same sins. If this were the case, there would be small hope of final victory. It is rather the result of the enlarging insight which comes with wider experience. This requires a continual re-interpreta-

---

[1] *Shorter Catechism*, question 87.

tion of the old ideal in the light of the new environment. The old duty is seen in new relations. The old principle receives new application. The claims of Christian love become more insistent, and the sacrifice which it requires takes on larger proportions. So, in new forms, the old battles have to be fought over again. This is an incident in Christian growth, the inevitable accompaniment of the life of progress.

We have elsewhere considered the place of progress in the Christian life.[1] We have seen that the Christian ideal is not one of changeless perfection, but of development toward an end. This end is the complete application of Christ's principle of self-sacrificing love to the life of individuals and the organization of society. It is in the consciousness of having some part in the promotion of this supreme end that the joy of Christian living consists.

By Christian joy is meant not simply the feeling of exhilaration which goes with all healthful activity; but that higher satisfaction which is the result of effort for a worthy end. It is the joy which springs from the consciousness of being fellow-workers with God for the upbuilding of his kingdom and the salvation of man.

Thus the sense of God's presence, which is the crown of the religious life, reaches over into the sphere of ethics and glorifies it. It gives the struggles and toils, the sacrifices and failures, which would otherwise dishearten, a divine meaning. Anticipating by faith the victory for which he strives, the Christian learns with the apostle to rejoice in all things, as he presses toward the goal which is set before him by God in Christ Jesus.[2]

[1] Chapter XIV, section 2, p. 218.
[2] Phil. iii, 13, 14; iv, 4.

It is in the light of this conception of the Christian life, as a life of filial trust and of brotherly service, that we must conceive the nature and functions of the Christian church.

4. *The Christian Life in its Social Expression (the Church).*

Both in its religious aspect as worship, and in its ethical aspect as service, the Christian life finds social expression in the church. We have elsewhere defined the nature of the church, and indicated its function as the means through which the revealing and redeeming work of Christ is perpetuated, and the Christ life mediated to the world.[1]   Here it is necessary only to indicate the way in which this mediatorial function is fulfilled.

As a worshipping body, the church gives social expression to that experience of communion with God which is characteristic of the individual Christian life. It is the recognition of the fact that on the religious side of his nature, which finds expression in prayer and praise, man is not an isolated individual, but a member of a community with common needs, aspirations and hopes. Nor is this communion confined to the living. Through the church the individual enters into relations with all those who have gone before him in the Christian life ; the prophets and teachers and saints of every age and land, who with him recognize their dependence upon the God whom Christ has revealed. Thus, through contact with those of deeper experience and profounder insight, both in the present and in the past, the spiritual life of the individual is quickened and enriched, and his worship made more intelligent and acceptable.

[1] Chapter V, section 1, p. 57.

As a working body, the church is the society through which the desire of the individual to serve his fellows is made practically effective for the solution of social problems. It represents the forces of unselfishness and righteousness, so far as they are organized for the pursuit of common social ends. It is related to the church as a worshipping body as the ethical life of the individual is related to his religious aspiration; namely, as the means by which the spiritual power and insight which man needs are brought to bear upon his wider life for its uplifting and ennobling.

Like all human societies, the church of Christ fulfils its ideal end only through outward organization. We have considered in another connection [1] the rise of institutional Christianity, and noted its various forms in doctrine, ritual and ministry. We have seen how natural and inevitable was this outward embodiment, yet at the same time how narrowing and cramping were its effects. We have seen how the conflict between vital and traditional Christianity expressed itself in the distinction between the church visible and the church invisible, and noted the various problems to which this distinction gave rise. These problems, acute even in Catholicism, became still more insistent in Protestantism, through the breaking down of the old distinction between the religious and the secular. Where all life is seen to be sacred, and every form of honest work may be a Christlike ministry, the question as to the true function of the church as an institution becomes a pressing one. Ought it to be extended till it takes in all the good work now performed by other organizations, or should it be restricted to a narrower sphere; and, if the latter, where shall its specific function be found?

[1] Chapter V, section 2, pp. 59 sq.

The former of these solutions is favored by those who advocate the so-called institutional church. They would add to the function of the church as a centre of common worship and religious instruction that of the organization and direction of all the charitable and philanthropic agencies of the community. It is no doubt the case that there are many neighborhoods where such extension is both practicable and desirable. This is notably true of the neglected quarters of great cities. It is true also on the foreign field, where, under the direct control of mission boards responsible to the churches, we see a great variety of Christian activity being carried on along educational, social, medical and even industrial lines. Yet, however far this extension may be carried, it cannot go far enough to take in all the ethical activities of Christians, or supersede the other natural forms of organization, the family, the school, the state and the various agencies to which these have given rise. A distinction must always be made between the church as an institution organized for worship and religious teaching, and the church as the society of men and women laboring to establish the kingdom of God. The former fulfils its true function not by attempting to rival other organizations in their own sphere, but by giving the men and women who come under its influence an inspiration which will enable them to apply Christ's principles and to exemplify his spirit under all the varying conditions of our complex modern life.

This is the justification for the prominent place given to worship in the ideal of the church. It is in worship that the spirit of man communes with God ; and it is through such communion that there comes upon the soul that sense of rest and peace, of attainment and mastery, which is the condition of the highest and the most effective living.

But if worship is to be central in the life of the church, it must be Christian worship; not the selfish absorption of the soul in God for its own sake, but such communion with the Father as gives strength and wisdom for the service of his children. The church should be the place where the lonely gain the sense of companionship, the discouraged new faith and hope, the perplexed fresh insight into duty, the weary renewed strength. It should be the place where those who have been working in isolation come to the consciousness of their oneness in Christ, and the purpose and resolution of each is reinforced by contact with the larger fellowship of which he is part. In a word it should be at once the source of inspiration and the bond of union for all who love and serve their fellow-men.

For this high work of inspiring and uniting there is no other social institution which can take the place of the Christian church. We have many agencies which have for their aim the promotion of ideal ends, and many organizations which are laboring manfully for the advancement and betterment of mankind. But each has its special field, and its fixed limits; and in this limitation each finds its strength. The church alone exists to remind men of their common origin as sons of God; of their common destiny as members of his kingdom ; of their common privilege as fellow-workers with Christ. The church alone has for its specific function the proclamation of the Gospel of Christ, as the message which all men alike need. And as long as it fulfils this function in fidelity and truth, it will find that it has a place in the organization of modern society which nothing else can take.

This is why the divisions in the Christian church give cause for such serious concern. It is not simply that they produce wastefulness and ineffectiveness in practical work, disheartening as this may be. It is because, through the misunderstanding and lack of sympathy which they cause, the church is prevented from fulfilling the highest and most important of its functions; that, namely, of providing a centre where all who would serve their fellows in the spirit of Christ may meet to renew their consecration through conscious communion with God.

The remedy for this situation is not to be found in any changes in the outward organization of the church, however desirable in themselves such changes may be ; but in a clearer vision of Christ's purpose for mankind, and a deeper experience of his transforming power. At the root of the outward differences which so baffle and perplex us, there will be found in every case a difference of ideal. It is in the realm of the ideal then, with which theology is concerned, that we must look for that ultimate adjustment, out of which effective co-operation will grow. When men have come to understand what Christ really desires for the world, and have had sufficient experience of the joy of his service to be willing to make the sacrifices he requires, then — and not till then — will the problem of church unity be solved.

CHAPTER XXII

In discussing the source of the Christian life, we have to distinguish its ultimate source in God, its beginnings in experience, and the outward means by which this experience is produced.

1. *The Divine Source (the Holy Spirit).*

The ultimate source of the Christian life is God, who not only in his providence provides the outward means by which the Christian experience is mediated; but through his Spirit acts directly upon the spirit of man, and is recognized by faith as himself the source of whatever is good and true in human life.

Historically, the doctrine of the Spirit is an inheritance from Israel. Originally denoting the energy of God which came upon men to fit them for special work connected with the upbuilding of the divine kingdom,[1] the Spirit comes to be conceived as the immanent life of God in the soul of man. Its marks become prevailingly ethical and spiritual, and the convincing proof of its presence is a character acceptable to God.[2] This conception of the Spirit of God as an abiding presence is further developed in Christianity, and finds its clearest expression in the writings of Paul and John. Here the Spirit is identified with that divine influence through which the Christ-

---

[1] *E. g.* Ex. xxxi, 3; Judg. vi, 34; xiv, 6.]
[2] Psalm li, 10, 11.

like life is realized in man. It is the means through
which the God who was outwardly manifest in Jesus
makes his presence inwardly felt in the life of his disciples. Hence, it is often difficult to distinguish in the
New Testament between the living Christ and the Spirit,
the two terms being used in more than one passage inter-
changeably, and the Spirit of God being described as
the Spirit of Christ.[1]

The theological interpretation of the doctrine of the
Spirit has varied with changing conceptions of the Trinity.
Some make the Spirit a separate personality within the
Godhead, having a self-consciousness as distinct as that of
Jesus; others regard the term as only a name for the
activity of the personal God himself, as manifest in the
consciousness of man. Our previous discussion has shown
the difficulty which besets any attempt to express the
difference between the Logos and the Spirit from the Godward side; and made it clear that the simplest view is
that which regards the Spirit as a term expressive of God's
activity in the soul of man, as distinct from his outward
manifestation in nature and history.[2]

Psychologically, the recognition of God as the source of
the Christian life is an expression of the fundamental religious experience of dependence. It is the obverse of that
consciousness of insufficiency and unworthiness which
grows with widening experience and deepening insight,
and is most marked in the best of men. It is a fact that
those who have gone farthest in the Christian life are most
conscious that they owe what they are, so far as it is
good, not to themselves, but to the God who worketh in

[1] 2 Cor. iii, 17; Gal. ii, 20; iv, 6; cf. John xiv, 16, 17, 26, with 18, 23;
1 Pet. i, 11; Rom. viii, 9.
[2] Chapter X, pp. 156 sq.

them both to will and to do of his good pleasure. We find parallels to this experience in the consciousness of the artist and of the poet. Even in our human relations it is often true that we owe what is deepest and best in us to others. Sonship is a matter of the spirit, as well as of the body ; and it is as an expression of spiritual dependence that the filial figure most adequately expresses the relation in which man stands to God.

Philosophically, the conception of the divine Spirit as the immanent life of God in man is involved in all the difficulties which beset our attempt to define the relation between the divine will and the human. Where the will of man is isolated from God as an independent cause, the Spirit will be conceived as one influence among others acting upon man, and the true relation between God and man be expressed in terms of co-operation. Where God is thought of as able to control the human will, the Spirit will include all the influences through which this control is exercised, of whatever nature they may be. It is in the description and estimate of these influences that the view taken of the nature of the Spirit is most clearly revealed, and the test furnished by which its Christian character may be determined.

Apart from the primitive conception which finds the proof of God's presence in extraordinary and abnormal manifestations, due to physical causes, we find three main views as to the way in which the divine life is produced in man. The first, or mystic, view holds that it is brought about by abstraction from all outward contacts ; and consists in an indescribable experience in which all ordinary influences are transcended. The second, or sacramentarian view, holds that the Spirit's influence is mediated by external objects divinely appointed for the purpose, and working *ex opere operato ;* and that the presence of the divine life is to be regarded as following the due performance of such acts even when other outward evidence is lacking. The third, which is the view of historic Protestantism, holds that whatever part may be played in the production of the divine life by subconscious influences, it requires for its normal development the appeal of the Gospel to man's reason and conscience, and is most clearly evidenced by the presence of the Christlike character which the Gospel is adapted to promote. It is in the light of the latter conception that we must judge of the nature and efficiency of those outward influences for promoting the Christian life which theology describes under the name of " means of grace."

2. *The Historic Media (the Means of Grace).*

As means of grace theology designates those outward influences by which God's historic revelation in Christ is brought to bear upon the lives of men for their salvation. In the Protestant conception these may all be summed up under the name of the *Gospel.* By the Gospel is meant the good news of God's redeeming love in Christ, as preserved in the Scriptures, preached by the living voice, pictured in the sacraments, and progressively verified in Christian experience. The unity of this conception is sometimes obscured by the familiar division of the means of grace into the Word and the sacraments, as though the two represented different principles. But in truth, Protestantism knows but one means of grace, namely, the *Word,* or message of God's love in Christ, of which the sacraments themselves are but one among other forms of expression.

This emphasis upon the Word, or Gospel, as the sole means of grace must not be understood as a narrowing of the conception. It is simply the expression of the fact that the God with whom we have to do in religion is a

rational and ethical being. If God be our Father and we
his children, then the means which he uses to make himself
known to us to-day must be moral and spiritual in character, appealing to the conscience and the will. This explains
the prominent place which Protestantism assigns to the
Bible among the means of grace.

Yet, important as is the function of the Bible as a means
of promoting the Christian life, it is only one of many ways
in which the Gospel is brought home to men. Before the
books of our New Testament were written, the good news
found expression in the preaching and personal witness of
the first disciples, and it continues to utter itself in the same
form to-day. It is in this form of personal witness, born of
experience, that the Gospel makes its most effective appeal
to the lives of men in every age, and the truths recorded in
the Bible are felt in their convincing power. So the Word
preached takes its place side by side with the written Word
as a means of grace.

This explains the central place which the sermon holds
in the religious worship of Protestantism. The sermon is
often contrasted with the other parts of the Sunday service
as that in which man addresses man. But, in truth, the
human and the divine should mingle in all parts of the
service ; and the ideal sermon, no less than the prayer and
the hymn, should promote that contact between the human
spirit and the divine in which worship consists. It is
through the sermon, with its direct message concerning a
God who is known in experience, that the truth of God is
made vivid, concrete, personal. It is through the sermon,
with its appeal to the reason and the conscience, that the
meaning of all the other acts of worship is made clear, and
so that sense of God's presence intensified, without which
all outward observances are superstitious and vain. It is

through the sermon, finally, that the will is most directly addressed and men are led to that consecration of self which is the truest worship.   In all these respects the sermon stands for that personal witness of man to man which is the most effective means for the propagation of the Gospel.

It follows that the ministry of the Word cannot be confined to those who have been formally set apart by ordination to the service of the church as an institution. Wherever a man has learned by experience the love and truth of God and is moved to express his knowledge to his neighbor, there we have a Christian minister in the true sense of the term.   The ideal of Protestantism, like that of Moses of old, is of a time when all the people shall be prophets, testifying of God with the authority which comes from personal experience of his redeeming grace.

Besides the written and the spoken Word, all branches of the Christian church, except the Friends, recognize certain symbolic acts called sacraments as means through which the grace of God is imparted to men.   The importance of this conception, both historically and practically, renders explanation and definition necessary.

In the broadest sense, the sacraments are the recognition within Christianity of that desire for the expression of the devout feeling in acts of outward ceremonial which is a common feature of all religions.   This connection is recognized in the Westminster Confession, which applies the term "sacraments" to the rites and ceremonies of the Old Testament, and conceives of them as fulfilling the same function in the religious life of Israel as the sacraments of the New Testament in Christianity.[1]

From the point of view of history the origin of the specific acts given sacramental character by the church

[1] *Conf. Faith*, chapter XXVII, 5.

is an entirely natural one, growing out of the circumstances of the case. Baptism has its parallel in the purifications practised by the Jews, and its direct anticipation in the work of John the Baptist. The Lord's Supper consecrates as memorials of the death of Christ the bread and wine which formed the staple of ordinary food, and was long observed by the primitive Christians in connection with the daily meal. It was only gradually, in connection with the growth of the church as an institution, that they lost their primitive simplicity and received the ecclesiastical character which has ever since characterized them. The same is true of the later sacraments. Each is the consecration to ecclesiastical usage of an earlier custom.

We have elsewhere considered the form taken by the sacramental conception in Catholicism.[1] By a sacrament in the Catholic sense is meant an outward act, performed by the priest who is Christ's representative, as the divinely appointed means for the impartation of a mystic grace, not to be obtained in any other way. As such, the due conditions on both sides having been fulfilled, it works *ex opere operato,* that is, without the necessity of the conscious participation of the receiver. In the course of time, this conception, at first applied indiscriminately to many religious acts, was more accurately defined, and the limits of its application settled. As at present held, the Catholic sacraments are seven in number: baptism, confirmation, the Eucharist, penance, marriage, ordination and extreme unction. Through these the grace of God is brought to bear upon all the more important crises of human life. Apart from them there is no ordinary possibility of salvation. So central are they in the religious life of Catholicism that the doctrines of the church gain their chief impor-

[1] Chapter XVIII, pp. 308 sq.

tance as explaining their presuppositions, and the methods of their activity; and the ministry owes its unique authority to the fact that it has the monopoly of their administration. Better than any other single word, sacramentarianism describes the Catholic conception of religion.

With the growth of the legal conception so prominent in Roman Catholicism, the sacrament of the Eucharist is given a Godward as well as a manward reference. In the change produced by the words of the priest in the elements offered on the altar (transubstantiation) Roman Catholicism sees a repetition of the sacrifice of Christ on the cross, and hence a means through which influence may be brought to bear upon God. As such, the mass becomes not only the centre of Catholic worship, but the most important instrument in that method of practical control and discipline known as the penitential system.

The Reformers rejected not only the conception of the mass as a sacrifice, but also the underlying sacramentarian conception of which it was a development. They restored the Word to its central place among the means of grace; rejected the later sacraments as superstitious corruptions, and gave to those which they retained a new significance. Baptism and the Lord's Supper were no longer regarded as embodying a different principle from the Word, but as one of the forms in which the Gospel was made known and its grace communicated. This appears in the Reform ers' rejection of the *ex opere operato* theory, and th insistence upon faith as the necessary condition, throu which alone the sacraments become effective for salvation.

As to the exact nature of the influence exercised by the sacraments the Reformers themselves were not agreed. While Zwingli and the Swiss reformers gave them a symbolic or pictorial significance, Luther insisted upon a real impartation of grace. Calvin occupied a middle position from which he tried in vain to bring about an understanding.

As defined in the Westminster Confession, a sacrament is an outward act instituted by God to be a " sign and seal of the covenant of grace," and " to represent Christ and his benefits " to believers.[1] While under ordinary circumstances of the highest importance, it is not absolutely essential to salvation.[2] Still less does the partaking of it by a person without faith confer any guarantee of his receiving its benefits.[3]

In the later interpretation of the sacraments we see the same disposition to vary between an internal and an external criterion, which we have already noted in connection with the older Protestant conception of the Bible. The sacrament is defined as an outward act immediately instituted by Christ, and depending for its efficacy upon the fidelity with which his directions are observed. Yet, when the qualities are described which give it its spiritual significance, the test is made inherent. The efficacy of the sacrament is declared to depend upon the inner relation between the sign and the thing signified, and hence its adaptation to produce the spiritual apprehension of truth to which faith is the response. In the same way we have seen how the Protestant conception of the Bible as a book to be received on internal grounds, because of the response of the spirit to the truth which it presents, was combined with a doctrine of inerrancy which had its origin in a very different conception of authority.

The conception of the sacrament as an outward rite depending for its efficacy upon the correct mode of its

[1] *Conf. Faith*, chapter XXVII, 1.
[2] *Ibid.*, chapter XXVIII, 5.
[3] *Ibid.*, chapter XXIX, 8.

administration has its most conspicuous illustration in the view that immersion is necessary to a valid performance of baptism. This is a relic of the legal conception of Christianity which conceives Jesus as the giver of a new law, rather than as the revealer of a new principle. It is the more singular that it should so often have been held by representatives of a body whose insistence upon the responsibility of the individual to God, and the sacredness of the rights of conscience, made them guardians of the principle of religious liberty at a time when other Christian bodies were in danger of neglecting it.

As opposed to this view it is to be maintained that the significance of the sacraments depends not upon the circumstances of their origin, but upon their inherent nature as rites adapted to illustrate the truths of the Gospel, and consecrated by centuries of Christian association and experience. Hence, the answer which scholarship may give to the questions which have been raised concerning the circumstances of their institution can no more destroy their significance for Christian faith than similar investigations into the human authorship and composition of the different Biblical books can overthrow the authority of the Scriptures, or undermine their influence as a means of grace.

Thus, in baptism we have a type of that purification of the soul from sin which is the result of personal consecration to God. It is a perpetual reminder of that great act of consecration by which the Master himself was set apart for his Messianic work, and the appeal to all who would be his disciples to follow him in like consecration.

In like manner, in the Lord's Supper we have the type of that spiritual feeding upon God through which the higher life of man is nourished. In the broken bread and the poured out wine we have the symbols of the life freely given for the world's salvation, and through this vivid presentation of the human love which led the Christ to Calvary, we realize more deeply the divine love which through all the ages has been bearing the sin of mankind. Thus, partaking with our fellow Christians of the symbols of divine sacrifice, we become conscious as in no other way of the ties which bind us together, and go forth with deeper sympathy and renewed consecration to take up the work to which our Master calls.

Thus to interpret the sacraments is not to resolve them into mere symbols. They are means through which spiritual influence is actually conveyed to men, and the communion between man and his Maker is rendered more real and vital. Here the witness of those who have used these means in faith and prayer is too explicit to be denied. Christian literature is full of testimony to the strength and inspiration, the comfort and peace which have come to men and women as they have publicly committed themselves to Christ's cause in baptism, and sat down with their fellow Christians at the table which commemorates his redeeming love.

Yet, however tender and sacred the associations which gather about these special acts, it is none the less true that the sacraments fulfil their true function only as they help us to carry into all of life such a sense of God's presence and power as to make all that we do alive with spiritual meaning. As the true Christian ideal of the ministry is realized, not through the destruction of the idea of priesthood, but through its enlargement till it takes in all humanity, so it should be in the case of the sacrament. What is true of baptism and the Supper as ecclesiastical acts should be true of every washing and of every eating. The true Christian sacrament is life itself; and every deed done in the spirit of Christ should be an outward sign of the inward grace received from God through him.

3.   *The Beginnings in Experience.*

The question as to the conscious beginnings of the Christian life is complicated theoretically with all the difficulties which surround the origin of consciousness itself. In practice, however, it is very simple.   The Christian life begins with the first appearance of the penitence and faith which are its distinguishing characteristics.   Some perception of the difference between right and wrong is necessary. Some acquaintance with the God whom Christ reveals is presupposed.   But, so soon as this knowledge bears fruit in conscious choice of the good rather than the evil, the unselfish rather than the self-centred life, so soon the Christian life has begun.   This turning from selfishness to service through penitence and faith is known in theology as conversion.

Historically, there have been two different conceptions of the nature and significance of conversion.   To the first, conversion constitutes a distinct crisis in the religious experience, involving a radical alteration in the prevailing tendencies of life.   It takes place comparatively late in life, and after a considerable period spent in more or less conscious abandonment to sin.   According to this view, the type of experience witnessed in the revival meeting and the inquiry room is to be regarded as normal; and something similar is to be expected even in the case of those whose lives have been lived from the beginning under Christian influences, and who have enjoyed from childhood the help afforded by the home and the church.

The other conception holds that the Christian life, being natural to man, may and normally should begin with the beginnings of conscious experience. This being the case, it is not necessary that a person should be able to remember the definite moment when he first turned from sin to God. The true proof that the Christian life has begun is to be found in the character of a man's present choices, and in his growing experience of dependence upon God and love for his service.

While it is, no doubt, true that in the case of men who have long been living in habits of self-indulgence and vice, an abrupt change, amounting in some cases to a revolution, is essential; it is yet the fact that the method of growth more accurately describes the normal course of the Christian life. To deny this would be to overlook altogether the part played by social influences in the production of character, and to lose the momentum afforded by previous generations of Christian living. In the influences which go to produce Christian manhood and womanhood the home plays a part no less important than the church ; and both alike fulfil their most important function in winning the children for Christ and training them for his service from the beginning. This is the truth which finds ecclesiastical recognition in the practice of infant baptism.

From Protestant principles the practice of infant baptism can only be defended as a recognition of the part played by parents in the formation of the character of their children. The faith essential to the spiritual significance of the sacrament is, in this case, parental faith. In presenting their children for baptism, parents consecrate them to Christ, so far as it is in their power, and promise to surround them with all the influences, both of teaching and example, by which the Christian life is fostered and developed. Apart from this conscious consecration, infant baptism is but a magical ceremony, not only superstitious but dangerous, since substituting reliance upon an external act, working *ex opere operato*, for those definite and conscious influences through which alone the Christian life, as we have defined it, can be brought into being. In this form it may be, and often is, a hindrance to true Christianity; and the protest of the Baptists has its justification. Yet, as a recognition of the social aspect of the Christian life, infant baptism has a positive significance. The testimony to its spiritual value in enhancing the sense of parental responsibility is too extensive to be disregarded. It is not the practice itself which is dangerous, but a superstitious conception of its efficacy; and this is a danger which attaches to the retention of the sacrament in any form.

It does not follow, because the normal Christian life can best be described in terms of growth, that there is no room for crisis. Environment may prepare the way for choice; it cannot supersede it. As our development along other lines takes place through repeated acts of the will, meeting the new conditions which arise with new decisions, so it is in the Christian life. It is not that conversion has no place in the Christian life, but that its place is too important to be exhausted in a single choice. The true life is a continual turning from the lower to the higher, from sin to God. The initial consecration for which baptism stands is repeated again and again as deeper insight reveals more fully what Christian service requires and Christian sacrifice costs. Thus, in a sense as true as we have already seen to be the case with the repentance and faith which are its elements, conversion may be said to enter as a constant element into the Christian life.

This does not mean, of course, that all decisions stand on the same level of importance. There are occasions when it becomes necessary to take long looks and to commit ourselves to a course of action which will affect our entire future. With the approach of manhood such serious weighing of the future becomes natural, and in the choice of life to which such self-examination leads, religious motives should play a determining part. This may explain the fact, to which recent investigations have called attention, that the experience of conversion, when conscious, is commonly associated with the age of puberty. This is the time when boyhood passes into manhood, and readjustment is natural all along the line. It is only to be expected that this readjustment should show its effects also in the sphere of religion.

This conception of the beginning of the Christian life has an important bearing upon the motive which should inspire missionary activity. It is not that by bringing Christ to men of other faiths we are bringing life to those who are wholly dead. God has not left himself anywhere without a witness; and the same choice between good and evil, self-seeking and self-sacrifice, presents itself in one form or another to every child of man. It is rather that, by bringing to men the higher revelation of God which has come to us through Christ, we are helping them to that better and truer life for which their own past has been preparing them; but to which, apart from such help, they are incapable of attaining. Such conscious entering into the purposes of the God before worshipped in ignorance is the necessary condition for the establishment of the kingdom of God; and, hence, for the enjoyment of the blessings which it is God's desire to impart to all men through Christ.

CHAPTER XXIII

THE GOAL OF THE CHRISTIAN LIFE

THE difficulties which meet us in our efforts to explain the beginnings of the Christian life are intensified when we attempt to conceive its goal. This is due, in part to the inherent difficulty of forecasting the future, in part to our ignorance of the specific conditions under which much of our future life is to be lived. More than anywhere else, in its conception of the future, faith is constrained to abandon the attempt at exact definition and to use the language of picture and symbol.

None the less is it true that, as hope enters as a necessary element into the Christian life, some definition of its objects is possible. These have to do with the realization of the Christian ideal, both in the individual and in society. In each case hope reaches out inevitably beyond the present life and expects its ultimate satisfaction in the life beyond death. We have, then, to consider (1) the Christian hope of individual perfection ; (2) the Christian outlook upon history; and (3) the Christian view of the final consummation.

1. *The Christian Ideal of Individual Perfection.*

So far as the individual is concerned, the goal of the Christian life can be described in a single word, — Christlikeness. The question in debate is as to the time and conditions under which this ideal can be realized; whether, in other words, the attainment of individual perfection is possible in this life, or whether it must be postponed to another. Those who take the former view are called perfectionists.

The word "perfection" is sometimes used in another sense. As understood by Ritschl,[1] it is a name which describes the qualities which enter into the Christian ideal, however incomplete may be their quantitative realization in the individual. Thus a man whose life is characterized by the qualities of faith, humility, patience and fidelity to his calling is perfect in Ritschl's sense of the term; since he is living in the right relation to God, however conscious he may be of occasional lapses from his own standard. So defined, Christian perfection is only a name for that assurance which should characterize all true Christian living, and which is possible in every walk of life. It is the rejection of the Catholic doctrine of a double standard by which the possibility of perfection is confined to those who give themselves to the monastic life.

In the present connection, however, the word is used in its more familiar sense to denote the complete realization of the Christian ideal, and the question to be decided is whether such realization of the ideal is possible in this life or no. Those who maintain the affirmative base their contention partly upon specific Biblical passages in which perfection is spoken of as already attained by Christians;[2] partly upon the general ground that if the ideal revealed by Christ be a true human ideal, its realization must be possible for others as well as for himself. The arguments on which their opponents rely are partly theoretical and partly practical. The former is based upon the inherent

[1] *Op. cit.*, pp. 646 sq.

[2] *E. g.* 1 Cor. ii, 6; Phil. iii, 15; cf. Matt. v, 48; Heb. v, 14; James iii, 2, and especially the passages in 1 John, which deny the possibility of sin in the regenerate (*e. g.* iii, 6, 9; v. 18).

contradiction between the idea of perfection and the limitations inseparable from finiteness. The latter consists in an appeal to experience, which is claimed to show that apart from Christ no individual has been found to whom the term "perfect" can properly be applied.

The theoretical argument against the possibilty of individual perfection has its psychological ground in the experience of incompleteness and limitation which is the natural characteristic of a developing life. Experience shows that we gain one height only to find another still unscaled; and the best of men describe their life, with the apostle, in terms of aspiration rather than of attainment. This sense of incompleteness is reinforced by a study of man's social nature. If it be true, as we have seen, that there is no such thing as an isolated personality, but that man realizes his true self through his relations to his fellows, then the necessary condition for the production of the perfect individual would seem to be a perfect society, and to hope to see this within the limits of time compassed by a single life is manifestly out of the question.

It is clear that if this be the true conception of perfection, the denial would apply with equal force to the case of the Master as to that of his disciples. He, too, experienced the limitations which belong to a developing life, and was hampered at every turn by an imperfect social environment. If we do not scruple to call him perfect, it must be because the word admits a different meaning from either which we have thus far considered; namely, that of the complete fulfilment, within the limits set by individual endowment and environment, of that ideal of trust, obedience and self-sacrifice, in pursuit of which man's true life consists. Such fulfilment we believe that we find in Jesus, and it is because of this that we call him perfect.

By perfection, then, as used in the present discussion, we mean such complete subordination of self to God in each new situation of life as characterized Jesus' experience. The question whether perfection be possible for us is the question whether, within the limitations set for us by our individuality and environment, we can attain such trust, obedience and self-sacrifice as we believe to have been realized in him. To answer this in the negative would be to set a gulf between Jesus and other men which would not only imperil the genuineness of his humanity, but would render impossible of accomplishment the end for which he gave his life.

But, if we refuse to follow the opponents of perfectionism in their theoretical denial of the possibility of individual perfection in this life, we must admit that the testimony of experience favors their contention that, as a matter of fact, such perfection is not here attained. The Biblical passages on which perfectionists base their claim are either expressions of that mystical point of view in which all that is relative and temporal fades away before the contemplation of eternal reality, or else refer to that victory over deliberate and wilful sin which ought to characterize the normal Christian experience. It is such mastery over the more obvious forms of sin that perfectionists commonly mean by Christian perfection. But it is not from these alone, but from the subtler forms of selfishness that God would set us free; and such victory comes only slowly and after many failures. Those who seem to us most advanced in the Christian life are most conscious of their own unworthiness and imperfection. Not here, they tell us, but in the better life which lies beyond, is the ideal to be realized.   So the hope of individual perfection requires as its complement faith in immortality.

2. *The Christian Outlook upon History.*

The same problem which meets us when we consider the ideal of individual perfection reappears on a larger scale when we pass to the social ideal.   The two are indeed only parts of the same problem, the Christian hope for the individual being indissolubly associated with his hope for society, and the personal ideal being realized in the measure in which the love of self is superseded by devotion to the welfare of others.   Inevitably, therefore, the idea of the perfect society takes its place among the objects of Christian hope.   This idea is expressed by the kingdom of God.

We have elsewhere considered the conception of the kingdom of God,[1] and seen that in Jesus' teaching it has both a present and a future meaning.   In the first case, it denotes the divine life, so far as it is actually realized in the Christian community; in the second case, it expresses that complete realization of Christ's principles in society as a whole which is the final object of Christian hope.   It is in the latter sense alone that we are concerned with it here.   The question is whether it is possible for us to expect this realization in this life, or whether it must be postponed to another.   In other words, it is a question as to the Christian outlook upon history.

Before we can answer intelligently, it is necessary, first, to consider what the complete Christianization of society means.   It involves, in the first place, the preaching of the Gospel to all mankind; and this, not simply in the outward sense of bringing to all men the *knowledge* of

---

[1] Chapter XII, section 1, pp. 183 sq.

the historic Christ, but in the deeper sense of making them realize the ideal of self-sacrificing love which Christ exemplifies. It involves the actual winning of men from selfishness to unselfishness, from indifference to love. It involves a like transformation in the life of nations, manifesting itself in the substitution of peace for war, and of international brotherhood and sympathy for rivalry and ambition. It requires, further, the complete organization of society according to the Christian principle; the reconstitution of social life in all its aspects, economic, educational, literary, artistic, in forms adapted to express and to further the relations of brotherly sympathy and service, of which Christ's own life was the example. It requires, finally, such changes in the physical environment as shall remove all preventable causes of ignorance and vice. All this, at least, with more which we cannot as yet perfectly express, is involved in the coming of Christ's kingdom upon earth. To the realization of such a social end our efforts as Christians must be directed.

But is this realization 'possible under the conditions of our present life? Here we find the same antithesis which we have already faced in our study of the individual ideal. On the one hand, we see the actual progress which has been made in the application of Christian principles to social problems, and are reminded of Jesus' own faith that the cause for which he gave himself would finally triumph. On the other hand, we face the limitation and incompleteness of our highest attainment, and are compelled to recognize that every victory of the Christian principle seems to call forth new and subtler manifestations of the forces of selfishness and oppression. If two thousand years have accomplished so little, what guarantee is there that it would be different after two hundred thousand?

It is only natural, therefore, that we should find in the interpretation of the social ideal the same two points of view which we have already considered in connection with that of the individual. On the one hand, we find those who are ready to abandon altogether the hope of a final victory of the good in this world, and to place the realization of God's kingdom wholly in the other. On the other hand, we find those who are as confident that the realization of the social ideal of Christianity is possible here and now, and who regard the other-worldly Christianity which despairs of the salvation of this world as a abandonment of the principles of Jesus, and an evidence of lack of faith in the Father whom he revealed. The analogy between this "social perfectionism" and the individual perfectionism already described is obvious.

The difference between these two points of view receives striking expression in the interpretation of the second advent, the doctrine under which theology brings to expression the Christian view of the outcome of history. In the former case, the advent marks the abandonment of the method which God has hitherto used in dealing with men in favor of another. It is the great catastrophe by which history is brought to a close and the perfect life of heaven introduced.[1] In the second, the advent is simply the expression in dramatic form of that progressive victory of Christ's principles in the world which is destined to issue at last in the complete Christianization of society.

If the principles which we have hitherto applied be correct, it would seem that neither of these solutions alone adequately represents the Christian hope. Against those who regard the Christian social ideal as inherently incapable of realization under present conditions, and base their

---

[1] Cf. chapter XII, pp. 185 sq.

hope of the kingdom upon a radical transformation of the conditions of life, it is to be maintained that our hope for the future lies not in the introduction of any new method, but simply in the more consistent application to the social problems of the same principle of self-sacrificing love through which all that is noblest and best in our present life has been achieved. Yet, at the same time, it must be admitted that experience makes it improbable that the complete realization of the Christian ideal, for society any more than for the individual, will fall wholly within the limits of this present life. If there were no other reason for retaining the other-worldly ideal, the fact that so many generations have passed away in incompleteness and failure would be sufficient. The kingdom of God belongs not to a single generation, but to all mankind; and those who have labored and suffered in the past, that we might attain a higher life, must have their part and share in the final fruition.

But, if this be the case, there is no necessity for believing that any single generation will witness the complete realization of the Christian ideal. This would be to give this world a finality for which the facts afford no warrant. Science tells us that, as this earth was formed out of pre-existing elements, so it shall be resolved into them again. It is not here, then, but in the unseen world for which this life is a training school, that we must look for the final realization of the Christian ideal. How faith conceives the realization we have finally to consider.

3. *The Christian View of the Final Consummation.*

The essential content of the Christian faith concerning the future life may be summed up in the sentence that it is the scene of the complete realization, both in the individual and in society, of that ideal of filial trust and brotherly service of which present experience gives us only partial anticipations.   Of the nature and grounds of this faith we have spoken elsewhere,[1] as well as of the limitations of our knowledge of the conditions under which the future life is to be lived.   Here it is necessary only to indicate in a word how the relation between this life and the next is to be conceived.

Historically, we find two different conceptions of the future life, corresponding to the two different ideals of perfection which we have already noted.   In the first, the contrast between this life and the next is magnified.   Death is regarded as introducing man into wholly new conditions, in which the principles which determine thought and conduct here no longer obtain, and the limitations of the present life, both in knowledge and in character, are abruptly transcended.   According to the second, death involves no such sudden break.   The life to come is only the continuation and completion of the life begun here, and the principles by which it is regulated do not differ essentially from those which govern our present experience.

An example of the first conception is found in the Protestant doctrine of instant sanctification at death.   According to the Westminster divines, the souls of believers are at death immediately " made perfect in holiness, and received into the highest heavens, where they behold the face of God in light and glory, waiting for the full redemption of their bodies." [2]   The truth for which this view stands is the fact that it is not necessary to wait for the last day to enjoy full communion with God, but that such communion is possible in the life immediately after death.

---

[1] Chapter XV, section 3, pp. 257 sq.

[2] *Larger Catechism*, question 86.

The difficulty with the doctrine, as stated, is that it makes no room for the conceptions of growth and progress which play so large a part in our experience here; and, especially, that it treats the whole problem from a purely individualistic standpoint, ignoring the fact that in the life to come, as here, the individual's full fruition and enjoyment must depend upon the extent to which the Christian ideal is realized in others also.

An example of the second point of view is the Catholic doctrine of purgatory. According to this view, the life after death is simply the continuation of the same process of training which has been begun here. For the individual it involves a progressive purification from sin, through the application of the same principles of penance and indulgence which characterize the Catholic conception of salvation here. For the church at large it involves the extension to the life to come of the same law of helpfulness and service through which the highest Christian ideal is realized here. The explanation of the strong hold of the doctrine upon the faith of Catholics, in spite of the superstition and abuses by which it is disfigured, is to be found in the reality and naturalness given to the thought of the future by this extension of present ideals and standards. It is evident that, if the future life is to have the same hold upon the imagination of Protestants, Protestant theology, too, must make place in a similar way for the ideas of progress and of service which play so large a part in the Christian life of the present.

The necessity for conceiving the future life as a life of progress is due in part to the immaturity and incompleteness of those who enter it; in part to the fact that our ideal of the finite life itself involves progress. The perfection for which we look is not the perfection which comes with the cessation of growth, but that which characterizes a development from which all that is hampering and abnormal has been removed; in which each new opportunity is instantly embraced, each new insight met with immediate response.

In like manner, the necessity for conceiving the future life as a life of service is due in part to the difference of attainment and ability already referred to; in part to the character of the Christian ideal itself. It is not an ideal of receptivity alone, but of activity as well; and this activity for the Christian must take the form of service. What work God may have for us to do in the life to come we may not know; but we may be sure that in a universe which still includes suffering, ignorance and need, we shall not be left with idle hands.

With the fact of service in a world still incomplete, there is involved the possibility of pain. If we conceive God as entering by sympathy into the sorrows and sufferings of humanity, there is no reason to doubt that those who share his fellowship in the heavenly life will share also his fellow-feeling for those who are in need. If pain fulfils a spiritual office here, it may do so there. It is not in its cessation, but in its transfiguration by the peace which comes with complete insight and perfect trust, that we are to find the blessedness of heaven.

Thus it is not in the radical alteration of the conditions of life, as we know them, that we must look for the difference between this life and the next; but rather in the extent to which that which is best and noblest here is there carried to fruition. For the individual, heaven will mean a life lived in the same consciousness of God's fellowship and fatherly care as characterized the life of Jesus on earth; for society it will mean the extension of this God-consciousness till it glorifies and transfigures all the relations of life. When all have come, through Christ, to the same knowledge and love of the Father which we see in him, then the goal of the Christian life will have been reached ; so far as it is possible to speak of finality at all in a life which involves, both for the individual and for society, boundless possibilities of progress. This social consummation is that far-off divine event of which Paul speaks in 1 Corinthians xv, 28, when Christ, his mediatorial work complete, shall surrender his authority to the Father that God may be all in all.

APPENDIX

A CLASSIFIED BIBLIOGRAPHY

I. The Idea and Relations of Christian Theology

SCHLEIERMACHER, F.: Kurze Darstellung des theologischen Studiums, 2d ed., Berlin, 1830, pp. 81–98; Eng. tr. by Farrar, Brief Outline of the Study of Theology, Edinburgh, 1850, pp. 161–172. Der christliche Glaube, Berlin, 1884, vol. I, pp. 1–113.

RITSCHL, A.: Die christliche Lehre von der Rechtfertigung und Versöhnung, 3d ed., vol. III, pp. 1–26; Eng. tr. by Mackintosh and Macaulay, The Christian Doctrine of Justification and Reconciliation, Edinburgh and New York, 1900, pp. 1–26.

SABATIER, A.: Esquisse d'une Philosophie de la Religion, d'après la Psychologie et l'Histoire, Paris, 1897, pp. 261–352; Eng. tr. Outlines of a Philosophy of Religion based on Psychology and History, New York, 1897, pp. 229–274.
La Vie Intime des Dogmes et leur Puissance d'Évolution, Paris, 1889; Eng. tr. by Christen, The Vitality of Christian Dogmas and their Power of Evolution, London, 1898.

LOBSTEIN, P.: Essai d'une Introduction à la Dogmatique Protestante, Paris, 1896; Eng. tr. by Smith, An Introduction to Protestant Dogmatics, Chicago, 1902.

SMITH, HENRY B.: Introduction to Christian Theology, New York, 1883, pp. 1–48.
The Idea of Christian Theology as a System (in Faith and Philosophy, New York, 1886, pp. 125 sq.).

WARFIELD, B. B.: The Right of Systematic Theology, Edinburgh, 1897.

HOGAN, J. B.: Clerical Studies, Boston, 1898, pp. 138–196 (Roman Catholic).

II. The Sources of Christian Theology

(1) *The Antecedents of Christian Theology.*

TOY, C. H.: Judaism and Christianity: A Sketch of the Progress of Thought from Old Testament to New Testament, Boston, 1890.

WEBER, F.: System der altsynagogalen palästinischen Theologie, ed. Delitzsch and Schnedermann, Leipzig, 1880.

MONTEFIORE, C. G. : Lectures on the Origin and Growth of Religion as illustrated by the Religion of the Ancient Hebrews, 2d ed., London, 1893.

BOUSSET, W. : Die Religion des Judentums im neutestamentlichen Zeitalter, Berlin, 2d. ed., 1906.

HATCH, E. : The Influence of Greek Ideas and Usages upon the Christian Church, ed. Fairbairn, London, 1890.

DRUMMOND, J. : The Jewish Messiah: A Critical History of the Messianic Idea among the Jews from the Rise of the Maccabees to the closing of the Talmud, London, 1877.

Philo Judaeus, or the Jewish-Alexandrian Philosophy in its Development and Completion, 2 vols., London, 1888.

(2) *Patristic and Medieval Theology.*

The Creeds of the early church collected in Hahn, Bibliothek der Symbole und Glaubensregeln der alten Kirche, 3d ed., Breslau, 1897.   The most important translated in Schaff, Creeds of Christendom, New York, 1881, 1882, vol. II, pp. 11–76.

The relevant sections in the Histories of Doctrine of Loofs (Leitfaden zum Studium der Dogmengeschichte, 3d ed., Halle, 1893), Harnack (Dogmengeschichte, 4th ed., Tübingen, 1905 sq.; Eng. tr., History of Dogma, from the 3d German ed., 7 vols., Boston, 1895-1900), Fisher, G. P. (History of Christian Doctrine, New York, 1896), and Bethune-Baker, J. F. (An Introduction to the Early History of Christian Doctrine to the Time of the Council of Chalcedon, London, 1903).

ORIGEN: De Principiis; Eng. tr. by Crombie in Ante-Nicene Library, vol. IV, pp. 239 sq.

GREGORY OF NYSSA : The Great Catechism; Eng. tr. by Moore, in Nicene and Post-Nicene Library, second series, vol. V, pp. 471 sq.

AUGUSTINE : Enchiridion ad Laurentianum de Fide, Spe et Caritate; Eng. tr. by Shaw, in Nicene and Post-Nicene Library, first series, vol. III, pp. 233 sq.

LANGEN, J. : Johannes von Damaskus: Eine patristiche Monographie, Gotha, 1879.

THOMAS AQUINAS : Summa Theologica, ed. Migne, 4 vols., Paris, 1853.

SEEBERG, R. : Die Theologie des Johannes Duns Scotus, Leipzig, 1900.

(3) *The Theology of Greek Catholicism.*

The Creeds of the Greek and Russian Churches in Schaff, Creeds, vol. II, pp. 275–542, and Michalcescu, J. : Die Bekenntnisse und die wichtigsten Glaubenszeugnisse der griechisch-orientalischen Kirche, Leipzig, 1904.

MAKARIUS: Handbuch zum Studium der christlichen orthodox-dogmatischen Theologie, ins deutsche übersezt von Dr. Blumenthal, Moscow, 1875.

(4) *The Theology of Roman Catholicism.*

The symbolical books of the Roman Church in Schaff, Creeds, vol. II, pp. 79–271, and Denzinger, Enchiridion Symbolorum et Definitionum, ed. Stahl, 9th ed., 1900. Most important of these are the Decrees and Canons of the Council of Trent, the Profession of Faith, and the Catechism of the same council, and the Decrees of the Vatican Council of 1870. The two former and the last are translated in Schaff. An English tr. of the Roman Catechism by Buckley, London, 1852.

PERRONE, G. : Praelectiones Theologicae, 9 vols., Vienna, 1838–43.
JANSSENS, L.: Summa Theologica, ad Modum Commentarii in Aquinatis Summam, Freiburg, 1900 sq.
BILLOT, L.: Commentarius in primam, secundam, tertiam partem S. Thomae, Rome, 1900 sq.
HEINRICH, J. B.: Lehrbuch der katholischen Dogmatik, ed. Huppert, 3 vols., Mainz, 1898–1900.
SCHEEBEN, M. J.: Handbuch der katholischen Dogmatik, 4 vols., Freiburg, 1873–1901; English abridgment by Wilhelm and Scannell, A Manual of Catholic Theology, based on Scheeben's Dogmatik, 2 vols., London, 1906.
SIMAR, T. H. : Lehrbuch der Dogmatik, 2 vols., 4th ed., Freiburg, 1889.
HURTER, H. : Theologiae Dogmaticae Compendium in Usum Studiosorum Theologiae, 10th ed., Innsbruck, 1900.
GIBBONS, J. : The Faith of our Fathers: being a plain exposition and vindication of the Church founded by our Lord Jesus Christ, 43d ed., Baltimore, 1893.
MÖHLER, J. A. : Symbolik, ed. Raich, Mainz, 1889; Eng. tr., Symbolism, or Exposition of the Doctrinal Differences between Catholics and Protestants, as shown by Their Symbolic Writings, New York, 1844.

(5) *Protestant Theology from the Reformation to Schleiermacher.*

The Creeds and Confessions of the Lutheran church, collected in Schaff, vol. III, and in Müller, J. T., Die symbolischen Bücher der evangelisch-lutherischen Kirche deutsch und lateinisch, 8th ed., Gütersloh, 1898.

Besides the three creeds of the ancient church, these are the *Augsburg Confession*, Luther's *Larger* and *Smaller Catechisms*, the

Articles of Smalcald, and the *Formula of Concord*, which together made up the so-called *Concordia* or *Book of Concord*.

The Creeds and Confessions of the Reformed Church collected in Schaff, vol. III, and in Müller, E. F. K., Die Bekenntnisschriften der reformirten Kirche in authentischen Texten, mit geschichtlicher Einleitung und Register, Leipzig, 1903.

> The most important continental creeds are the I and II *Helvetic Confessions*, the *Gallic* and *Belgic Confessions*, the *Heidelberg Catechism*, and the Articles and Canons of the Synod of Dort.
>
> The most important English creeds are John Knox's *Scotch Confession* of 1560, the *Thirty-nine Articles* of the Church of England, the *Irish Articles of 1615*, and the *Westminster Confession* and *Catechisms*.
>
> The extreme of Protestant orthodoxy is represented by the *Helvetic Consensus Formula* of 1675 (in Müller, E. F. K., op. cit. pp. 861 sq.).

The articles of the Remonstrants (Arminian) in Schaff, vol. III, pp. 545 sq.; the Socinian doctrine in the *Racovian Catechism* (Eng. tr. by Rees, London, 1818).

GASS, F. W. J. H.: Geschichte der protestantischen Dogmatik in ihrem Zusammenhange mit der Theologie überhaupt, 4 vols., Berlin, 1854–67.

DORNER, J. A.: Geschichte der protestantischen Theologie, Munich, 1867; Eng. tr., 2 vols., History of Protestant Theology, Edinburgh, 1871.

MELANCHTHON, P.: Loci Communes: in ihrer Urgestalt nach G. L. Plitt, ed. Kolde, 3d ed., Leipzig, 1900.

HERRLINGER: Die Theologie Melanchthons, Gotha, 1879.

KÖSTLIN, J.: Luthers Theologie in ihrer geschichtlichen Entwicklung und ihrem inneren Zusammenhange, 2d ed , 2 vols., Stuttgart, 1883 ; Eng. tr. by C. E. Hay, The Theology of Luther in its Historical Development and Inner Harmony, 2 vols., Philadelphia, 1897.

ZWINGLI, U. : De Vera et Falsa Religione Commentarius, 1525 (Opera, Zurich, 1828–42, vol. III, pp. 145–325).

BAUR, A.: Zwinglis Theologie, ihr Werden und ihr System, 2 vols., Halle, 1885, 1889.

CALVIN, J.: Institutio Religionis Christianae, 1536, 1839–54, 1859, ed. Reuss and Cunitz, Brunswick, 1863 sq. ; Eng. trs. by Allen (3 vols., Philadelphia, 1816) and Beveridge (Calvin Translation Society, 3 vols., Edinburgh, 1845 sq.).

HEPPE, H.: Dogmatik des deutschen Protestantismus im 16ten Jahrhundert, 3 vols., Gotha, 1857.

HASE, K: Hutterus Redivivus: Dogmatik der evangelisch-lutherischen Kirche, 12th ed., Leipzig, 1883.

GERHARD, J. : Loci Theologici, 9 vols., ed. Preuss, Berlin, 1863–75 (the greatest of the Lutheran systems).

CALIXTUS, G. : Epitome Theologiae, Goslar, 1619; ed. Titius, Helmstädt, 1661 (the representative of a liberal and mediating tendency).

SCHWEIZER, A.: Die Glaubenslehre der evangelisch-reformirten Kirche, 2 vols., Zürich, 1844, 1847.

AMES, W.: Medulla Theologiae, Amsterdam, 1623 ; Eng. tr., The Marrow of Sacred Divinity, London, 1642; new ed. by Candlish, London, 1874.

COCCEJUS, J.: Summa Doctrinae de Foedere et Testamento Dei, Frankfort, 1648.

TURRETINE, F.: Institutio Theologiae Elencticae, 2d ed., Geneva, 1688 sq.

Compendium Theologiae, Amsterdam, 1695.

ARMINIUS, J. : Works ; Eng. tr. by Nichols, 3 vols., London, 1825.

GROTIUS, H. : Opera Omnia, 4 vols., Amsterdam, 1679, esp. De Veritate Religionis Christianae (vol. IV, pp. 1–96).

LIMBORCH : Theologia Christiana, Amsterdam, 2d ed. 1700; Eng. tr., A Complete System or Body of Divinity, 2 vols., London, 1702 (the most important dogmatic treatise of Arminianism).

FREYLINGHAUSEN: Grundlegung der Theologie, Halle, 1774, Eng. tr., An Abstract of the Whole Doctrine of the Christian Religion, London, 1804 (pietistic).

WEGSCHEIDER, J. A. L. : Institutiones Theologiae Christianae Dogmaticae, Halle, 1815, 7th ed. 1833 (rationalistic).

(6) *European Theology since Schleiermacher.*

DORNER, J. : Geschichte der protestantischen Theologie, Munich, 1867 ; Eng. tr., History of Protestant Theology, 2 vols., Edinburgh, 1871.

LICHTENBERGER, F.: Histoire des Idées Religieuses en Allemagne depuis le XVIIIme Siècle j'usqu' à nos jours, 2d ed., Paris, 1888; Eng. tr. by Hastie, History of German Theology in the Nineteenth Century, Edinburgh, 1889.

PFLEIDERER, O. : The Development of Theology in Germany since Kant, and its Progress in Great Britain since 1825, London, 1890.

SCHLEIERMACHER, F. : Der Christliche Glaube, nach den Grundsätzen der evangelischen Kirche im Zusammenhange dargestellt, 1821 ; 2d ed. 1830 ; a convenient reprint, 2 vols., Berlin, 1884.

HEGEL, G. W. F.: Vorlesungen über die Philosophie der Religion, 2 vols., 2d ed., Berlin, 1840 ; Eng. tr. by Speirs and Sanderson, The Philosophy of Religion, 3 vols., London, 1895 sq.

STRAUSS, D. F.: Christliche Glaubenslehre, 2 vols., Tübingen and Stuttgart, 1840, 1841.

Der alte und der neue Glaube, Leipzig, 1872; 14th ed., Bonn, 1895.

BIEDERMANN, A. E.: Christliche Dogmatik, 2d ed., 2 vols., Berlin, 1884, 1885.

PFLEIDERER, O.: Grundriss der christlichen Glaubens-und Sittenlehre, 4th ed., Berlin, 1888.

FRANK, F. H. R.: System der christlichen Gewissheit, 2d ed., 2 vols., Erlangen, 1881, 1884; Eng. tr. by Evans, System of the Christian Certainty, 2d ed., Edinburgh, 1886.
System der christlichen Wahrheit, 3d ed., Leipzig, 1894.

PHILIPPI, F. A.: Die kirchliche Glaubenslehre, 6 vols., Gütersloh, 1864–1879.

KAHNIS, K. F. A.: Die lutherische Dogmatik historisch-genetisch dargestellt, 2 vols., Leipzig, 1874.

OETTINGEN, A. VON: Lutherische Dogmatik, 3 vols., Munich, 1897–1902.

HASE, C. A.: Gnosis, oder protestantisch-evangelische Glaubenslehre für die Gebildeten in der Gemeinde, wissenschaftlich dargestellt, 2d ed., 2 vols., Leipzig, 1869, 1870.

VON HOFMANN, J. C. K.: Der Schriftbeweis, 3 parts, 2d ed., Nördlingen, 1857–60.

KÄHLER, M.: Die Wissenchaft der christlichen Lehre von dem evangelischen Grundartikel aus im Abriss dargestellt; 2d ed. Leipzig, 1893.

LUTHARDT, C. E.: Kompendium der Dogmatik, 9th ed., Leipzig, 1893.

ROTHE, R.: Zur Dogmatik, 2d ed., Gotha, 1869.
Dogmatik, 2 vols., ed. Schenkel, Heidelberg, 1870.
Theologische Ethik, 2d ed., 5 vols., Wittenberg, 1867–71.

EBRARD, J. H. A.: Christliche Dogmatik, 2d ed., Königsberg, 2 vols., 1862, 1863.

DORNER, J. A.: System der christlichen Glaubenslehre, 2d ed., Berlin, 1886, 1887; Eng. tr. by Cave and Banks, A System of Christian Doctrine, Edinburgh, 1880.

MARTENSEN, H.: Die christliche Dogmatik, Berlin, 1856; Eng. tr. by Urwick, Christian Dogmatics, Edinburgh, 1866.

VAN OOSTERZEE, J. J.: Christian Dogmatics, Eng. tr. by Watson and Evans, 2 vols., New York, 1874.

LIPSIUS, R. A.: Lehrbuch der evangelisch-protestantischen Dogmatik, 3d ed., Brunswick, 1893.

RITSCHL, A.: Die christliche Lehre von der Rechtfertigung und Versöhnung, 3 vols., Bonn, 1870–74; 2d ed. 1882, 1883; 3d ed. 1888, 1889; 1895, reprint of vol. III from 3d ed., unchanged; Eng. tr. of vol. I, by Black, The Christian Doctrine of Justification and Reconciliation, Edinburgh, 1872; of vol. III, by Mackintosh and Macaulay, New York and Edinburgh, 1900.
Unterricht in der christlichen Religion, Bonn, 1875; 5th ed.

1895; Eng. tr. by Swing, in The Theology of Albrecht Ritschl, London and New York, 1901.

NITZSCH, F. : Lehrbuch der evangelischen Dogmatik, Freiburg, 1892, 2d ed. 1896.

KAFTAN, J. : Dogmatik, Freiburg, 1897, 3d and 4th ed., Tübingen, 1901.

SCHULTZ, H. : Grundriss der evangelischen Dogmatik, 2d ed., Göttingen, 1892.

REISCHLE, M. : Christliche Glaubenslehre in Leitsätzen, 1899, 2d ed., Halle, 1902.

GRÉTILLAT, A. : Exposé de la Theologie Systématique, 4 vols., Paris, and Neuchatel, 1885–90.

BOVON, J. : Étude sur l'Œuvre de la Rédemption, Part II. Dogmatique Chrétienne, Lausanne, 2 vols., 1895–96.

MATTER, A. : Étude de la Doctrine Chrétienne, 2 vols., Paris, 1892.

(7) *The Theology of the Anglican and Protestant Episcopal Churches.*

HUNT, J. : Religious Thought in England from the Reformation to the End of the Last Century : a contribution to the History of Theology, 3 vols., London, 1870–73.

Religious Thought in England in the Nineteenth Century, London, 1896.

PFLEIDERER, O. : The Development of Theology in Germany since Kant, and its Progress in Great Britain since 1825, London, 1890.

TULLOCH, J. : Movements of Religious Thought in Britain during the Nineteenth Century, St. Giles Lectures, New York, 1885.

HOOKER, R. : The Laws of Ecclesiastical Polity, 1592 sq., ed. Keble, Oxford, 1836 sq.

USHER, J. : A Body of Divinity, or the Summe and Substance of the Christian Religion, 6th ed., London, 1670 ; new ed. by Robinson, London, 1841.

HOBBES, T. : Leviathan, or the Matter, Forme and Power of a Common-wealth, ecclesiastical and civill, London, 1651 ; reprint, Cambridge English classics, ed. Waller, London, 1904.

BUTLER, J. : The Analogy of Religion, Natural and Revealed, to the Constitution and Course of Nature, vol. I of Works, ed. Gladstone, Oxford, 1896.

BURNET, G. : Exposition of the Thirty-Nine Articles of the Church of England, Oxford, 1845.

PEARSON, J. : An Exposition of the Creed, 7th ed., London, 1701, New York, 1889.

COLERIDGE, S. T. : Aids to Reflection, 6th ed., New York, 1847.

MAURICE, F. D. : The Kingdom of Christ, 4th ed., London, 1891.

MASON, A. J. : The Faith of the Gospel, London, 1888.

MOULE, H. C. G.: Outlines of Christian Doctrine, London, 1889, 18th ed. 1902.

STRONG, T. B.: A Manual of Theology, London and Edinburgh, 1892.

RYLE, J. R.: Knots Untied; being plain statements on disputed points in religion from the standpoint of an evangelical churchman, 10th ed., London, 1898.

LUX MUNDI: A series of studies in the religion of the Incarnation, ed. Gore, 3d ed., London, 1890.

CONTENTIO VERITATIS: Essays in constructive theology by six Oxford Tutors, 2d ed., London, 1902.

KEDNEY, J. S.: Christian Doctrine Harmonized, and its Rationality Vindicated, 2 vols., New York, 1889.

(8) *Presbyterian Theology.*

HILL, G.: Lectures in Divinity, Edinburgh, 1821; new ed. New York, 1872.

CUNNINGHAM, W.: Discussions on Church Principles, Popish, Erastian and Presbyterian, Edinburgh, 1863.

CHALMERS, T.: Institutes of Theology, 2 vols., Edinburgh, 1849.

McPHERSON, J.: Christian Dogmatics, Edinburgh, 1898.

DENNEY, J.: Studies in Theology, New York, 6th ed., 1901.

ORR, J.: The Christian View of God and of the World as Centring in the Incarnation, Edinburgh, 1893.

CAIRD, J.: Fundamental Ideas of Christianity, Gifford Lectures for 1892–93, 1895–96, 2 vols., Glasgow, 1899.

BRECKENRIDGE, R. J.: The Knowledge of God Objectively Considered, New York, 1859.

    The Knowledge of God Subjectively Considered, New York, 1859.

RICHARDS, J.: Lectures on Mental Philosophy and Theology, New York, 1846.

DABNEY, R. L.: Syllabus and Notes on Course of Systematic and Polemic Theology, taught in Union Theological Seminary, Virginia, 2d ed., St. Louis, 1878.

SHEDD, W. G. T.: Dogmatic Theology, 3 vols., New York, 1888.

HODGE, C.: Systematic Theology, 3 vols., Philadelphia, 1865.

HODGE, A. A.: Outlines of Theology, rewritten and enlarged, New York, 1900.

    Popular lectures on Theological themes, Philadelphia, 1887.
    Commentary on the Confession of Faith, Philadelphia, 1869.

SMITH, H. B.: System of Christian Theology, 4th ed., New York, 1890.

MORRIS, E. D.: Theology of the Westminster Symbols, Columbus, 1900.

BEATTIE, F. R. : The Presbyterian Standards: An Exposition of the Westminster Confession of Faith and Catechisms, Richmond, 1896.

BROWN, W. A. : Changes in the Theology of American Presbyterianism (American Journal of Theology, July, 1906, pp. 387 sq.).

FOSTER, R. V. : Systematic Theology, Nashville, 1898 (Cumberland Presbyterian).

(9) *Methodist Theology.*

WESLEY, J. : Works, 14 vols., London, 1829 sq. ; 10 vols., New York, 1826.

FLETCHER, J. : Works, 4 vols., New York, 1833 (esp. his Checks to Antinomianism, vols. I and II).

WATSON, R. : Theological Institutes, new ed., 2 vols., New York, 1850.

POPE, W. B. : Compendium of Christian Theology, 2d ed., 3 vols., London, 1879.

BANKS, J. S. : A Manual of Christian Doctrine, 5th ed., London, 1895.

MILEY, J. : Systematic Theology, 2 vols., New York, 1892, 1894.

FOSTER, R. S. : Studies in Theology, 6 vols., New York and Cincinnati, 1889 sq.

SHELDON, H. C. : System of Christian Doctrine, New York, 1903.

CURTIS, O. A. : The Christian Faith, Personally Given in a System of Doctrine, New York, 1905.

COE, G. A. : The Religion of a Mature Mind, New York, 1902.

(10) *Congregational Theology.*

WALKER, W. : The Creeds and Platforms of Congregationalism, New York, 1893.

EDWARDS, J. : Works, 10 vols., New York, 1829 sq.; 4 vols., New York, 1868.

　　An unpublished essay on the Trinity, ed. G. P. Fisher, New York, 1903.

EMMONS, N. : Works, ed. Ide, 6 vols., Boston, 1842.

BELLAMY, J. : Works, 2 vols., Boston, 1850.

HOPKINS, S. : Works, 3 vols., Boston, 1854.

TAYLOR, N. W. : Lectures on the Moral Government of God, 2 vols., New York, 1859.

BUSHNELL, H. : Collected Works, New York, 1891 sq.

PARK, E. A. : Discourses on Some Theological Doctrines, Andover, 1885.

FINNEY, C. G. : Lectures on Systematic Theology, new ed., London, 1851.

DALE, R. W.: Christian Doctrine: A Series of Discourses, London, 1894.
HARRIS, S.: God, the Creator and Lord of All, 2 vols., New York, 1896.
STEARNS, L. F.: Present-Day Theology, New York, 1893.
HYDE, W. DeW.: Outlines of Social Theology, New York, 1895.
GORDON, G. A.: Ultimate Conceptions of Faith, Boston, 1903.
FAIRCHILD, J. H.: Elements of Theology, Natural and Revealed, Oberlin, 1892.
STEVENS, G. B.: Doctrine and Life, Boston, 1895.
KING, H. C.: Reconstruction in Theology, New York, 1901.
    Theology and the Social Consciousness, New York, 1902.
BECKWITH, C. A.: Realities of Christian Theology: An Interpretation of Christian Experience, Boston, 1906.

(11) *Baptist Theology.*

ROBINSON, E. G.: Christian Theology, Rochester, 1894.
JOHNSON, E. H.: Outline of Systematic Theology, Philadelphia, 1891.
STRONG, A. H.: Systematic Theology, 7th ed., New York, 1902.
CLARKE, W. N.: An Outline of Christian Theology, New York, 1898.

(12) *Unitarian Theology.*

PRIESTLEY, J.: Institutes of Natural and Revealed Theology, 2d ed., Birmingham, 1782.
MARTINEAU, J.: The Seat of Authority in Religion, 2d ed., London, 1890.
    Essays, Reviews and Addresses, 4 vols., London, 1890–91.
CARPENTER, J. E., AND WICKSTEED, P. H.: Studies in Theology, London, 1903.
CHANNING, W. E.: Works, Boston, 1875.
PARKER, T.: Collected Works, 14 vols., London, 1863–71.
SAVAGE, M.: Our Unitarian Gospel, Boston, 1900.

(13) *Other Bodies.*

BARCLAY, R.: An Apology for the True Christian Divinity, 8th ed., London, 1780.
SPRECHER, S.: Groundwork of a System of Evangelical Lutheran Theology, Philadelphia, 1879.
JACOBS, H. E.: A Summary of the Christian Faith, Philadelphia, 1905 (Lutheran).
GERHART, E. V.: Institutes of the Christian Religion, 2 vols., New York, 1894.

III. The Christian Religion

(1) *The View of Religion presupposed by Christianity.*

SCHLEIERMACHER, F. : Reden über die Religion, Berlin, 1799, ed. Otto, 2d ed., Göttingen, 1906; Eng. tr. by Oman, On Religion, London, 1893.

HEGEL, G. W. F. : Vorlesungen über die Philosophie der Religion, 2 vols., 2d ed., Berlin, 1840; Eng. tr. by Speirs and Sanderson, The Philosophy of Religion, 3 vols., London, 1895 sq.

JASTROW, M. : The Study of Religion, New York, 1901.

TIELE, C. P. : Elements of the Science of Religion, Gifford Lectures for 1896, 2 vols., New York, 1897.

JAMES, W. : The Varieties of Religious Experience, Gifford Lectures for 1901–02, London and New York, 1902.

KNOX, G. W. : The Direct and Fundamental Proofs of the Christian Religion, New York, 1903, pp. 52 sq.

EVERETT, C. C. : The Psychological Elements of Religious Faith, New York, 1902.

CAIRD, E. : The Evolution of Religion, Gifford Lectures for 1890–91, and 1891–92, 2 vols., New York, 1893.

MARTINEAU, J. : A Study of Religion, its Sources and Contents, 2 vols., Oxford and New York, 1888.

CAIRD, J. : An Introduction to the Philosophy of Religion, the Croall Lectures for 1878–79, New York, 1880.

CALDECOTT, A. : The Philosophy of Religion in England and America, New York, 1901.

BOUSSET, W. : Das Wesen der Religion, dargestellt an ihrer Geschichte, Halle, 1904.

STARBUCK, E. D. : The Psychology of Religion : An Empirical Study of the Growth of Religious Consciousness, London, 1899.

PFLEIDERER, O. : Religionsphilosophie auf geschichtlicher Grundlage, 3d ed., 2 vols., Berlin, 1896; Eng. tr. by Stewart and Menzies, The Philosophy of Religion on the Basis of its History, 4 vols., London, 1886 sq.

RAUWENHOFF, L. W. E. : Religionsphilosophie, German tr. by Hanne, Brunswick, 2d ed., 1894.

EUCKEN, R. : Die Wahrheitsgehalt der Religion, Leipzig, 1901.

HÖFFDING, H. : The Philosophy of Religion, translated from the German by B. E. Meyer, London, 1906.

SABATIER, A. : Philosophie de la Religion, Paris, 1897 ; Eng. tr., Outlines of a Philosophy of Religion, New York, 1897.

LADD, G. T. : The Philosophy of Religion, 2 vols., New York, 1905.

JORDAN, L. H. : Comparative Religion, its Genesis and Growth, Edinburgh, 1905.

MENZIES, A.: History of Religion, a sketch of primitive religious beliefs and practices, and of the origin and character of the great systems, New York, 1895.

DE LA SAUSSAYE, P. D. C.: Lehrbuch der Religionsgeschichte, 2 vols., 3d ed., Tübingen, 1905.

(2) *Christianity as a Distinctive Religion.*

KAFTAN, J.: Das Wesen der christlichen Religion, 2d ed., Basle, 1888.

HARNACK, A.: Das Wesen des Christentums, Leipzig, 1900; Eng. tr. by Saunders, What is Christianity? London and New York, 1901.

BROWN, W. A.: The Essence of Christianity: A Study in the History of Definition, New York, 1902.

CAIRD, J.: The Fundamental Ideas of Christianity, 2 vols., Glasgow, 1899.

DRUMMOND, J.: Via, Veritas, Vita, London, 1894.

LOISY, A.: L'Évangile et l'Église, Eng. tr. by C. Home, The Gospel and the Church, New York, 1904.

GARDNER, P.: Exploratio Evangelica: A Brief Examination of the Basis and Origin of Christian Belief, London and New York, 1899.

GUNKEL: Zum religionsgeschichtlichen Verständnis des Neuen Testaments, Göttingen, 1903.

WERNLE, P.: Die Anfänge unserer Religion, Tübingen, 1901; Eng. tr. by Bienemann, The Beginnings of Christianity, 2 vols., New York, 1903, 1904.

(3) *The Finality of the Christian Religion.*

SCHULTZ, H.: Grundriss der christlichen Apologetik, 2d ed., Göttingen, 1902.

STEARNS, L. F.: The Evidence of Christian Experience, New York, 1890.

FAIRBAIRN, A. M.: The Philosophy of the Christian Religion, London and New York, 2d ed., 1902.

FOSTER, G. B.: The Finality of the Christian Religion, Chicago, 1906.

TROELTSCH, E.: Die Absolutheit des Christentums und die Religionsgeschichte, Tübingen, 2d ed., 1902.

KAFTAN, J.: Die Wahrheit der christlichen Religion, 2d ed, Basle, 1888; Eng. tr. by Ferries, The Truth of the Christian Religion, 2 vols., Edinburgh, 1894.

KNOX, G. W.: The Direct and Fundamental Proofs of the Christian Religion, New York, 1903.

CLARKE, W. N.: What Shall We Think of Christianity? New York, 1899.

BRUCE, A. B.: Apologetics, or Christianity Defensively Stated, New York, 1892.

IV. THE CHRISTIAN REVELATION

(1) *The Nature and Test of Revelation.*

BRUCE, A. B.: The Chief End of Revelation, 2d ed., London, 1887.

HARRIS, S.: The Self-Revelation of God, 2d ed., New York, 1892.

CAMPBELL, J. McL.: Thoughts on Revelation, 2d ed., London, 1874.

FISHER, G. P.: The Nature and Method of Revelation, New York, 1890.

MEAD, C. M.: Supernatural Revelation, New York; 1889.

MARTINEAU, J.: The Seat of Authority in Religion, 2d ed., 1890.

BALFOUR, A. J.: The Foundations of Belief, New York, 1895.

STANTON, V. H.: The Place of Authority in Matters of Religious Belief, London, 1891.

STERRETT, J. McB.: The Freedom of Authority, London and New York, 1905.

BRIGGS, C. A.: The Bible, the Church and the Reason, New York, 1892.

MANSEL, H. L.: The Limits of Religious Thought, 5th ed., London, 1867.

NEWMAN, J. H.: An Essay in Aid of a Grammar of Assent, new ed., London and New York, 1891.

(2) *The Bible, its Nature and Inspiration.*

BRIGGS, C. A.: General Introduction to the Study of Holy Scripture, New York, 1899.

GARDINER, J. H.: The Bible as English Literature, New York, 1906.

CLARKE, W. N.: The Use of the Scriptures in Theology, New York, 1905.

MOORE, E. C.: The New Testament in the Christian Church, New York, 1904.

GARDNER, P.: A Historic View of the New Testament, London, 1901.

DODS, M.: The Bible, its Origin and Nature, New York, 1905.

RYLE, H. E.: The Canon of the Old Testament, London, 1892.

WESTCOTT, B. F.: A General Survey of the History of the Canon of the New Testament, 6th ed., Cambridge and New York, 1889.

MUZZEY, D. S.: The Rise of the New Testament, New York, 1900.

BARRY, W.: The Tradition of Scripture, New York, 1906.

SANDAY, W.: Inspiration, Bampton Lectures for 1893, London, 1893.

DE WITT, J.: What is Inspiration? New York, 1893.

EVANS, L. J., and SMITH, H. P.: Biblical Scholarship and Inspiration, Cincinnati, 1891.

LEE, W.: Inspiration of Holy Scripture, New York, 1857 ; republ. New York, 1892.

HODGE, A. A., and WARFIELD, B. B.: Inspiration (Presbyterian Review, April 1881, pp. 225 sq.).

KUYPER, A.: Encyclopedia of Sacred Theology: its Principles, Eng. tr. by De Vries, New York, 1898, pp. 341–563.

ORR, J.: The Problem of the Old Testament considered with Reference to Recent Criticism, New York, 1906.

V. THE CHRISTIAN CHURCH

(1) *The Definition and Ideal of the Church.*

BANNERMAN, D. D.: The Scripture Doctrine of the Church, Edinburgh, 1887.

HATCH, E.: The Organization of the Early Christian Churches, London, 1881.

SOHM, R.: Kirchenrecht, vol. I, Leipzig, 1892.

LOWRIE, W.: The Church and its Organization in Primitive and Catholic Times, New York, London and Bombay, 1904.

STANLEY, A. P.: Christian Institutions, London, 1882.

ALLEN, A. V. G.: Christian Institutions, New York, 1897.

HORT, F. J. A.: The Christian Ecclesia, London, 1898.

RITSCHL, A.: Ueber die Begriffe "sichtbare und unsichtbare Kirche," in *Gesammelte Aufsätze*, vol. I, pp. 68–99, Freiburg, 1893.

SEEBERG, R.: Studien zur Geschichte des Begriffes der Kirche, Erlangen, 1885.

DORNER, A.: Kirche und Reich Gottes, Gotha, 1883.

HOOKER, R.: The Laws of Ecclesiastical Polity (in his collected works, ed. Keble, 4 vols., Oxford, 1836 sq.).

WARD, W. G.: The Ideal of a Christian Church, London, 1844.

MAURICE, F. D.: The Kingdom of Christ, 4th ed., 2 vols., London, 1891.

GORE, C.: The Mission of the Church, New York, 1892.

HADDAN, A. W.: Apostolic Succession in the Church of England, London, 1869.

MASON, A. J.: The Principles of Ecclesiastical Unity, London and New York, 1896.

HUNTINGTON, W. R.: A National Church, New York, 1898 (with a full bibliography).

CUNNINGHAM, W.: Discussions on Church Principles, Popish, Erastian and Presbyterian, Edinburgh, 1863.

KILLEN, W. D.: The Framework of the Church, Edinburgh, 1890.

BRIGGS, C. A.: Whither? New York, 1889, pp. 225 sq.

CHURCH UNITY: Lectures delivered in the Union Theological Seminary, New York, 1896.

Cf. also the works cited under XI–XIV (2) on The Kingdom of God.

(2) *The Types of Historic Christianity.*

McGIFFERT, A. C. : Primitive and Catholic Christianity, New York, 1893.

MÖHLER, J. A. : Symbolik, new ed. by Raich, Mainz, 1889 ; Eng. tr., Symbolism, New York, 1844.

SABATIER, A. : Les Religions de l'Autorité et la Religion de l'Esprit, Paris, 1894 ; Eng. tr. by Houghton, The Religions of Authority and the Religion of the Spirit, New York, 1904.

MARTINEAU, J. : The Seat of Authority in Religion, 2d ed., London, 1890.

HARNACK, A. : What is Christianity? pp. 190 sq.

FAIRBAIRN, A. M. : Catholicism, Roman and Anglican, New York, 1899.

INGE, W. R. : Christian Mysticism, London, 1899.

REISCHLE, M. : Ein Wort zur Controverse über die Mystik in der Theologie, Freiburg, 1886.

VI. THE TASK OF MODERN THEOLOGY

BROWN, W. A. : Christ, the Vitalizing Principle of Christian Theology, New York, 1898.

FAIRBAIRN, A. M. : The Place of Christ in Modern Theology, New York, 1893.

KÄHLER, M. : Der sogenannte historische Jesus, und der geschichtliche biblische Christus, 2d ed., Leipzig, 1896.

ROTHE, R. : Zur Dogmatik, 2d ed., Gotha, 1869.

WENDT, H. H. : Die Norm des echten Christentums, Leipzig, 1893.

Die Aufgabe der systematischen Theologie, Göttingen, 1894.

KING, H. C. : Reconstruction in Theology, New York, 1901.

FISHER, G. P. : The Historical Method in Theology (address before the Congregational Council, 1899), New Haven.

BURTON, E. DE W. : The Function of Interpretation in Its Relation to Theology (American Journal of Theology, January, 1898, pp. 52–79).

CLARKE, W. N. : The Use of the Scriptures in Theology, New York, 1905.

REISCHLE, M. : Historische und dogmatische Methode der Theologie (review of recent articles by Niedergall, Tröltsch, Wobbermin, Rolffs and Deissmann), Theologische Rundschau, vol. IV, pp. 261 sq., 305 sq.

VII–X. The Christian Idea of God

(1) *The Sources of the Christian Idea.*

DAVIDSON, A. B.: Article "God" in Hastings' Dictionary of the Bible, vol. II, pp. 196–205.

TOY, C. H.: Judaism and Christianity, pp. 77–140.

HATCH, E.: On the Influence of Greek Ideas, etc., pp. 171–282.

WENDT, H. H.: Die Lehre Jesu, Göttingen, 1901, pp. 464 sq.; Eng. tr., The Teaching of Jesus, vol. II, pp. 184 sq.

HOLTZMANN, O.: Der christliche Gottesglaube, seine Vorgeschichte und Urgeschichte, Giessen, 1905.

(2) *The Christian Definition of God.   The Being and Attributes of God.*

CANDLISH, J.: The Christian Doctrine of God (Handbooks for Bible Classes), Edinburgh, 1891.

STEENSTRA, P. H.: The Being of God in Unity and Trinity, New York, 1891.

MEAD, C. H.: The Fatherhood of God (American Journal of Theology for July, 1897, pp. 577–600).

LIDGETT, T. S.: The Fatherhood of God in Christian Truth and Life, Edinburgh, 1902.

FISKE, J.: The Idea of God, as Affected by Modern Thought, Boston and New York, 1886.

ROYCE, J.: The Conception of God: A Philosophical Discussion Concerning the Nature of the Divine Idea as a Demonstrable Reality, New York, 1898.

MOORE, A.: The Christian Doctrine of God (in Lux Mundi, chapter II).

RITSCHL, A.: Christian Doctrine of Justification and Reconciliation; Eng. tr. of vol. III, pp. 226 sq. (on the Personality of God).

ILLINGWORTH, J. R.: Personality, Human and Divine, Bampton Lectures for 1894, London, 1894.

SIMON, D. W.: The Redemption of Man, Edinburgh, 1889 (chapter V, on the Anger of God).

RASHDALL, H.: The Murtle Lecture on Personality in God and Man (in Doctrine and Development, London, 1898, pp. 268 sq.).
    Personality, Human and Divine, (in Personal Idealism, ed. Sturt, London, 1902, pp. 369 sq.).

DORNER, J. A.: Gesammelte Schriften aus dem Gebiet der systematischen Theologie, Berlin, 1883, pp. 188–377 (on the Immutability of God).

STEINMANN, T.: Die lebendige Persönlichkeit Gottes; seine Immanenz und Transzendenz als religiöses Erlebnis (Zeitschrift für Theologie und Kirche, 1904, pp. 389–461).

WOBBERMIN, G.: Die christliche Gottesglaube in seinem Verhältnis zur gegenwärtigen Philosophie, Berlin, 1902.

(3) *The Proof of the Christian Idea.*

HARRIS, S.: The Philosophical Basis of Theism, rev. ed., New York, 1886.

FLINT, R: Theism, new ed., New York, 1890.
  Anti-theistic Theories, 3d ed., Edinburgh, 1885.
  Agnosticism, New York, 1903.

BOWNE, B. P.: Theism, New York, 1902.

KNIGHT, W.: Aspects of Theism, London, 1893.

SETH, A.: Two Lectures on Theism, New York, 1897.

DIMAN, J. L.: The Theistic Argument, Lowell Lectures, Boston, 1882.

LINDSAY, J.: Recent Advances in Theistic Philosophy and Religion, Edinburgh, 1897.

SCHURMAN, J. G.: Belief in God, Winkley Lectures for 1890, New York, 1892.

ROMANES, G. J.: Thoughts on Religion, ed. Gore, Chicago, 1895.

WARD, J.: Naturalism and Agnosticism, 2 vols., New York, 1899.

FISHER, G. P.: Grounds of Theistic and Christian Belief, rev. ed., New York, 1902.

CLARKE, W. N.: Can I Believe in God the Father? New York, 1899.

RITSCHL, A.: Christian Doctrine of Justification and Reconciliation, Eng. tr. of vol. III, pp. 214 sq.

(4) *The Trinity.*

The relevant sections in the Histories of Doctrine, especially Harnack (Eng. tr., vol. IV, pp. 1–137), Loofs (pp. 146–159), Fisher (pp. 134–147), Bethune-Baker (pp. 119–238).

BAUR, F. C.: Die christliche Lehre von der Dreieinigkeit und Menschwerdung Gottes, 3 vols., Tübingen, 1841–43.

KRÜGER, G.: Das Dogma von der Dreieinigkeit und Gottmenschheit, in seiner geschichtlichen Entwicklung dargestellt, Tübingen, 1901.

ROBERTSON, A.: Introduction to Athanasius (Nicene and Post-Nicene Library, second series, vol. IV, pp. xv. sq.).

AUGUSTINE, A.: On the Trinity (Nicene and Post-Nicene Library, first series, vol. II, pp. 1–128).

GWATKIN, H. M.: Studies of Arianism, Cambridge, 1882.

CALVIN, J.: Institutes, Bk. I, chapter XIII (Eng. tr. by Beveridge, vol. I, pp. 144 sq.).

EDWARDS, J.: An Unpublished Essay on the Trinity, ed. G. P. Fisher, New York, 1903.

STEENSTRA, P. H.: The Being of God in Unity and Trinity, pp. 159 sq.

STEVENS, G. B.: Doctrine and Life, Boston, 1895, pp. 87 sq.

KAFTAN, J.: Dogmatik, pp. 189-225.

CLARKE, W. N.: Outline of Christian Theology, pp. 161-181.

FAIRBAIRN, A M.: The Place of Christ in Modern Theology, New York, 1893, pp. 391 sq.

STRONG, T. B: The History of the Theological Term "Substance" (in Journal of Theological Studies, vol. II, pp. 224 sq.; vol. III, pp. 22-40).

CHANNING, W. E.: Works, Boston, 1875, pp. 302-336, 367-407.

MARTINEAU, J.: Essays, Reviews and Addresses, esp. vol. II, pp. 371 sq., The Unitarian Position; pp. 525 sq., A Way out of the Trinitarian Controversy.

WICKSTEED, P. H.; The Significance of Unitarianism as a Theology (Studies in Theology, by Carpenter and Wicksteed, London, 1903).

BROOKS, P.: Sermons, vol. I, No. XIII, pp. 228 sq.; vol. II, No. XVIII, pp. 305 sq.

BROWN, W. A.: The Trinity and Modern Thought: An Experiment in Theological Reconstruction, New York, 1906.

XI-XIV. THE CHRISTIAN VIEW OF THE WORLD

(1) *The Sources of the Christian View.*

The relevant sections in the Biblical Theologies and in the Histories of Doctrine, esp. Harnack (Eng. tr., vol. III, pp. 241-287).

HATCH, E.: On the Influence of Greek Ideas, etc., pp. 171 sq.

DRUMMOND, J.: The Jewish Messiah: A Critical History of the Messianic Idea among the Jews, London, 1877

Philo Judaeus, or the Jewish Alexandrine Philosophy in its Development and Completion, 2 vols., London, 1888 (esp. vol. II, pp. 156-273, on the Logos)

SCHÜRER, E.: A History of the Jewish People in the Time of Christ, Eng. tr., by Macpherson, Edinburgh, 1890 sq., div. II, vol. II, pp. 126-187.

MATTHEWS, S: The Messianic Hope in the New Testament, Chicago, 1905.

KAFTAN, J.: Dogmatik, pp. 226-242.

WHITE, A. D.: A History of the Warfare of Science with Theology in Christendom, 2 vols., New York, 1896.

KENT, C. F. : The Student's Old Testament: The Beginnings of Hebrew History, New York, 1904, pp. 360–370 (on the Babylonian accounts of creation).

PEAKE, A. S. : The Problem of Suffering in the Old Testament, London, 1904.

GUNKEL, H. : Schöpfung und Chaos in Urzeit und Endzeit, Göttingen, 1895.

(2) *Of God's Plan for the World.   The Kingdom of God.*

EDWARDS, J. : Dissertation on the End for Which God Created the World (Works, New York, 1869, vol. II, pp. 193 sq.).

RITSCHL, A. : Christian Doctrine of Justification and Reconciliation, Eng. tr. of vol. III, pp. 238–326.

TOY, C. H. : Judaism and Christianity, pp. 303–371.

WENDT, H. H. : Teaching of Jesus, 2d ed. pp. 249 sq., Eng. tr., vol. I, pp. 364 sq.

BRUCE, A. B. : The Kingdom of God, Edinburgh, 1890.

WEISS, J. : Die Predigt Jesu vom Reiche Gottes, 2d ed., Göttingen, 1900.

   Die Idee des Reiches Gottes in der Theologie, Giessen, 1901.

AUGUSTINE, A. : The City of God, Eng. tr. by Dods in Nicene Library, second series, vol. II, pp. 1–511.

BOARDMAN, G. D. : The Kingdom, New York, 1899.

ROBERTSON, A. : Regnum Dei ; eight Lectures on the Kingdom of God in the History of Christian Thought, New York, 1901.

FREMANTLE, W. H. : The World as the Subject of Redemption, 2d ed., London, 1895.

SEISS, J. A. : The Last Times, Philadelphia, 1878.

ANDREWS, S. J. : Christianity and Anti-Christianity in Their Final Conflict, 2d ed., New York, 1899.

(3) *The Christian View of the World.   The Problem of Evil.*

LEIBNITZ, G. W. : Essais de Theodicée (Works, ed. Gerhardt, Berlin, 1875 sq., vol. VI, pp. 1 sq.).

BELLAMY, J. : On the Wisdom of God in the Permission of Sin, (Sermons, Boston, 1758, pp. 71 sq.).

TAYLOR, N. : Lectures on the Moral Government of God, 2 vols., New York, 1859

YOUNG, J. : Evil not from God, New York, 1858.

HALL, C. C. : Does God Send Trouble ?   Boston, 1895.

HINTON, J. : The Mystery of Pain: A Book for the Sorrowful, new ed., London, 1879.

HARRIS, S. : God, the Creator and Lord of All, New York, 1896, vol. I, pp. 210–293.

MARSHALL, H. R. : Pain, Pleasure and Æsthetics. London and New York, 1894, pp. 167 sq. (the physical basis of pleasure and pain).

(4) *God's Relation to the World.   Creation.   Providence.*
Nature and the Supernatural.

HARRIS, S. : God, the Creator and Lord of All, vol. I, pp. 463–518.
MARTINEAU, J. : A Study of Religion, vol. I, pp. 374 sq.
BRUCE, A. B. : The Providential Order of the World, Gifford Lectures for 1897, New York, 1897.
ILLINGWORTH, J. A. : The Divine Immanence : An Essay on the Spiritual Significance of Matter, New York, 1898.
BOWNE, B. P. : Immanence of God, London, 1905.
BUSHNELL, H. : Nature and the Supernatural, New York, 1858.
MOZLEY, J. B. : Bampton Lectures on Miracles, 3d ed., London, 1872.
MEAD, C. H. : Supernatural Revelation, 2d ed., New York, 1889, pp. 87–228.
STEARNS, L. F. : Present-Day Theology, New York, 1893, pp. 58–74.
ROTHE, R. : Zur Dogmatik, 2d ed., Gotha, 1869, pp. 54 sq.
BRUCE, A. B. : The Miraculous Element in the Gospels, New York, 1886, pp. 11–78.
HUXLEY, T. H. : Hume, New York, 1894, pp. 153–165.
SABATIER, A. : Philosophie de la Religion, pp. 64 sq. ; Eng. tr., Outlines of a Philosophy of Religion, pp. 67–95.
KAFTAN, J. : Dogmatik, pp. 263 sq.

XV. THE CHRISTIAN IDEA OF MAN

(1) *Origin and Primitive State.*

LAIDLAW, J. : The Bible Doctrine of Man, new ed., Edinburgh, 1895.
HEPPE, H. : Die Dogmatik der evangelisch-reformirten Kirche, Elberfeld, 1861 (Locus XI, De Homine, pp. 158 sq.).
MÖHLER, J. : Symbolism, pp. 113–167 (the Roman Catholic view).
SHEDD, W. G. T. : Dogmatic Theology, vol. II, pp. 95–114 (the older Calvinistic view).
MILEY, J. : Systematic Theology, vol. I, pp. 394–428 (the Arminian view).
DARWIN, C. : The Descent of Man, and Selection in Relation to Sex, 2 vols., London, 1891.
DRUMMOND, H. : The Ascent of Man, Lowell Lectures, New York, 1894.

(2) *Freedom and Responsibility.*

EDWARDS, J. : A Careful and Strict Inquiry into the Modern Prevailing Notions of that Freedom of the Will which is supposed to be essential to Moral Agency, Virtue and Vice, Reward and Punishment, Praise and Blame (Works, New York, 1869, vol. II, pp. 1 sq.).

HYSLOP, J. : Elements of Ethics, New York, 1895, pp. 150 sq. (definition of terms).

SETH, J. : A Study of Ethical Principles, 3d ed., New York, 1898, pp. 360–397 (indeterministic).

RIEHL, A. : Science and Metaphysics, Eng. tr. by Fairbanks, London, 1894, pp. 206–267 (deterministic).

SIDGWICK, H. : The Methods of Ethics, 5th ed., 1893, pp. 57–76.

GREEN, T. H. : Prolegomena to Ethics, 3d ed., Oxford, 1890, pp. 90 sq.

FULLERTON, G. S. : A System of Metaphysics, New York, 1904, pp. 550 sq.

TAYLOR, A. E. : Elements of Metaphysics, London, 1903, pp. 359 sq.

HOWISON, G. H. : The Limits of Evolution and other Essays, 2d ed., New York, 1904, pp. 313–380.

(3) *Immortality.*

The relevant sections in the Biblical Theologies.

TOY, C. H. : Judaism and Christianity, pp. 372–414.

CHARLES, R. H. : A Critical History of the Doctrine of a Future Life in Israel, in Judaism, and in Christianity, London, 1899.

SCHULTZ, H. : Die Voraussetzungen der christlichen Lehre von der Unsterblichkeit, Göttingen, 1861.

GAYE, R. K. : The Platonic Conception of Immortality, and its connection with the Theory of Ideas; an Essay which obtained the Hare prize, New York, 1903.

SALMOND, S. D. F. : The Christian Doctrine of Immortality, 2d ed., Edinburgh, 1895.

WHITE, E. : Life in Christ, London, 1846, 3d ed., New York, 1878.

PETAVEL, E. : The Problem of Immortality, tr. from the French by F. A. Freer, London, 1892.

FISKE, J. : The Destiny of Man, viewed in the Light of his Origin, 21st ed., Boston, 1898.

SABATIER, ARMAND : Essai sur l'Immortalité au point de vue du Naturalisme Évolutioniste, 2d ed., Paris, 1895.

GORDON, G. A. : Immortality and the New Theodicy, Boston, 1897.

JAMES, W. : Human Immortality, Boston, 1898.

MYERS, F. W. H. : Human Personality and Its Survival of Bodily Death, 2 vols., New York, 1903.

HOWISON, G. H. : Limits of Evolution, pp. 279–312.

SCHILLER, F. C. S. : Humanism. Philosophical Essays, London, 1903, pp. 228–289.

XVI, XVII. The Christian Idea of Sin

(1) *The Nature and Origin of Sin.*

Müller, J. : Die christliche Lehre von der Sünde, 6th ed., 2 vols., Stuttgart, 1877; Eng. tr. by Urwick, The Christian Doctrine of Sin, 2 vols., Edinburgh, 1868.

Clemen, C. : Die christliche Lehre von der Sünde. Eine Untersuchung zur systematischen Theologie, vol. I, Göttingen, 1897.

Toy, C. H. : Judaism and Christianity, pp. 183–220.

Tulloch, J. : The Christian Doctrine of Sin, New York, 1876.

Tennant, F. R. : The Origin and Propagation of Sin, the Hulsean Lectures for 1901–2, Cambridge, 1902.

The Sources of the Doctrines of the Fall and Original Sin, Cambridge, 1903.

### (2) *The Consequences of Sin.	Guilt and Penalty.*

The relevant sections in the Systematic Theologies of Shedd (vol. II, pp. 168–257), Strong (pp. 308–357), C. Hodge (vol. II, pp. 227–254), H. B. Smith (pp. 314–323), Miley (vol. I, pp. 441–533), for a discussion of the older views of Original Sin and Imputation.

Placæus, J. : Disputatio de Imputatione Primi Peccati Adami, 1655. (Works, Franeker, 1699 sq., vol. I., pp. 159–479.)

Landis, R. W. : The Doctrine of Original Sin as received and taught by the Churches of the Reformation, Richmond, 1884 (a criticism of Hodge).

Shedd, W. G. T. : Doctrine of Endless Punishment, New York, 1887.

Row, C. A. : Future Retribution viewed in the Light of Reason and Revelation, 2d ed., London, 1889.

Farrar, F. W. : The Eternal Hope, 5 sermons, London, 1892. Mercy and Judgment, 1880, 1881.

Pusey, E. B. : What is of Faith concerning Everlasting Punishment? 2d ed., London, 1880 (an answer to Farrar's Eternal Hope).

Petavel, E. : The Problem of Immortality, London, 1892.

XVIII. The Christian Idea of Salvation

Brown, W. A. : art., Salvation, in Hastings' Dictionary of the Bible, vol. IV, pp. 357 sq.

Du Bose, W. P. : Soteriology of the New Testament, New York, 1892.

Titius, A. : Die neutestamentliche Lehre von der Seligkeit, 4 parts, Freiburg, 1895–1900.

Ritschl, A.: Die christliche Lehre von der Rechtfertigung und Versöhnung, 3 vols., 3d ed., Bonn, 1888, 1889, Eng. tr. of vol. I, Edinburgh, 1872 ; of vol. III, Edinburgh, 1905.

Baur, F. C.: Die christliche Lehre von der Versöhnung, Tübingen, 1838.

Rivière, J.: Le Dogme de la Rédemption, Paris, 1905.

Simon, D. W.: The Redemption of Man, Edinburgh, 1889.

Reconciliation by Incarnation, Edinburgh, 1898.

Stevens, G. B.: The Christian Doctrine of Salvation, New York, 1905.

Ziegler, K. W.: Die Versöhnung mit Gott : Bekenntnisse und Erkenntniswege, Tübingen, 1902.

Cf. also the literature cited under XX.

XIX. The Person of Christ.

Sanday. W.: art., Jesus Christ in Hastings' Dictionary of the Bible, vol. II, pp. 603 sq.

The Creed statements in Schaff, Creeds of Christendom, and for the early Church in Hahn, Bibliothek der Symbole und Glaubensregeln der alten Kirche, Breslau, 1897.

The relevant sections in the Histories of Doctrine, especially Harnack (Eng. tr., vol. IV, pp. 138–267); Loofs (pp. 159 sq.); Nitzsch, (Grundriss der christlichen Dogmengeschichte, Berlin, 1870, vol. I, pp. 302–328) ; and Bethune-Baker, (pp. 239–300).

Dorner, J. A.: Entwicklungsgeschichte der Lehre von der Person Christi, 2d ed., 3 pts., Stuttgart, 1845 sq.; Eng. tr. by Alexander and Simon, History of the Development of the Doctrine of the Person of Christ, 5 vols., Edinburgh, 1861–63.

Ottley, R. L.: The Doctrine of the Incarnation, 2 vols., London, 1896.

Koestlin, J.: Luthers Theologie, vol. II, pp. 385 sq. ; Eng. tr., vol. II, pp. 370 sq.

Calvin, J.: Institutes, Bk. II, chapters XII–XIV (Eng. tr. by Beveridge, vol. II, pp. 1 sq.).

The Racovian Catechism: Eng. tr., ed. Rees, pp. 51 sq. (Socinian).

Shedd, W. G. T.: Dogmatic Theology, vol. II, pp. 261 sq., pp. 311 sq.

Godet, F.: Commentary on St. John's Gospel, Eng. tr., vol. I, pp. 358 sq., pp. 394 sq. (kenotic).

Thomasius, G.: Christi Person und Werk. Darstellung der evangelisch-lutherischen Dogmatik vom Mittelpunkte der Christologie aus, 3d ed., 2 vols., Erlangen, 1886–88.

Gess, W. F.: Christi Person und Werk, nach Christi Selbstzeugniss und den Zeugnissen der Apostel, 3 vols., Basle, 1870–87.

Dorner, J. A.: System der christlichen Glaubenslehre, vol. II, pp. 384 sq.; Eng. tr., System of Christian Doctrine, vol. III, pp. 279 sq.

RITSCHL, A. : Christian Doctrine of Justification and Reconciliation
Eng. tr. of vol. III, pp. 385 sq.

Unterricht in der christlichen Religion, pp. 17 sq. ; Eng. tr.
by Swing, The Theology of Albrecht Ritschl, pp. 194 sq.

KAFTAN, J. : Dogmatik, pp. 372 sq.

SCHULTZ, H. : Die Lehre von der Gottheit Christi ; Communicatio
Idiomatum, Gotha, 1881.

BRUCE, A. B. : The Humiliation of Christ, in its physical, ethical and
official aspects, 2d ed., New York, 1887.

ULLMANN, C. : The Sinlessness of Jesus, Edinburgh, 1858.

FORREST, D. W. : The Christ of History and Experience, Kerr
Lectures for 1867, Edinburgh, 1899.

GORDON, G. : The Christ of To-day, Boston, 1895.

WALKER, W. L. : The Spirit and the Incarnation, 2d ed., Edinburgh,
1901.

VAN DYKE, H. : The Gospel for an Age of Doubt, New York,
1896.

LIDDON, H. P. : The Divinity of Jesus Christ, Bampton Lectures,
for 1866, New York, 1868.

GORE, C. : The Incarnation of the Son of God, Bampton Lectures
for 1891, New York, 1898.

Dissertations on Subjects Connected with the Incarnation, New
York, 1895.

MASON, A. J. : The Conditions of our Lord's Life on Earth, Paddock
Lectures for 1896, New York, 1896.

GIFFORD, E. H. : The Incarnation : a study of Philippians ii, 5–11,
New York, 1897.

POWELL, H. C. : The Principle of the Incarnation, New York, 1896.

HALL, F. J. : The Kenotic Theory, considered with particular reference to its Anglican forms and arguments, New York, 1898.

INGE, W. R. : The Person of Christ (Contentio Veritatis, pp. 59–
104).

BRIGGS, C. A. : The Incarnation of the Lord, New York, 1902.

SCHMIDT, N. : The Prophet of Nazareth, New York, 1905.

WEINEL, H. : Jesus im neunzehnten Jahrhundert, Tübingen, 1903.

SCHWEITZER, A. : Von Reimarus zu Wrede : eine Geschichte der
Leben-Jesu-Forschung, Tübingen, 1906.

LOBSTEIN, P. : La Notion de la Préexistence du Fils de Dieu : Frag-
ment de Christologie experimentale, Paris, 1883.

Die Lehre von der übernatürlichen Geburt Christi : christolo-
gische Studie, 2d ed., Freiburg, 1896 ; Eng. tr., The Virgin Birth of
Christ, An Historical and Critical Essay ; tr. Leuliette, ed. Morri-
son, New York, 1903.

La Christologie Traditionelle et la Foi Protestante, Paris, 1894.

ADAMSON, T. : Studies in the Mind of Christ, Edinburgh, 1898.

XX. The Work of Christ

(1) *Prophetic.*

On this subject cf. the literature cited under IV.

(2) *Priestly.*

Moore, G. : art., Sacrifice in Encyclopædia Biblica, vol. IV.

Cave, A. : The Scriptural Doctrine of Sacrifice, Edinburgh, 1877.

Sanday, W. : Priesthood and Sacrifice, London and New York, 1900.

Ménégoz, E. : La Théologie de l'Epitre aux Hebreux, Paris, 1894.

Everett, C. C. : The Gospel of Paul, Boston, 1893.

Athanasius : On the Incarnation of the Word, Eng. tr. by Robertson, in Nicene and Post-Nicene Library, second series, vol. IV, pp. 31 sq.

Anselm : Cur Deus Homo ; Eng. tr. by Deane, St. Anselm, Chicago, 1903, pp. 173 sq.

Abelard : On Romans iii, 22–26 (Migne, Patrologia, vol. CLXXVIII, pp. 833 sq.)

Aquinas : Summa, part III, questions 46–49.

Köstlin, J. : The Theology of Luther, Eng. tr., vol. II, pp. 338–424.

Calvin, J. : Institutes, Bk. II, chapters XV–XVII (vol. II, pp. 35 sq.).

The Racovian Catechism : Eng. tr., ed. Rees, pp. 349–359.

Grotius, H.: Defensio Fidei. . . De Satisfactione Christi, in his Collected Works, vol. IV, pp. 297–336; Eng. tr. by Foster, A Defence of the Catholic Faith Concerning the Satisfaction of Christ, Andover, 1889.

The Atonement : Discourses and Treatises by Edwards, Smalley, Maxcy, Emmons, Griffin, Burge and Weeks, with an introductory essay by Park, Boston, 1859.

Thomasius, G. : Christi Person und Werk, 4 vols., Erlangen, 1853.

Gess, W. F. : Christi Person und Werk, Basle, 1870.

Simon, D. W. : The Redemption of Man, Edinburgh, 1889. Reconciliation through Incarnation, Edinburgh, 1898.

Hodge, A. A. : The Atonement, Philadelphia, 1867.

Shedd, W. G. T. : Dogmatic Theology, vol. II, pp. 378 sq.

Barnes, A. : The Atonement in its Relation to Law and Moral Government, Philadelphia, 1859.

Candlish, R. S. : The Atonement : its Efficacy and Extent, Edinburgh, 1867.

Clarke, W. N. : Outline, pp. 321–362.

Campbell, J. McL. : The Nature of the Atonement, and its Relation to Remission of Sins and Eternal Life, 6th ed., New York, 1895.

Bushnell, H. : The Vicarious Sacrifice, grounded in principles interpreted by human analogies, 2 vols., New York, 1891.

Oxenham, H. N. : The Catholic Doctrine of Atonement, London, 1865.

Lidgett, J. S. : The Spiritual Principle of the Atonement, London, 1901.

Kaftan, J. : Dogmatik, pp. 531 sq.

Walker, W. L. : The Cross and the Kingdom as Viewed by Christ Himself and in the Light of Evolution, Edinburgh, 1902.

Tymms, T. V. : The Christian Idea of Atonement, London, 1904.

Moberly, R. C. : Atonement and Personality, New York, 1901.

Sabatier, A. : The Doctrine of the Atonement and its Historical Evolution, Eng. tr. by Leuliette, New York, 1904.

Denney, J. : The Death of Christ : its Place and Interpretation in the New Testament, 2d ed., New York, 1903.

The Atonement and the Modern Mind, London, 1903.

Stevens, G. B. : The Christian Doctrine of Salvation, pp. 136 sq.

(3) *Kingly.*

Brown, W. A. : Arts., Millennium and Parousia in Hastings' Dictionary of the Bible, vol. III, pp. 370 sq.; 674 sq.

Warren, I. P. : The Parousia, Portland, 1884.

Russell, J. S. : The Parousia, London, 1887.

Terry, M. S. : Biblical Apocalyptics, New York, 1898.

Edgar, W. McC. : The Gospel of a Risen Saviour, Edinburgh, 1892.

Milligan, W. : The Resurrection of Our Lord, London, 1881.

Salmond, S. D. F. : The Christian Doctrine of Immortality, 2d ed., Edinburgh, 1895.

Seiss, J. A. : The Last Times, Philadelphia, 1878.

Andrews, S. J. : Christianity and Anti-Christianity in Their Final Conflict, 2d ed., New York, 1899.

Charles, R. H. : A Critical History of the Doctrine of a Future Life in Israel, in Judaism, and in Christianity, Jowett Lectures for 1898–99, London, 1899.

XXI–XXIII. The Christian Life

(1) *The Nature of the Christian Life.*

Luther, M. : On the Freedom of a Christian Man, Eng. tr., in First Principles of the Reformation, ed. Wace and Buchheim, London, 1883.

Herrmann, W. : Der Verkehr des Christen mit Gott, 2d ed., Stuttgart, 1892 ; Eng. tr. by Stanyon, The Communion of the Christian with God, London, 1895, New York, 1906.

Inge, W. R. : Christian Mysticism, Bampton Lectures for 1899, New York, 1899.

PEABODY, F. G.: Jesus Christ and the Christian Character, New York, 1905.

KÖSTLIN, J.: Der Glaube, und seine Bedeutung für Erkenntnis, Leben und Kirche, Berlin, 1895.

FERRIES, G.: The Growth of Christian Faith, Edinburgh, 1905.

BUCHANAN, J.: The Doctrine of Justification, Cunningham Lectures, Edinburgh, 1867.

BRIGGS, C. A.: Whither? New York, 1889, pp. 141 sq.

RITSCHL, A.: Christian Doctrine of Justification and Reconciliation, Eng. tr. of vol. III, pp. 609 sq.

HERRMANN, W.: Roman and Evangelical Morality (Faith and Morals, New York, 1904).

NEWMAN, J. H.: Lectures on Justification, London, 1838.

(2) *The Source of the Christian Life. The Holy Spirit. The Means of Grace.*

SMEATON, G.: The Doctrine of the Holy Spirit, Cunningham Lectures, Edinburgh, 1882.

DENIO, F. B.: The Supreme Leader: A study of the nature and work of the Holy Spirit, Boston, 1900.

WOOD, I. F.: The Spirit of God in Biblical Literature, New York, 1904.

GUNKEL, H: Die Wirkungen des heiligen Geistes nach der populären Anschauung der apostolischen Zeit, und nach der Lehre des Apostels Paulus, Göttingen, 1888.

WEINEL, H.: Die Wirkungen des Geistes und der Geister im nachapostolichen Zeitalter bis auf Irenaeus, Freiburg, 1899.

COUNCIL OF TRENT: Dogmatic Decrees (Schaff, Creeds, vol. II, pp. 119–206).

GIBBONS, J.: The Faith of our Fathers, Baltimore, 1897, pp. 303 sq.

LEA, H. C.: History of Auricular Confession and Indulgence, 3 vols. Philadelphia, 1896.

GORE, C.: The Body of Christ, 3d ed., New York, 1902.

ALLEN, A. V. G.: Christian Institutions, New York, 1897.

NEVIN, J. W.: The Mystical Presence, Philadelphia, 1846.

WHITE, E. N.: Why Infants are Baptized, Philadelphia, 1900.

(3) *The Goal of the Christian Life. Christian Perfection. The Final Consummation.*

RITSCHL, A.: Die christliche Vollkommenheit, 2d ed., Göttingen, 1889.

WENDT, H. H.: Die christliche Lehre von der menschlichen Vollkommenheit, Göttingen, 1882.

DAHLE, L. N. : Life after Death and the Future of the Kingdom of
    God, Edinburgh, 1896.
BEET, J. A. : The Last Things, New York, 1897.
SALMOND, S. D. F. : Christian Doctrine of Immortality, Edinburgh,
    1895
Cf., also, the works cited under XV, (3) and XX, (3).

INDEX

INDEX